lonely planet

Beijing

Robert Storey

Beijing

3rd edition

Published by
 Lonely Planet Publications
 Head Office: PO Box 617, Hawthorn, Vic 3122, Australia
 Branches: 150 Linden St, Oakland, CA 94607, USA
 10a Spring Place, London NW5 3BH, UK
 1 rue du Dahomey, 75011 Paris, France

Printed by
 SNP Printing Pte Ltd, Singapore

Photographs by
David Andrew	Glenn Beanland	Patrick Horton
Diana Mayfield	Damien Simonis	Tony Wheeler

Front cover: Detail of the main entrance to Beijing's most colourful temple, Lama Temple
 (Damien Simonis)

First Published
 February 1994

This Edition
 July 1998

Although the authors and publisher have tried to make the information as accurate as possible, they accept no responsibility for any loss, injury or inconvenience sustained by any person using this book.

National Library of Australia Cataloguing in Publication Data

Storey, Robert.
Beijing.

3rd ed.
Includes index.
ISBN 0 86442 547 3.

1. Peking (China) - Guidebooks. I. Title.

915.11560459

text & maps © Lonely Planet 1998
photos © photographers as indicated 1998

Robert Storey

Robert has a colourful past, starting with his first job as a monkey-keeper at a zoo and continuing with a stint as a 'taco-flipper' at Jack-In-The-Box. He received what he describes as a worthless liberal arts degree from the University of Nevada, working evenings as a slot machine repairman in a Las Vegas casino. After graduation, he travelled to Asia and finally got his first respectable job (as an English teacher). Somewhere along the way it was discovered that Robert could write, and he has written and/or updated 13 Lonely Planet guides.

From Robert

I'd like to express my gratitude to a number of visitors to Beijing, both long-termers and transients. Special thanks must go to Chiu Miaoling, Bruce A Douglas, Lars-Olof Lindgren, Ola Svensson, RJ Berry and Mark Lyseyko. I'm deeply grateful to a number of Chinese people I also met along the way who provided helpful advice, companionship, hospitality and some terrific dumplings.

From the Publisher

This book, the 3rd edition of *Beijing*, was edited and proofed at the Lonely Planet office in Melbourne by David Andrew and Mic Looby. Tim Fitzgerald was responsible for maps, design and layout – not to mention those snazzy special sections and chapter ends. Ta to Rachael Scott for working a bit of last-minute magic with the subway map.

Thanks to Russ Kerr (and his little historical helper, Kevin Frost), Alex English, Martin Hughes and Linda Jaivin for providing fresh asides. Three cheers as well to Amy Soileau for beefing up the Places to Eat chapter, and to William Lindesay for walking the wild wall for us.

Gratuitous thanks must also go to Kristin Odijk for love and light, Chris Love for cracking the whip, Michael Weldon for the scratchboard illustrations and icons, Mic Looby for a couple of dodgy cartoons, David Kemp for designing the front and back covers, Dan Levin for programming the

pinyin and Chinese script, Charles Qin and Quentin Frayne for untying the language tangles.

Thanks

Many thanks must go to the following travellers who used the last edition of *Beijing* and wrote to us with helpful hints, useful advice and interesting anecdotes:

Joachim Bergmann, Neil Bonnell, Helen Chivuer, Pauline Connolly, Ted Cook, Mark Creasy, Peggy & Stan Douglas, Jocelyne Finazzi, Ralph Gebhard, Harlan Hague, Richard Heap, Catherine Hunt, Marie-Paule Kellner, Dr Jane Lawson, Julie Leigh, Apara Mahal, Barrie McCormick, Sam McFerran, Pamela McVoy, Celia Mesure, G N Munn, K O'Hara, Mark Plescia, Marco Ropke, Yvonne Rowe, Diane Ryley, Hack E Sack, John Senior, Ton Spitsbaard, Bettina Standrasser, Vesna Stankovic, Francois Tonnellier, Stefaan Van Ryssen, Andrew Williams, Ian Winter.

Warning & Request

Things change – prices go up, schedules change, good places go bad and bad places go bankrupt – nothing stays the same. So, if you find things better or worse, recently opened or long since closed, please tell us and help make the next edition even more accurate and useful.

We value all the feedback we receive from travellers. Julie Young coordinates a small team which reads and acknowledges every letter, postcard and email, and ensures every morsel of information finds its way to the appropriate authors, editors and publishers.

Everyone who writes to us will find their name in the next edition of the appropriate guide and will receive a free subscription to our quarterly newsletter, *Planet Talk*. The very best contributions will be rewarded with a free Lonely Planet guide.

Excerpts from your correspondence may appear in new editions of this guide; in our newsletter, *Planet Talk*; or in updates on our Web site or email newsletter – so please let us know if you don't want your letter published or your name acknowledged.

Contents

SHOPPING 146

EXCURSIONS 151

GLOSSARY 187

INDEX 189

MAPS 201

Introduction

For centuries, Beijing has been the promised land of China. Originally a walled bastion for emperors and officials, it remains a majestic political and architectural marvel. Today, poor peasants still flock to the city in search of the elusive pot of gold at the end of the rainbow; many wind up camped out on the pavement in front of the railway station. The government encourages them to go home, but the lure of the capital proves too enticing. Meanwhile, down the road by the Friendship Store, smartly attired customers clutching cellular telephones head for the nearest banquet or disco.

As the capital of the People's Republic of China, Beijing is home to bureaucrats, generals, nouveau-riche cadres and *lǎobǎixìng* (the common people); host to reporters, disgruntled diplomats, English-teaching expatriates and tourists; a labyrinth of doors, walls, tunnels, gates and entrances, temples, pavilions, parks and museums. As far away as Xinjiang they run on Beijing's clock; all over the land they chortle in *pǔtōnghuà*, the Beijing dialect; in remote Tibet they struggle to interpret the latest half-baked directives from the capital. This is where they move the cogs and wheels of the Chinese universe, or try to slow them down if they're moving in the wrong direction.

Perhaps nowhere else in China is the generation gap more visible. Appalled by the

The city's Western Gate was an imposing sight for travellers such as Thomas Allom, who recorded this scene in the early 19th century. While the giant gates and walls have long gone, the Forbidden City remains as Bejing's well preserved ancient heart.

current drive to 'modernisation', many older people still wax euphoric about Chairman Mao and the years of sacrifice for the socialist revolution. But most youngsters disdain socialist sacrifice and are more interested in money, motorbikes, fashion, video games, sex and rock music – not necessarily in that order.

All cities in China are equal, but some are more equal than others. Beijing has the best of everything in China bar the weather: the best food, the best hotels, the best transport, the best temples. But its vast squares and boulevards, its cavernous monoliths, militaristic parades, ubiquitous police, luxury high-rises and armies of tourists may leave you with the impression that Beijing is China's largest theme park. Foreign residents sometimes call it 'the Los Angeles of China' – traffic-choked freeways plus a surreal imitation of Disneyland.

Foreigners seem to enjoy Beijing – the city offers plenty to see and do. Yet until the 1990s, it was arguably one of the poorest-looking capitals in all of Asia. Things have changed drastically – gone are the years of austerity and ration coupons. The Beijing of today is a forest of construction cranes, bulldozers and 24 hour work crews scrambling to build the new China. Plush shopping malls and five-star hotels rise from the rubble. Whatever one says about Beijing, it probably won't be true tomorrow – the city is metamorphosing so rapidly it makes you dizzy. Travellers of the 1980s remember Beijing as a city of narrow lanes with single-storey

homes built around courtyards – these have given way to the high-rise housing estates of the 1990s. TV sets and washing machines – unimaginable luxuries in the 1980s – are commonplace now. Whereas bicycles and ox carts were the main form of transport a decade ago, both are prohibited on the new freeways and toll roads which now encompass the city.

Whatever impression you come away with, Beijing is one of the most fascinating places in China. It may be something of a showcase, but what capital city isn't? And with a bit of effort you can get out of the make-up department – Beijing houses some of China's most stunning sights: the Forbidden City, Summer Palace, Great Wall, Lama Temple and Tiantan Park, to name just a few. During the Cultural Revolution of the 1960s, these and other historical treasures of China literally took a beating. Now that the damage has been repaired, the temples have been restored and everything is being spruced up.

Group tourists are processed through Beijing in much the same way the ducks are force-fed on the outlying farms – the two usually meet on the first night over the dinner table. But individual travellers will have no trouble getting around. For visitors, Beijing is for the most part user-friendly – the biggest problem is that it's just so big.

Any effort you make to get out and see things will be rewarding. The city offers so much of intrinsic interest that the main complaint of most visitors is that they simply run out of time before seeing it all.

Facts about Beijing

HISTORY

Beijing is a time-setter for China, but it actually has a short history as Chinese timespans go. Although the area south-west of the city was inhabited by primitive humans some 500,000 years ago, the earliest records of settlement date from around 1000 BC. It developed as a frontier trading town for the Mongols, Koreans and the tribes from Shandong Province and central China. By the Warring States Period (453–221 BC) it had grown to be the capital of the Yan Kingdom and was called Ji, a reference to the marshy features of the area. The town underwent a number of changes as it acquired new warlords, the Khitan Mongols and the Manchurian Jurchen tribes among them. What attracted the conquerors was the strategic position of the town on the edge of the North China Plain. During the Liao Dynasty (916–1125 AD) Beijing was referred to as Yanjing (Capital of Yan) – the name now used for Beijing's most popular beer.

In 1215 AD, the great Mongol warrior Genghis Khan thoroughly set fire to the preceding paragraph and razed everything in sight. From the ashes emerged Dadu (Great Capital), alias Khanbaliq, the Khan's town. By 1279 Genghis' grandson Kublai had made himself ruler of the largest empire the world has ever known, with Khanbaliq as his capital. Thus was China's Yuan Dynasty (1215–1368) established.

When the Mongol emperor was informed by his astrologers that the old site of Beijing was a breeding ground for rebels, he shifted his capital further north. The great palace he built no longer remains, but was visited by the great Italian traveller, Marco Polo, who later described what he saw to an amazed Europe. Polo was equally dazzled by the innovations of gunpowder and paper money. The latter was not without its drawbacks – in history's first case of paper-currency inflation, the last Mongol emperor flooded the country with worthless bills. This, coupled with a large number of natural disasters, provoked an uprising led by the mercenary Zhu Yanhang, who took Beijing in 1368. During the Ming Dynasty (1368–1644) which followed, the city was rechristened Beiping (Northern Peace), though for the next 35 years the imperial capital was situated in Nanjing.

In the early 1400s Zhu's son Yong Le shuffled the court back to Beiping and renamed it Beijing (Northern Capital). Millions of taels of silver were spent on refurbishing the city. Many of Beijing's most famous structures, like the Forbidden City and Tiantan, were first built in Yong Le's reign. In fact, he is credited with being the true architect of the modern city. The Inner City grew to encircle the imperial compound, and a suburban zone was added to the south – a bustle of merchants and street life. The basic grid of present-day Beijing had been laid.

Under the Manchus, who invaded China and established the Qing Dynasty (1644–1911), and particularly during the reigns of the emperors Kangxi and Qianlong, Beijing was expanded and renovated; summer palaces, pagodas and temples were built.

In the last 120 years of Manchu rule, Beijing and much of China were subject to invaders and rebels: the Anglo-French troops, who in 1860 marched in and burnt the Old Summer Palace to the ground; and the disastrous Boxer Rebellion of 1900 against the corrupt regime of Empress Dowager Cixi (1834–1908), who grabbed control of the dragon throne in 1860. When Cixi died, she bequeathed power to a two-year-old boy, Puyi, who was to be China's last emperor. The Qing, brutal and incompetent at the best of times, was now rudderless and quickly collapsed. The revolution of 1911 ostensibly brought the Kuomintang (Nationalist Party) to power and the Republic

Chiang Kaishek

later established a power base in Shanghai and entered into an uneasy alliance with the Kuomintang to reunify China.

In 1926, the Kuomintang embarked on the Northern Expedition to wrest power from the remaining warlords. Chiang Kaishek (1886-1975) was appointed commander-in-chief by the Kuomintang and the Communists. The following year, Chiang turned on his Communist allies and slaughtered them en masse in Shanghai; the survivors carried on a civil war from the countryside. By the middle of 1928 the Northern Expedition had reached Beijing, where a national government was established with Chiang holding both military and political leadership.

In 1937 the Japanese invaded Beijing and by 1939 had overrun eastern China. The Kuomintang retreated west to the city of Chongqing, which became China's temporary capital during WWII. After Japan's defeat in 1945 the Kuomintang returned, but their days were numbered; by this time the Chinese Civil War was in full swing. The Communists, now under the leadership of Mao Zedong, achieved victory in 1949 – the

of China (ROC) was declared with Sun Yatsen as president. However, real power remained in the hands of warlords who carved China up into their own fiefdoms. One such warlord, General Yuan Shikai, tried to declare himself emperor in Beijing during 1915.

Yuan's scheme ended abruptly when he died in 1916, but other warlords continued to control most of northern China while the Kuomintang held power in the south. The country was badly splintered by private Chinese armies, while foreigners controlled important economic zones (called Concessions) in major ports like Shanghai and Tianjin.

China's continuing poverty, backwardness and control by warlords and foreigners was a recipe for rebellion. Beijing University became a hotbed of intellectual dissent, attracting scholars from all over China. Karl Marx's *The Communist Manifesto*, translated into Chinese, became the basis for countless discussion groups. One of those attending was a library assistant named Mao Zedong (1893-1976).

The Communists, including Mao Zedong,

Mao Zedong

Kuomintang leaders fled to Taiwan, which they control to this day, and the People's Liberation Army (PLA) entered Beijing in January 1949. On 1 October of the same year, Mao Zedong proclaimed the People's Republic of China (PRC) to an audience of 500,000 in Tiananmen Square.

After the Revolution

After 1949 came a period of urban reconstruction in Beijing. Down came the walls and commemorative arches. Blocks of buildings were reduced to rubble to widen the boulevards and Tiananmen Square. Soviet technicians poured in and left their mark in the form of Stalinesque architecture.

Progress of all kinds came to a halt in 1966 when Mao launched what became known as the Cultural Revolution. Seeing his power-base eroding, Mao officially sanctioned wall posters and criticisms of party members by university staff and students, and before long students were being issued with red armbands and were taking to the streets. The Red Guards *(hóngwèibīng)* had been born. By August 1966 Mao was reviewing mass parades of the Red Guards in Tiananmen Square, who were chanting while fanatically waving copies of his famous 'little red book'.

There was nothing sacred enough to be spared the brutal onslaught of the Red Guards. Universities and secondary schools were shut down; intellectuals, writers, artists and monks were dismissed, killed, persecuted or sent to labour camps in the countryside; the publication of scientific, artistic, literary and cultural periodicals ceased; temples were ransacked and monasteries disbanded; and many physical reminders of China's 'feudal', 'exploitative' or 'capitalist' past (including temples, monuments and works of art) were destroyed. Red Guard factions often battled each other and in the end the PLA was forced to bring them under control.

China was to remain in the grip of chaos for the next decade. It wasn't until around 1979 that Deng Xiaoping – a former protégé of Mao who had emerged as a pragmatic leader – launched a 'modernisation' drive.

Deng Xiaoping

The country opened up and westerners were finally given a chance to see what the Communists had been up to for the past 30 years.

Beijing saw considerable change during the 1980s – private businesses, once banned by the Communists, were allowed again. Most temples, monuments and libraries wrecked during the Cultural Revolution were repaired. Unfortunately, the decade ended on a tragic note in June 1989, when PLA troops crushed a student-led pro-democracy movement in Tiananmen Square. For a couple of years China was frozen out of the international community. These days, both the Cultural Revolution and the Tiananmen Square massacre are taboo topics among officials.

Nonetheless, in 1994 the Chinese leadership was confident that their nation had re-established its reputation on the world stage. When cities were being polled to host the 2000 Olympics, the Chinese assumed Beijing would win. They took the rebuff badly when Sydney, Australia, was chosen.

Nor did the Chinese win many friends in 1995 when Beijing played host to the United

Nations' Conference on Women. Having lobbied the UN hard to get the conference, the Chinese then denied visas to at least several hundred people who wanted to attend because they were regarded as politically incorrect. About 20,000 representatives of non-governmental organisations did in fact attend, but were isolated in a fenced compound 50km from the capital because the Chinese deemed their activities potentially subversive.

China found itself at loggerheads with the West again in early 1996 when the leadership decided to fire missiles at the coastal waters just off Taiwan to 'influence' Taiwan's presidential election. The net effect was to greatly increase support for Lee Tenghui, the candidate that Beijing had vilified (Lee was re-elected with 54% of the vote). The crisis also brought US warships into the area and threats from China to 'nuke Los Angeles'.

Things have cooled down since then and Beijing has been trying to polish its tarnished image. The funeral of the paramount leader Deng Xiaoping in early 1997 was a momentous event, with huge crowds of grieving Beijingers lining the streets. There was no public talk of succession, leaving journalists to speculate on just what sort of power struggles might be taking place behind the scenes.

China's takeover of Hong Kong in July 1997 was predictably accompanied by fireworks, parades and an orgy of nationalistic chest-thumping in Beijing. All of which seemed to delight the Chinese public, and reminded the West that, as always, China is a country that cannot be ignored.

GEOGRAPHY

The city limits of Beijing extend some 80km, including the urban and the suburban areas and the nine counties under its administration. Mountainous along the north and west, and flat in the south-east, Beijing municipality has a total area of 16,800 sq km.

In the western corner of Beijing municipality is Lingshan which, at 2303m, is the region's highest peak. The southern extremity of Beijing is the lowest point at 44m above sea level.

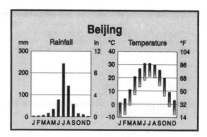

CLIMATE

Autumn (from September to early November) is the perfect time to visit: there's little rain, it's not dry or humid, and the city wears a pleasant cloak of foliage.

Winter can be interesting if you don't mind the cold. Although the temperature can dip as low as -20°C and the northern winds cut like a knife through bean curd, parts of the capital appear charming in this season. Burning coal to heat buildings produces pollution, but the resulting subdued light renders the capital oddly photogenic, with contrasting blacks and whites and some extra-sooty greys. Winter clothing is readily available – the locals tend to wear about 15 layers each.

Spring is short, dry and dusty. From April to May a phenomenon known as 'yellow wind' plagues the Chinese capital – fine dust particles, blown all the way from the Gobi Desert in the north-west, sandpaper everything in sight, including your face. Beijing women run around with mesh bags over their heads to protect their smooth complexions.

In summer (June to August) the average temperature is 26°C – hot with sticky humidity, plus heavy afternoon thunder showers and mosquitoes in July.

ECOLOGY & ENVIRONMENT

With 12 million residents and a rapidly expanding economy, Beijing's environment has taken a beating.

Beijing before 1980 had a few monolithic socialist-style buildings, but most of the city consisted of narrow lanes (hútòng), walls and single-storey homes built in traditional rectangular courtyards *(sìhéyuàn)*. For better or worse, the new Beijing is a landscape of wide boulevards, building cranes and concrete high-rises.

The consumer boom of the past few years has led to all the usual problems of people using more throwaway packaging and power-hungry electrical devices. Rising affluence has led many to abandon bicycles and buses for motorbikes, cars and taxis.

Air pollution has been recognised as a serious health hazard and the government has made an effort to move smoke-belching factories out to rural areas. Air pollution has also been reduced by replacing coal with natural gas as a heating fuel. Unfortunately, these improvements in air quality have been sullied by the increase in motor vehicles.

In response, the municipal government has embarked on a massive road improvement scheme in the hopes of reducing both traffic congestion and pollution. But as many predicted, this has simply tempted even more people to buy cars and motorbikes.

Mass transit should be the answer. The neglected bus and subway systems are beginning to get some attention, but the short-term prognosis seems to be more traffic, noise and pollution.

FLORA & FAUNA

Most of the land around Beijing has either been heavily cultivated or urbanised, to such an extent that the native flora and fauna long ago perished.

However, there are two nature reserves on the far reaches of Beijing municipality. At the eastern tip of Beijing is the Wulingshan (fog spirit mountain) Nature Reserve *(wùlíngshān zìrán bǎohù qū)* with a peak reaching a height of 2116m. On the northwest outskirts of town is the Songshan (pine mountain) Nature Reserve *(sōngshān zìrán bǎohù qū)* which contains Haituoshan at 2241m. Both reserves have conifer forests and a rich assortment of migratory birds during the warmer months. However, all the large animals (such as tigers) were long ago hunted to extinction.

GOVERNMENT & POLITICS

Although Beijing is the home of China's central government and thus at the apex of the Communist pyramid, it also has a mayor and is an independent municipality situated within Hubei Province. However, like many national capitals, Beijing is directly under the control of the central government and subject to factional struggles within the Chinese Communist Party (CCP).

Villages in China with a population under 10,000 are permitted to elect local leaders, but no such elections are permitted in big cities such as Beijing. Everyone from the

Model Citizen

Comrade Lei Feng was a young soldier who in 1963, one year after dying in a traffic accident at the age of 22, was lionised by the Communist Party as a model worker, warrior, Party member and all-round PRC model citizen. The masses were urged by top Party officials to 'learn from Comrade Lei Feng', whose feats included washing his fellow soldiers' laundry in his spare time, helping old ladies cross the street, and making sure everyone in his home town and army platoon was up-to-date on the latest Party doctrine.

Lei Feng was not the only model citizen dreamed up by the Communist leadership, but he certainly was (and remains) the most famous. He was made into a great hero during the Cultural Revolution of the 1960s, then forgotten for about 25 years. He resurfaced again in 1990 in a bid to counter the widespread disillusionment with the Party that followed the Tiananmen Square massacre. Soon thereafter, he disappeared from the billboards again, but in 1997 a new movie about the life and times of Comrade Lei Feng had its debut in Beijing.

Lei Feng's patriotism and sacrifices for the revolution are well known, but what about his love life? The authorities have been mum on this sensitive topic, but shortly after the movie debut, a 60-year-old woman emerged claiming to have been Lei Feng's girlfriend when she was young. If China had a tabloid press in the tradition of Fleet St, it's easy to imagine what they could have done with a story like that.

It's a great disappointment that Beijing doesn't have a museum dedicated to this national hero; however, there is one outside Lei Feng's home town – Changsha in Hunan Province – should you happen to be there. ■

mayor down is appointed by someone higher up the ladder.

A number of top Beijing officials fell from grace early in 1995 when the central government launched a merciless anti-corruption drive. Victims of that particular purge included Beijing's highest official, Mayor Chen Xitong, and Treasurer Wang Baosen; the latter committed suicide while under arrest.

The basic unit of social organisation outside the family is the work unit. Every Chinese person is theoretically a member of one. However, many Chinese nowadays slip through the net by being self-employed or by working in a private operation.

The work unit is a perfect organ of social control, and very little proceeds without it. The work unit approves marriages, divorces and even childbirth. It assigns housing, sets salaries, handles mail, recruits Party members, keeps files on each unit member, arranges job transfers, and gives permission to travel abroad.

Follow the Yellow Brick Road

China's youth are again on the move and older generations are trying to prepare – but which way are they headed?

The latest generation of young, mostly urban, 'middle class' Chinese – often referred to as 'little emperors' – are growing up in times of peace, prosperity and promise. Goodies unimaginable to earlier 'lost generations' are available, from discmans to designer jeans. Some of the items are even free, such as the right to kiss in public, Western-style individualism and aggressive nationalism.

In number-crunching China, children are also called 'four-two-ones' (four grandparents, two parents, one child), which reflects the new family structure created by the 'one child' policy. Like many draconian directives, this one's had some unintended results, compounding a generational problem which already has enough complex causes.

The contrast on the streets between Mao suits and mini-skirts typifies generational conflicts and contradictions. According to the parents and grandparents who've pampered them from birth and put children's careerist educations ahead of all else, these kids lack morals, maturity and manners, and not many people are looking forward to the day the 'little emperors' rule the country.

But if the young can't be blamed for their upbringing, neither can the parents trying to do the right thing. Most Chinese will say that the choices available to the young offer a richer life than parents have endured. Yet lack of blame doesn't resolve dilemmas (though it may be a good start), such as in isolation-scared China, few people really want to 'do it all' themselves. (This is true for nationalist enthusiasm, too: the youthful hope is for China to be recognised as a 'unique yet modern nation' – just like those in the West.)

Older generations also wonder if the young will reciprocate and look after them when parents have grown old. It doesn't look likely. This Confucian expectation (which many youth regard somewhat conveniently as 'feudal') doesn't sit well with modern individualism. In bad economic times, sons set up house on their own, but as a matter of necessity. For the first time in China, boys and girls now grow up to live 'their own lives', ideally where and with whom they want; the rest of the family lives with the consequences.

So what's in store for generations X, Y and Z? Career choices for China's gilded youth are best illustrated by what's called 'the four roads' to success: the Red Road, the Black Road, the Yellow Road and the Green Road.

Following the Red Road means joining the Communist Party and becoming a high official: security, influence and connections (*guanxi*) are the rewards. The Black Road is the artist/intellectual's way, neither paved with gold nor influence, but it's a moral, self-sacrificing path, leading to long-term change in the country. (There's not much company on this particular route.) The Yellow Road is lined with slogans like 'To Get Rich Is Glorious'; it takes you into business and (hopefully) a ride on a truck full of money. The plethora of street hawking, joint-venture firms, and stock and share gamblers testifies to the decision by most urban Chinese (not only youth) to follow this rocky road. Finally, if all else fails, there's the Green Road – it's named for the Green Card, the ticket to success in the USA.

By the time these options have run their course, expect new generation gaps to have emerged: a lot of those teenagers speeding down the road to success will slow down long enough to have a child of their own ...

Russ Kerr & Alex English

ECONOMY

After 1949, when the Communists took over China, the Chinese could claim to be some of the most devout practitioners of Marxist economic theory. All forms of capitalism were banned and foreign investors were shut out. After 30 years of following this path, China suddenly awoke to find it had fallen behind almost every country in the region.

China started experimenting with capitalist-style economic reforms in 1980, initiated by the all-seeing Party Leader Deng Xiaoping. The reforms proceeded in fits and starts for nearly a decade, and almost came to a halt with the Tiananmen incident in 1989. But since then, the economic shackles of state control have been thrown off and foreign money and technology have poured in. For the past decade, economic growth has averaged a dizzying 10% a year. Flush with cash, the Chinese government has poured money into their capital city, essentially turning it into a boom town. This has transformed the face of Beijing – just 10 years ago it was one of Asia's most austere capital cities. Nowadays, it's looking frighteningly modern.

By some predictions, in another decade China will have the world's largest economy. Others are not so sure – the country's messy politics may yet again cause economic grief. Another problem is that the enormous State sector continues to lose money, but the government is ideologically opposed to privatisation (it would essentially mean the death of socialism). Inflation, bottlenecks in the economy and an underdeveloped infrastructure are other sources of concern. Still, no one is predicting China's imminent collapse. The pace of economic liberalisation has gone so far so fast that it has taken on a momentum of its own. Putting the capitalist toothpaste back into the tube seems well near impossible.

POPULATION & PEOPLE

The population of Beijing municipality is over 12 million souls, with perhaps eight million in the central city. The majority of Beijingers (over 95%) are Han Chinese. The rest of China's 56 official ethnic minorities are scattered about, but a few have established little enclaves. As China has opened up to the outside world, the capital has acquired a fast-growing foreign business community.

ARTS

Music

Traditional Other than in conservatories, it is becoming rare to hear traditional instrumental Chinese music. More often, opera and other vocal forms tend to predominate. Such recitals as there are usually take the form of soloists or small groups of musicians performing on traditional instruments. These include the flute *(shēng)*, two stringed fiddle *(èrhú)*, viola *(húqín)*, guitar *(yùeqín)* and lute *(pípá)* – all used in Beijing opera. Others are the three stringed lute *(sānxúan)*, vertical flute *(dòngxiāo)*, horizontal flute *(dízi)*, piccolo *(bāngdí)*, zither *(gǔzhēng)*, ceremonial trumpet *(sǔonà)* and ceremonial gongs *(dàlúo)*. Tapes and CDs of traditional music music can be bought at places such as the Foreign Languages Bookstore in Wangfujing (see Map 11, Wangfujing Area).

Modern China's music market is heavily influenced by the already well established music industries in Taiwan and Hong Kong. The advent of satellite TV and the popularity of MTV – broadcast via Hong Kong's Star TV network – is also having an impact.

Hip young urban Chinese are into disco. Taiwanese love songs have been enormously successful in China, and Mandarin versions of Hong Kong pop music (the original songs are Cantonese) produced for the Taiwan and China markets are frequently chart hits. While Chinese tastes generally run towards soft melodies, Beijing has a nascent heavy metal and punk scene, and impromptu performances are often held in the shopping malls of Beijing's outer suburbs. In an attempt to show that the geriatric leadership is also hip, government officials authorised a disco version of 'The East is Red', theme song of the Mao generation – though sales figures are not available.

The older generation got a jolt in 1989 with the release of 'Rock & Roll for the New

Long March', by Cui Jian, one of China's foremost singers. Despite being put on hold after Tiananmen, he continues to produce ambiguously worded lyrics, as well as featuring in *Beijing Bastards*, a shoestring film by Zhang Yuan about the fringes of the city's rock scene. More jolts to the system came with heavy metal sounds by the bands, Tang Dynasty and Black Panther, though the latter now look and sound like Bon Jovi. The cassette tape *Rock & Roll Beijing* (Volumes I, II & III so far) has impressed many foreigners – the quality of the music could compete with some of the best offerings in the west. One feature of the recording was an all-female rock group, Cobra. Perhaps integral to the growing influence of Chinese rock as the voice of urban youth is the fact that it no longer blandly copies foreign models.

There are dance halls in most major hotels, generally alternating between jazz, disco, live music and a karaoke session. For details on venues, see the Entertainment chapter.

Opera

After decades in the shade of political operas like 'Taking Tiger Mountain by Strategy', Beijing opera *(píngjù)* has made a comeback. Although only one of many versions of the art, it is the most famous, though in fact it's only got a short history. The year 1790 is the key date; in that year a provincial troupe performed before Emperor Qianlong on his 80th birthday.

Beijing opera bears little resemblance to its European counterpart. The mixture of singing, dancing, speaking, mime, acrobatics and dancing can go on for five or six hours, but two hours is more typical. The screeching music can be searing to western ears, but plots are fairly simple and easy to follow.

Art

Foreigners struggling to read shop signs might not be so impressed, but calligraphy has traditionally been regarded in China as the highest form of visual art. This derives from the use of ink and brush, which has always been the main mode of Chinese painting. Landscape paintings regularly include calligraphy as part of the composition, and connoisseurs debate the merits of a painting mainly in terms of its brushwork. For 1500 years, the Chinese have been producing fine ink and watercolour paintings, particularly landscapes, flower paintings and imperial portraits. Although painting as high art was mainly the province of the scholar-gentry, much was also produced for temples and religious sites.

There is also a tradition of incredibly elegant and refined porcelain, which the Chinese first began to produce during the Tang Dynasty (618–907 AD). Stoneware was first produced much earlier. Bronze vessels of great sophistication have been discovered dating from around 1200 AD. Silk embroidery, jade jewellery and sculpture in clay, wood and stone are other notable areas of Chinese art.

Acrobatics

Acrobatics *(tèjì biǎoyǎn)* are pure fun. Donating pandas may have soothed international relations, but it's the acrobats who are China's true ambassadors. Some people find the animal acts a bit sad, but in general foreigners have reacted to the shows enthusiastically. Sometimes performing tigers and pandas (not together) show up as an added bonus.

Circus acts go back 2000 years in China. Effects are obtained using simple props: sticks, plates, eggs and chairs; and apart from the acrobatics there's magic, vaudeville, drama, clowning, music, conjuring, dance and mime thrown in to complete the performance. Happily it's an art which gained from the Communist takeover and which did not suffer during the Cultural Revolution.

Acts vary from troupe to troupe. Some traditional acts haven't changed over the centuries, while others have incorporated roller skates and motorcycles. A couple of time-proven acts that are hard to follow include 'balancing in pairs', with one man balanced upside down on the head of another mimicking every movement of the partner below, even drinking a glass of water! Hoop-

Top: Rows of mythological beasts, such as these at the Forbidden City, guard the rooftops of Beijing's temples and palaces.
Middle: Old buildings reflected in the Forbidden City moat.
Bottom: Late morning sun bakes a peeling pavillion, Beihai Park.

DAMIEN SIMONIS

DAMIEN SIMONIS

DAMIEN SIMONIS

DAMIEN SIMONIS

GLENN BEANLAND

GLENN BEANLAND

DAMIEN SIMONIS

God – or Buddha, in this case – is in the details. Many of the capital's historic and religious buildings will reward the eagle-eyed visitor who is prepared to take a closer look at the finer points of traditional Chinese architecture.

jumping is another: four hoops are stacked on top of each other; the human chunk of rubber going through the top hoop may do a backflip with a simultaneous body twist.

The 'Peacock Displaying its Feathers' act involves an array of people balanced on one bicycle – a Shanghai troupe holds the record at 13. The 'Pagoda of Bowls' is a balancing act where the performer, usually a woman, does everything with her torso except tie it in knots, all the while balancing a stack of porcelain bowls on foot, head or both – and perhaps also balancing on a partner.

Film

The most dramatic development in Chinese cinema over the last 15 years has been the appearance of films made by the so-called Fifth Generation directors. Although better known abroad than within China, their films, such as *Yellow Earth*, *Horse Thief* and *Raise the Red Lantern*, have set a new benchmark for the local film industry after the troughs of socialist propaganda. However, the popular market is given over to martial arts and historical epics copied from Hong Kong cinema.

Literature

Fiction Classic works of Chinese literature now available in English translations include *Outlaws of the Marsh*, *The Dream of the Red Chamber* (also known as *The Dream of Red Mansions* and *The Story of the Stone*) and *Journey to the west* (also known as *Monkey*).

The most famous author to have called

A Brush with Fame

Wander down an historic country road or pass through a city gate and you'll likely be greeted by a carved or painted sample of imperial calligraphy. Old steles, plaques and scrolls dot Beijing and its environs. And they're multiplying – like old tomcats, China's modern leaders can't resist the chance to mark their territory.

Until 1905, a successful career as a scholar in the imperial civil service hinged on one's skills as a calligrapher. But while the examination system declined, calligraphy remained. However, the purpose had changed: from a means of practising the virtues of Chunzi (the 'upright man' of Confucianism), calligraphy became a tool of mass mobilisation. Mao Zedong was well respected as a calligrapher and never hesitated to inscribe his newest slogans or poems in his own hand. Many of Mao's revolutionary comrades left poems or names inscribed in red on rocks around the country.

After Mao's death in 1976, the government tried to revive the work of many artists and academics. This was most successful in Beijing and was even termed a cultural renaissance, with many calligraphers and painters taking on non-revolutionary subjects for the first time. Calligraphy returned as a popular discipline and hobby, making a visit to one of the galleries around the city an interesting and rewarding experience. The newer work was needed, too: sadly for Beijingers, many of the city's pre-revolutionary art holdings were taken by the fleeing Nationalists to Taiwan.

Hua Guofeng, Mao's successor, scrawled his calligraphic thoughts all over the place too. But Hua was a bit of a joke as a calligrapher; in fact, his unworthy brush strokes partly justified his removal from office. Hua's attempt to mimic Mao led to a weakening of the link between calligraphy and politics – by 1980 the Party had imposed a number of restrictions on the use of calligraphy by Party officials.

But it wasn't long before Deng Xiaoping was brandishing a brush, first on a visit to the Special Economic Zones in 1984, then during the 1989 crisis that led to the Tiananmen massacre. To mark his departure from Mao, Deng – the motivational speaker for free-market reform – replaced his early mentor's calligraphy with artistic slogans of his own.

If his ubiquitous artistic displays are anything to go by, the current chairman, Jiang Zemin, seems a little concerned that people will forget him all too quickly. Officially, Jiang is, of course, a 'master' of the brush, but his eventual departure may bring more objective assessments of his style and prose.

Jiang's technocrat background hasn't impeded his style, but has led to fears that calligraphy will be reduced to a mere political commodity. When one considers the extent of signs carrying the mark of the political elite, this fear is no exaggeration. Whether it's a magazine or newspaper banner, the title of a TV series or restaurant sign, the marks of the men at the top are hard to miss.

Alex English

Beijing home is Lu Xun (1881–1936). Considered by many Chinese to be their greatest 20th-century writer, he first achieved fame with *A Madman's Diary*, a paranoiac fable of Confucian society. His most famous work, *The Story of Ah Q*, examines the life of a man who is chronically unable to recognise the setbacks in his life, just as China itself seemed unable to accept the apparently desperate need to modernise. Because his work reflects the need for revolution, the Communists have canonised Lu Xun and his house in Beijing has been preserved as a museum.

Lao She, another important novelist of the early 20th century, is famous for *The Rickshaw Boy*, a social critique of the living conditions of rickshaw drivers in Beijing.

Since the Communists came to power in 1949, writing has become a particularly dangerous occupation. During the Cultural Revolution, the safest thing a writer could do was to churn out slogans in praise of Chairman Mao. Things have eased up, but social critics are still kept on a short leash.

One of the most interesting writers in contemporary China is Zhang Xianliang, whose book *Half of Man is Woman* was extremely controversial in China for its sexual content.

Blood Red Dusk by Lao Gui (literally 'old devil') is a fascinatingly cynical account of the Cultural Revolution years. Feng Jicai is a writer known for his horrific accounts of the same period, and is most famous for his *Voices From the Whirlwind*. More recently, Wang Shuo's short stories have given a voice to Beijing's growing underclass of unemployed and disaffected youth.

SOCIETY & CONDUCT
Traditional Culture
Fengshui The ancient Chinese world view included the belief that the earth, like a human body, has 'channels' or veins, along which benevolent and evil influences flowed. This belief, known as *fēngshuǐ*, or geomancy, plays an important role in the choice of sites for buildings or tombs. An example of fengshui in practice is Jingshan, an artificial hill on the north side of the Forbidden City. It was built specifically as a

barrier to block 'evil influences' from penetrating the emperor's palace.

T'ai chi Previously spelled 'taichichuan' and usually just called t'ai chi (or taiji), this art form has been popular in China for centuries. It's translated into English as 'slow-motion shadow boxing'. It's basically a martial art aimed at improving and maintaining health.

T'ai chi is traditionally performed early in the morning. If you want to see it, visit any major park in Beijing around 6 am or so.

Gongfu One form of the martial arts, *gōngfu* has been popular in the west mostly thanks to Hong Kong movies. Previously spelled 'kungfu', gongfu differs from t'ai chi in that it's performed at a much higher speed and is intended to do bodily harm.

Qigong This is another variation on the gongfu theme. *Qì* represents life's vital energy, and *gōng* is from gongfu. Qigong is a form of energy management, and seems to work almost like magic. Through daily practice, practitioners hope to maintain good mental and physical health. The real masters take the process a step further – they try to project their qi to perform various miracles, including healing others and driving nails through boards with their bare fingers. It's a standard feature of Hong Kong gongfu movies – bad guys are blown away without actually being physically touched, while mortally wounded heroes are healed with a few waves of the hands. Qigong is gaining an increasing number of fans in the west.

Beijing's Qigong Club is within the Wuta Temple grounds (near the Beijing Zoo).

Dos & Don'ts
Dress Cynics say that the Communists are the worst-dressed people in the world. Certainly in the days of blue Mao suits there was a lot of truth to that statement, but Beijingers are now far more fashion-conscious than they once were. Suits and ties for men and flamboyant dresses for women are no longer regarded as unusual. In summer, women now wear miniskirts and shorts which would

Tickled Red

Adam and Eve (whose scintillating sex life is, of course, well documented) have lent their names to Beijing's first sex shop. This is appropriate, since there isn't much 'Chinese' about the concept of better sex through shopping; on the other hand, some of the products inside could only come from China.

Shoppers won't find that fetching '*Pulp Fiction* Gimp Get-Up' for the folks back home, but still, with products that promise to prevent AIDS (eg 'Playman Oil', or a special bathtub liner), who needs leather?

The shop's been around for a few years, and has recently spawned similar ventures in other mainland cities. The story goes that the Adam & Eve Sex Health Shop's founder got official approval for the project by convincing the Party that the store's merchandise would enable the physically disabled to have a sex life (former paramount leader Deng Xiaoping's son is paraplegic).

The official touch appears in the large portrait of Karl Marx (the noted sexologist?) on the wall, and in the store's motto 'Eliminate Sexual Ignorance; Respect Sexual Science'. It's hard to say who's more interested in open-eyed, scientifically sanctioned nooky, the trickle of Beijingers pondering the Claudia Schiffer-like blow-up dolls on display or the prudish government.

Certainly those peeking in from outside keep coming back for more. The shop has attracted some attention in the overseas media, where articles regularly relay the poor state of sexual affairs in China. The line taken is predictable: reduced to puritan status by statistics ('foreplay for 34% of urban couples in China lasts less than one minute' etc), the Chinese are now apparently undergoing a 'sexual awakening' – just like the west (apparently) has.

Lurid statistics take us a long way from the days when the juicier bits of classical Chinese novels were left in Latin by blushing translators. China's moved a long way too: from Taoist and Tantric ideals of sexual relations aimed at loosening the bonds of ego and attachment (for both men and women), the Middle Kingdom appears ready to embrace the essentially Victorian notion that sex is a matter of possessive self-identity ('repression and liberation' of your 'true' self in all its flowering *jouissance*).

But if it looks like China has completely surrendered to a missionary position on sex, look again –

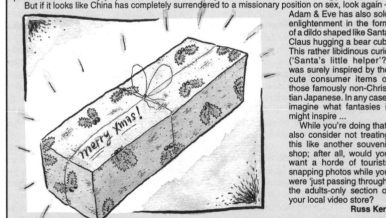

Adam & Eve has also sold enlightenment in the form of a dildo shaped like Santa Claus hugging a bear cub. This rather libidinous curio ('Santa's little helper'?) was surely inspired by the cute consumer items of those famously non-Christian Japanese. In any case, imagine what fantasies it might inspire ...

While you're doing that, also consider not treating this like another souvenir shop; after all, would you want a horde of tourists snapping photos while you were 'just passing through' the adults-only section of your local video store?

Russ Kerr

---

have been scandalous a decade ago. But skimpy bikinis and see-through blouses are stretching the definition of 'acceptable' somewhat – Beijing has a long way to go before catching up with Hong Kong.

If wearing sandals outdoors, there is an unwritten rule that the back of the ankle must be covered with a strap – thongs (flip-flops) are not acceptable, and many backpackers run afoul of this regulation.

Face Face can be loosely defined as 'status' and many Chinese people will go to great lengths to avoid 'losing face'. For example, a foreigner may front up to a hotel desk and have a furious row with the receptionist because the foreigner believes that the hotel bill contains hidden charges (often true) while the receptionist denies it. The receptionist is less likely to admit the truth (and 'lose face') if the foreigner throws a tantrum.

In such situations, you can accomplish a great deal more with smiles, talking about other things for a while ('Where did you learn such good English?'), showing some of your photos from your trip etc, before putting forward your case in a quiet manner (in the case of a hotel bill, a diplomatic solution is to ask for a 'discount').

Avoid direct criticisms of people. If you have to complain about something, like the hot water not working, do so in a fairly quiet tone. Confrontation causes loss of face and that leads to trouble. Venting your rage in public and trying to make someone lose face will cause the Chinese to dig in their heels and only worsen your situation. Business travellers should take note here – a lot of westerners really blow it on this point.

Chopsticks Two chopsticks stuck vertically into a rice bowl resemble incense sticks in a bowl of ashes. This is considered a death sign in China and many other Asian countries – it's rude and should be avoided. However, younger people care less about this.

Red Ink If giving someone your address or telephone number, write in any colour but red. Red ink conveys unfriendliness. If you're teaching, it's OK to use red to correct papers, but if you write extensive comments on the back, use some other colour.

Public Etiquette The Chinese are not nearly as innocent as they pretend to be when it comes to sexual matters. However, the Communist regime is one of the most prudish in the world. Walking around hand in hand is becoming more common but is still considered risqué. Few people get passionate in public; refrain from it yourself. It goes without saying that topless sunbathing and so on is asking for big trouble.

Splitists versus the Motherland Politics is something most Beijingers wisely avoid discussing. Ignorant foreigners sometimes offend their Chinese hosts with what seems like an innocent remark. A good way to create a near riot is to call Taiwan a country – it's firmly hammered into every Chinese head that Taiwan is part of the 'Motherland', and those who say otherwise are passionately denounced as 'splitists' which is just about the worst thing you can be called. Tibet is another sore spot – the Dalai Lama is lambasted in the Chinese press as the devil incarnate – so if you're a closet Lamaist, keep it to yourself. Indeed, it's a good idea to keep negative comments about China to a minimum (this holds true in most countries).

RELIGION

While religions such as Islam and Christianity exist in large areas of China and in a few pockets in Beijing, Confucianism, Taoism and Buddhism dominate. Ancestor worship is also widely practised.

The three main religions have gradually combined over the centuries. Confucianism, in effect state policy for the last two millennia, advocated loyalty to the emperor and to the patriarchal structure below him as its main tenets. These were originally set out by Confucius in the 5th century BC. Taoism has existed in two forms: firstly in the philosophical outlook advocated by the semi-mythical Laotzu (6th century BC) which stresses acceptance of the 'way', of 'going with the flow'; and secondly in a popular form, having many gods and devils in its pantheon. Taoism has also been a strong influence in the Chinese tradition. Mahayana Buddhism, imported from India during the Han Dynasty(206 BC–24 AD) has had fluctuating fortunes but by the 10th century was as entrenched as the other two religions.

The Cultural Revolution devastated Chinese religion – it's yet to recover fully. Temples were destroyed, monks were sent to labour in the countryside where they often perished, and believers were prohibited from worship. But the temples are now being restored and worshippers are returning.

While freedom of religion now exists in China, it's worth noting that membership in the Chinese Communist Party (CCP) is not permitted for anyone practising religion.

LANGUAGE

The official language of the PRC is the Beijing dialect, usually referred to in the west as 'Mandarin Chinese'. The word 'Mandarin' derives from the use of the Beijing dialect as a standard language by the scholar class in centuries past. The official name for Mandarin in China is *pŭtōnghuà*, or 'common speech'.

Lonely Planet publishes a *Mandarin Chinese phrasebook*. A small dictionary with English, romanisation and Chinese characters can also be very helpful.

Chinese & Computers

After long delays, the information revolution has finally arrived in China. Not so long ago the Chinese government frowned on personal ownership of photocopiers and fax machines. Nowadays it's recognised that computer access is a necessity in the drive to modernise. Although access to politically sensitive Internet sites is blocked and Internet users must register with the police, getting an online account is no longer the trauma it once was. And there has been a slow but steady increase in the number of cybercafes permitted to open.

One catch is that Chinese doesn't lend itself to computer environments very well. A computer keyboard is designed for keying in alphabetic languages, not languages like Chinese with thousands of pictographs. A true Chinese 'keyboard' would have to have thousands of keys. Not surprisingly, Chinese software developers have opted for input methods that use a standard alphabetic keyboard.

The easiest input method is to use Romanised Chinese (*Pinyin*), which the computer translates into characters. But when a Romanised Chinese word such as *yi* pulls up over 100 choices, the going can be slow. Moreover, not many Chinese people are familiar with the Romanised version of their language. Another input method allows the user to find the correct character by the order of the strokes used in normal Chinese writing – this method works well but is very slow. A similar but much faster method called *cangjie* breaks every character down into four component parts – it's fast but the main drawback is that it's hard to learn. Yet another system (*neima*) requires the operator to memorise a code number for each character – thousands of them!

Programmers in China, Singapore and Taiwan have been looking for solutions. One option is to input with an electronic pad and pen – however, it's not fast, and prone to errors if your calligraphy is sloppy. Experiments have been tried with voice input, bypassing the need to use your hands entirely. After countless hours of effort and millions of dollars in research grants, the results have been poor – no-one has found an adequate substitute for typing or pen input.

Input is one side of the equation – the other is how to store the characters on disk so they can be outputted when needed. All the original programming work was done in Taiwan, which has an official list of 13,000 traditional Chinese characters to deal with. The Taiwanese produced a coding system called BIG5. Back on the Chinese mainland, where simplified characters are used, the Taiwanese system couldn't be accepted for political reasons so a new system called GB2312 was developed (it supports 7000 characters only). Alas, the two systems are incompatible. Hong Kong chips in by having 3000 specialised Cantonese characters not supported by either system. Then the Internet came along and a new incompatible system called HZ was introduced in an attempt to satisfy everybody, but then the Chinese government introduced the GBK system which supports 20,000 characters. Meanwhile, Microsoft started offering the Unicode system which works with Windows NT but not Windows 97.

To put it in a word, the market is 'confused'. In the meantime, the number of computers in China is increasing exponentially. The proliferation of incompatible 'standards' is perhaps the greatest obstacle to Chinese computing. Most experts believe that Unicode will win out in the long term, but in the meantime it's chaos out there in the computing world.

Meanwhile, computer manufacturers are flocking to China, lured by the promise of cheap labour and the so far mythical market of over one billion souls. But the market is growing – most Chinese companies, as well as many schools and well-to-do individuals, now own PCs. And just what are all these machines being used for? Sometimes for accounting, and sometimes for keeping business records – but mostly for playing video games.

And sometimes for making mischief. Software pirating is rife in China and so are computer viruses. The dreaded 'Li Peng virus' has appeared: it asks if you like Premier Li Peng and if you answer 'yes' your hard disk will be wiped out. ■

Tones

Chinese is a language with a large number of homonyms (words of different meaning but identical pronunciation), and if it were not for its tonal quality it probably would not work very well as a language. Mandarin has four tones: in the first the voice is pitched quite high; in the second it rises rather like when asking a question; in the third the voice dips and then rises; and in the fourth the voice falls away. The following provides an example of how tones can change the meaning:

(1st)	high tone	*mā*	mother
(2nd)	rising tone or numb	*má*	hemp
(3rd)	falling-rising tone	*mǎ*	horse
(4th)	falling tone	*mà*	to scold or swear

Pinyin

In 1958 the Chinese officially adopted a system known as *pīnyīn* as a method of writing their language using the Roman alphabet. Pinyin is helpful in that it is often used, at least in major cities, on shop fronts, street signs and advertising billboards. However, don't expect the average Beijinger to be able to use it. Unless you speak Mandarin you will need a good user-friendly phrasebook with Chinese characters.

The Pinyin system replaces the old Wade-Giles and Lessing systems of romanising Chinese script. Thus under Pinyin, 'Mao Tse-tung' becomes *Mao Zedong*; 'Chou En-lai' becomes *Zhou Enlai*; and 'Peking' becomes *Beijing*.

Pronunciation

The letter **v** is not used in Pinyin. The trickiest sounds in Pinyin are **c**, **q** and **x**. The following is a description of the sounds produced in spoken Mandarin:

Vowels

a	like the 'a' in 'father'
ai	like the 'i' in 'I'
ao	like the 'ow' in 'cow'
e	like the 'u' in 'blur'
ei	like the 'ei' in 'weigh'
i	like the 'ee' in 'meet'
ian	like in 'yen'
ie	like the English word 'yeah'
o	like the 'o' in 'or'
ou	like the 'oa' in 'boat'
u	like the 'u' in 'flute'
ui	like 'way'
uo	like 'w' followed by an 'o' as in 'or'
yu	like German umlaut 'ü' or French 'u' in 'union'
ü	like German umlaut 'ü'

Consonants

c	like the 'ts' in 'bits'
ch	like in English, but with the tongue curled back
h	like in English, but articulated from the throat
q	like the 'ch' in 'cheese'
r	like the 's' in 'pleasure'
sh	like in English, but with the tongue curled back
x	like the 'sh' in 'shine'
z	like the 'ds' in 'suds'
zh	like the 'j' in 'judge', but with the tongue curled back

With the exception of **n**, **ng**, and **r**, syllables never have a consonant at the end. In Pinyin, apostrophes can serve to separate syllables – writing *ping'an* prevents pronunciation as *pin'gan*.

To confuse matters, Beijingers have their own distinct accent sometimes referred to as *r-hua* because nearly every word ends with an 'r' sound. The word for park *(gongyuan)* becomes *gongyuar*. The Chinese word for tea *(cha)* becomes *char*. And so on.

Gestures

The Chinese have a system for counting on their hands and it's worth your while to learn this system of finger counting. The symbol for number 10 is to form a cross with the index fingers, but in many locations the Chinese just show a fist.

Written Language

Chinese characters look like little pictures, and hence are often referred to as a language of 'pictographs'. Many of the basic Chinese characters are in fact highly stylised pictures of what they represent, but often characters give clues to the pronunciation as well.

A well-educated Chinese person should know about 7000 characters. Students would need to understand around 1300 characters to get the gist of a Chinese newspaper, but they'd probably need between 2000 and 3000 before the going started to get easy.

Simplification To increase literacy, the Committee for Reforming the Chinese Language was set up in Beijing in 1954. The committee simplified 2238 characters, reducing the number of strokes by about half.

The reforms were implemented successfully on the mainland, but Taiwan and Hong Kong continue to use traditional characters. The last few years have seen a return of the full-form characters to China, mainly in advertising (where the traditional characters are considered more attractive) and restaurant, hotel and shop signs.

Greetings & Civilities

Hello.
  Nǐ hǎo. 你好
Goodbye.
  Zàijiàn. 再见
Thank you.
  Xièxie. 谢谢
You're welcome.
  Búkèqi. 不客气
I'm sorry.
  Duìbùqǐ. 对不起
No, don't have.
  Méiyǒu. 没有
No, not so.
  Búshì. 不是
I'm a foreign student.
  Wǒ shì liúxuéshēng. 我是留学生
What's to be done now?
  Zěnme bàn? 怎么办?
It doesn't matter.
  Méishì. 没事
I want ...
  Wǒ yào ... 我要
No, I don't want it.
  Búyào. 不要
I don't understand.
  Wǒ tīngbudǒng. 听不懂
I understand.
  Wǒ tīngdedǒng. 我听得懂
Do you understand?
  Dǒng ma? 懂吗?

Toilets

toilet (restroom)
  cèsuǒ 厕所
toilet paper
  wèishēng zhǐ 卫生纸
bathroom (washroom)
  xǐshǒu jiān 洗手间

Money

How much is it?
  Duōshǎo qián? 多少钱?
Is there anything cheaper?
  Yǒu piányi yìdiǎn de ma?
  有便宜一点的吗?
That's too expensive.
  Tài guìle. 太贵了
I want to change money.
  Wǒ yào huàn qián. 我要换钱

Accommodation

hotel
  lǚguǎn 旅馆
tourist hotel
  bīnguǎn/fàndiàn/jiǔdiàn
  宾馆/饭店/酒店宾馆
reception desk
  zǒng fúwù tái 总服务台
dormitory
  duōrénfáng 多人房
single room
  dānrénfáng 单人房
twin room
  shuāngrénfáng 双人房
bed
  chuángwèi 床位
economy room (no bath)
  pǔtōngfáng 普通房
standard room
  biāozhǔn fángjiān 标准房间

studio suite
tàofáng 套房
deluxe suite
háohuá tàofáng 豪华套房
Is there a vacant room?
Yŏu méiyŏu kōng fángjiān? 有没有空房间?
Yes, there is.
Yŏu. 有
No, there isn't.
Méiyŏu. 没有
Can I see the room?
Wŏ néng kànkan ma? 我能看房间吗?
I don't like this room.
Wŏ bù xĭhuan zhèijiān fángjiān.
我不喜欢这间房间
book a whole room
bāofáng 包房
Are there any messages for me?
Yŏu méiyŏu liú huà? 有没有留话?
May I have a hotel namecard?
Yŏu méiyŏu lǚguăn de míngpiàn?
有没有旅馆的名片?
Could I have these clothes washed, please?
Qíng bă zhè xiē yīfú xĭ gānjìng, hăo ma?
请把这些衣服洗干净, 好吗?

Post

post office
yóujú 邮局
letters
xìn 信
envelope
xìnfēng 信封
package
bāoguŏ 包裹
air mail
hángkōng xìn 航空信
surface mail
píngyóu 平邮
stamps
yóupiào 邮票
postcard
míngxìnpiàn 明信片
aerogramme
hángkōng xìnjiàn 航空信件
poste restante
cúnjú hòulĭnglán 存局候领栏
express mail (EMS)
yóuzhèng tèkuài zhuāndì 邮政特快专递
registered mail
guà hào 挂号

Telecommunications

telephone
diànhuà 电话
telephone office
diànxùn dàlóu 电讯大楼
telephone card
diànhuà kă 电话卡
international call
guójì diànhuà 国际电话
collect call
duìfāng fùqián diànhuà 对方付钱电话
direct-dial call
zhíbō diànhuà 直拨电话
fax
chuánzhēn 传真

Directions

map
dìtú 地图
Where is the ...?
... zài nălĭ? ... 在哪里?
I'm lost.
Wŏ mílùle 我迷路
turn right
yòu zhuăn 右转
turn left
zuŏ zhuăn 左转
go straight
yìzhí zŏu 一直走
turn around
wăng huí zŏu 往回走

Bicycle

bicycle
zìxíngchē 自行车
I want to hire a bicycle.
Wŏ yào zū yíliàng zìxíngchē 我要租一辆自行车
How much is it per day?
Yìtiān duōshăo qián? 一天多少钱?
How much is it per hour?
Yíge xiăoshí duōshăo qián?
一个小时多少钱?
How much is the deposit?
Yājīn dūoshăo qián? 押金多少钱?

Transport

I want to go to ...
Wŏ yào qù ... 我要去...
I want to get off.
Wŏ yào xiàchē. 我要下车

luggage
  xínglǐ　　　行李
left-luggage room
  jìcún chù　　　寄存处
one ticket
  yìzhāng piào　　　一张票
What time does it depart?
  Jǐdiǎn kāi?　　　几点开?
What time does it arrive?
  Jǐdiǎn dào?　　　几点到?
How long does the trip take?
  Zhècì lǚxíng yào huā duōcháng shíjiān?
　　　这次旅行要花多长时间?

buy a ticket
  mǎi piào　　　买票
refund a ticket
  tuì piào　　　退票
taxi
  chūzū chē　　　出租车
microbus ('bread') taxi
  miànbāo chē, miàndì　　　面包车, 面的
Please use the meter.
  Dǎ biǎo.　　　打表

Bus

bus
  gōnggòng qìchē　　　公共汽车
minibus
  xiǎo gōnggòng qìchē　　　小公共汽车
long-distance bus station
  chángtú qìchē zhàn　　　长途汽车站
When is the first bus?
  Tóubān qìchē jǐdiǎn kāi?　　　头班汽车几点开?
When is the last bus?
  Mòbān qìchē jǐdiǎn kāi?　　　末班汽车几点开?
When is the next bus?
  Xià yìbān qìchē jǐdiǎn kāi?　下一班汽车几点开?

Train

train
  huǒchē　　　火车
ticket office
  shòupiào chù　　　售票处
railway station
  huǒchē zhàn　　　火车站
hard-seat
  yìngxí, yìngzuò　　　硬席, 硬座
soft-seat
  ruǎnxí, ruǎnzuò　　　软席, 软座
hard-sleeper
  yìngwò　　　硬卧

soft-sleeper
  ruǎnwò　　　软卧
platform ticket
  zhàntái piào　　　站台票
Which platform?
  Dìjǐhào zhàntái?　　　第几号站台?
upgrade ticket (after boarding)
  bǔpiào　　　补票
subway (underground)
  dìxiàtiě　　　地下铁
subway station
  dìtiě zhàn　　　地铁站

Air Transport

airport
  fēijīchǎng　　　飞机场
charter flight
  bāojī　　　包机
one-way ticket
  dānchéng piào　　　单程票
round-trip ticket
  láihuí piào　　　来回票
reconfirm
  quèrèn　　　确认
cancel
  qǔxiāo　　　取消
bonded baggage
  cúnzhàn xínglǐ　　　存栈行李
CAAC ticket office
  zhōngguó mínháng shòupiào chù
　　　中国民航售票处

Emergency

emergency
  jǐnjí qíngkuàng　　　紧急情况
hospital emergency room
  jízhěn shì　　　急诊室
police
  jǐngchá　　　警察
Public Security Bureau (PSB)
  gōng'ān jú　　　公安局
Foreign Affairs Branch
  wàishì kē　　　外事科
Fire!
  Zháo huǒle!　　　着火了
Help!
  Jiùmìng a!　　　救命啊
Thief!
  Zhuā xiǎotōu!　　　抓小偷

Medical & Pharmaceutical

I'm sick.
Wǒ shēngbìngle. 我生病了
I'm injured.
Wǒ shòushāngle. 我受伤了
hospital
yīyuàn 医院
laxative
xièyào 泻药
anti-diarrhoeal medicine
zhǐxièyào 止泻药
aspirin
āsīpǐlín 阿斯匹林
antibiotics
kàngjūnsù 抗菌素
condom
bìyùn tào 避孕套
tampon
wèishēng mián tiáo 卫生棉条
sanitary napkin (Kotex)
wèishēng mián 卫生棉

Numbers

0	*líng*	零
1	*yī, yāo*	一, 幺
2	*èr, liǎng*	二, 两
3	*sān*	三
4	*sì*	四
5	*wǔ*	五
6	*liù*	六
7	*qī*	七
8	*bā*	八
9	*jiǔ*	九
10	*shí*	十
11	*shíyī*	十一
12	*shí'èr*	十二
20	*èrshí*	二十
21	*èrshíyī*	二十一
100	*yibǎi*	一百
200	*liǎngbǎi*	两百
1000	*yìqiān*	一千
2000	*liǎngqiān*	两千
10,000	*yíwàn*	一万
20,000	*liǎngwàn*	两万
100,000	*shíwàn*	十万
200,000	*èrshíwàn*	二十万

Facts for the Visitor

WHEN TO GO

Summer is considered peak season, when hotels typically raise their rates and the Great Wall nearly collapses under the weight of marching tourists. Autumn has the best weather and fewer tourists. Spring is less pleasant – not many tourists but lots of wind and dust. In winter, you'll have Beijing to yourself, and many hotels offer substantial discounts – just remember it's an ice box outside. Be sure to avoid the Chinese New Year, when everything is chock-a-block (see the Public Holidays & Special Events section later in this chapter).

ORIENTATION

Though it may not appear so in the shambles of arrival, Beijing is a place of very orderly design. Long, straight boulevards and avenues are crisscrossed by a network of lanes. Places of interest are either very easy to find if they're on the avenues, or impossible to find if they're buried down the narrow alleys. To make sense of addresses and maps, it's useful to know just a little Chinese terminology (see box below).

The Forbidden City acts like a bullseye, surrounded by a chessboard of roads (with the First Ring Road marking the outline of what was once a walled enclosure encompassing the Forbidden City). The symmetry folds on an ancient north-south axis passing through Qianmen (Front Gate).

There is a certain logic to street names in Beijing: Jianguomenwai Dajie, for example, means 'the avenue *(dajie)* outside *(wai)* Jianguo Gate (Jianguomen)'; whereas Jianguomennei Dajie means 'the avenue inside *(nei)* Jianguo Gate'. This is purely an academic exercise since the gate in question no longer exists.

Streets are also split along compass points. For example, Andingmen Dong Dajie is East Andingmen Avenue, and Andingmen Xi Dajie is the western part of the same street. These streets tend to head off from an intersection, usually where a gate – in this case Andingmen – once stood. A major boulevard can change names six or eight times along its length.

Then there are the 'villages' *(li)*. Beijing was once surrounded by many tiny villages, though over time these have in fact become neighbourhoods within the megalopolis. Thus you find addresses like Yulinli (Yulin Village). Many addresses also refer to bridges *(qiao)* long gone, such as Anhuaqiao (Anhua Bridge).

There are four 'ring roads' around Beijing, circumnavigating the city centre in concentric circles. The First (innermost) Ring Road is a mapmaker's fiction and just part of the

Map Terms					
Road		lane		east	
lù	路	*xiàng*	巷	*dōng*	东
street		inner		west	
jiē	街	*nèi*	内	*xī*	西
avenue		outer		village	
dàjiē	大街	*wài*	外	*lǐ*	里
boulevard		north		gate	
dàdào	大道	*běi*	北	*mén*	门
alley		south		bridge	
hútong	胡同	*nán*	南	*qiáo*	桥

grid around the Forbidden City. However, the Second *(èrhuán)* and Third Ring Roads *(sānhuán)* should be taken seriously – they are multi-lane freeways that get you around town quickly. Construction of the Fourth Ring Road *(sìhuán)* is nearly complete and a fifth is on the drawing boards.

The Beijing Municipality is carved up into 10 districts and eight counties. Roughly within the Second Ring Road are the four central districts: Xicheng (north-west), Dongcheng (north-east), Chongwen (south-east) and Xuanwu (south-west). Outside the Second Ring Road, the so-called 'suburban' (now urbanised) districts are Chaoyang (east), Fengtai (south-west), Haidian (north-west) and Shijingshan (central west).

MAPS

This Month in Beijing is a freebie handed out at many big hotels. It comes with a basic English map of the city along with a good deal of up-to-date tourist information.

Good bilingual maps of Beijing showing the bus routes are a rare find. There are some still around (try hotel gift shops and the Friendship Store) – but they tend to be out of date.

If you can deal with Chinese characters you'll find a wide variety of up-to-date maps to choose from. New editions printed by different companies are issued every couple of months. Street vendors hawk these maps (for about Y2) near subway stations, park entrances and other likely places.

The Foreign Languages Bookstore on Wangfujing sells several excellent atlases of Beijing, but these are entirely in Chinese characters.

TOURIST OFFICES

Beijing doesn't yet have a real walk-in tourist office like you find in Hong Kong or Macau. The closest thing to it is the Beijing Tourism Administration (☎ 6515-8844), but don't ring them up (unless you want to host a convention or sporting event). For tourist pamphlets, try the China International Travel Service (CITS) – although they can be a little reluctant to hand them out.

Individual travellers would be better served by calling the tourist hotline (☎ 6513-0828), which operates 24 hours and is run by the Beijing Tourism Administration.

For more information on the major government-owned travel agencies – CITS and China Travel Service (CTS) – look under Travel Agents in the Getting There & Away chapter. These two agencies also have branch offices abroad (see the Getting There & Away chapter, page 64).

Individual travel agencies have some useful tourist information, but remember they're in the business of organising tours in return for cold hard cash. Don't expect them to be very charitable with their time.

DOCUMENTS

Visas

Visas are readily available from Chinese embassies and consulates in most western and many other countries (see the list under Embassies later in this chapter).

The Chinese government requires that your passport must be valid for at least six months after the expiry date of your visa.

When you check into a hotel, there is usually a question on the registration form asking what type of visa you have. The letter specifying your visa category is usually stamped on the visa itself. There are seven categories of visas, as follows:

L	travel *(lǚxíng)*
F	business *(fǎngwèn)*
D	resident *(dìngjū)*
G	transit *(guòjìng)*
X	student *(liúxué)*
Z	working *(rènzhí)*
C	steward/ess *(chéngwù)*

Most people get a one-month single-entry visa. These visas are valid from the date of entry that you specify on the visa application. But all other visas are valid from the date of issue, *not* from the date of entry, so there's no point in getting such a visa far in advance of your planned entry date.

If you request it, you can also receive a dual-entry travel visa (each entry valid for 30 days) or a single-entry three-month visa. These visas cost more than the standard 30-day visa, but may be worth it to you depending on your itinerary.

Business visas are multiple-entry and permit a stay of 30 days per visit – the visa remains valid for three to six months from date of issue (depending on how much you paid for it). These visas are easy to get – you do not need to prove that you will be doing business. However, business visas are hard to extend, so don't get one if you plan to be in China for more than 30 days. Obviously, this is the visa to get if you'll be making frequent short trips to China.

Hong Kong and Macau are both good places to get Chinese visas. Normally it takes three days to issue a visa, but it can be done overnight or even the same day if you're willing to pay a surcharge.

Visa Extensions

The Public Security Bureau (PSB) is the name given to China's police force, and visa extensions are handled by the PSB's Foreign Affairs Section. The Beijing PSB (Map 11) (☎ 6525-5486) is at 85 Beichizi Dajie, the street running north-south at the east side of the Forbidden City. It's open from 8.30 to 11.30 am and 1 to 5 pm Monday to Friday; from 8.30 to 11.30 am Saturday; and closed on Sunday. Extensions can cost nothing for some but Y110 for most nationalities. It's free for nationals of Cuba and Tanzania.

The general rule is that if you entered on a one-month visa you can get one extension of one month's duration. You may be able to wangle more, especially with cogent reasons such as illness (except AIDS) or transport delays, but second extensions are usually only granted for one week with the understanding that you are on your way out of China. Similarly, if you entered on a three-month visa, you'll probably only get a one-week extension. To extend a business visa, you need a letter from a Chinese work unit willing to sponsor you. If you're studying in China, your school can of course sponsor you for a visa extension.

The penalty for overstaying your visa is a Y300 fine per day!

Photocopies

If married and travelling with your spouse, a copy of your marriage certificate can save some grief if you become involved with the police, hospitals or other bureaucratic institutions. If you're thinking about working or studying in China, photocopies of college or university diplomas, transcripts and letters of recommendation could prove helpful.

It might be useful to have a photocopy of your passport in the unfortunate event that your real passport gets lost or stolen. Even better is to bring along an old expired passport if you have one – it can be used as proof of your identity so that your embassy can issue you with a replacement passport.

Travel Insurance

It's very likely that a health insurance policy which you contribute to in your home country will *not* cover you in China – if unsure, ask your insurance company. If you're not covered, it would be prudent to purchase travel insurance. The best policies will reimburse you for a variety of mishaps such as accidents, illness, theft and even the purchase of an emergency ticket home. The policies are usually available from travel agents, including student travel services. Read the small print: some policies specifically exclude 'dangerous activities', which may include motorcycling, scuba diving and even hiking. Obviously, you'll want a policy that covers you in all the circumstances you're likely to find yourself in.

To make a claim for compensation, you will need proper documentation (hopefully in English). This can include medical reports, police reports, baggage receipts from airlines etc.

Driving Licence

Foreign tourists are not permitted to drive in China without special permission, and getting such permission will cost you dearly. In other words, it's highly unlikely that you'll get any use out of either your home country's licence or an International Driving Permit.

It's a different story if you plan to take up residence in Beijing. If you have a Chinese residence certificate, you can obtain a Chinese driver's licence after some bureaucratic wrangling. The process will be much less complicated if you bring a valid licence from your home country – otherwise you'll have to take a driving course and a driving test in China, which is a major hassle and best avoided. The procedure is basically that the Chinese authorities exchange your original driver's licence for a Chinese one. They will keep your original licence until you depart China, at which time it will be returned to you in exchange for the Chinese one.

One stumbling block is that you may be asked to prove that you first own a car before the licence can be issued!

Name Cards

Business name cards are essential, even if you don't do business – exchanging name cards with someone you've just met goes down well. It's particularly good if you can get your name translated into Chinese and have that printed just next to your English name. You can get name cards made cheaply in China, but it's better to have some in advance of your arrival.

Chinese Documents

Foreigners who live, work or study in China will be issued with a number of documents, and some of these can be used to obtain substantial discounts for flights, hotels, museums and tourist sites.

Student Card A very common but not-too-useful document is the so-called 'white card'. This is a simple student ID card with a pasted-on photo which is usually kept in a red plastic holder (some call it a 'red card' for this reason). A white card is easily forged – they can be reproduced with a photocopy machine – and the red plastic holders are on sale everywhere. For this reason, you might be approached by touts wanting to sell you a fake one. The fact is that outside Beijing and

other major cities railway clerks really have no idea what a white card is supposed to look like – fake ones sometimes work when real ones don't! One French student had a knock-down drag-out battle with a smug booking clerk who threw her absolutely genuine white card into the rubbish bin and told her it was a fake.

Residence Permit The 'green card' is a residence permit, issued to English teachers, business people, students and other foreigners who are authorised to live in the PRC. It's such a valuable document that you'd better not lose it if you have one, or the PSB will be all over you. Foreigners living in China say that if you lose your green card, you might want to leave the country rather than face the music.

A green card will sometimes mean you'll get you a discount on flights, hotels, tourist sites and elsewhere. However, don't count on this – no law says they have to give you a discount.

The green card is not really a card but resembles a small passport – it would be extremely difficult to forge without modern printing equipment and special paper. Green cards are issued for one year and must be renewed annually.

Marriage Certificate Foreigners married to Chinese nationals must have their marriage certificates to check into a hotel. If you don't have the certificates (husband's and wife's both), then you're talking about two rooms for sure. The certificate has a red cover and looks much like a passport (which, in a sense, it is ... nudge nudge, wink wink).

Dog Licence Expats can own a legally licensed dog in Beijing provided it isn't taller than 35cm. The licence has to be applied for at the PSB office (Map 11) (☎ 6525-5486) at 85 Beichizi Dajie, which is also the same place you go for visa extensions. The dog will need to get a physical examination at the Veterinary Clinic (☎ 6491-5708) at 96 Huizhongsi, Chaoyang District.

EMBASSIES
Chinese Embassies Abroad
Some of the addresses of Chinese embassies and consulates in major cities overseas include:

Australia
15 Coronation Drive, Yarralumla, ACT 2600 (☎ (02) 6273-4780, 6273-4781)
Consulates: Melbourne, Perth and Sydney
Austria
Metternichgasse 4, 1030 Vienna (☎ (06) 713-6706)
Belgium
Boulevarde General Jacques 19, 1050 Bruxelles (☎ (02) 640-4006)
Canada
515 St Patrick St, Ottawa, Ontario K1N 5H3 (☎ (613) 789-3509)
Consulates: Toronto and Vancouver
Denmark
Oregards Alle 25, 2900 Hellerup, Copenhagen (☎ (039) 625806)
France
11 avenue George V, 75008, Paris (☎ (01) 47 23 36 77)
Germany
Kurfürstenallee 125300 Bonn 2 (☎ (0228) 361 095)
Hungary
Budapest VI-1068 (☎ 122-4872)
Italy
00135 Roma Via Della Camilluccia 613, Rome (☎ (06) 3630-8534, 3630-3856)
Consulate: Milan
Japan
3-4-33 Moto-Azabu, Minato-ku, Tokyo 106 (☎ (03) 3403-3380, 3403-3065)
Consulates: Fukuoka, Osaka and Sapporo
Netherlands
Adriaan Goekooplaan 7, 2517 JX The Hague (☎ (070) 355-1515)
New Zealand
104A Korokoro Rd, Petone, Wellington (☎ (04) 587-0407)
Consulate: Auckland
Poland
00-203 Warsaw St, Bonifraterska 1 (☎ 313836)
Singapore
70 Dalvey Rd (☎ 734-3361)
South Korea
83 Myŏng-dong 2-ga, Chung-gu (☎ (02) 319-5101)
Spain
Arturo Soria 111, 28043 Madrid (☎ (341) 519-4242)
Consulate: Barcelona

Sweden
Ringvagen 56, 18134 Lidingo (☎ (08) 767 87 40, 767 40 83)
Switzerland
7 JV Widmannstrasse, 3074 Muri Bern (☎ (031) 951 14 01, 951 14 02)
UK
31 Portland Place, London, W1N 5AG (☎ (0171) 636-9756)
USA
2300 Connecticut Ave NW, Washington DC 20008 (☎ (202) 328-2517)
Consulates: Chicago, Houston, Los Angeles, New York and San Francisco

Foreign Embassies in Beijing
A visit to Beijing's embassy-land is a trip in itself – sentry boxes with Chinese soldiers, fancy residences for the diplomats and fancy stores, restaurants, discos and nightclubs for entertainment. There are two main embassy compounds – Jianguomenwai and Sanlitun.

Embassies in the Jianguomenwai area (Map 9) include:

Austria
5 Xiushuinan Jie (☎ 6532-2061; fax 6532-1505)
Bangladesh
42 Guanghua Lu (☎ 6532-2521; fax 6532-4346)
Czech Republic
Ritan Lu (☎ 6532-1531; fax 6532-5653)
India
1 Ritandong Lu (☎ 6532-1908; fax 6532-4684)
Ireland
3 Ritan Dong Lu (☎ 6532-2691; fax 6532-2168)
Israel
Room 405, West Wing, China World Trade Centre, 1 Jianguomenwai Dajie (☎ 6505-0328)
Japan
7 Ritan Lu (☎ 6532-2361; fax 6532-4625)
Mongolia
2 Xiushuibei Jie (☎ 6532-1203; fax 6532-5045)
New Zealand
1 Ritan Dong 2-Jie (☎ 6532-2731; fax 6532-4317)
North Korea
Ritanbei Lu (☎ 6532-1186; fax 6532-6056)
Philippines
23 Xiushuibei Jie (☎ 6532-1872; fax 6532-3761)
Poland
1 Ritan Lu (☎ 6532-1235; fax 6532-5364)
Romania
Ritan Lu Dong 2-Jie (☎ 6532-3315; fax 6532-5728)
Singapore
1 Xiushuibei Jie (☎ 6532-3926; fax 6532-2215)

South Korea
 3rd and 4th floors, China World Trade Centre, 1 Jianguomenwai Dajie (☎ 6505-2608; fax 6505-3458)
Slovak Republic
 Ritan Lu (☎ 6532-1531; fax 6532-4814)
Sri Lanka
 3 Jianhua Lu (☎ 6532-1861; fax 6532-5426)
Thailand
 40 Guanghua Lu (☎ 6532-1903; fax 6532-1748)
UK
 11 Guanghua Lu (☎ 6532-1961; fax 6532-1937)
USA
 3 Xiushuibei Jie (☎ 6532-3831; fax 6532-6057)
Vietnam
 32 Guanghua Lu (☎ 6532-1155; fax 6532-5720)

The Sanlitun compound (Map 7) is home to the following embassies:

Australia
 21 Dongzhimenwai Dajie (☎ 6532-2331; fax 6532-6957)
Belgium
 6 Sanlitun Lu (☎ 6532-1736; fax 6532-5097)
Cambodia
 9 Dongzhimenwai Dajie (☎ 6532-1889; fax 6532-3507)
Canada
 19 Dongzhimenwai Dajie (☎ 6532-3536; fax 6532-4072)
Denmark
 1 Sanlitun Dong 5-Jie (☎ 6532-2431; fax 6532-2439)
Finland
 1-10-1 Tayuan Diplomatic Building, 14 Liangmahenan Lu (☎ 6532-1817; fax 6532-1884)
France
 3 Sanlitun Dong 3-Jie (☎ 6532-1331; fax 6532-4841)
Germany
 5 Dongzhimenwai Dajie (☎ 6532-2161; fax 6532-5336)
Hungary
 10 Dongzhimenwai Dajie (☎ 6532-1431; fax 6532-5053)
Italy
 2 Sanlitun Dong 2-Jie (☎ 6532-2131; fax 6532-4676)
Kazakhstan
 9 Sanlitun Dong 6-Jie (☎ 6532-6182; fax 6532-6183)
Malaysia
 13 Dongzhimenwai Dajie (☎ 6532-2531; fax 6532-5032)
Myanmar (Burma)
 6 Dongzhimenwai Dajie (☎ 6532-1584; fax 6532-1344)

Nepal
 1 Sanlitun Xi 6-Jie (☎ 6532-1795; fax 6532-3251)
Netherlands
 4 Liangmahenan Lu (☎ 6532-1131; fax 6532-4689)
Norway
 1 Sanlitun Dong 1-Jie (☎ 6532-2261; fax 6532-2392)
Pakistan
 1 Dongzhimenwai Dajie (☎ 6532-2504)
Portugal
 2-15-1 Tayuan Diplomatic Building, 14 Liangmahe Nan Lu(☎ 6532-3497; fax 6532-4637)
Russia
 4 Dongzhimen Beizhong Jie, west of the Sanlitun Compound in a separate compound (☎ 6532-1267; fax 6532-4853)
Spain
 9 Sanlitun Lu (☎ 6532-1986; fax 6532-3401)
Sweden
 3 Dongzhimenwai Dajie (☎ 6532-3331; fax 6532-5008)
Switzerland
 3 Sanlitun Dong 5-Jie (☎ 6532-2736; fax 6532-4353)
Ukraine
 11 Sanlitun Dong 6-Jie (☎ 6532-6359; fax 6532-6765)

CUSTOMS

Chinese border crossings have gone from being severely traumatic to exceedingly easy – at least in most cases. There are now clearly marked 'green channels' and 'red channels', the latter reserved for those with such everyday travel items as refrigerators, washing machines, microwave ovens and television sets.

Take note that antiques, or even things which look antique, could cause you a few hassles with Customs:

If you plan to take antiques out of China, you need a certificate or red seal to clear Customs. I bought a bronze Buddha head (Customs found it when they x-rayed my baggage). I spent US$600 on it, and had it confiscated by Customs upon leaving China. At this point, I may or may not be able to recover it, but it will require a trip back to China to get it. To add insult to injury, I will be required to pay Customs for storage. If I am not able to recover the Buddha, Customs will apparently sell it and keep the money they receive!

Nancy Parshall

GLENN BEANLAND

DAMIEN SIMONIS

The many faces of Beijing: a woman burns incense at the Lama Temple (top left); old men play Chinese dominoes (*pai gow*) near Tiantan Park (top right); a budding maestro munches on an apple (bottom left); Mao-style jackets and caps are still worn by older Beijingers (bottom right).

DIANA MAYFIELD

DAMIEN SIMONIS

GLENN BEANLAND

GLEN'... ...ANLAND

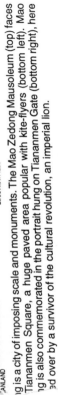

DIANA MAYFIELD

...g is a city of imposing scale and monuments. The Mao Zedong Mausoleum (top) faces Tiananmen Square, a huge paved area popular with kite-flyers (bottom left). Mao ...g is also commemorated in the portrait hung on Tiananmen Gate (bottom right), here ...d over by a survivor of the cultural revolution, an imperial lion.

Indeed, there's a standing joke that the duty-free shop in Beijing's airport simply 'recycles' Chinese relics by selling them to tourists, only to have these items seized moments later by Customs and returned to the shop.

A very peculiar restriction is the Y300 limit (Y150 if going to Hong Kong or Macau) on taking herbal medicines out of the country. One would think that China would like to encourage the export of Chinese medicine, a profitable (and mostly state-run) industry.

Duty free, you're allowed to import 400 cigarettes or the equivalent in tobacco products, two litres of alcoholic drink and 50g of gold or silver. Importation of fresh fruit is prohibited. You can legally only bring in or take out Y6000 in Chinese currency. There are no restrictions on foreign currency, however you should declare any cash that exceeds US$5000 (or its equivalent in another currency).

It's illegal to impot printed material, film, tapes etc which are 'detrimental to China's politics, economy, culture and ethics'. But don't be too concerned about what you take to read. As you leave China, any tapes, manuscripts, books etc 'which contain state secrets or are otherwise prohibited for export' can be seized. Mainly, the authorities are interested in things written in Chinese – they seldom pay much attention to English publications.

MONEY
Cash
Australian, Canadian, US, UK, Hong Kong, Japanese and most west European currencies are acceptable in China, but US dollars are still the easiest to change.

Travellers Cheques
Besides the advantage of safety, travellers cheques are useful to carry in China because the exchange rate is actually more favourable than the rate you get for cash. Cheques from most of the world's leading banks and issuing agencies are acceptable in Beijing – stick with the major players such as Citibank,

American Express and Visa and you should be OK.

Some foreign banks have representative offices in Beijing, but these offices are by no means full-service banking operations. Some can issue replacements for lost or stolen traveller's cheques, or at least process the paperwork for you.

American Express (☎ 6505-2888; fax 6505-4972) is in Room L115D, Shopping Arcade, China World Trade Centre, 1 Jianguomenwai Dajie, 100004 (Map 9). Citibank (☎ 6500-4425; fax 6512-7930) is in Room 1, 18th floor, CITIC Building, 19 Jianguomenwai Dajie, 100004 (Map 9).

ATMs
There is currently no way to use a foreign-issued ATM (Automatic Telling Machine) card in Beijing, though this may change in the near future. On the other hand, foreigners can indeed open bank accounts in China and apply for a local ATM card, although a card issued in Beijing will not work in Shanghai (or any other province outside the Beijing municipality).

Accounts can be opened in both Chinese yuan and US dollars (the latter only at special foreign-exchange banks), but the ATMs only pay in Chinese yuan. You do not need to have resident status – a tourist visa is sufficient.

American Express has an ATM in the China World Trade Centre shopping arcade. If you have an American Express card you can make a withdrawal here.

Credit Cards
Plastic money is gaining more acceptance in Beijing. Useful cards now include Visa, MasterCard, American Express, JCB and Diners Club. Expats can be issued a genuine made-in-China Peony, Jinsui or Great Wall credit card. It's possible to get a cash advance against any of these cards at CITIC Bank, 19 Jianguomenwai Dajie (Map 9), but there is a steep (5%) commission.

International Transfers
Inter-bank money transfers using China's wobbly banking system can take weeks. If

you have to use a bank, try CITIC at 19 Jianguomenwai Dajie (first open an account, then have the money wired to it).

There's also a very efficient money transfer service which is a joint venture between Western Union Financial Services in the USA and China Courier Service Corporation. China Courier (☎ 6318-4285) is at 173 Yong'an St in Beijing. There are branches also at the Asian Games Village (National Olympic Sports Centre) post office and Jianguomennei Dajie post office. For now, only US currency is handled.

Currency

The basic unit of Chinese currency is the *yuan* – designated in this book by a capital 'Y'. In spoken Chinese, the word *kuai* or *kuaiqian* is often substituted for yuan. Ten *jiao* – in spoken Chinese, it's pronounced *mao* – make up one yuan. Ten *fen* make up one *jiao*, but these days fen are very rare because they're worth next to nothing.

Renminbi (RMB), or 'people's money', is issued by the Bank of China. Paper notes are issued in denominations of one, two, five, 10, 50 and 100 yuan; one, two and five jiao; and one, two and five fen. The one-fen note is small and yellow, the two-fen note is blue, and the five-fen note is small and green – all are hardly worth the paper they're printed on. Coins are in denominations of one yuan; five jiao; and one, two and five fen.

Currency Exchange

Exchange rates against the yuan at the time of publication include the following:

Australia	A$1	=	Y5.49
Canada	C$1	=	Y5.83
France	FF1	=	Y1.34
Germany	DM1	=	Y4.51
Hong Kong	HK$1	=	Y1.06
Japan	¥1	=	Y0.06
Netherlands	G1	=	Y4.01
New Zealand	NZ$1	=	Y4.65
Switzerland	SFr1	=	Y5.52
UK	UK£1	=	Y13.80
USA	US$1	=	Y8.29

Changing Money

Foreign currency and travellers cheques can be changed at main branches of the Bank of China, CITIC, tourist hotels, the Friendship Store and some other big department stores. Hotels usually give the official rate, but some will add a small commission. A bigger problem is that a few up-market hotels only change money for their own guests.

Hong Kong dollars, Japanese yen and most western European currencies can be exchanged at major banks, but US dollars are still the easiest to change.

Whenever you change foreign currency into Chinese currency you'll be given a money-exchange voucher recording the transaction. Theoretically you need to show this to change Chinese yuan back to foreign currency – in practice, there is no problem. It's easier to buy and sell Chinese yuan in Hong Kong and Macau. Try not to get stuck with a lot of Chinese currency on departure, because outside China RMB is hard to unload.

At Beijing's capital airport there is only a single money changer on duty, and when several large international flights arrive at once you may have to queue for an hour or more! People have complained about this for years to no avail. The best bet is to have several hundred yuan before arrival – you can then change money at a bank or your hotel though this may not work if you arrive late in the evening.

Black Market

Forget it – black-market money changers are nothing but thieves. Don't even bother talking to them unless you enjoy getting ripped off.

As for bringing things to Beijing to sell, you'll probably find that the Chinese strike too much of a hard bargain to make it worth the trouble.

Costs

Beijing can be more expensive than New York or London, a somewhat ridiculous situation given the fact that beneath the veneer,

China's capital is still a poor city where most workers earn a pittance.

How much it actually costs pretty much depends on the degree of comfort you desire. Hotels are going to be the biggest expense, but food and transport can add up quickly too. Excluding the cost of getting to Beijing, ascetics can survive on US$15 per day. This means you must stay in dormitories, travel by bus or bicycle rather than taxi, eat from street stalls or small cafes and refrain from buying anything.

Travelling, however, is something to be enjoyed, not an endurance contest. Staying in some dump, eating badly and fighting your way aboard the Neolithic buses will probably make the whole endeavour more trouble than it's worth.

On the opposite end of the spectrum, rooms at five-star hotels can be over US$200 per day and meals at up-market restaurants can be US$50. And there is an increasing number of classy department stores charging western prices.

China has long had an official policy of tacking all sorts of ridiculous surcharges onto foreigners. The state-owned airlines, for example, add 50% to the price of tickets purchased by foreigners. And parks, museums and other tourist scenic sites often force foreigners into buying special (read 'overpriced') admission tickets. However, noting plunging tourist revenues and loud complaints from China's trading partners, there is at last an attempt being made to redress this grievance. You may still be hit with some ridiculous foreigner surcharges, but the situation is at least improving.

You may also encounter outright cheating by taxi drivers, waiters and others in the various tourist service industries. After so many years of official support for cheating tourists, it's not surprising that many of these people feel that ripping off foreigners is their patriotic duty.

Tipping & Bargaining

As some compensation for being frequently overcharged, Beijing is at least one of those wonderful cities where tipping is not done and almost no one asks for it. This applies throughout China. Porters at up-market hotels will, of course, expect a tip.

Bargaining is something else. As the government has long made it policy to charge foreigners at least double for everything, many private businesses pitch in by charging three or four times the Chinese rate; this leaves considerable room for negotiation.

In large department stores where prices are clearly marked, there is usually no latitude for bargaining. In the smaller shops, bargaining is sometimes possible, especially where there are no price tags. At street stalls, it is expected. In all cases, there is one important rule to follow – be polite. There is nothing wrong with asking for a 'discount', if you do so with a smile. The worst they can say is 'no'. Some foreigners seem to think that bargaining is a battle of wits, involving bluff, screams and threats. This is not only unpleasant for all concerned, it seldom results in you getting a lower price – indeed, in 'face-conscious' China, intimidation is likely to make the vendor more recalcitrant and you'll be overcharged.

You should keep in mind that entrepreneurs are in business to make money; they aren't going to sell anything to you at a loss. Your goal should be to pay the Chinese price, as opposed to the foreigners' price – if you can do that, you've done well.

Taxes

Although big hotels and fancy restaurants may add a tax or 'service charge' of 15%, all other consumer taxes are included in the price tag.

Discounts

Especially at hotels, there is some latitude when it comes to price. The price for hotel rooms in Beijing is ridiculously high for what's on offer, so discounts are not all that difficult to obtain. During the off season (winter, except Chinese New Year) discounting is common, and you may be able to negotiate a better rate for a longer stay, especially at better hotels. On the other hand there's not much discounting at the few budget backpackers' dormitories; prices are low but firmly fixed.

If you have a residence permit to live or work in China, you can often pay the Chinese price for many things (transport, hotel rooms, admission fees etc).

It's also worth knowing that government-owned travel agencies (CITS, CTS etc) can get you sizeable discounts at the top-end hotels. See under Travel Agents in the Getting There & Away chapter.

DOING BUSINESS

In bureaucratic China, even simple things can be made difficult. Renting property, getting a telephone installed, hiring employees, paying taxes and so on, can generate mind-boggling quantities of red tape. Many foreign business people working in Beijing and elsewhere say that success is usually the result of dogged persistence and finding cooperative officials.

If you have any intention of doing business in Beijing, be it buying, selling or investing, it's worth knowing that most urban districts *(shìqū)* have a Commerce Office *(shāngyè jú)*. If you approach one of these offices for assistance, the reaction you get can vary from enthusiastic welcome to bureaucratic inertia. In the case of a dispute (the goods you ordered are not what was delivered etc), the Commerce Office could assist you, provided they are willing.

Buying is simple, selling is more difficult, but setting up a business in Beijing is a whole different can of worms. If yours is a high-technology company, you can go into certain economic zones and register as a wholly foreign-owned enterprise. In that case you can hire people without going through the government, enjoy a three-year tax holiday, obtain long-term income tax advantages and import duty-free personal items for corporate and expat use (including a car!). The alternative is listing your company as a representative office, which does not allow you to sign any contracts in China – these must be signed by the parent company.

It's easier to register as a representative office. First find out where you want to set up (the city or a special economic zone), then go through local authorities (there are no national authorities for this). Go to the local Commerce Office, Economic Ministry, Foreign Ministry, or any ministry that deals with foreign economic trade promotion. In Beijing, the Haidian High-Technology Zone is recommended if you can qualify, but where you register depends on what type of business you're involved in. Contact your embassy first – they can advise you.

The most important thing to remember when you go to register a company is not to turn away when you run into a bureaucratic barrier. Bureaucrats will tell you that everything is 'impossible'. In fact, anything is possible – it all depends on your *guānxi* (relationships). Whatever you have in mind is negotiable, and all the rules are not necessarily rules at all.

Tax rates vary from zone to zone, authority to authority. It seems to be negotiable but 15% is fairly standard in economic zones. Every economic zone has a fairly comprehensive investment guide, available in English and Chinese – ask at the economic or trade section of your embassy, which might have copies of these. These investment guides are getting to be very clear, although even all their printed 'rules' are negotiable!

The Foreign Enterprise Service Corporation (FESCO) is an organisation that most foreign businesses would like to avoid – it's where you are supposed to go to hire employees (its address is given under Useful Organisations later in this chapter). Bits of the bureaucracy which foreign business people should become familiar with are listed under the same heading as FESCO.

Business Services You may find the following service-based companies handy:

Accounting: Arthur Anderson (☎ 6505-3333; fax 6505-1828), Unit 26-29, Level 28, China World Tower, 1 Jianguomenwai Dajie; Price Waterhouse (☎ 6606-7514; fax 6606-7507), Room 409, East Wing Office, China World Trade Centre, 1 Jianguomenwai Dajie

Advertising: Beijing PEI (☎ 6595-0501; fax 6595-0499; email bpcbpacn@public3.bta.net.cn), Building 17A, Guanghuali, Jianguomenwai, Chaoyang District, 100020; Guo An Advertising (☎ 6235-1634; fax 6204-0572), Building 1, Huayanli Qijiahuozi, Deshengmenwai Dajie, Chaoyang District

Attorneys: Graham & James (☎ 6500-2255 ext 3564; fax 6500-2557), Suite 2002, CITIC Building, 19 Jianguomenwai Dajie, 100004; Paul, Weiss, Rifkin, Wharton & Garrison (☎ 6512-3628 ext 363; fax 6512-3631), Room 1910, Scitech Tower, 22 Jianguomenwai Dajie

Banking: China International Trust & Investment Corporation (CITIC), main branch, CITIC Building, 19 Jianguomenwai Dajie, 100004; CITIC Headquarters (☎ 6512-2233; fax 6466-1059), Capital Mansion, 6 Xinyuannan Lu, 100004

Computers: Pandata Software (☎ 6435-7929; email info@pandata.co.cn; http://www.pandata.co.cn)

Insurance: John Hancock Mutual (☎ 6506-8040; fax 6506-8041), Room 1107, Landmark Building, 8 Dongsanhuanbei Lu; Prudential (☎ 6465-1238; fax 6465-1236), Lufthansa Centre, 50 Liangmaqiao Lu

Printing (namecards, etc): Alphagraphics (☎ 6465-1907; fax 6465-1906), S122 Lufthansa Centre, 50 Liangmaqiao Lu, Chaoyang District; Empire Quick Print (☎ 6592-9511; fax 6592-9510), 63 Dongdaqiao Lu, Jianguomenwai Dajie, 100004

Translations: Herald Translations (☎ 6505-5533; email 105172.1504@compuserve.com); Sinofile (☎ 6605-9198; email andrewr@sinofile.com; http://www.sinofile.com)

Visa Photos: Beijing Photo, 263 Wanfgujing Dajie; Friendship Store Instant Photo, 17 Jianguomenwai Dajie; Landao Instant Photo, Landao Department Store, 8 Chaoyangmenwai Dajie; Lily Photo, ground floor, CITIC Building, 19 Jianguomenwai Dajie; Lufthansa Instant Photo, 4th floor, Lufthansa Centre, 50 Liangmaqiao Lu

POST & COMMUNICATIONS
Post

Letters and parcels marked 'Poste Restante, Beijing Main Post Office' will wind up at the International Post Office (Map 9) on Jianguomenbei Dajie, not far from the Friendship Store. Hours are from 8 am to 7 pm. The staff even file poste restante letters in alphabetical order, a rare occurrence in China, but you pay for all this efficiency – there is a Y1.50 fee charged for each letter received.

Some major tourist hotels will hold mail for their guests, but this doesn't always work.

Officially, the PRC forbids several items from being mailed to it – the regulations specifically prohibit 'reactionary books, magazines and propaganda materials, obscene or immoral articles'. You are also considered very naughty if you mail Chinese currency abroad, or receive it by post. Like elsewhere, mail-order hashish and other recreational substances will not amuse the authorities.

The international postal service seems efficient, and airmailed letters and postcards will probably take around five to 10 days to reach their destinations. If possible, write the country of destination in Chinese as well as English, as this should speed up the delivery. Domestic post is amazingly fast, perhaps one day from Beijing to Shanghai. Within Beijing, same-day delivery is possible.

You can post letters at the reception desks of all major hotels. Even at cheap hotels you can do this – reliability varies but in general it's OK. There is a small but convenient post office in the CITIC building (Map 9). Another useful post office is in the basement of the China World Trade Centre (Map 9).

Overseas parcels are sent and received at the International Post & Telecommunications Building on Jianguomen Bei Dajie. Both outgoing and incoming packages will be opened and inspected here. Obviously, if sending a parcel, don't seal the package until you've had it inspected. If someone sends a parcel to you, what you will receive from the mail carrier is a slip of paper (in Chinese only) – you must bring this and your passport to the post office and the package will be opened in front of you and the contents inspected.

Most countries impose a maximum weight limitation (10kg is typical) on packages received. This rate varies from country to country, but Chinese post offices should be able to tell you what the limitation is. If you have a receipt for the goods, then put it in the box when you're mailing it, since it may be opened again by Customs further down the line.

Like elsewhere, China charges extra for registered mail, but offers cheaper postal rates for printed matter, small packets, parcels, bulk mailings and so on. Rates are as follows:

Letters Up to 20g: domestic Y0.50; Hong Kong, Macau and Taiwan airmail Y2.50; Asia-Pacific Y4.70; other countries Y5.40.

Postcards Domestic Y0.30; Hong Kong, Macau and Taiwan airmail Y2; Asia-Pacific Y3.70; other countries Y4.20.

Aerogrammes Hong Kong, Macau and Taiwan Y1.80; Asia-Pacific Y4.50; other countries Y5.20.

EMS Domestic Express Mail Service (EMS) parcels up to 200g cost Y15; each additional 200g costs Y5. International EMS charges vary according to country. Some sample minimal rates (up to 500g parcels) are as follows:

Australia Y195; Eastern Europe Y382; Hong Kong and Macau Y105; Japan and Korea Y135; Middle East Y375; North America Y217; South America Y262; South Asia Y255; South-East Asia Y150; and western Europe Y232

Private Carriers There are a number of private couriers in Beijing which offer international express posting of documents and parcels. None of these private carriers is cheap, but they're fast and secure. These companies have pick-up service as well as drop-off centres, so call for the latest details. The major players in this market are:

DHL (☎ 6466-2211; fax 6467-7826), 45 Xinyuan Jie, Chaoyang District, 100027 (24-hour service)
Federal Express (☎ 6462-3253; fax 6462-3259), 401 EAS Tower, 21 Xiaoyun Lu, Sanyuan Dongqiao, Dongsanhuan Beilu, Chaoyang District, 100027
TNT Skypak (☎ 6465-2227; fax 6462-4018), 8A Xiangheyuan Zhongli, Chaoyang District, 100028
United Parcel Service (☎ 6593-2932), Unit A, 1st floor, Tower B, Beijing Kelun Building, 12A Guanghua Lu, Chaoyang District, 100020

Telephone
China's state-run telephone monopoly has long been known for providing lousy service at high prices. The good news is that this is starting to change – both international and domestic calls can be made with a minimum of fuss from your hotel room. Even card phones are now becoming increasingly widespread.

Many hotel rooms are equipped with phones from which local calls are free. Local calls can be made from public pay phones (there are some around, but not enough to meet demand). Beijing's budding entrepreneurs try to fill the gap – people with a private phone run a long cord out the window and stand with it on a street corner, where they allow you to use their phone to place local calls for around about Y1 each. Long-distance domestic and international calls should be possible on these phones, but ask first. A few restaurants and hotels use the same system – free calls for guests, Y1 for non-guests, and long-distance calls are charged by the minute.

You can place both domestic and international long-distance phone calls from main telecommunications offices, but it's usually more trouble than it's worth. Domestic long-distance rates in China vary according to distance but are cheap. By contrast, international phone calls are expensive. At the International Post & Telecommunications Building, phone and fax service cost the same: domestic Y50, international Y200 for three minutes (a three-minute minimum charge applies).

If you are expecting a call, try to advise the caller beforehand of your hotel room number. The operators frequently have difficulty understanding western names, and the hotel receptionist may not be able to locate you. If this can't be done, then try to inform the operator that you are expecting the call and write down your name and room number – this increases your chances of success.

Card Phones Card phones can be found in hotel lobbies and in most telecommunications buildings. Calls made on card phones are charged by the minute, so you avoid the expense of making a three-minute minimum call. The cards are currently available in two flavours – magnetic phone cards and 'Smartcards'.

The magnetic cards are an older design. The phone company has a problem with these – they can be magnetically recharged using a simple device readily available on the black market. The cards do eventually wear out, but it is possible to recharge it over 100 times – thus, a Y100 phone card can be used to make over Y10,000 worth of phone calls! This situation is not unique to China.

The phone company's response has been to introduce the so-called Smartcards. The cards aren't really smart, but they are resistant to tampering and – as far as is known – nobody has yet built a device to recharge them.

At the present time you'll find both kinds of card phones, but the phone company will definitely phase out the magnetic cards over the next couple of years. Note that magnetic cards can only be used in the province where you buy them, but Smartcards can be used throughout China (provided you can find a Smartcard phone).

The international access code is 00 (same throughout China). Add the country code, then the local area code (omitting the 0 before it) and the number you want to reach. Another option is to dial the home country direct dial number (108), which puts you straight through to a local operator there. You can then make a reverse-charge (collect) call or a credit card call with a telephone credit card valid in the destination country.

With domestic direct dialling, it's useful to know the area codes of China's cities. These all begin with zero, but if you're dialling into China from abroad, omit the first zero from each code.

Hotel Phones You can also dial direct from the phones found in hotel business centres, but this will cost more than using a card phone. Business centres usually charge a three-minute minimum regardless of how briefly you talk.

International Country Codes		
Country	Direct Dial	Home Country Direct
Australia	00-61	108-61
Canada	00-1	108-1
Hong Kong	00-852	108-852
Japan	00-81	108-81
Netherlands	00-31	108-31
New Zealand	00-64	108-64
UK	00-44	108-44
USA	00-1	108-1*

* For the USA you can dial 108-11 (AT&T), 108-12 (MCI) or 108-13 (Sprint)

If your hotel lacks card phones or a business centre, you should be able to dial direct from your hotel room. You'll have to ask the staff at your hotel what's the dial-out code for a direct line (usually a '7' on most switchboards, or sometimes a combination like '78'). Once you have the outside line, dial 00 (the international access code) followed by the country code, area code and the number you want to reach.

The equipment used on most hotel switchboards is not very sophisticated. It's often a simple timer and it begins charging you starting from 30 seconds after you dial '7' (or '78' or whatever). The timer does not know if your call succeeds or not so you get charged if you stay on the line over 30 seconds, even if you just let the phone ring repeatedly or get a busy signal! On the other hand, if you complete your conversation within 30 seconds and hang up, you don't get charged at all. The hotel switchboard timer keeps running until you hang up, not when the other party hangs up, so replace the receiver as soon as the conversation ends. Many business centres use this same system, so be careful.

The usual procedure is that you make the call and someone comes to your room five or 10 minutes later to collect the cash. If the hotel does not have International Direct Dialling (IDD), you can usually book calls from your room through the switchboard and the operator calls you back, but this procedure will be more expensive.

Useful Phone Numbers There's at least a 50% chance that the person answering the phone will speak no English, so you get to practise your Chinese. With that warning in mind, the following might prove useful:

Useful\Emergency Numbers	
Ambulance hotline	☎ 120
Car accident hotline	☎ 122
Car accident hotline (foreigners)	☎ 6839-9971
Domestic long-distance directory assistance	☎ 113, 173
Fire hotline	☎ 119
International directory assistance	☎ 115
Local directory assistance	☎ 114
Phone repair	☎ 112
Police hotline	☎ 110
Post code check	☎ 6303-7131
Time	☎ 117
Tourist hotline	☎ 6513-0828
Transport hotline	☎ 1601688
Weather	☎ 121

Telephone Codes	
International access code	00
China's country code	86
Beijing's area code	010
Guangzhou's area code	020
Shanghai's area code	021
Tianjin's area code	022

Rent A Phone You can gain instant status in Beijing by renting a cellular phone. These are available from Phone Rent (☎ 6422-3287; 6422-9335; fax 6837-2831; email 105371.3152@compuserve.com), Rooms 812 & 819, 1 Binhe Lu, Hepingli, Dongcheng District, 100013. You can rent a phone for as short a time as one day.

Your Own Phone The cost of installing a phone has dropped tremendously in the past couple of years, and the long waiting lists for service have disappeared. The cost for installing a regular phone is now Y2000, or Y7000 for a cellular phone. The cost per minute to both make and receive a local call

is Y0.8. To get your own phone line a residence permit is required.

Cellular telephones are all the rage with cadres and other status-conscious urban Chinese with money to burn. Previously, the Ministry of Post & Telecommunications had a monopoly on cellular phone service in China, but in 1995 the China United Telecommunications Corporation joined the marketing fray.

If you will be staying in China for more than a few months and make frequent overseas calls, it's worthwhile to sign up with a callback service. Virtually all such services are based in the USA (to take advantage of America's cheap phone rates). Some of the choices available include:

Justice Technology (☎ (310) 526-2000; fax 526-2100; http://www.justicecorp.com)
Kallback (☎ (206) 599-1992; fax 599-1982; email info@kallback.com; http://www.kallback.com)
Kallmart (☎ (407) 676-1717; fax 676-5289; email sales@kallmart.com; http://www.kallmart.com)
New World Telecommunications (☎ (201) 488-5811; email economist@newworldtele.com; http://www.newworldtele.com)

The cheapest (if not the most convenient) way to make overseas calls is through the Internet. Getting this to work requires making prior arrangements with the person you wish to call, having the proper software, a fast modem connection and a bit of luck. There are various publications which explain how to do it, but it's beyond the level of this travel guide.

Pagers Those living on a budget, such as foreign students, may well find pagers a more realistic option than having a phone installed. Though considered a luxury in the west, pagers are far more common in China than telephones. Pagers are hot-selling items among the face-conscious Chinese, though cellular phones are the ultimate status symbol (next to a car). China is the world's second largest pager market after the USA and will probably soon be the largest.

Pagers for use in Beijing cost Y15 a month. For a pager useable throughout

Upwardly Mobile ...
Statistically China may still be a poor country, but you wouldn't think so judging by the number of people in the PRC who can be seen toting cellular phones and pagers. Even some street vendors have them.

The other big status symbol are driver's licences. Although there are only a few thousand privately owned cars in Beijing, it's everyone's aim to be ready for the day when they can afford to buy one. In the meantime, driving schools are doing great business. ∎

China, the price rises to Y80 per month. The paging market was opened to free competition in 1993 – there are now about 1700 paging firms in China so it's difficult to say which company is best. The leading manufacturers of cellular phones and pagers are the USA's Motorola and Sweden's Ericsson. The Chinese don't yet manufacture cellular phones, but they do make pagers which even the locals will tell you are junk.

Fax, Telegraph & Email

All but the most rock-bottom hotels offer international telephone and fax services. You can send a telegraph from the Telegraph Service Centre (☎ 6603-4900), at 11 Xichang'an Jie, Xicheng District.

Email is in its infancy in China. A major stumbling block is that the government monopolises telecommunications, so only State-run companies offer email services.

Foreign companies such as CompuServe have tried to come into Beijing and set up local nodes, but the government gives them so little band-width that their systems soon overload. As a result, you'll have much difficulty getting online in Beijing if you want to use a foreign-based Internet Service Provider (ISP). If you're travelling with a portable computer and want to access your email, your only alternative may be to make an expensive call to Hong Kong or abroad.

If you're travelling with a portable computer and modem, all you need is an IDD line with an RJ-11 phone jack to call to your favourite email service abroad. However, it's risky to attach your modem to the phone in your hotel room and dial out through the switchboard – if the switchboard is digital (as opposed to analog) you risk frying your modem. Ironically, this is a bigger problem at newer hotels – old hotels usually have analog equipment.

One of the few companies to come up with a solution to the tricky connection problem is Konexx (http://www.konexx.com), which sells a device called a 'mobile konnector' which protects the modem and allows you to hook up to the phone's handset cord.

There are a small but growing number of Internet cafes in Beijing. Probably the cheapest way to keep in touch while on the road is to sign up for a free account with Hotmail (http://www.hotmail.com/), Rocketmail (http://www.rocketmail.com/) or NetAddress (http://netaddress.usa.net) and access your account from a cybercafe. These services are free because you have to put up with advertising. If you're willing to spend US$15 per year, you can get your email forwarded by signing up with Pobox (http://www.pobox.com) – this service can also block advertising and mail bombs.

Things are a lot easier if you're a legal foreign resident of China and wish to set up a local Internet account. Chinese ISPs are all government run, but the service is gradually improving and costs have come down. You do have to put up with some censorship – the Chinese government has blocked access to sites that peddle pornography or contain political content deemed unsuitable for the masses. Nevertheless, you can get quite a lot of useful work done on the Internet. Some companies in Beijing offering Internet service are as follows:

3CNET (☎ 6496-1814; http://www.netchina.co.cn)
Eastnet (☎ 6529-2268; http://www.home.eastnet.co.cn)
International United Online (☎ 6492-3076; http://www.iuol.cn.net)

The Chinese packet-switching network, CHINAPAC, should be avoided as the charges are nothing short of outrageous (about three times more expensive than an IDD call).

The Sparkice Internet Cafe (Map 10) (☎ 6833-5335; email cafe@sparkice.co.cn; http://www.sparkice.co.cn) *(shíhuá wǎngluò kāfēi shì)* in the west wing of the Capital Gymnasium (west of Beijing Zoo) charges Y30 per hour for use of their machines. It's open daily except Monday. There are two other Sparkice Internet Cafes in Beijing. The second is on the ground floor of the Vantone Shopping Centre, 2-8 Fuchengmenwai Dajie, Xicheng District (Map 5). The third branch is in the China World Trade Centre, 1 Jianguomenwai Dajie (Map 9).

Noticeboards

No discussion of communications in Beijing would be complete without some mention of the various expat noticeboards around town. This is where expats can buy used furniture and computers from those who are giving up and leaving town; find a Chinese tutor; advertise your skills to others (therapeutic massage?); or search for flats to rent.

Expat-oriented supermarkets arguably have the best noticeboards – the Wellcome supermarket in the basement of the China World Trade Centre (Map 9) has a classic. Some expat pubs and/or restaurants, such as the Mexican Wave (Map 9) are good. It's definitely worthwhile asking some of the other expats you'll no doubt encounter just where the latest and best noticeboards can be found.

BOOKS

There is enough literature on China to keep you reading for the next 5000 years of their history, but relatively little dealing with Beijing exclusively. Another irony is that Beijing itself is not a good place to look for books about Beijing – the widest selection in China is in Hong Kong.

Guidebooks

The perennial guide for business travellers is the red-covered *The China Phone Book &* *Business Directory* (China Phone Book Company). It's dry reading, but vital to those who need it. It's most easily purchased in Hong Kong (not Beijing), and don't mistake it for the phone book published by the government, which is mostly useless.

The *Beijing Scene Guidebook* has good information, but the binding falls apart in a matter of hours. The book can be ordered online (http://www.beijingscene.com). To find it in Beijing, ring up their office (☎ 6592-2715; fax 6593-1625).

The *Beijing Insight Guide* by APA Publications of Singapore is a more portable coffee table book with much information about Chinese culture.

Peking Opera by Colin MacKerras is part of the pictorial 'Images of Asia' series.

In Search of Old Peking by Arlington and Lewisohn is one of the great classic guidebooks of the city. It's currently out of print though it can often be found in libraries or second-hand bookshops.

Biking Beijing by Diana Kingsbury has a useful selection of self-guided tours around the thoroughfares and back alleys of the capital. This book is also becoming a little difficult to find.

The Palace Museum: Peking, Treasures of the Forbidden City by Wango and Boda (Yang Weng) is a pricey hardcover guide (over US$50), but covers its subject in microscopic detail.

Beijing by Deborah Kent, Rudolf Steiner is part of the 'Cities of the World' series published mainly for library reference .

The *Beijing Official Guide* is published four times a year by the Chinese government. Though the information is far from complete, it's at least up to date. You can find free copies around the lobbies of various tourist hotels.

The government toots its own horn in *Place of Interest in Beijing* by the China Travel & Tourism Press – actually, it's not bad. A much slimmer volume is simply entitled *Beijing* by the China Esperanto Press. Look for both of these at the Friendship Store (Map 9) or Foreign Languages Bookstore in Beijing (Map 11).

History

An interesting aside to current intellectual history is provided by Perry Link in his *Evening Chats in Beijing*.

Dragon Lady: The Life and Legend of the Last Empress of China by Sterling Seagrave is the definitive biography of Cixi, who ruled China in the late 19th century. A fascinating read.

The Private Life of Chairman Mao by Li Zhisui offers some amazing insights into the hidden world behind the great walls of Zhongnanhai, China's so-called 'new Forbidden City'.

Rickshaw Beijing: City People and Politics in the 1920s by David Strand is, amazingly, still in print. Ditto for *The IG in Peking; Letters of Robert Hart, Chinese Maritime Customs, 1868-1907*. Also look for *Jesuits at the Court of Peking*.

Old Peking: City of the Ruler of the World by Chris Elder is a most recent work (1997).

Hard to find but worth tracking down (at least in libraries) is *Twilight in the Forbidden City* by Reginald F Johnston. It was written by a British colonial official who tutored China's last emperor from 1919 to 1924.

Other books in the 'special order' category include *The Lion and the Dragon: The Story of the First British Embassy to the Court of the Emperor Qianlong in Peking 1792-1794* by Aubrey Singer; and *Old Madam Yin: A Memoir of Peking Life, 1926-1938* by Ida Pruitt.

General

Peking by Anthony Grey is your standard blockbuster by the author of *Saigon*. Not bad. The foregoing should not be confused with *Peking* by Juliet Bredon, another great book.

Letter from Peking by Pearl S Buck is a classic novel currently out of print. Ms Buck lived most of her life in 19th century China, and was a prolific writer. Her most famous (and still in print) book was *The Good Earth*.

For books published within China, see 'Literature' in the Arts section of the Facts about Beijing chapter.

NEWSPAPERS & MAGAZINES

China publishes various newspapers, books and magazines in a number of European and Asian languages. The government's favourite English-language mouthpiece is the *China Daily*. First published in June 1981, it now has two overseas editions (Hong Kong and USA). Overseas subscriptions can be obtained from the following sources:

China Daily Distribution Corporation (☎ (212) 219-0130; fax 210-0108), Suite 401, 15 Mercer St, New York, NY 10013, USA

Wen Wei Po (☎ 2572-2211; fax 2572-0441), 197 Wanchai Rd, Hong Kong

Surely the most interesting English-language publication in Beijing is the *Beijing Scene* which is published twice monthly. Free copies pop up around hotels and expat hang-outs, but it's also available by subscription (☎ 6592-2715; fax 6593-1625; http://www.beijingscene.com).

Although you might stumble across some of the English-language magazines in luxury

Subversive Trash

When a Communist Party committee in Beijing investigated the bustling black market in foreign literature, they discovered that the city's hotel staff and garbage collectors were very well placed intermediaries for this business. Foreign hotel guests can be relied on to leave behind several tonnes of foreign books, magazines and newspapers every month, and resident foreigners throw out nearly 20 tonnes.

The Beijing committee analysed printed matter left behind at the Xinqiao Hotel and was pleased to discover that nearly half of the publications had good or relatively good contents. The remaining items contained 'partly erroneous' or 'problematic' material such as 'half-naked advertisements'. When the courageous committee delved into diplomatic rubbish bins, they discovered that 15% of their haul was 'anti-Communist, anti-Chinese, obscene and pornographic' – definitely bottom of the barrel. ■

hotels and the Friendship Store, they are most readily available by subscription. These can be posted to you overseas. The place to contact is the Beijing Foreign Cultural Exchange Service Centre (☎ 6512-3388 ext 2338; fax 6512-3415), Baihe Hall, 2nd floor, Scitech Hotel, 22 Jianguomenwai Dajie, Beijing 100004 (Map 9). This outfit produces the *Beijing Official Guide*, *Beijing This Month* and *Business Beijing*.

In Beijing, it's easy enough to score copies of the popular imported English-language magazines including *Time, Newsweek, Far Eastern Economic Review* and *The Economist*. Occasionally you might find European magazines in French or German. Foreign newspapers like the *Asian Wall Street Journal* and *International Herald-Tribune* are available. Hong Kong's *South China Morning Post* produces a whitewashed China edition which is not worth reading. Imported magazines are most readily available from the big tourist hotels and the Friendship Store.

RADIO & TV

Domestic radio broadcasting is controlled by the Central People's Broadcasting Station (CPBS). Broadcasts are made in *pǔtōnghuà*, the standard Chinese speech, as well as in local Chinese dialects and minority languages. Even if you can't understand what's being said, the classical music requires no translation. 'Easy FM' broadcasts in English 12 hours a day at 91.5 mHz.

If you want to hear world news broadcasts in English, a short-wave radio receiver would be worth bringing with you. You can buy these in China, but Japanese-made ones are more compact and better quality.

The Chinese Central Television operates two stations (CCTV 1 and 2). Beijing Television (BTV) operates three channels. At the time of writing, CCTV 2 does an English-language news program from 11 to 11.30 pm every evening. BTV 1 has English-language news at 11.45 pm. Unless you want to practise your Chinese, you'll probably find most of the local stuff boring.

But the situation is not hopeless – satellite TV is all the rage in China. Hong Kong's Star TV has taken the country by storm because it broadcasts in Chinese and does not require a decoder (advertising revenues pay the bill) to receive it. Star TV also has an English channel, available in your hotel room (if you've got the right kind of room). The news, of course, has been sanitised so as not to offend the Chinese government. Some up-market hotels also offer in-house video. If you can't live without TV, you should inquire at a hotel to see what's available before checking in.

PHOTOGRAPHY & VIDEO

Beijing is a very photogenic city, and there are 11 million potential human portraits as well. Some Chinese shy away from having their photo taken and even duck for cover. Others are proud to pose and will ham it up for the camera – and they're especially proud if you're taking a shot of their kid. Nobody expects any payment for photos, so don't give any or you'll set a precedent. What the Chinese would go for is a copy of a colour photo, which you could mail to them.

There are three basic approaches to photographing people. One is the polite 'ask for permission and pose it' shot, which is sometimes rejected. Another is the 'no-holds barred and upset everyone' approach. The third is surreptitious – standing 500m away with a metre-long telephoto lens. Many Chinese will disagree with you on what constitutes good subject matter; they don't really see why anyone would want to take a street scene, a picture of a beggar or a shot of an old man driving a donkey cart.

The Chinese are obsessed with photos of themselves standing in front of something. A temple, waterfall, heroic statue or important vintages of calligraphy are considered suitable backgrounds. At amusement parks, Mickey Mouse and Donald Duck get into nearly every photo, while Ronald McDonald and the Colonel of Kentucky Fried fame are favourite photo companions in Beijing. If you hang around these places you can sometimes clip off a few portrait photos for yourself, but don't be surprised if your photo subjects suddenly drag you into the picture as an exotic prop!

Big-name colour print film (Kodak, Fuji etc) is available almost everywhere, but is almost exclusively 100 ASA (21 DIN). Black and white film can be found at a few select photo shops, but its use is not common as colour photos are now the big thing. Colour slide film is seldom used by the Chinese, but can be bought in Beijing at speciality shops. It's cheapest at the Friendship Store and photo shops on Wangfujing Dajie. Major hotels also sell it, but at a significant mark-up.

Genuine Chinese brands of film are a rarity. Polaroid film is rumoured to exist, but if you know you'll need it bring your own supply. Lithium batteries can generally be found at photo shops, but it doesn't hurt to carry a spare.

Many of Beijing's scenic spots (Summer Palace, Forbidden City etc) impose special fees on video cameras or ban them outright. It's not clear if this is to prevent you from stealing state secrets, or from filming a sequel to 'The Last Emperor' without paying the Chinese government.

Big hotels and stores along Wangfujing are equipped with the latest Japanese photoprocessing machines. Quality colour prints can be turned out in one or two hours for a reasonable cost.

It's a different situation with colour slides. Ektachrome and Fujichrome can be processed in Beijing, but this is normally slow and expensive and quality is not assured. There is no place in China to develop Kodachrome.

Undeveloped film can be sent out of China and, going by personal experience only, the dreaded X-ray machines do not appear to be a problem.

Religious reasons for avoiding photographs are absent among the Han Chinese. Some guy isn't going to stick a spear through you for taking a picture of his wife and stealing part of her soul. On the other hand, photographing monks and the interiors of temples is generally prohibited.

Photography from planes and photographs of airports, military installations, harbour facilities, train terminals and bridges can be a touchy subject. Of course, these rules only get enforced if the enforcers happen to be around.

Taking photos is not permitted in most museums, at archaeological sites and in many temples, mainly to protect the postcard and colour slide industry. It prevents westerners from publishing their own books about these sites and taking business away from the Chinese-published books. It also prevents valuable works of art from being damaged by countless flash photos.

TIME

All of China runs on Beijing's clock, which is set eight hours ahead of Greenwich Mean Time/UTC and daylight-saving time was abandoned in 1992. When it's noon in Beijing, it's 4 am in London, 5 am in Frankfurt, Paris and Rome, noon in Hong Kong, 2 pm in Melbourne, 4 pm in Wellington, 8 pm in Los Angeles, and 11 pm in Montreal and New York.

ELECTRICITY

Electricity is 220 volts, 50 cycles AC. Plugs come in at least four designs – three-pronged angled pins (like in Australia), three-pronged round pins (like in Hong Kong), two flat pins (US-style but without the ground wire) or two narrow round pins (European-style). Conversion plugs are easily purchased in Hong Kong but are damned near impossible to find in Beijing. Battery rechargers are widely available, but these are generally the bulky style which aren't ideal for travelling – buy a travel-friendly one in Hong Kong or elsewhere.

LAUNDRY

On just about every floor of just about every hotel in China there is a service desk. The job of the attendants at these desks is mainly to clean the rooms, make the beds and collect and deliver laundry. Almost all tourist hotels have a laundry service, and if you hand in clothes in the morning you should get them back the same evening or the next day. If the hotel doesn't have a laundry, the staff can usually direct you to one. Hotel laundry services tend to be expensive and if you're on a tight budget you might wind up doing what many travellers do – hand-washing your own clothes. If you plan on doing this, dark clothes are better since the dirt's not so obvious. Laundry prices can vary widely. Budget hotels charge around Y1 or Y2 per item, while ritzier hotels can demand around Y10 per item.

WEIGHTS & MEASURES

China officially subscribes to the international metric system. However, ancient Chinese weights and measures persist. The most likely ones that tourists will encounter are the *tael (liǎng)* and the *catty (jīn)*.

One catty is 0.6kg (1.32 lbs). There are 16 taels to the catty, so one tael is 37.5g (1.32 oz). Most fruits and vegetables in China are sold by the jin, while tea and herbal medicine are sold by the liang.

The other unit of measure that you might encounter is the *ping*. Pings are used to measure area, and one ping is approximately 1.82 sq metres (5.97 sq feet). When you buy cloth or carpet, the price will be determined by the number of pings. It's the same deal for leasing or purchasing an apartment or house.

HEALTH

Beijing is a reasonably healthy city – the cold climate means you needn't fear tropical bugs like malaria.

Some basic precautions are advisable. It's worth having your own medicine kit, for example. A traveller's first-aid kit really need contain only paracetomol, vitamins, sunscreen lotion and anti-diarrhoea tablets. Other items you might like to include are laxatives, contraceptives and a thermometer. If you wear spectacles, take a prescription with you in case they get broken. If you require a particular medication, take an adequate supply because your drug of choice may not be available locally. Also, take the prescription with the generic rather than the brand name, which may be unavailable, as it will make getting replacements easier. See

the boxed text 'Medical Kit Check List' for more suggestions on what to take.

Immunisations

There are no vaccination requirements for entry to China except yellow fever if you are coming from an area infected with yellow fever (most of sub-Saharan Africa and parts of South America; there is no risk of yellow fever in China). As a basic precaution before travelling, it's a good idea to ensure that your

---

Medical Kit Check List
Consider taking a basic medical kit including:

☐ **Aspirin** or **paracetamol** (acetaminophen in the USA) – for pain or fever.

☐ **Antihistamine** (such as Benadryl) – useful as a decongestant for colds and allergies, to ease the itch from insect bites or stings, and to help prevent motion sickness. Antihistamines may cause sedation and interact with alcohol so care should be taken when using them; take one you know and have used before, if possible.

☐ **Antibiotics** – useful if you're travelling well off the beaten track, but they must be prescribed; carry the prescription with you.

☐ **Loperamide** (eg Imodium) or **Lomotil** for diarrhoea; **prochlorperazine** (eg Stemetil) or **metaclopramide** (eg Maxalon) for nausea and vomiting.

☐ **Rehydration mixture** – for treatment of severe diarrhoea; particularly important for travelling with children.

☐ **Antiseptic** such as **povidone-iodine** (eg Betadine) – for cuts and grazes.

☐ **Multivitamins** – especially for long trips when dietary vitamin intake may be inadequate.

☐ **Calamine lotion** or **aluminium sulphate spray** (eg Stingose) – to ease irritation from bites or stings.

☐ **Bandages** and Band-aids.

☐ **Scissors, tweezers** and a **thermometer** (note that mercury thermometers are prohibited by airlines).

☐ **Cold and flu tablets** and **throat lozenges.** Pseudoephedrine hydrochloride (Sudafed) may be useful if flying with a cold to avoid ear damage.

☐ **Insect repellent, sunscreen, chap stick** and **water purification tablets.**

☐ **A couple of syringes,** in case you need injections in a country with medical hygiene problems. Ask your doctor for a note explaining why they have been prescribed.

tetanus, diphtheria and polio vaccinations are up to date (boosters are required every 10 years). Discuss your requirements with your doctor, but other diseases you should consider having vaccinations against before you leave are hepatitis A, which is a common food and water-borne disease, and hepatitis B, which is transmitted through sexual activity and blood (hepatitis B is highly endemic in China). Other vaccinations for a long term stay might include typhoid, tuberculosis, Japanese B encephalitis and rabies. Malaria has nearly been eradicated in China and is not generally a risk for travellers visiting cities. If you will be living in Beijing for a while, a vaccination every autumn against influenza wouldn't be a bad idea, especially for seniors.

Food & Drink

Salads and fruit should be washed with purified water or peeled where possible. Ice cream is usually OK if it is a reputable brand name, but beware of ice cream which is sold on the street or has melted and refrozen. Shellfish such as mussels, oysters and clams should be avoided as well as undercooked meat, particularly in the form of mince. Steaming does not make shellfish safe for eating.

Water supplies are fairly good, but it's still recommended that you drink only boiled or bottled water. If you don't know for certain that the water is safe, then assume the worst. Milk should be treated with suspicion as it is often unpasteurised, though boiled milk is fine if it is kept hygienically. Drinking tea should be OK – after all, it's boiled.

Bottled water or soft drinks are fine – the main problem is that the exterior of the bottle may be encrusted in dust (or worse) as Chinese vendors don't give a damn about where they store the stuff. Try to find a place to wash the bottle or can before opening it.

Diseases

China Syndrome *(liúxíngxìng gǎnmào)*
The most likely illness to befall you in Beijing is influenza. China is notorious for outbreaks of nasty strains of flu and pneumo-nia is a possible complication. Expats simply call it 'the China Syndrome'. The problem is especially serious during winter, though you can catch it any time of the year. The situation is exacerbated by the Chinese habit of spitting anywhere and everywhere, which spreads respiratory illnesses. You can protect yourself up to a limited extent with a flu vaccine, but 100% protection would require that you live in total quarantine or give up breathing.

Diarrhoea *(lā dùzi)* Travellers' diarrhoea has been around a long time – even Marco Polo had it. Simple things like a change of water, food or climate can all cause a mild bout of diarrhoea, but a few rushed trips to the toilet with no symptoms do not indicate a major problem. If you're not drinking unboiled water, the most likely way to get a bad case of diarrhoea is to eat salads (the Chinese use unprocessed faeces as fertiliser). The solution is to stick to cooked vegetables.

Dehydration is the main danger with any diarrhoea, particularly in children or the elderly because dehydration can occur quite quickly.

Under all circumstances *fluid replacement* (at least equal to the volume being lost) is the most important thing to remember. Weak black tea with a little sugar, soda water, or soft drinks allowed to go flat and diluted 50% with clean (boiled or bottled) water are all good. With severe diarrhoea a rehydrating solution is preferable to replace minerals and salts lost. Commercially available oral rehydration salts (ORS) are very useful; add them to boiled or bottled water. In an emergency you can make up a solution of six teaspoons of sugar and half a teaspoon of salt to a litre of boiled or bottled water. You need to drink at least the same volume of fluid that you are losing in bowel movements and vomiting. Urine is the best guide to the adequacy of replacement – if you have small amounts of concentrated urine, you need to drink more. Keep drinking small amounts often. Stick to a bland diet as you recover. High-fibre or spicy foods like hot pickled chillies, raw vegetables and fruits are a disaster – you'll be running for the toilet within minutes.

Lomotil or Imodium can be used to bring relief from the symptoms, although they do not actually cure the problem. Use these drugs only if you do not have access to toilets eg if you *must* travel. For children under 12 years Lomotil and Imodium are not recommended. Do not use these drugs if the person has a high fever or is severely dehydrated.

In certain situations antibiotics may be required: diarrhoea with blood or mucus

Chinese Medicine

Many foreigners visiting China never try Chinese herbal medicine *(zhōng yào)* because they either know nothing about it or don't believe in it. It's understandable: Western medical authorities often dismiss herbalists as no better than witch doctors, the ingredients may include exotic animal bits and the mind-boggling array of herbs on offer can make for some very bitter experiences.

Chinese herbs may be remarkably effective but some warnings are in order. Herbs are not miracle drugs, despite the extravagant claims sometimes made. Such medicine works best for the relief of unpleasant symptoms (such as a sore throat or toothache) and for chronic ailments like migraines and asthma.

There are relatively few side effects to herbal medicine. Nevertheless, herbs are medicine, not candy, and there is no need to take them if you're feeling fine to begin with. In fact, some herbs are mildly toxic and if taken over a long period of time can actually damage the liver and other organs. There is good advice on when to avoid common products like red ginseng (bad for the elderly or for anyone in summer) and what to avoid while taking it (such as coffee). Conversely, resist the urge to stop taking the medicine as soon as you feel a bit better – most treatments are not designed as a quick fix.

Some manufacturers falsely claim that their product contains numerous potent and expensive ingredients, such as rhinoceros horn. As the rhino is a rare and endangered species, these products are highly questionable in any case. Counterfeiting is another problem: if the herbs you take seem to be totally ineffective, it may be because you've bought sugar pills rather than medicine.

Although a tonic such as snake gall bladder may be good for treating colds, there are many different types of colds. See a doctor versed in herbal medicine and get a specific prescription; otherwise, the medicine may not suit your condition. If you can't get to a doctor, you can try your luck at a pharmacy.

Chinese medicine is often described as 'holistic': it seeks to treat the whole body rather than focusing on a particular organ or disease. A herbal doctor will almost certainly take your pulse (more than 30 kinds of pulse are considered). The doctor may then examine your tongue. Having discovered that you have, say, 'damp heat', as evidenced by a 'slippery' pulse and a 'red greasy' tongue, the doctor will prescribe the herbs that will help restore your body's yin-yang balance and *qi* (vital energy) flow.

Many Chinese deal with motion sickness, nausea and headaches by smearing liniments on their stomach or head. Look for White Flower Oil *(bái huā yóu)*, probably the most popular brand. Then there are salves, the most famous being Tiger Balm (which originated in Hong Kong). Back strain? Try 'sticky dog skin plaster'. You might be relieved to know that these days it's no longer made from real dog skin. ■

(dysentery), any diarrhoea with high fever, persistent diarrhoea not improving after 48 hours and severe diarrhoea. In these situations gut-paralysing drugs like Imodium or Lomotil should be avoided. The Chinese have a few useful herbal medicines which can also bring diarrhoea under control. Seek medical help.

Sexually Transmitted Diseases & AIDS
(xìng bìng) The Cultural Revolution may be over but the sexual revolution is booming in China, and Sexually Transmitted Diseases (STDs) are spreading rapidly. Therefore it pays to be cautious in sexual activity, particularly as you could be unlucky enough to catch herpes (incurable) or, worse still, Acquired Immune Deficiency Syndrome (AIDS). Apart from sexual abstinence, condoms provide the most effective protection and are available in China. The word for condom is *bǎoxiǎn tào* which literally translates as 'insurance glove'.

As most people know by now, AIDS can also be spread through infected blood transfusions, and by dirty needles – vaccinations, acupuncture, ear piercing and tattooing can potentially be as dangerous as intravenous drug use if the equipment is not clean. Much of the blood supply in China is *not* tested for AIDS, so if you really need a transfusion it is safest to find a healthy friend to donate blood to you rather than rely on the stocks in hospitals. You may choose to buy your own acupuncture needles, which are widely available in Beijing, if you're intending having that form of treatment. Medical clinics which cater to foreigners all use disposable needles and syringes. Fear of HIV/AIDS should never preclude treatment for serious medical conditions.

Medical Facilities
Asia Emergency Assistance (AEA ; ☎ 6462-9100; fax 6462-9111) has the biggest market share with the foreign community. The staff is mostly expats, and emergency service is available 24 hours. AEA is at 2-1-1 Tayuan Diplomatic Building, 14 Liangmahe Nanlu, in the Sanlitun embassy area (Map 7). AEA

offers emergency evacuation from China for the critically ill or injured.

The handy International Medical Centre (☎ 6465-1561; fax 6465-1984) is inside the Lufthansa Centre, at 50 Liangmaqiao Lu. An emergency service is available 24 hours, although there are regular office hours and it's a good idea to phone first and make an appointment.

Also good is the Sino-German Policlinic (Map 7) (☎ 6501-1983) *(zhōngdé zhěnsuǒ)*. The clinic is in the basement of Landmark Tower B-1, adjacent to the Great Wall Sheraton Hotel.

The Sino-Japanese Friendship Hospital (Map 3) (☎ 6422-1122 ext 3411) *(zhōngrì yǒuhǎo yīyuàn)* is at Yinghuadong Lu, Hepingli (Hepinglibei Jie and Hepinglidong Jie) in the north-east. There is a foreigners' clinic on the 4th floor.

Beijing Union Hospital (Map 11) *(xiéhé yīyuàn)* has a 24-hour emergency room *(jízhěn shì)* (☎ 6529-5269; emergency 6529-5284) and a foreigners' clinic *(wàishìbàn gōng shì)* on the 6th floor. The address is 1 Shifuyuan, Wangfujing.

The Hong Kong International Medical Clinic (☎ 6501-2288 ext 2346) *(guójì yīliáo zhōngxīn)*, 3rd floor, Hong Kong-Macau Centre, 2 Chaoyangmenbei Dajie, is a Hong Kong joint-venture staffed by Chinese.

Beijing United Family Health Centre (Map 3) (☎ 6527-0154), 2 Jiangtai Lu (near the Holiday Inn Lido), is geared primarily to the needs of women and children.

TOILETS
There has been much improvement in Beijing's toilet scene in recent years – in the not-too-distant past you basically had to squat over a very smelly hole or a ditch. However, it's still like that in some of the outlying areas around the city.

Better hotels and restaurants supply toilet paper in their public toilets, but many other places (public parks, department stores, railway and bus stations) do not. Always keep a stash of this vital stuff with you.

The Chinese plumbing system has problems digesting used toilet paper, and the issue of just what to do with it has caused some concern.

In general, if you see a waste basket next to the toilet, that's where you should throw the toilet paper. The problem is that in many hotels, the sewage system can't handle toilet paper. This is especially true in old hotels with antiquated plumbing systems. In rural areas there's no sewage treatment – the waste empties into an underground septic tank and toilet paper will really create a mess. For the sake of international relations, throw the paper in the waste basket. In some hotels the staff will get angry if you flush paper down the loo. In other places it's quite OK.

Remember:

men	男
women	女

WOMEN TRAVELLERS

In general, foreign women are unlikely to suffer serious sexual harassment in Beijing. There have been reports of foreign women being harassed by Chinese men in parks or while cycling alone at night, but rape cases involving foreign women are not common and most Chinese rapists appear to target Chinese women.

Police tend to investigate crimes against foreigners more closely than they do crimes against locals, and more severe penalties (like execution) are often imposed. This provides non-Chinese women with a small but important aura of protection.

GAY & LESBIAN TRAVELLERS

Local law is ambiguous on this issue, but generally the authorities take a dim view of gays and lesbians. Certainly a scene exists in Beijing (and regular haunts are plentiful), but few dare say so too loudly. While the cops tend not to care what foreigners do, things can get heavy when Chinese nationals are involved. Even heterosexual affairs between foreigners and Chinese are frowned on, so openly gay involvement with locals is liable to make the authorities go ballistic.

For excellent and up-to-date information on the latest gay and lesbian hot spots in Beijing and elsewhere throughout China, have a look at their Internet site (http://www.utopia-asia.com/tipschin.htm).

See also under Discos in the Entertainment chapter.

DISABLED TRAVELLERS

While Beijing is not particularly user-friendly to disabled travellers, it's not the worst offender in this regard. Compared to the narrow lanes of other Asian cities, Beijing's wide boulevards and pedestrian footpaths make it easier to manoeuvre wheelchairs or for blind people to avoid being run over. On the downside, there are a number of places where the only way to cross the street is via an underground walkway with many steps. Uneven pavements can be a hazard too. Another drawback is that the city is very spread out.

SENIOR TRAVELLERS

As already noted in the Health section, China is one vast reservoir of the influenza virus. The elderly are particularly prone, and pneumonia can be a fatal complication. Older travellers should be sure that their influenza vaccines are up to date and should not hesitate to seek medical care or leave the country if problems arise.

Aside from this, Beijing poses no particular problems for seniors.

BEIJING FOR CHILDREN

Beijing is a city notable for its history and architecture. Many children enjoy running around atop the Great Wall or peddling a paddleboat on Beihai Lake, but most kids are not much impressed by architectural and historical masterpieces such as the Forbidden City and Lama Temple.

In short, if you want to bring the kids, you may have trouble keeping them happy. Salvation lies in some of Beijing's theme parks (see the Entertainment chapter). Other places offering children-oriented entertainment include the rides at Badachu and the Kangxi Grasslands (see the Excursions chapter).

LIBRARIES
Chinese
The Beijing National Library (Map 10) *(běijīng túshūguǎn)* holds around 10 million books and four million periodicals and newspapers, over a third of which are in foreign languages. Access to books is limited and access to rare books is even more limited, though you might be shown a microfilm copy. The large collection of rare books includes surviving imperial works such as the *Yong Le Encyclopedia* and selections from the old Jesuit library. Of interest to Ming-Qing scholars is the special collection, the *Shanbenbu* – you will not be permitted to check it out for home use. The library is across Baishiqiao Lu west of the zoo and is open from 8 am to 5 pm every day except Sunday.

The Capital Library *(shǒudū túshūguǎn)* is attached to the Confucius Temple (see the Things to See & Do chapter).

Western
Various embassies maintain libraries in English and other languages. Though the selection of books is limited, it's certainly better than what you can hope to find at the Chinese libraries. Some of the more notable embassy libraries include:

American Centre for Educational Exchange, Room 2801, Jingguang New World Hotel, Hujialou, Chaoyang District (☎ 6532-2331)
Australian Embassy, 21 Dongzhimenwai Dajie, Chaoyang District (☎ 6532-2331)
Canadian Embassy, 19 Dongzhimenwai Dajie, Chaoyang District (☎ 6532-3536)
Cultural & Educational Section, 4th floor, British Embassy Annex, Landmark Tower, 8 Dongsanhuanbei Lu, Chaoyang District (☎ 6501-1903)

CAMPUSES
Beijing is host to some 50 universities and colleges. The majority are in the Haidian District (north-west Beijing). If you're looking to make contact with foreign students, the largest concentration is to be found at the Beijing Language Institute (Map 10). Each campus with a foreign student population has at least one pub-restaurant where everyone goes to socialise in the evening. Finding these places isn't hard – locate the foreign student dormitory *(liúxuéshēng lóu)* on any campus and ask any likely looking person where the local hangout is.

To make contact with the locals, the various pubs, clubs and discos (see the Entertainment chapter) opposite the Beijing University (Map 10) in the Haidian District where students congregate after hours.

CULTURAL CENTRES
China's ethnic minorities do exhibits, song and dance shows at the Nationalities Cultural Palace (☎ 6602-2530) *(mínzúgōng lǐtáng)*, 49 Fuxingmennei Dajie, Xicheng District, which is next to the Minzu Hotel.

USEFUL ORGANISATIONS
Bureaucracy Some important addresses of government institutions include:

First Commercial Bureau, 38 Qianliang Hutong, Dongcheng District, 100010 (☎ 6401-2462).
Foreign Enterprise Service Corporation (FESCO), 14 Chaoyangmen Nan Jie (☎ 6512-0547)
Foreign Investment Service, 3A Jianguomenwai Dajie (☎ 6701-7766 ext 2048); 7K Kaiqi Building, 21 Beisanhuan Zhong Lu (Third Ring Road) (☎ 6202-3332 ext 2707)
Industry & Commerce Office, 360B Caihuying Dong Jie (☎ 6346-9955)
Tax Bureau, 13B Xin Zhong Jie, Gongtibei Jie (☎ 6466-0568)

Foreign Organisations Several countries have full-time commercial offices in Beijing. The largest ones are:

American Chamber of Commerce, Room 444, Great Wall Sheraton Hotel (Map 15B2), 8 Dongsanhuanbei Lu, Chaoyang District, 100026 (☎ 6500-5566 ext 444 & 2271; fax 6501-8273)
Australia-China Chamber of Commerce, Room 314, Great Wall Sheraton Hotel (Map 15B2), 8 Dongsanhuanbei Lu, Chaoyang District, 100026 (☎ 6500-5566 ext 314)

British Chamber of Commerce, Room 31, ground floor, 15 Guanghuali, Jianguomenwai Dajie (☎ 6500-8399, 6500-2255 ext 1463 and 2464; fax 6500-4337)

Canada-China Business Council, 19th floor, CITIC Building, 19 Jianguomenwai Dajie, Chaoyang District, 100004 (☎ 6512-6120; fax 6512-6125)

Clubs There are lots of small organisations in Beijing run by volunteers, examples being the Arts & Crafts Club, the International Choir and even Alcoholics Anonymous. There are also clubs which focus on a particular nation or group of nations, such as the Dutch Club, African Solidarity Association, the Commonwealth Society and Nordic Club. However, the contact phone numbers for these organisations change frequently depending on who is willing to act as the club's liaison – it may even change several times a year. Check with your embassy to find out what is on offer and who to contact.

Schools for Expat Children A number of schools have set up in Beijing catering to the expat market. The language of instruction is mostly English, though some offer instruction in other western languages and in Chinese. The current line-up includes:

Beanstalk; nursery and pre-school; Sino-Japanese Youth Exchange Centre, 40 Liangmaqiao Lu, Chaoyang District (☎ 6466-3311 ext 3312)

Beijing ISS International School; nursery school to grade 10; Building 17, Anzhen Xili, Area 4, Chaoyang District (☎ 6428-3151; fax 6428-3156)

Beijing No 55 Middle School; instruction in Chinese for foreign children grades 7 to 12; 12 Xinzhong Jie, Chaoyang District (☎ 6467-1356)

French School of Beijing; kindergarten through high school; 13 Sanlitun Dongsiji, Chaoyang District (☎ 6532-3498; fax 6532-5245)

German School of Beijing, Holiday Inn Lido Complex, Jichang Lu, Jiangtai Lu, Chaoyang District (☎ 6437-6688 ext 2571; fax 6436-1952)

International School of Beijing (ISB); the largest expat school in Beijing offers kindergarten through high school instruction; Building 7, Holiday Inn Lido Complex, Jichang Lu, Jiangtai Lu, 100004 (☎ 6437-6688 ext 1242; fax 6437-6989)

Lido Kindergarten, Holiday Inn Lido Complex, Jichang Lu, Jiangtai Lu, Chaoyang District (☎ 6437-6688 ext 1640)

Montessori School of Beijing (MSB), 7 Sanlitun Beixiao Jie, Chaoyang District (☎ 6532-6713; fax 6532-6997)

New School of Collaborative Learning; both English and Chinese instruction; Shangdi Information Technology Park, Shangdixi Lu, Haidian District, 100085 (☎ 6298-1620; fax 6298-2017)

Swedish School, East Lake Villas, 35 Dongzhimenwai Dajie, Chaoyang District (☎ 6466-9442; fax 6467-7072)

Western Academy of Beijing (WAB); nursery school through to grade 8; 7A Beisihuandong Lu, Chaoyang District, 100015 (☎ 6437-5935; fax 6437-5936; email: leny@wab.hk.net)

Yew Chung International School; English-Chinese instruction for children age 3 to 12 years, will be moving to new location before year 2000; Honglingjin Park, 5 Houbalizhuang, Chaoyang district 100025 (☎ 6594-1731)

All in One? CITS has created Europe Assistance (☎ 6505-3195; fax 6505-3196) whose mission is to provide services covering a wide spectrum of expat needs: medical assistance, housing search, education for expat children, translators, travel services and paperwork handling. It's geared towards corporate accounts, though individuals can join. You can telephone or write for a brochure: Apt 9C, North Lodge, China World Trade Centre, 1 Jianguomenwai Dajie, Chaoyang District, 100004.

DANGERS & ANNOYANCES
Theft

Some would say that the ridiculous overcharging of foreigners is the most common form of theft in China, but that happens to be legal. As for illegal crime, pick-pocketing is a problem you need to carefully guard against. In back alleys, a thief might try to grab your bag and run away, but far more common is the razoring of bags and pockets in crowded places like buses and railway stations. If you want to avoid opening wallets or bags on the bus, keep a few coins or small notes ready in an accessible pocket before launching yourself into the crowd.

Hotels are usually safe places to leave your stuff; each floor has an attendant watching who goes in and out. If anything is missing from your room then they're going to be obvious suspects since they've got keys to the rooms. Don't expect them to watch over your room like a hawk, though, because they won't.

Dormitories could be a problem; there have been a few reports of thefts by staff, but the culprits are more likely to be other foreigners! There are at least a few people who subsidise their journey by ripping off their fellow travellers.

Most hotels have storage rooms where you check your bags in; some insist that you do. Obviously, do not leave your valuables (passport, travellers cheques, money, air tickets) lying around anywhere.

A money belt is the safest way to carry valuables, particularly when travelling on buses and trains. During the cooler weather, it's more comfortable to wear a vest (waistcoat) with numerous pockets, but you should wear this under a light jacket or coat since visible pockets invite wandering hands even if sealed with zips.

Perhaps the best way to avoid getting ripped off is to avoid bringing stuff you don't need – Walkmans, video cameras, expensive watches and jewellery all invite theft.

Spitting

The national sport, spitting is practised by everyone. All venues are possible – buses, trains, and even restaurants. Never walk too close to a bus full of passengers, and try not to get caught in the crossfire elsewhere!

Technically, spitting is illegal in Beijing. But while anti-spitting wars (with fines for violators) are waged periodically – usually coinciding with a visit by an important

Us & Phlegm

Beijing residents will tell you there's a good reason to take off your shoes indoors. Sure, it's polite. But it's also practical, if you check the spit-soaked soles of your shoes. The usual tourist responses to the popular pastime of spitting range from resignation to rank fear and loathing. This may be hard to swallow, but maybe there's something to learn from this slippery habit. Beijingers don't like the slime on the street any more than you do, but it doesn't make their stomachs turn. How come?

Norbert Elias, a scholar who'd lost his parents in Nazi camps (he therefore had an interest in these things), argued that 'civilised' behaviour in Europe began as a 16th century attempt by an emerging, uncertain middle class to define their social standing. Until this time, behaviour on the street or at the table was pretty much the same for every social order. Kings and queens might wipe their hands on dogs at dinner, but so did anyone who owned a fur-bearing napkin. Aristocrats, being aristocrats, didn't need to distinguish themselves from lower orders.

Enter the brand new idea of 'manners', especially of 'good' and 'bad' ones (courtesy of reformers like Erasmus). The middle class seized on these rules as a way to distinguish themselves from peasants, pay back the indifferent upper order and identify themselves to each other as a class. Bourgeois wives laid out the table in 'proper' fashion from then on. It worked, and even the aristocracy had to follow on.

The security-giving function of manners is new to China: while imperial Chinese merchants self-consciously hung scrolls on their walls in imitation of what scholar-officials did by nature, merchants already knew where they fitted in (at the bottom of China's social rank).

But things change – Chinese business has new status, and you'll see far fewer middle-class neckties dangling over grates in Beijing than was the case some years ago. As the advice now given in Beijing anti-spitting campaigns (if you have to hack up a lung on the street, step on it etc) is just like what Erasmus wrote, it's quite possible that 'manners' soon will differentiate the masses.

If all that doesn't help, consider this: 'manners' aren't good or bad in themselves. To many Chinese, rubbing the sleep from your eyes in public is pretty much uncouth.

One more thing: before passing judgement, consider who the 'civilised' folks are. While Europeans were still swinging from the branches of Black Forest trees (to quote Goethe), Chinese bottoms were being wiped with toilet paper.

Still, it's all relative: the 9th century Arab traders who reported this custom thought the Chinese were 'dirty', since they didn't wash themselves with water, but used paper instead ...

Russ Kerr

foreign dignitary – but in the countryside, it's a free-for-all.

Queues

Basically, there are none. People tend to 'huddle' rather than queue, resembling American-style football but without the protective gear. You're most likely to encounter the situation when trying to board a bus or buy a train ticket. Good luck.

Beggars

The Beijing authorities have made an effort to reduce the number of beggars in the city (mostly by evicting them), but the destitute folks just won't disappear. While one should certainly be sympathetic to the poor, a real problem exists with professional beggars. Worst of all are the child beggars who practically have to be removed with a crowbar once they've seized your trouser leg. Child beggars are usually an organised operation, working under instructions from nearby older women who supervise them and collect most of the cash. There have even been stories of children being kidnapped, taken hundreds of kilometres from their homes and forced into these begging gangs.

Sex Vigilantes

For all the Communists' talk of the equality of women in Chinese society, the fact remains that China is a bastion of male chauvinism. There seems to be nothing as upsetting to the average Chinese male as seeing a western male being accompanied by a Chinese woman. In the opposite scenario (where a Chinese male is being accompanied by a western woman), the male is likely to receive knowing winks and snide remarks about his sexual prowess.

The reason this is important is because it can occasionally lead to trouble. Racially mixed couples often receive verbal abuse and occasionally find themselves being followed by gangs of semi-drunk males looking for trouble. If you're caught in this situation, don't expect much help from the police. The Beijing police have been known to arrest foreigners for 'insulting Chinese women',

---

How Much Is That Doggy in the Window?

You'll come up against the hard reality of China's treatment of animals in Beijing's back streets and markets, which are sometimes more like take-away zoos than the markets you're probably familiar with. The sight of dog meat or the on-site slaughter of chickens is not for the faint-hearted, and gentle stomachs should avoid those Beijing restaurants which sell bear paws and whole sheep that are skinned alive.

One of the most inhumane practices involves the regular round-up and slaughter of dogs, mainly strays, but also unlicensed pets (dog licences are very expensive in the city). Until recently, the preferred method of killing was to stuff the dogs in a sack and beat them to death in front of their owners.

For information on animal welfare issues contact WSPA, (☎ (0171) 793 0540; fax (0171) 793 0208; email: wspa@wspa.org.uk; http://www.way.net/wspa.) 2 Langley Lane, London SW8 1TJ, United Kingdom

Martin Hughes

---

while the women being 'insulted' may be arrested for prostitution (even though they are not prostitutes).

The situation is actually not so bad in parts of Beijing where foreigners are common and the locals have grown accustomed to western ways. The further one travels away from the cosmopolitan centre, the more likelihood there is of encountering this strange form of sexual harassment.

LEGAL MATTERS
Crime & Punishment

Only the most serious cases are tried in front of a judge (never a jury). Most lesser crimes are handled administratively by the Public Security Bureau. The PSB acts as police, judge and executioner – they will decide what constitutes a crime, regardless of what the law says, and they decide what the penalty will be. The ultimate penalty is execution, which serves the purpose of 'killing the rooster to frighten the monkey' or, to phrase this in official terms, 'It's good to have people executed to educate others'.

Chinese prisons generally operate at a

profit. The prisoner's family often has to pay the cost of imprisonment, as well as the cost of the bullet if execution is the penalty.

Foreigners are very rarely executed, and imprisonment is only reserved for the most serious crimes. In most cases, foreigners who have had a run in with the PSB are persuaded to write a confession of guilt and pay a fine. In some cases, foreigners are expelled from China (at their own expense).

Drugs

China takes a particularly dim view of opium and all its derivatives. The Chinese suffered severely from addiction after opium was foisted upon them by British traders in 1773 – they haven't forgotten! Marijuana is less well known by the Chinese, though some minority groups (including members of Beijing's Uighur community) have a habit of smoking it. It's difficult to say what attitude the Chinese police will take towards foreigners caught using marijuana – they often don't care what foreigners do if Chinese aren't involved. Then again, you have to remember the old story about 'killing the rooster to frighten the monkey'. If you're planning to use drugs and don't want to become that rooster, discretion is strongly advised!

Getting caught smuggling drugs in China is bad news. Don't even think about it.

Embassies

If you're arrested for something serious, it's best to contact your embassy as soon as possible. Don't think that your embassy can get you out of hot water if you've really committed a serious crime – they can't. The best they can do is to ensure that you're treated fairly, and perhaps put you in touch with an attorney and inform your family of the situation.

BUSINESS HOURS

China officially converted to a five-day working week in 1995, though some businesses still force their workers to put in six days. Banks, offices and government departments are normally open Monday to Friday. As a rough guide only, they open around 8 to 9 am, close for two hours in the middle of the day, then reopen until 5 or 6 pm. Saturday and Sunday are both public holidays, but most museums stay open on weekends and make up for this by closing for one or two days mid-week. Travel agencies, the Friendship Store, foreign-exchange counters in the tourist hotels and some of the local branches of the Bank of China have similar opening hours, but are generally open on Saturday and Sunday as well, at least in the morning.

Many parks, zoos and monuments have similar opening hours; they're also open on weekends and often at night. Shows at cinemas and theatres end around 9.30 pm.

The restaurant situation has improved dramatically; nowadays it is always possible to find something to eat at any hour of the day, especially around railway and bus stations.

Long-distance bus stations and railway stations open their ticket offices around 5 am, before the first trains and buses pull out. Apart from a one or two-hour break for lunch, they often stay open until midnight.

PUBLIC HOLIDAYS & SPECIAL EVENTS

Weekends and holidays aren't good for sightseeing. From the Great Wall to the shopping malls, it's like one giant phone-booth stuffing contest. Crowds thin out on Monday, but many museums are closed at that time.

Aside from Saturday and Sunday, the PRC has nine national holidays during the year:

New Year's Day (yuándàn); 1 January

Spring Festival (chūn jié); otherwise known as Chinese New Year, it starts on the first day of the first moon according to the traditional lunar calendar. Although officially lasting only three days, many people take a week off work. This is a bad time for a visit – hotels are booked solid, many places shut down totally and those that remain open may double their rates. The Chinese New Year will fall on the following dates: 16 February 1999, 5 February 2000, 24 January 2001 and 12 February 2002.

International Working Women's Day (fúnǚ jié); celebrated in most Communist countries; 8 March

International Labour Day (láodòng jié); the closest thing the Communists have to a worldwide religious holiday; 1 May

Youth Day (qīngnián jié); commemorates the student demonstrations in Beijing on 4 May 1919, when the Versailles Conference decided to give Germany's 'rights' in the city of Tianjin to Japan; 4 May

Children's Day (értóng jié); 1 June

Anniversary of the Founding of the Chinese Communist Party (zhōngguó gòngchǎndǎng qìng); 1 July

Anniversary of the Founding of the PLA (jiěfàng jūn jié); 1 August

National Day (guóqīng jié); celebrates the founding of the PRC in 1949; 1 October

Beijing is probably at its prettiest on May Day (1 May), a holiday for Communists and officially known as International Labour Day. During this time, the whole city (especially Tiananmen Square) is decorated with flowers. Beijing also rolls out its marching bands and militaristic displays on National Day (1 October).

Special prayers are held at Buddhist and Taoist temples on days when the moon is either full or just a sliver. According to the Chinese lunar calendar, the full moon falls on the 15th and 16th days of the lunar month and on the last (30th) day of the month just ending and the first day of the new month.

The Lantern Festival *(yuánxiāo jié)* is not a public holiday, but it's a relatively colourful time to visit Beijing. People take the time to walk the streets at night carrying coloured paper lanterns. It falls on the 15th day of the 1st moon, and will be celebrated on: 2 March 1999, 19 February 2000, 7 February 2001 and 27 February 2002.

The birthday of Guanyin *(guānshìyīn shēngrì)*, the Goddess of Mercy, is a good time to visit Taoist temples. Guanyin's birthday is the 19th day of the 2nd moon and will fall on: 5 April 1999, 24 March 2000, 13 March 2001 and 1 April 2002.

Tomb Sweep Day *(qīng míng jié)* is a day for worshipping ancestors; people visit the graves of their dearly departed relatives and clean their gravesites. They often place flowers on the tomb and burn 'ghost money' (for use in the afterworld) for the departed. It falls on 5 April in the Gregorian calendar in most years, 4 April in leap years.

The Mid-Autumn Festival *(zhōngqiū jié)* is also known as the Moon Festival and is the time to eat tasty moon cakes. Gazing at the moon and lighting fireworks are popular activities, and it's also a traditional holiday for lovers. The festival takes place on the 15th day of the 8th moon, and will be celebrated on: 5 October 1998, 24 September 1999, 12 September 2000, 1 October 2001 and 21 September 2002.

WORK

As Chairman Mao used to say, 'We all must be happy in our work'. Foreigners seeking happiness in Beijing usually wind up teaching English or foreign languages. Teaching in China is not a way to get rich – pay is roughly Y2000 a month. This is about four times what the average urban Chinese worker earns. There are usually some fringe benefits like free or low-cost housing and subsidised medical care. If you possess certain technical skills much in demand, you could possibly land a good-paying job with a foreign company in Beijing but such plum jobs aren't easy to come by. The majoity of foreign professionals working in Beijing are recruited from overseas; many have spent years employed in the company in their home countries.

The main reason to work in China is to experience the country at a level not generally available to travellers. Unfortunately, just how close you will be able to get to the Chinese people depends on what the PSB allows. In Beijing, where the local PSB is almost hysterical about controlling evil foreign 'spiritual pollution', your students may be prohibited from having any contact with you beyond the classroom, though you may secretly meet them far away from the campus.

Foreign teachers are usually forced to live in separate apartments or dormitories. Chinese students wishing to visit you at your room may be turned away at the reception desk; otherwise they may be required to register their name, ID number and purpose of visit. Since many people are reluctant to draw attention to themselves like this (and they could well be questioned by the police later), they may be unwilling to come visiting at all.

In other words, teaching in Beijing can be a lonely experience unless you spend all your free time in the company of other expats, which of course deprives you of that 'foreign experience' you may be seeking. If you're interested in working in Beijing, contact a Chinese embassy or the universities directly.

Two topics which cannot be discussed in the classroom are politics and religion. Foreigners teaching in Beijing have reported spies being placed in their classrooms. Other teachers have found microphones hidden in their dormitory rooms (one fellow took revenge by attaching his Walkman to the microphone wires and blasting the snoops with punk music!).

Rules change – Beijing is becoming more liberal. But just because the Chinese can now listen to rock music and wear miniskirts doesn't mean it's a free society.

MOVING TO CHINA

If you're moving heavy stuff like furniture or all your household goods, you'll need an international mover or freight forwarder. In Beijing, you can try any one of the following:

Asian Express
    A6-16 Shilihe, Zuoanmenwai, Chaoyang District, 100021 (☎ 6774-6146; fax 6774-8621)
Crown Worldwide Group
    Room 1103, CITIC Building, 19 Jianguomenwai Dajie, Chaoyang District, 100004 (☎ 6500-2255 ext 1140; fax 6500-7487; email crownpek @public.bta.net.cn)
Mitsubishi Warehouse & Transportation
    Room 1826, China World Trade Centre, 1 Jianguomenwai Dajie, Chaoyang District, 100004 (☎ 6505-0330; fax 6505-1029)
Sea-Land Service Inc
    Room 2205, Landmark Office Building, 8 Dongsanhua Beilu, Chaoyang District, 100004 (☎ 6501-1978; fax 6501-1923)
Sino Santa Fe
    4th floor, East Lake Office Building, 35 Dongzhimenwai, Chaoyang District (☎ 6467-7777; fax 6467-8050)

Getting There & Away

AIR

Beijing's aerial web spreads out in every conceivable direction with something like 630 domestic air routes. There are also numerous international air routes, though in this regard Hong Kong is far ahead of Beijing.

The China Aviation Administration of China *(zhōngguó mínháng)*, also known as CAAC, is the national carrier of the PRC. Officially CAAC has been broken up into some 30 domestic and international airlines. This doesn't mean that CAAC is out of business, but it now assumes the role of 'umbrella organisation' for its numerous subsidiaries, which include Air China (its major international carrier), China Eastern, China Southern, China Northern, China Southwest, China Northwest etc.

CAAC publishes a comprehensive international and domestic timetable in both English and Chinese, which comes out in April and November each year. These can be bought in Beijing for Y10 at the CAAC office inside the World Trade Centre (Map 9). In Hong Kong the CAAC office hands them out for free.

Foreigners must pay a surcharge of 50% on top of the fare charged to local Chinese people. A student or foreign expert with a legitimate residence permit *might* get a discount on the surcharge. If you do somehow happen to score the Chinese price without the proper credentials, your ticket will be confiscated at the check-in counter and no refund given. Children over 12 years are charged the adult fare.

On domestic flights, if you cancel 24 hours before departure you lose 10% of the fare; if you cancel between two and 24 hours before the flight you lose 20%; and if you cancel less than two hours before the flight you lose 30%. If you don't show up for a domestic flight you are entitled to a refund of 50%.

In theory you can reserve seats without paying for them. In practice, this often leads to disappointment. The staff at some booking offices will hold a seat for more than a week, while other offices will hold a seat for only a few hours so you can run to the bank and change money. Until you've actually paid for and received your ticket, nothing can be guaranteed. Usually, competition for seats is keen and people with connections can often jump the queue. Stand-by tickets exist, a fact worth knowing if you're desperate.

Other Countries

Although Hong Kong was 'reunited' with China in 1997, this doesn't apply to the airline business. Flights between Hong Kong and the rest of China are treated as international flights. This means you not only go through Immigration and Customs, but you also pay international rates (including international departure taxes). On the positive side, it also means that international standards of service and safety are maintained. That said, the government of the PRC allows only two carriers at present to fly the Beijing-Hong Kong route: CAAC and Dragonair *(gǎnglóng hángkōng)*, the latter a CAAC-Cathay Pacific joint venture. Dragonair has better service than CAAC and even charges lower prices, but its flights are often fully booked. As Dragonair is closely integrated with Hong Kong's Cathay Pacific Airlines, you can book Dragonair flights from Cathay Pacific offices around the world.

Aside from Hong Kong and Macau, Beijing's international air routes are served by a wide variety of airlines. However, there is not much free market competition because China regulates prices to keep them high – Beijing is an expensive city to fly into. Also, (and this is crucial, so read it twice) tickets bought within China are much more expensive than those bought elsewhere. A London-Beijing return-trip ticket may cost twice as much if bought in Beijing rather than London! If you're stuck in Beijing and looking to get out cheaply, the best you can hope for is a train to Hong Kong or the boat from Tianjin (near Beijing) to South Korea.

International departure tax in Beijing is Y90. Domestic departure tax is Y50. On both international and domestic flights in China the free baggage allowance for an adult passenger is 20kg in economy class and 30kg in 1st class. You are also allowed a maximum of 5kg of hand luggage, although this is hardly ever weighed.

Airline Offices in Beijing

Although CAAC goes by a variety of aliases (Air China, China Eastern Airlines etc), you can purchase tickets for all of them at the Aviation Building (Map 8) (domestic ☎ 6601-3336; international ☎ 6601-6667) *(mínháng dàshà)*, 15 Xichang'an Jie, Xidan District. You can buy the same tickets at the CAAC office in the China World Trade Centre (Map 9) or from the numerous other CAAC service counters like the one in the Beijing Hotel (Map 11) or the CITS counter in the International Hotel (Map 9).

Inquiries for all airlines can be made at Beijing's Capital Airport (☎ 6456-3604). Other international airlines offices include:

Aeroflot
  Jinglun Hotel, 3 Jianguomenwai Dajie (☎ 6500-2412)
Air France
  Room 2716, China World Trade Centre, 1 Jianguomenwai (☎ 6505-1818)
Air Macau
  Room 807, Scitech Tower, 22 Jianguomenwai (☎ 6515-8988)
Alitalia
  Room 143, Jianguo Hotel, 5 Jianguomenwai (☎ 6591-8468)
All Nippon Airways
  Room 1510, China World Trade Centre, 1 Jianguomenwai (☎ 6505-3311)
American Airlines
  c/o Beijing Tradewinds, 114 International Club, 11 Ritan Lu (☎ 6500-4837)
Asiana Airlines
  Room 134, Jianguo Hotel, 5 Jianguomenwai (☎ 6506-1118)

Austrian Airlines
  Great Wall Sheraton Hotel, 10 Dongsanhuanbei Lu (☎ 6591-7861)
British Airways
  Room 210, 2nd Floor, Scitech Tower, 22 Jianguomenwai (☎ 6512-4070)
Canadian Airlines
  Unit C201, Lufthansa Centre, 50 Liangmaqiao Lu (☎ 6463-7901)
Dragonair
  1st Floor, L107, China World Trade Centre, 1 Jianguomenwai (☎ 6505-4343)
El Al Airlines
  Room 2906, Jingguang New World Hotel (☎ 6501-4512)
Ethiopian Airlines
  Room 0506, China World Trade Centre, 1 Jianguomenwai (☎ 6505-0134)
Finnair
  Room 204, Scitech Tower, 22 Jianguomenwai (☎ 6512-7180)
Garuda Indonesia
  Unit L116A, West Wing, China World Trade Centre, 1 Jianguomenwai (☎ 6505-2901)
Japan Airlines
  Ground floor, Changfugong Building, Hotel New Otani, 26A Jianguomenwai (☎ 6513-0888)
KLM - Royal Dutch Airlines
  Suite 2432, China World Trade Centre, 1 Jianguomenwai (☎ 6505-3505)
Korean Air
  Room 401, West Wing, China World Trade Centre, 1 Jianguomenwai (☎ 6505-0088)
LOT Polish Airlines
  Room 2002, Chains City Hotel, 4 Gongren Tiyuchangdong Lu (☎ 6500-7215)
Lufthansa
  S101, Lufthansa Centre, 50 Liangmaqiao Lu (☎ 6465-4488)
Malaysia Airlines
  W115A/B Level One, West Wing Office Block, China World Trade Centre, 1 Jianguomenwai (☎ 6505-2681)
MIAT Mongolian Airlines
  China Golden Bridge Building, East Gate, A1 Jianguomenwai (☎ 6507-9297)
Northwest Airlines
  Room 104, China World Trade Centre, 1 Jianguomenwai (☎ 6505-3505)
Pakistan International
  Room 106A, China World Trade Centre, 1 Jianguomenwai (☎ 6505-1681)
Qantas
  Suite S120B, ground floor, East Wing Office Building, Kempinski Hotel, Lufthansa Centre, 50 Liangmaqiao Lu (☎ 6467-4794)
Scandinavian Airlines
  18th floor, Scitech Tower, 22 Jianguomenwai (☎ 6512-0575)

Singapore Airlines
  Room 109, China World Trade Centre, 1 Jiang-
  uomenwai (☎ 6505-2233)
Swissair
  Room 201, Scitech Tower, 22 Jianguomenwai
  (☎ 6512-3555)
Tarom
  Jianguo Hotel, 5 Jianguomenwai (☎ 6500-2233
  ext 111)
Thai Airways International
  S102B Lufthansa Centre, 50 Liangmaqiao Lu
  (☎ 6460-8899)
United Airlines
  Lufthansa Centre, 50 Liangmaqiao Lu (☎ 6463-
  1111)
Yugoslav Airlines
  Room 414, Kunlun Hotel, 2 Xinyuannan Lu
  (☎ 6500-3388 ext 414)

BUS

There are no international buses serving
Beijing, but there are plenty of long-distance
domestic buses. In general, arriving in
Beijing by bus is easier than departing
mainly because it's very confusing figuring
out which bus station has the bus you need.

The basic rule is that long-distance bus
stations are on the perimeter of the city in the
direction you want to go. The four major
ones are at Beijiao (north – also called
Deshengmen) (Map 3), Dongzhimen (north-
east) (Map 7), Majuan (east) (Map 9) and
Haihutun (south) (Map 3). Near the entrance
to the Beijing-Tianjin Expressway is the
Zhaogongkou bus station (Map 3), where
you get buses to Tianjin. The Tianqiao bus
statiion (Map 9) and Lianhuachi bus station
(Map 8) are two places where you can get
buses to sites south-west of Beijing.

There are a few small bus stations where
tour buses and minibuses gather (usually just
in the morning) looking for passengers
heading to the Great Wall and other sites in
the outlying areas. The most important of
these is the Qianmen bus station (Map 11)
(which has two parts) just to the south-west
of Tiananmen Square. Also useful is the
Zhanlanguan Lu Tour bus station (Map 4)
which is just to the south of Beijing Zoo. A
few tour buses also depart from the car park
at the Workers Stadium (Map 7) and the
Beijing railway station (Map 9).

TRAIN
Domestic Trains

Most of China's railway system was blown
to pieces in WWII and the subsequent civil
war that brought the Communists to power.
Since 1949, some 52,000km of railway lines
have been built in China, a truly revolutionary achievement that would have made
Chairman Mao proud. After coming to
power, Mao himself travelled in a specially-
built luxury coach – all other rail traffic had
to be diverted, causing chaos with the schedule. Nowadays this problem no longer exists
and the trains run mostly on time.

China's trains are small towns in themselves, with populations typically well over
1000. Though crowded, trains are the best
way to get around in reasonable comfort. The
network covers every province except Tibet.

The safety record of the railway system is
good. Other than having your bags pinched
or suffering a heart attack when you see the
toilets, there isn't much danger on trains.
However, the Chinese have a habit of throwing rubbish out the windows even as the train
moves through a station. Avoid standing too
close to a passing train, lest you get hit by
flying beer bottles or chicken bones.

Stations All express trains (international
and domestic) go through Beijing station
(Map 9) *(běijīng zhàn)* or Beijing west
station (Map 8) *(běijīng xī zhàn)*. Beijing
west is China's largest and plushest station.

The other main stations are Beijing north
(Map 10) *(běijīng běi zhàn)* and Beijing
south (Map 8) *(běijīng nán zhàn)*. Both
these stations are served by suburban trains.

All railway stations have left-luggage
rooms *(jìcún chù)*, though sometimes you'll
find them just outside the station itself. It
usually costs about Y5 per day to store a bag.

Tickets Both Beijing station and Beijing
west station have special counters for foreigners to purchase tickets (the signs say
'International Passenger Booking Office').
The staff here speak passable English, but
even if you can speak fluent Chinese you'll
appreciate these special ticket windows as it

saves you having to queue with the masses. The ticket windows are open daily from 5.30 to 7.30 am, 8 to 5.30 pm and from 7 pm until midnight. At least those are the official times, but foreigners have often found the staff opening late and closing early.

Outside Beijing, obtaining tickets is not so straightforward. Shanghai and a few other cities also have booking offices for foreigners, but in many cases your only hope of obtaining a sleeper is to seek the assistance of a travel agent. Most hotels employ an in-house travel agent to book train tickets, so inquire at the reception desk.

Depending on which station you book from, tickets can be purchased up to six days in advance.

An alternative to all the above is to board the train with only a platform ticket *(zhàntái piào)*. These are available from the station's information booth for a few jiao. You then buy a proper ticket on the train. This method is usually more hassle than it's worth, but may be necessary if you arrive at the station with no time to get your ticket.

Hard-Seat Except on the trains which serve some of the branch or more obscure lines, hard-seat is in fact padded. But it's hard on your sanity – the hard-seat section tends to be spectacularly dirty, noisy and smoky, and you'll get little sleep in the upright seats.

Since hard-seat is the only thing most locals can afford it's packed to the gills. If you're lucky, you'll get a ticket with an assigned seat number, but in many cases you'll have no seat reservation and will have to battle for a seat or piece of floor space with 5000 other hopefuls.

Hard-seat can be endured for a day trip; some foreigners can't take more than five hours of it, while others have a threshold of 12 hours or even longer. A few brave, penniless souls have even been known to travel *long-distance* this way – some roll out a mat on the floor under the seats and go to sleep on top of the peanut shells, chicken bones and spittle.

Because hard-seat tickets are relatively easy to obtain, you may have to travel hard-seat even if you're willing to pay more for a higher class.

Hard-Sleeper The carriage is made up of doorless compartments with half a dozen bunks in three tiers, and sheets, pillows and blankets are provided. It does very nicely as an overnight hotel. The best bunk to get is a middle one since the lower one is invaded by all and sundry who use it as a seat during the day, while the top one has little headroom and loudspeakers which spew forth an indecipherable cacophony of military music and pleas in Chinese not to spit or throw beer bottles out the windows. Lights and speakers in hard-sleeper go out at around 10 pm.

Hard-sleeper tickets are the most difficult of all to buy; you almost always need to buy these far in advance.

Soft-Seat On shorter journeys (such as Beijing to Tianjin) some trains have soft-seat carriages. The seats are comfortable and overcrowding is not permitted. Smoking is prohibited, a significant advantage unless you enjoy asphyxiation. If you want to smoke in the soft-seat section, you can do so only by going out into the corridor between cars. Soft-seats cost about the same as hard-sleeper and are well worth it. Unfortunately, soft-seat cars are a rarity.

Soft-Sleeper Luxury. Softies get the works with four comfortable bunks in a closed compartment – complete with straps to stop the top fatso from falling off in the middle of the night, wood panelling, potted plants, lace curtains, teacup sets, clean washrooms, carpets (so no spitting) and often air-conditioning. As for those speakers, not only do you have a volume control, you can turn the bloody things off! Soft-sleeper costs twice as much as hard-sleeper, and almost the same price as flying (on some routes even *more* than flying!). Soft-sleeper tickets are easier to come by than hard-sleeper simply because of the high price. However, with China growing more affluent, even soft-sleeper tickets are becoming elusive.

Travel Times & Train Fares from Beijing

Destination	Soft-Sleeper (Y)	Hard-Sleeper (Y)	Hard-Seat (Y)	Soft-Seat (Y)	Approx Travel Time (hours)
Baotou	316	208	112	-	15
Beidaihe	-	-	62	97	6
Changchun	379	248	136	-	17
Changsha	529	344	190	-	23
Chengde	-	-	28	51	5
Chengdu	642	417	230	-	34
Chongqing	658	430	237	-	40
Dalian	369	236	121	-	19
Dandong	400	262	142	-	19
Datong	162	108	54	-	7
Fuzhou	705	457	252	-	43
Guangzhou	705	457	252	-	35
Guilin	658	429	237	-	31
Hangzhou	529	345	190	-	24
Harbin	442	289	157	-	20
Hohhot	254	169	91	-	12
Hong Kong	1027	776	-	-	29
Ji'nan	205	136	72	-	9
Kunming	890	577	319	-	59
Lanzhou	600	389	214	-	35
Liuyuan	892	511	309	-	59
Luoyang	298	196	105	-	14
Nanjing	417	273	149	-	20
Nanning	748	472	289	-	39
Qingdao	326	214	115	-	17
Qinglongqiao	-	-	14	21	2
Qiqihar	353	225	113	-	22
Shanghai	520	347	199	-	17
Shenyang	298	202	115	-	11
Shenzhen	720	466	256	-	33
Shijiazhuang	139	95	41	-	4
Suzhou	452	288	149	-	25
Tai'an	241	149	92	-	10
Taiyuan	345	183	110	-	11
Tangshan	-	-	40	61	3
Tianjin	-	-	22	34	2
Turpan	985	639	354	-	72
Urumqi	1005	650	361	-	75
Xi'an	417	273	149	-	22
Xining	658	430	237	-	44
Yinchuan	452	270	176	-	25
Zhengzhou	264	174	93	-	12

Upgrading If you get on the train with an unreserved seating ticket, you can find the conductor and upgrade (bǔpiào) yourself to a hard-sleeper, soft-seat or soft-sleeper if there are any available. This is sometimes the only way to get a sleeper or even a seat, but there are no guarantees.

If the sleeper carriages are full then you may have to wait until someone gets off. That sleeper may only be available to you until the next major station which is allowed to issue sleepers, but you may be able to get several hours' sleep. The sleeper price will be calculated for the distance that you used it for.

The desperate may be allowed to sleep in the dining car after it closes. There is usually a small charge for this. It's not terribly comfortable but is less horrible than hard-seat.

Timetables Paperback railway timetables are available, but in Chinese only. They are so excruciatingly detailed that it's a drag working your way through them; even the Chinese complain about this. Thinner versions listing the major trains can be bought at railway stations for about Y2.

Food Food is available on the trains and at stations. On all long-distance trains, railway staff regularly walk through the trains with pushcarts offering instant noodles, bread, bologna, beer and soft drinks. Journeys longer than 12 hours, qualify for a dining car.

Toilets The toilets in hard-seat are unspeakable horrors – a clear human rights violation if there ever was one. The facilities get a bit cleaner and nicer in hard-sleeper and soft-seat. However, all these devices are of the squat variety, and balancing yourself can be tricky. All the nasty waste goes out a tube and straight onto the tracks, and for this reason you're not allowed to use the toilets while the train is stopped (the staff sometimes lock up the toilets if someone violates this rule).

Be sure to bring toilet paper. It's never supplied free, though you can sometimes buy it from vendors on the train.

International Trains

Trans-Siberian The much-lauded Trans-Siberian Railway connects Europe to Asia via Moscow. The Beijing-Moscow run is very popular, but it takes about six days and it's yet another two days between Moscow and western Europe. For Beijing-Moscow you have two routes to choose from, the Trans-Mongolian (7865km), across Mongolia, or the Trans-Manchurian (9001km), which takes a little longer. A stop-off in Mongolia can be arranged with some difficulty, but in either case you *cannot* stop off in Russia unless you've booked a tour.

There are many things to consider in making the Trans-Siberian journey (costs, visas, accommodation in Moscow etc) and it's beyond the scope of this book. Lonely Planet's *China* guide has more information. At http://www.monkeyshrine.com and http://www.russia-rail.com you'll find good Trans-Siberian Railway Internet sites.

Two agents offering reasonably priced

tour packages (including stop-offs) include Moonsky Star (☎ 2723-1376; fax 2723-6653), 4th floor, Block E, Flat 6, Chungking Mansions, 30 Nathan Rd, Tsimshatsui, Kowloon, Hong Kong; and The Russia Experience (☎ (0181) 566-8846; email: 100604.764@compuserve.com) in the UK.

Beijing-Vietnam There is a twice-weekly international train running between Beijing and Hanoi, which stops at Friendship Pass (the border checkpoint). You can board or exit the train at numerous stations in China. The entire Beijing-Hanoi run is 2951km and takes approximately 55 hours, including a three-hour delay at the border. Schedules are subject to change, but at present train No 5 departs Beijing on Monday and Friday, arriving in Hanoi on Thursday and Monday, respectively. Going the other way, train No 6 departs Hanoi on Tuesday and Friday, arriving in Beijing on Friday and Monday, respectively. Arrival and departure times are as follows:

Station	To Hanoi Train No 5	To Beijing Train No 6
Beijing	11.20 pm	9.21 am
Shijiazhuang	2.54 am	5.58 am
Zhengzhou	7.53 am	12.53 am
Xinyang	11.50 am	8.53 pm
Hankou (Wuhan)	2.59 pm	5.35 pm
Wuchang (Wuhan)	3.34 pm	4.56 pm
Yueyang	6.47 pm	1.46 pm
Changsha	8.56 pm	11.42 am
Hengyang	11.49 pm	8.46 am
Lengshuitan	2.07 am	6.26 am
Guilin North	5.38 am	2.31 am
Guilin	5.59 am	2.12 am
Liuzhou	8.45 am	11.07 pm
Nanning	3.10 pm	6.49 pm
Pinxiang	10.04 pm	noon
Friendship Pass	10.00 pm*	8.00 am*
Dong Dang	1.00 am*	5.00 am*
Hanoi	6.30 am*	11.00 pm*

* *Vietnamese Time*

Beijing-Hong Kong Although Hong Kong is now officially part of mainland China, the Beijing-Hong Kong train is an international route subject to Immigration and Customs controls (based at Changping in Guangdong Province).

This is the most luxurious train in China. It's also fast by (China's standards), taking 29 hours to make the journey of 2470km (an average speed of 85km/h). There are three classes: hard-sleeper (Y776), soft-sleeper (Y1027) and deluxe soft-sleeper (Y1310).

At present, the train runs every other day. Train No 97 departs Hong Kong's Hunghom station at 7.30 am, arriving in Beijing west station the next day at 1.10 pm. Train No 98 departs Beijing at 3 pm, arriving in Hong Kong at 8.40 pm. Note that the timetables on display in Beijing west station say 'Jiulong', the official Pinyin spelling for Kowloon.

BOAT

While Beijing is not on the ocean, there is a seaport 2½ hours away by train at Tianjin's port district of Tanggu. There are boats running between Tianjin and Kobe in Japan, and also to Inch'ŏn in South Korea.

For details on cruises between Inch'ŏn and Tianjin, ring the Tianjin Ferry Company (☎ (022) 331-6049). This popular ferry sails once every five days from Tianjin at 10 am and the journey takes a minimum of 28 hours. Expect to pay no less than US$120.

TRAVEL AGENTS

China has two main government travel agencies and many smaller ones. Private agencies exist, but they have a hard time competing without the state subsidies.

The two biggest government-owned travel agents in Beijing are China International Travel Service (CITS) and China Travel Service (CTS) which are located in the same building. China Youth Travel Service (CYTS) is smaller but known for cheaper service. Aside from the big travel agents, there are booking counters in most of the major hotels. The key players are:

Beijing Overseas Tourism Corporation, 6th floor, Beijing Tourist Building, 28 Jianguomenwai Dajie, Chaoyang District, 100022 (☎ 6515-8573; fax 6515-8381)

Beijing Travel Service, 13 Xiagongfu Jie, 100006 (☎ 6512-2441; fax 6512-2219)
Cathay International Tourist Corporation, 19 Xinyuannan Lu, Dongzhimenwai, Chaoyang District, 100027 (☎ 6460-4813; fax 6467-7307)
China International Travel Service (CITS), ground floor, Beijing Tourist Building, 28 Jianguomenwai Dajie, 100022, behind the New Otani Hotel (☎ 6515-8562; fax 6515-8603)
China Peace International Tourism Corporation, 14 Chaoyangmen Nan Dajie, 100020 (☎ 6512-2504; fax 6512-5860)
China Travel Service (CTS), Beijing Tourist Building, 28 Jianguomenwai Dajie, 100022 (☎ 6515-8264; fax 6515-8557)
China Women Travel Service, 103 Dongsi Nan Dajie, Dongcheng District, 100010 (☎ 6523-1439; fax 6512-9021)
China Youth Travel Service (CYTS), 23C Dongjiaomin Xiangnei, 100006 (the alley behind the Capital Hotel) (☎ 6524-3388; fax 6524-9809)

Those Tricky Bits ...

Although Hong Kong is now technically part of China, and Macau soon will be, the two cities remain in limbo in most travellers' minds – so we've grouped their CTS and CITS branches on their own below:

CTS

Hong Kong
    Head Office, 4th Floor, CTS House, 78-83 Connaught Rd (GPO Box 6016), Central (☎ 2583-3888; fax 2854-1383; Kowloon Branch, 1st floor, Alpha House, 27-33 Nathan Rd, Tsimshatsui (☎ 2315-7188; fax 2721-7757)
Macau
    Xinhua Building, Rua de Nagasaki (☎ 705506; fax 706611)

CITS

Hong Kong
    CITS, 12th floor, Tower A, New Mandarin Plaza, 14 Science Museum Rd, Tsimshatsui East (☎ 2732-5888; fax 2721-7154)

Branches Abroad

CITS Outside China and Hong Kong, CITS is usually known as the China National Tourist Office (CNTO). CITS (or CNTO) representatives include:

Australia
    CNTO, 19th floor, 44 Market St, Sydney NSW 2000 (☎ (02) 9299-4057; fax 9290-1958)

France
> Office du Tourisme de Chine, 116, avenue des Champs Elysées, 75008, Paris (☎ (01) 44 21 82 82; fax 44 21 81 00)

Germany
> CNTO, Ilkenhansstr 6, D-60433 Frankfurt am Main (☎ (069) 520135; fax 528490)

Israel
> CNTO, 19 Frishman St, PO Box 3281, Tel-Aviv 61030 (☎ (03) 522-6272; fax 522-6281)

Japan
> China National Tourist Administration, 6th floor, Hamamatsu-cho Building, 1-27-13 Hamamatsu-cho, Minato-ku, Tokyo (☎ (03) 3433-1461; fax 3433-8653)

Singapore
> CNTO, No 17-05 Robina House, 1 Shenton Way, Singapore 0106 (☎ 221-8681; fax 221-9267)

Spain
> CNTO, Gran Via 88, Grupo 2, Planta 16, 28013 Madrid (☎ (01) 548-0011; fax 548-0597)

UK
> CNTO, 4 Glenworth St, London NW1 (☎ (0171) 935-9787; fax 487-5842)

USA
> CNTO, Los Angeles Branch, Suite 201, 333 West Broadway, Glendale CA 91204 (☎ (818) 545-7504; fax 545-7506); New York Branch, Suite 6413, Empire State Building, 350 Fifth Avenue, New York, NY 10118 (☎ (212) 760-9700; fax 760-8809)

Japan
> 103 Buyoo Building, 3-8-16, Nihombashi, Chuo-Ku, Tokyo (☎ (03) 3273-5512; fax 3273-2667)

Malaysia
> Ground floor, 112-114 Jalan Pudu, 55100, Kuala Lumpur (☎ (03) 201-8888; fax 201-3268)

Philippines
> 801-803 Gandara St (corner Espeleta St), Santa Cruz, Manila (☎ (02) 733-1274; fax 733-1431)

Singapore
> 1 Park Rd, No 03-49 to 52, People's Park Complex, Singapore, 059108 (☎ 532-9988; fax 535-4912)

South Korea
> 8th floor, Chung Oh Building, 164-3 Samsung-dong, Kangnam-gu, Seoul (☎ (02) 566-9361; fax 557-0021)

Thailand
> 559 Yaowarat Rd, Sampuntawang, Bangkok 10100 (☎ (02) 226-0041; fax 226-4701)

UK
> CTS House, 7 Upper St Martins Lane, London WC2H 9DL (☎ (0171) 836-9911; fax 836-3121)

USA
> Main Office, L/F, 575 Sutter St, San Francisco, CA 94102 (☎ (800) 332-2831, (415) 398-6627; fax 398-6669); Los Angeles Branch, Suite 303, US CTS Building, 119 South Atlantic Blvd, Monterey Park, CA 91754 (☎ (818) 457-8668; fax 457-8955)

CTS Overseas representatives include the following:

Australia
> Ground floor, 757-759 George St, Sydney, NSW 2000 (☎ (02) 9211-2633; fax 9281-3595)

Canada
> 556 West Broadway, Vancouver, BC V5Z 1E9 (☎ (800) 663-1126, (604) 872-8787; fax 873-2823); Suite 306, 438 University Ave, Box 28, Toronto, Ontario M5G 2K8 (☎ (800) 387-6622, (416) 979-8993; fax 979-8220)

France
> 32, rue Vignon, 75009, Paris (☎ (01) 44 51 55 66; fax 44 51 55 60)

Germany
> Düsseldorfer Strasse 14, D-60329, Frankfurt am Main (☎ (69) 2238522; Beusselstrasse 5, D-10553, Berlin (☎ (30) 393-4068; fax 391-8085)

Indonesia
> PT Cempaka Travelindo, Jalan Hayam Wuruk 97, Jakarta-Barat (☎ (21) 629-4452; fax 629-4836)

ORGANISED TOURS

Tours do ease the hassle, but that assumes your tour operator gives a damn. There have been numerous negative comments from travellers who have booked through CITS and CTS, but service is slowly improving.

A number of travel agents in the west do China tours, but most are forced into some sort of cooperative joint venture with CITS or other government bodies, which means high prices.

WARNING

Prices are volatile and anything quoted today is sure to be obsolete tomorrow. China's rate of inflation has slowed down in recent years, but greed has not, so be mentally and financially prepared for sudden price hikes.

Getting Around

THE AIRPORT

Beijing's Capital airport is 27km from the centre (Forbidden City area), but add another 10km if you're going to the backpacker fortresses at the southern end of town.

At the airport you'll be presented with a bewildering choice of buses into town: several companies offer a service and new routes are being added all the time. The fact that the destinations are written exclusively in Chinese also adds a measure of confusion. Nevertheless, you shouldn't be intimidated as it's fairly easy to find a bus that will take you close to where you want to go.

Inside the airport terminal itself there's a service desk that sells tickets. All buses into town cost Y16, so just plop down the money and tell them where you want to go. With ticket in hand, walk outside and keep muttering your destination – somebody will see that you get onto the right bus. In fact, almost any bus that gets you to a subway station will probably do. Save your ticket stub as you may have to return it to the bus driver when you disembark from the vehicle.

One company called 'Airbus' currently operates two routes. Route A goes to Beijing Railway Station *(běijīng zhàn)* (Map 9) and this is probably the most popular bus with travellers. Route B goes to the Xinxing Hotel (Map 8) over on the west side of town near Yuyuantan Park. Both of these buses can drop you at a subway station.

The Anle Bus Company offers three routes. The most popular route is to Xidan, which is close to the CAAC office west of the Forbidden City (Map 8). Another route is to Zhongguancun near Beijing University (north-west Beijing). The third route is to the China Art Gallery *(zhōngguó měishù guǎn)* north of Wangfujing (central area).

The official schedule for all of the above buses is once every 30 minutes between 5.30 am and 7 pm, but during peak demand times they put on additional buses.

Some of the big hotels also run minibus shuttles. You do not necessarily have to be a guest of the hotel to use these, but you do have to pay. The price for the minibuses is higher than the price for the regular airport buses.

There is one bus that runs directly from the airport to the nearby port city of Tianjin, taking about three hours for the trip. It costs about Y70.

Going from the city to the airport by bus can be quite complicated because it's hard to figure out exactly where the bus stops are. It's probably easiest to pick up the shuttle bus at the Aviation Building *(mínháng dàshà)* on Xichang'an Jie, Xidan District (Map 8) – this is the location of the CAAC ticket office. The bus departs on the opposite side of the street (south side of Xichang'an Jie), not from the car park of the Aviation Building. Lots of taxi drivers congregate here too. You may well have to ask someone where to find the bus stop, but don't bother asking any of the taxi drivers – they'll insist that the bus is either out of order, has gone bankrupt, or driven off a cliff.

A taxi (using its meter) should cost only about Y85 from the airport to the centre. Going the other way, drivers may ask for Y20 extra because they are not assured of getting a return passenger. They will also expect you to pay the Y10 toll if you take the airport expressway. The yellow microbus taxis may be unwilling to take you to the airport because they are not permitted to pick up return passengers there.

There is a well-established illegal taxi operation at the airport that attempts to lure weary travellers into a Y250 ride to the city. They pass themselves off as legitimate taxi drivers. One man acts as a taxi pimp for a squad of drivers – he will usually solicit you while you're still inside the airport terminal building. It is advisable to ignore him, head out the doors and cross the road to the queue for the official taxis.

Andrew Williams

Beijing's capital airport is an overcrowded mess forever undergoing renovation. In peak season (summer and holidays) you can expect long queues at both the domestic and international departure areas. It can take an awfully long time to clear security – you'd best arrive at the airport early if you don't want to miss your departing flight. Keep a close lookout as well; not all departures are announced, and sometimes departures are not from the area you expect.

In the departure area for domestic flights there are a couple of cheap but pathetic restaurants. In the international section there is nothing once you pass the first security check except for an overpriced coffee bar serving drinks and cakes only. If you'll be hanging out for a while in the departure lounge, bring some food from outside or be prepared to survive on chocolate-covered macadamia nuts from the duty-free shop.

BUS

Sharpen your elbows, chain your wallet to your underwear and muster all the patience you can because you'll need it. Overstuffed buses are in vogue in Beijing, and you'd be wise to avoid these sardine cans at rush hours or on holidays. Given the crowds and lack of air-conditioning, you can expect the buses to be unbearably hot during summer. They're cosy in winter if you haven't frozen at the bus stop by the time the trolley arrives, but difficult to exit from – try the nearest window. Fares are typically five jiao depending on distance, but often it's free because you can't see (let alone reach) the conductor. Smoking is prohibited but spitting is not.

There are about 140 bus *(gōnggòng qìchē)* and electric trolley *(diànchē)* routes. This makes navigation rather tricky, especially if you can't see out of the window in the first place. Bus maps save the day.

One or two-digit bus numbers are city core buses, 100-series buses are trolley-style, 200-series are night buses only, the 300 designation is for inner suburban lines and Nos 400 to 999 are for the outer suburbs. Buses run from around 5 am to 11 pm.

Minibus

These are more comfortable than the buses and definitely faster, but figuring out where the minibuses come and go from is tricky. Many simply follow the busiest bus routes and even display the same bus numbers, while others have only a sign in Chinese indicating the destination. Fares are between Y1 and Y6.

Double Decker Bus

A special two-tiered bus for tourists and upper-crust locals, the double deckers run in a circle around the city centre. These cost Y2 but you are spared the traumas of normal public buses – passengers are guaranteed a seat! There are four routes on offer, as follows:

Double Decker Bus Routes

Route 1
Beijing West railway station, heading eastward along Fuxingmen Dajie, Xichang'an Jie, Dongchang'an Jie, Jianguomenei Dajie, Jianguomenwai Dajie, Jianguo Lu and terminating at a major bus stop called Bawangfen (intersection of Jianguo Lu and Xidawang Lu)

Route 2
Qianmen, north on Dongdan Beidajie, Dongsi Nandajie, Dongsi Beidajie, Lama Temple, the China Ethnic Minorities Park, Asian Games Village

Route 3
Jijia Temple (the south-west extremity of the Third Ring Road), Grand View Garden, Leyou Hotel, Jingguang New World Hotel, Tuanjiehu Park, Agricultural Exhibition Centre, Lufthansa Centre

Route 4
Beijing Zoo, Exhibition Centre, Second Ring Road, Holiday Inn Downtown, Yuetan Park, Fuxingmen Dajie flyover, Qianmen Xidajie, Qianmen

---

SUBWAY

Originally constructed as part of Beijing's botched air-raid shelter system, the east-west underground line (opened in 1969) was for a time restricted to Chinese citizens with special passes. Foreigners weren't permitted to ride the subway until 1980.

The Underground Dragon now boasts two lines. Unlike most other subways, the crime rate is low (there is the odd pickpocket), graffiti is nonexistent and messy suicides are said to be rare. You will find ashtrays installed in the subway stations, just below the 'No Smoking' signs. There are no toilets in the subway stations – staying dehydrated may be a smart move. The subway is less crowded than the buses, and trains run at a frequency of one every few minutes during peak times. The carriages have seats for 60 and standing room for 200. Platform signs are in Chinese and Pinyin. The trains are *not* air-conditioned, so you suffer in summer but can enjoy a toasty ride in winter. The fare is a flat Y2 regardless of distance; like other subways around the world, it loses money, several million yuan per year. Trains run from 5 am to 11 pm.

The subway looks its age, and certainly needs upgrading. Lots of new lines are urgently needed to accommodate Beijing's ever-expanding population. Sadly, it seems that former Mayor Chen Xitong (now in prison) and his Treasurer, Wang Baosen (now dead) siphoned off much of the city's construction funds to pay for their Mercedes' and mistresses – the till is dry and expansion of the subway system has suffered a major setback. However, at the time of writing the East-West Line was being expanded further east and some new stations will probably be open by the time you read this. Unfortunately, the names of these stations was not yet determined when we went to press.

To recognise a subway station, look for the subway symbol which is an English capital 'D' with a circle around it. The 'D' stands for *dìtie* (subway). Another way of recognising a substation station is to look for an enormous cluster of bicycles.

Circle Line

This 16km line presently has 18 stations: Beijing Zhan (the main railway station), Jianguomen, Chaoyangmen, Dongsishitiao, Dongzhimen, Yonghegong, Andingmen, Gulou, Jishuitan, Xizhimen (the north railway station and zoo), Chegongzhuang, Fuchengmen, Fuxingmen, Changchunjie, Xuanwumen, Hepingmen, Qianmen and Chongwenmen.

East-West Line

This line has 13 stops and runs from Xidan to Pingguoyuan which is – no, not the capital of North Korea – but a western suburb of Beijing whose name translates as 'Apple Orchard' (unfortunately, the apple trees have long since vanished). It takes about 40 minutes to travel the length of the line. From east to west the stops are: Xidan, Fuxingmen, Nanlishilu, Muxidi, Junshibowuguan (Military Museum), Gongzhufen, Wanshoulu, Wukesong, Yuquanlu, Babaoshan, Bajiaocun, Guchenglu, and, lastly, Pingguoyuan. Fuxingmen is where the Circle Line meets the East-West Line and there is no additional fare to make the transfer.

Seven new stops are currently being added to the eastern end of the line. When completed, the East-West Line will extend eastwards almost as far as the Fourth Ring Road.

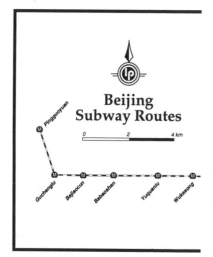

Beijing Subway Routes

CAR & MOTORCYCLE

The use of private vehicles by foreigners is tightly controlled. Resident expats with a Chinese driver's licence are allowed to drive their own cars anywhere within the environs of Beijing, Tianjin and their suburbs. They are not permitted to drive further afield without special permission. Expats in Beijing say that the rule can be stretched a bit, but the further from the capital you go the greater the risk of trouble with the local authorities. Foreigners busted for this particular offence have mostly been caught when checking into hotels far from Beijing.

Resident foreigners can also purchase a motorcycle, but the number of motorcycle licence plates available is tightly restricted – the Beijing municipal government wants to cut down on motorcycle use. Interestingly, these restrictions do not apply if you buy a motorbike with a sidecar – it's officially treated as a car! Sidecar or not, bikes are liable to be left lying around unused during Beijing's fierce winters, but they can be fun when the weather cooperates. In China both driver and passenger are required to wear a safety helmet. As in the USA, vehicles drive on the right.

The licence plates issued to foreigners are different from those issued to Chinese, and this is a bigger hassle than you might first imagine. Since the licence plates go with the car, this essentially means that a foreigner wanting to buy a used car must buy it from another foreigner.

Driving standards are not particularly good – nobody yields if they don't have to. Leaning on the horn is *de rigueur* – taxis might as well have a permanent siren attached. Half-eaten apple cores, lit cigarette butts and spittle get unexpectedly launched out the open window of the car in front of you. If you get into an accident, call the special hotline for foreigners (☎ 6839-9003, 6839-9971) which functions 24 hours. If that doesn't work and you speak Chinese, call the Chinese accident hotline (☎ 122).

Rather than do the driving yourself, it is much less hassle to hire a chauffeur-driven car. This can be arranged at major hotels, CITS or other travel agencies. However, depending on the type of vehicle, a chauffeur-driven car could cost you as much as Y1000 per day. It would be far cheaper to hire a microbus taxi by the day (see the following Taxi section).

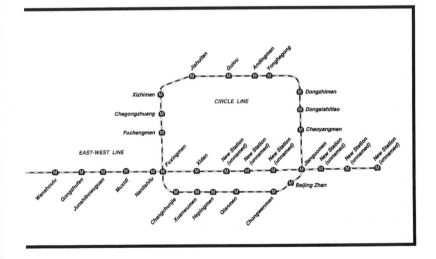

TAXI

In 1986 there were fewer than 1000 taxis available in the capital, so if you wanted one, it had to be booked hours in advance. By 1997, the number of taxis exceeded 80,000 and it is expected to reach 100,000 soon.

In other words, finding a cab is seldom a problem, though surging demand means that during rush hours you may have to battle it out with the other 12 million residents of Beijing. Taxis always become scarce during heavy rainstorms, and at such times the drivers often won't even take you if you want to go someplace far afield (they earn more by making numerous short hops).

One government brochure claims that 80% of Beijing taxi drivers can speak English. Perhaps they meant 80 drivers, since out of the total 60,000 that would be just about the right percentage. If you don't speak Chinese, bring a map or have your destination written down in characters. It helps if you know the way to your destination; sit in the front with a map. If you seem totally ignorant, you could be taken for quite a long ride.

The vehicles usually have a sticker on the window indicating their per kilometre charge, which varies all the way from Y1 to Y2 with a Y10 minimum. If you don't get one with a meter, be sure to negotiate the fare for the trip in advance. Cabs can be hired for distance (use the meter), by the hour ,or by the day for Y50 to Y100. You can usually get a cheaper rate if you say in advance, 'I don't need an official receipt' *(wǒ bùbì fāpiào)*.

The yellow microbuses – affectionately called 'bread taxis' *(miǎndì)* by the Chinese because they're shaped like a loaf of bread – are cheapest. However, they suffer much discrimination from the authorities – they are not permitted on some major roads or in the left (express) lane on the ring roads; many hotels will not allow them to stop in the driveway to discharge passengers; and they are prohibited from picking up passengers at the usual taxi stops. The authorities plan to phase them out and replace them with the recently-introduced 'bullet taxis' (so-called because of their sleek shape). The bullets

cost Y7 at flagfall which gets you 4km, after which you pay Y1.20 for each additional km.

Next up in the pecking order are the *xiali* taxis, small economy cars that cost Y1.40 to Y1.80 per km. Top of the line are the petrol-guzzling limousine taxis which cost Y12 for the first 4km and Y2 for each kilometre thereafter. Between 11 pm and 6 am a 20% surcharge is added to the metered fare.

Taxis can be hailed in the street or summoned by phone. For phone bookings, contact Beijing Taxi (☎ 6701-5113), Capital Taxi (☎ 6491-3309), Beijing Tourism Taxi (☎ 6515-8605), or Beichen Taxi (☎ 6491-2051). There is also a number to call for making taxi complaints (☎ 6601-2620).

If you're staying for a long time and you meet a taxi driver you like, ask for a name card. Most drivers have home phones, cellular phones or pagers (or all three) and can be hired for the day.

PEDICAB

Three-wheeled bicycles can accommodate one or two passengers in the back plus the driver up front. These look like a charming way to get around, but sadly they're not. What ruins it is that the drivers are aggressive and almost universally dishonest. The government should put meters on these things, because whatever fare you've agreed on in advance almost always gets multiplied by 10 when you arrive at your destination. Indeed, the final price is usually several times what a taxi would cost! Unless you enjoy vociferous arguments and confrontations, this mode of transport is not recommended.

Be especially wary if the driver wants his 'brother' to come along for the ride or ride alongside you in his own vehicle. The whole purpose of having brother along is so that you'll be up against two of them when the inevitable argument over the fare begins. This can also apply to taxis, but not usually.

BICYCLE

The scale of Beijing is much reduced on a bike, which can also give you a great deal of freedom. Beijing's rush hour can be rather astounding, consisting of a roving popula-

On Your Bike

It's Beijing's broad avenues, tree-lined side streets and narrow hutongs (ancient, atmospheric, winding lanes) that lend the city its unique character. A taxi goes either too quickly for you to catch the details, or too slowly to sustain interest. Chronic traffic jams can make bike travel not just more adventurous, but more efficient as well.

Being flat, Beijing city is ideal for cycling. You can bike past people flying kites in Tiananmen Square in the evenings, or see one generation cavorting to rock, while another enjoys ballroom dancing. Then there's clusters of neighbours squatting under streetlights to gossip and play cards; street stalls offering kitchenware, silk, noodles and even banquets; dentists extracting teeth; teenage boys shooting pool; or old men taking constitutionals, caged birds in hand. All the while, street performers compete for attention and brawlers tumble out of bars and karaoke clubs.

The bustle can seem daunting, but you quickly learn to weave around the horse-drawn carts and negotiate the buses that dip into the bike lanes from nowhere. You'll soon discover that large intersections are best tackled in packs and that, unless it's very late, you're never far from a roadside bicycle repairman.

Some Beijing sights really only ought to be seen by bicycle; places of such magic that only the breeze on your face convinces you they're for real. One is the moat around the Forbidden City, traversable around the eastern side of the palace. On one side of the path the clay-red wall of the Imperial Palace, with its crenellated battlements, rears up. Ornamental guard towers with flying eaves and roofs of gold jag into view at each corner. On the other, lotuses and fishermen lounge as pleasure boats stir ripples in the moat. If you start at the front of the palace, by Tiananmen Square, when you come out the back you're just a short ride to the even more spectacular 'back lakes' – Houhai and Shishahai.

Villas that once belonged to princes, now the abodes of the Communist nomenklatura, line these man-made lakes and the majestic Drum Tower, where once imperial timekeepers beat out the hours of the day, looms over the scene. In winter, a blanket of snow freshens the Beijing grey; no sooner does the lake freeze over than it swarms with skaters.

Linda Jaivin

Linda Jaivin is a writer and translator. Her books include Confessions of an S&M Virgin, Eat Me *and* Rock n Roll Babes from Outer Space.

---

tion of three million plus bicycles – a fact explained by the agony of bus rides.

Hotels often have bike hire, especially budget hotels. Bike hire agencies tend to congregate around hotels and tourist spots – look for signs in English. Costs vary wildly depending on the type of bike and where you rent it. Around the Jinghua Hotel you can score a heavy workhorse bike for Y5 per day, but a spiffy mountain bike can go for Y100 per day over at the Palace Hotel! There's a popular bike rental station in front of Scitech Plaza on Jianguomenwai. A passport (use an old expired one) or cash deposit is necessary.

Beware of a scam some unscrupulous renters will try. They rent you a bike which includes a lock and key. But the renter's brother or cousin has a key to the same lock. He follows you and at the first opportunity,

steals the bike. You then have to pay for a new bike to replace the 'stolen' one, or forfeit your deposit (or passport!). The solution – always use your own cable lock, and make sure it's a good one (preferably foreign-made). Bike theft is a big problem anyway; cable locks are a good idea and can be bought from department stores.

Several shopping areas are closed to cyclists from 6 am to 6 pm; Wangfujing is an important one. Bike parks are everywhere and cost peanuts – compulsory peanuts since your trusty steed can be towed away if you're not careful. Roadside puncture repair kits cost around Y5.

Billboards around Beijing depict the gory result of cyclists who didn't look where they were going and wound up looking like Y5 worth of fried noodles. These displays also give tips on how to avoid accidents and show 're-education classes' for offenders who have had several accidents.

To avoid becoming a feature in the next billboard display, bear the following advice in mind:

- Beijing in winter presents special problems, like slippery roads (black ice) and frostbite. The fierce winds during springtime present another challenge – not exactly optimum cycling conditions, but if you follow the example of the locals nothing will deter you.
- Dogs – the bane of cyclists the world over – are less of a problem in China than elsewhere. This is because Fido is more likely to wind up stir-fried than menacing cyclists on street corners.
- Riding at night can be hazardous, in large part because few Chinese bikes are equipped with lights.
- Bringing your own bike to China is not particularly recommended, because local ones are cheap and good enough for all but long-distance tours.

ORGANISED TOURS

CITS offers a number of 'Dragon Tours' – the name may refer as much to the price as to the cute logo on the side of the tour bus. Of course, the tours may mean you only see what the guides want you to see.

Bookings can be made at the CITS office or from the service counters at the Jianguo Hotel, Scitech Hotel, Kunlun Hotel, Landmark Hotel and Radisson SAS Hotel. On tours that extend past noon, lunch is thrown in 'free'. There are pick-up points at many hotels, so inquire about that when you book. There are seven Dragon Tours (see box).

Tour No 5 (hutongs by pedicab) is cheaper if you don't book through CITS. To do this, phone the Beijing Hutong Tourist Agency (☎ 6615-9097, 6400-2787), in which case

---

Dragon Tours

Tour 1
Badaling Great Wall and Ming Tombs; daily; departure at 8.30 am; return 5.30 pm; price Y290.

Tour 2
Tiananmen, Forbidden City and Temple of Heaven; Monday, Wednesday, Friday (Sunday optional); departure 8.30 am; return 3.30 pm (5.30 pm for special 'enhanced tour'); price Y280 (Y340 for enhanced tour).

Tour 3
Summer Palace, Lama Temple and Beijing Zoo; Tuesday, Wednesday and Saturday; departure 8.30 am, return 3.30 pm; price Y260.

Tour 4
Mutianyu Great Wall; Tuesday, Thursday and Saturday; departure noon; return 5 pm; price Y200.

Tour 5
Old Beijing on Rickshaw (explore the hutongs by pedicab); daily; departure 8.30 am; return 11.30 am; price Y230.

Tour 6
Beijing at Night (Beijing opera and duck dinner); Wednesday and Saturday; departure 8 pm; return 11 pm; price Y330.

Tour 7
Morning Exercises by Local Chinese (see taijiquan in the park and then eat breakfast); Tuesday, Thursday and Saturday; departure 7 am; return 9.30 am; price Y120.

---

the tariff is only Y180. If you do it this way you won't be picked up – you'll have to get yourself to the meeting point just west of the north gate of Beihai Park. The morning tour meets at the gate at 8.50 am and there's an optional afternoon tour at 1.50 pm. Many travellers have recommended this tour.

Things to See & Do

HIGHLIGHTS

Beijing has so much worth seeing that it's difficult to know where to begin. Many start with Qianmen, Tiananmen Square and the Forbidden City, followed by a jaunt through nearby Jingshan and Beihai parks. Another busy day could be spent at the Summer Palace and Fragrant Hills. A major excursion out of town is the journey to the Great Wall and nearby Ming Tombs. Those with an extra day may wish to explore Tianjin. (For the Great Wall and Ming Tombs, see the Excursions chapter.)

SQUARES, GATES & HALLS

Tiananmen Square (Map 11)
(tiān'ānmén guǎngchǎng)

Though it was a gathering place and the site of government offices in the imperial days, Tiananmen Square is Mao's creation, as is Chang'an Jie – the street leading onto it. It's the world's largest square, a vast desert of pavement and photo booths. Major rallies took place here during the Cultural Revolution when Mao, wearing a Red Guard armband, reviewed parades of up to a million people. In 1976 another million people jammed the square to pay their last respects. In 1989 PLA tanks and soldiers cut down pro-democracy demonstrators here. Today the square is a place for people to wander and fly kites or buy balloons for the kiddies.

Surrounding or studding the square is a mish-mash of monuments past and present: Tiananmen (Gate of Heavenly Peace), the Chinese Revolution History Museum (see the Museums section for details), the Great Hall of the People, Qianmen (Front Gate), the Mao Mausoleum and the Monument to the People's Heroes.

If you get up early you can watch the flag-raising ceremony at sunrise, performed by a troop of PLA soldiers drilled to march at precisely 108 paces per minute, 75cm per pace. The same ceremony in reverse gets performed at sunset, but you can hardly see the soldiers for the throngs gathered to watch. Most foreigners don't find it all that inspiring, but the Chinese queue for hours to get a front-row view.

Tiananmen Gate (Map 11)
(tiān'ānmén)

Tiananmen (Gate of Heavenly Peace) is a national symbol which pops up on everything from airline tickets to policemen's caps. The gate was built in the 15th century and restored in the 17th. From imperial days it functioned as a rostrum for dealing with or proclaiming to the assembled masses. There are five doors to the gate, and in front of it are seven bridges spanning a stream. Each of these bridges was restricted in its use, and only the emperor could use the central door and bridge. The dominating feature is now the gigantic portrait of Mao, the required backdrop for any photo the Chinese take of themselves at the gate. To the left of the portrait is a slogan in Chinese, 'Long Live the People's Republic of China' and to the right is another, 'Long Live the Unity of the Peoples of the World'.

You pass through Tiananmen Gate on your way into the Forbidden City (assuming you enter from the south side). There is no fee for walking through the gate, but to go upstairs and look down on the square costs a whopping Y30 for foreigners, Y10 for Chinese. It's hardly worth it, since you can get a similar view of the square from inside Qianmen for a quarter of the price.

Qianmen (Map 11)
(qiánmén)

Qianmen (Front Gate) sits on the south side of Tiananmen Square. Qianmen guarded the wall dividing the ancient Inner City and the outer suburban zone, and dates back to the reign of Emperor Yong Le in the 15th century. With the disappearance of the city walls, the gate has had its context removed, but it's still an impressive sight.

There are two gates – the southern one is known as the Arrow Tower *(jiàn lóu)* and the northern (or rear) one is called the Main Gate *(zhèngyángmén,* or the City Building *(chéng lóu)*. You can go upstairs into the Main Gate for Y3.

Great Hall of the People (Map 11)
(rénmín dàhuì táng)

The Great Hall of the People is the venue of the rubber-stamp legislature, the National People's Congress. It's open to the public when the Congress is not sitting, and to earn some hard currency it's even rented out occasionally to foreigners for conventions! You tramp through the halls of power, many of them named after provinces and regions of China and decorated appropriately. You can see the 5000-seat banquet room and the 10,000-seat auditorium with the familiar red star embedded in a galaxy of lights in the ceiling. The hall was completed over a 10-month period from 1958 to 1959.

The hall is on the west side of Tiananmen Square and admission costs Y35. Photography *is* permitted so you needn't check in cameras or bags.

MONUMENTS & MAUSOLEUMS
Monument to the People's Heroes (Map 11)
(rénmín yīngxióng jìnìan bēi)

On the site of the old Outer Palace Gate at the southern end of Tiananmen Square, the Monument to the People's Heroes was completed in 1958. The 36m obelisk, made of Qingdao granite, bears bas-reliefs of key revolutionary events (one relief shows the Chinese destroying opium in the 19th century) as well as appropriate calligraphy from Mao Zedong and Zhou Enlai.

Mao Zedong Mausoleum (Map 11)
(máo zhǔxí jìnìan bēi)

A fun visit with Chairman Mao's carcass is a must for every Chinese visitor to Beijing. The '*Mao*soleum' (as the expats call it) was opened in 1977 and is where Mao's body is kept on display for all to see.

Mao died on 8 September 1976; the ruling Politburo voted just hours later to preserve his body for two weeks then extended the mandate to 'perpetuity'. Mao's personal physician, Dr Li Zhisui, was most alarmed about this as he had no idea how to preserve a dead body permanently. In his book, *The Private Life of Chairman Mao*, Dr Li reveals that a wax Mao figure was constructed just in case the preservation techniques didn't work. According to Dr Li, both the real Mao and the wax dummy are stored in a vault below the public viewing area, and a lift is used to move the body (or the wax, as the case might be) to where it can be seen by the public.

However history will judge Mao, his impact on its course was enormous. Easy as it now is to vilify his deeds and excesses, many Chinese show deep respect when confronted with the physical presence of the man. CITS guides freely quote the old 7:3 ratio on Mao that first surfaced in 1976 – Mao was 70% right and 30% wrong (what, one wonders, are the figures for CITS itself?) and this is now the official Party line.

The atmosphere in the inner sanctum is one of hushed reverence. Foreigners are advised to avoid loud talk, not to crack jokes ('Is he dead?') nor indulge in other behaviour that will get you arrested.

The mausoleum is open daily from 8.30 to 11.30 am and occasionally from 2 to around 4 pm; entry is free but bags and cameras must be left at a booth outside which charges Y10. Join the enormous queue of Chinese sightseers, but don't expect more than a quick glimpse of the body as you file past the sarcophagus. At certain times of year, the body (or wax) requires maintenance and is not on view.

Whatever Mao might have done to the Chinese economy while he was alive, sales of Mao memorabilia are certainly giving the free market a boost these days. At the souvenir stalls near the mausoleum you can pick up Chairman Mao key rings, thermometers, face towels, handkerchiefs, sun visors, address books and cartons of cigarettes (a comment on his chain-smoking habit?).

MUSEUMS

As far as foreigners are concerned, Beijing's museums are worthwhile but pretty poorly presented. Signs and other information in the museums are very rarely in English.

Chinese Revolution History Museum (Map 11)

(zhōngguó gémìng lìshǐ bówùguǎn)

Housed in a sombre building on the east side of Tiananmen Square, the Chinese Revolution History Museum was for a long time made impenetrable by special permission requirements. From 1966 to 1978 the museum was closed so that history could be revised in the light of recent events.

The presentation of history poses quite a problem for the Chinese Communist Party. It has failed to publish anything of note on its own history since it gained power, before, during or since the Cultural Revolution. This would have required reams of carefully worded revision according to what tack politics (here synonymous with history) might take, so it was better left unwritten.

There are actually two museums here combined into one – the Museum of History and the Museum of the Revolution. Explanations throughout most of the museums are entirely in Chinese, so you won't get much out of this labyrinth unless you're fluent or pick up an English-speaking student. An English text relating to the museum is available inside.

The Museum of History contains artefacts and cultural relics (many of them copies) from year zero to 1919, subdivided into primitive communal groups, slavery, feudalism and capitalism/imperialism, laced with Marxist commentary. Without a guide you can discern ancient weapons, inventions and musical instruments.

The Museum of the Revolution is divided into five distinct sections: the founding of the Chinese Communist Party (1919-21), the First Civil War (1924-27), the Second Civil War (1927-37), resistance against Japanese forces (1937-45) and the Third Civil War (1945-49).

Imperial Archives Museum (Map 11)

(huángshǐchéng)

Just to the south-east of the Forbidden City on Nanchizi Lu is a small museum which houses the archives of the Ming and Qing empires. Some of the books and documents here go back 450 years, which is about as long as you can expect paper to hold up under less than ideal conditions. To their credit, the Ming and Qing emperors were good about keeping notes. Then, like now, it was necessary to make accurate records of whatever laws, edicts and rantings emanated from the imperial palace. This monumental task was given to a small army of eunuchs who did their tedious work with ink and brush pens.

Keeping the imperial family tree up to date was an especially complex affair given the level of marital infidelity within the Forbidden City. The family archives is the most amazing book in the entire collection, a mind-boggling tome 1m thick and weighing in at 150kg. You won't be allowed to casually flip through the pages, but it's still incredible to see.

The Imperial Archives Museum is open daily from 9 am to 4 pm.

Military Museum (Map 8)

(jūnshì bówùguǎn)

Perhaps more to the point than the Revolution History Museum, the Military Museum traces the genesis of the PLA from 1927 to the present and has some interesting exhibits: pictures of Mao in the early days, astonishing socialist-realist artwork, captured American tanks from the Korean War and other tools of destruction.

The museum is on Fuxing Lu on the western side of the city; to get there take the subway to Junshibowuguan.

Natural History Museum (Map 9)

(zìrán bówùguǎn)

This is the largest such museum in China and gets good reviews from travellers. The four main exhibition halls are devoted to flora and fauna, ancient fauna and human evolution. Some of the more memorable exhibits include a human cadaver cut in half to show the insides and a complete dinosaur skeleton. There is also plenty of pickled wildlife, though nothing worse than what you see for sale in some of the street markets. Some of the exhibits were donated by the British Museum, the American Museum of Natural History and other foreign sources.

The Natural History Museum is at 126 Tianqiao Nan Dajie, just west of Tiantan Park, Chongwen District, just north of the park's west gate. Admission is Y15. The museum is open daily except Monday, from 8.30 am until 4 pm.

Wax Museum (Map 6)
(làxiàng guǎn)
Here we have Beijing's answer to Madame Tussaud's in London. Although, in order to be immortalised in wax here, you have to be dead. There is a wax Mao on show, and rumour has it that Deng Xiaoping will soon join the exhibit.

The Wax Museum is in Ditan Park in the Dongcheng District, within walking distance of the Lama Temple. It's open from 9 am to 4 pm, but closed on Thursday and Friday. Admission costs Y5.

China Art Gallery (Map 11)
(zhōngguó měishù guǎn)
Back in Cultural Revolution days one of the safest hobbies for an artist was to retouch classical-style landscapes with red flags, belching factory chimneys or bright red tractors. You can get some idea of the state of the arts in China at the China Art Gallery. At times very good exhibitions of current work including photo displays are held in an adjacent gallery. Check the *China Daily* for listings. The arts and crafts shop inside has an excellent range of woodblock prints and papercuts (intricate designs cut from coloured paper). The gallery is west of the Dongsi intersection and admission is free.

Xu Beihong Museum (Map 5)
(xú bēihóng jìnìan guǎn)
This place displays oil paintings, gouaches, sketches and assorted memorabilia of the famous artist Xu Beihong, noted for his gal-loping horse paintings. Albums of paintings are on sale here, as well as reproductions and Chinese stationery.

The Xu Beihong Museum is at 53 Xinjiekou Bei Dajie, Xicheng District. It's open Tuesday through Sunday from 9 am to 5 pm (but closed noon to 1 pm for lunch), and admission costs Y1.

FORMER RESIDENCES
Unless you are pursuing a particular historical interest, most of the famous former residences are a wipeout. A notable exception is the Song Qingling Former Residence which is very classy.

Song Qingling Former Residence (Map 5)
(sòng qìnglíng gùjū)
Madam Song was the wife of Sun Yatsen, founder of the Republic of China. After 1981 her large residence was transformed into a museum dedicated to her memory and to that of Sun Yatsen. On display are personal items and pictures of historical interest such as clothing and books. The Song Qingling Museum is on the north side of Shisha Houhai Lake at 46 Beiheyan Lu. Admission costs Y10.

Lu Xun Museum (Map 10)
(lǔ xùn bówùguǎn)
Dedicated in no small way to the nation's 'No 1 Thinking Person's Revolutionary', the Lu Xun Museum has manuscripts, diaries, letters and inscriptions by the famous writer. Lu Xun (1881–1936) was the pen name of Zhou Shuren, often regarded as the father of modern Chinese literature. Before his time, Chinese authors saw themselves as scholars and insisted on writing in a literary style which was all but unintelligible to the masses. Lu Xun broke this tradition once and for all. His most famous work is *The True Story of Ah Q*.

The museum is off Fuchengmennei Dajie, west of the Xisi intersection. Admission is just Y1.

continued on page 92

The Palaces of Beijing

紫
禁
城

The capital of China for a number of centuries, Beijing has acquired a substantial number of up-market residences for emperors and empresses. In addition, the royal families required housing for their various servants, consorts, concubines, eunuchs and so on. It should not be forgotten that this is still the capital, and the construction of 'palaces' is an ongoing process.

FORBIDDEN CITY (Forbidden City Map page 82)
(zǐjìn chéng)

The Forbidden City, so called because it was more or less off limits for 500 years, is the biggest and best preserved cluster of ancient buildings in China. It was home to two dynasties of emperors, the Ming and the Qing, who didn't stray from this pleasure dome unless they absolutely had to.

The Beijing authorities insist on calling this place the Palace Museum *(gùgōng)*. Whatever its official name, it's open daily from 8.30 am to 5 pm – and last admission tickets are sold at around 3.30 pm. The foreigners' ticket allows admission to all the special exhibition halls; if you pay the Chinese price, the special exhibition

Title Page: Thomas Allom travelled through China in the early to mid-1800s, recording what he saw. This etching, showing a scene within the Forbidden City, is from his 1843 book, China, its Scenery, Architecture & Social Habits.

Right: The Qing Dynasty Emperor Daoguang (reigned 1821–1850) reviewing his palace guards in the Forbidden City.

紫
禁
城

halls cost extra, although it would still work out much cheaper if you could get the Chinese price (foreign residents of Beijing are supposedly entitled to the local Chinese price). Your Y85 includes rental of a cassette tape for a self-guided tour, though you can enter for Y60 without the tape. Tape players are available for free but require a refundable Y100 deposit (or passport, but this is not recommended) – you can use your own personal stereo instead if you prefer. For the tape to make sense you must enter the Forbidden City from the south gate (the Tiananmen Square end) and exit from the north (the Jingshan Park end). The tape is available in a myriad of languages.

A Forbidden City by Any Other Name ...

A Chinese riddle: when is a secret not a secret? Answer: when it's forbidden. The solution to this puzzle is the name of Beijing's heart (if not its soul): the Forbidden City. Visitors may leave the Meridian Gate feeling like they must have missed something inside – a certain emptiness seems to follow you up the marble cloud banisters to the vacant throne rooms. Turning the palace into a movie set helped fill the void – you might catch a glimpse of the ghost of Peter O'Toole rattling round a quiet courtyard on a push-bike. But to most people, it's the name that really entices and haunts.

The 'Forbidden City' is now officially called *gugong* – within the character *gu*, a 'former' palace is also a modern 'museum'. This isn't the first time the place has changed names. The French intellectuals' love affair with Mao took off with a visit to the 'Purple City' by Jean-Paul Sartre and Simone de Beauvoir in 1955. The foreigners weren't actually colour-blind – the magnificent Ming structure built by Emperor Yongle (reigned 1403–1424) was called Zi Jincheng, and *zi* (purple) signified the steady, axial North Star that the Celestial Empire should follow.

It's bizarre enough that *cheng* means both 'city' and 'wall', but the most curious character in 'Zi Jincheng' is *jin* – it can signify 'forbidden', but it also means 'secret'. The 'Forbidden City' might just as readily be known as the 'Secret City'; if it isn't, it's probably because something got lost in the political translation. Zi Jincheng was only crudely 'forbidden'; more exactly, it embodied the Chinese distinction between inner, outer and hidden, and the place of each social 'caste' in the imperial cosmic order. Thus, the emperor's winter palace was not open to the 'hundred surnames' (nowadays reduced to 'the common people'), but more to the point, scholar-officials (and this included foreign diplomats) weren't welcome beyond the outer court.

It's not clear when Zi Jincheng became known to 'barbarians' as the 'Forbidden City'. It might have been during the tenure of early, frustrated Jesuits or in the wake of the late-18th century ambassador to China, Lord George Macartney. Macartney's demands for British concessions (including the right to reside in Beijing's inner city) were finally answered by Emperor Qianlong (reigned 1736–1795) at the Jehol summer palace, not at the Forbidden City (at Jehol the British subject may have managed to fudge the issue of kowtowing to the Son of Heaven, but real estate matters weren't open to discussion).

Of course, the secret side of the imperial palace recedes further into the shadows as light is let in – the more 'open' the imperial palace is (even Sir Paul McCartney is allowed in these days), the more 'forbidden' it once must have been.

Russ Kerr

紫
禁
城

Don't believe the shifty characters loitering in front of the Forbidden City – you *don't* need an official guide to get inside, and you definitely don't have to give them any money for their troubles. It's also worth mentioning that many foreigners get Tiananmen Gate confused with the Forbidden City entrance because the two are physically attached and there are no signs in English. As a result, some people wind up purchasing the Tiananmen Gate admission ticket by mistake, not realising that this only gains you admission to the upstairs portion of the gate. To find the Forbidden City ticket booths, keep walking north until you can't walk any further without paying.

Behind the Wall

If ceremonial and administrative duties occupied most of the emperor's working hours, then behind the high walls of the Forbidden City it was the pursuit of pleasure which occupied much of his attention during the evenings. One of the imperial bedtime systems was to keep the names of royal wives, consorts and favourites on jade tablets near the emperor's chambers – sometimes as many as 50 of them.

By turning the tablet over the emperor made his request for the evening, and the eunuch on duty would rush off to find the lucky lady. Stripped naked and therefore weaponless, she was gift-wrapped in a yellow cloth, and the little bound-footed creature was piggybacked over to the royal boudoir and dumped at the feet of the emperor; the eunuch recorded the date and time to verify legitimacy of a possible child.

Aside from having fun, all this activity had a more serious purpose – prolonging the life of the emperor. An ancient Chinese belief that frequent sex with young girls could sustain one's youth even motivated Mao Zedong to follow the same procedure.

Financing the affairs of state probably cost less than financing the affairs of the emperor; keeping the pleasure dome functioning drew heavily on the resources of the empire. During the Ming Dynasty there were an estimated 9000 maids of honour and 70,000 eunuchs serving the court. Apart from the servants and the prize concubines, there were also the royal elephants to maintain. These were gifts from Myanmar (Burma) and were stabled south-west of the Forbidden City. Accorded rank by the emperor, when one died a period of mourning was declared. Periodically the elephant keepers embezzled the funds intended for elephant chow. When this occurred, the ravenous pachyderms went on a rampage.

While pocketing this cash was illegal, selling elephant dung for use as shampoo was not – it was believed to give the hair that extra sheen. Back in the harem the cosmetic bills piled up to 400,000 taels of silver. Then, of course, the concubines who had grown old and were no longer in active service were still supposed to be cared for. Rather than cut back on expenditure, the emperor sent out eunuchs to collect emergency taxes whenever money ran short.

As for the palace eunuchs, the royal chop was administered at the Eunuch Clinic near the Forbidden City, using a swift knife and a special chair with a hole in the seat. The candidates sought to better their lives in the service of the court, but half of them died after the operation. Mutilation of any kind was considered grounds for exclusion from the next life, so many eunuchs carried their appendages around in pouches, believing that at the time of death the spirits might be deceived into thinking of them as whole. ∎

紫
禁
城

History

The basic layout of the city was established between 1406 and 1420 by Emperor Yong Le, commanding battalions of labourers and craftspeople – some estimate up to a million of them. From this palace the emperors governed China, often rather erratically as they tended to become lost in this self-contained little world and allocate real power to the court eunuchs.

The buildings now seen are mostly post-18th century, as are a lot of restored or rebuilt structures around Beijing. The palace was constantly going up in flames – a lantern festival combined with a sudden gust of Gobi wind would easily do the trick, as would a fireworks display. Fires were also deliberately lit by court eunuchs and officials who could get rich from the repair bills. In 1664 the Manchus stormed in and burned the palace to the ground.

It was not just the buildings that went up in smoke, but rare books, paintings, calligraphy and anything else flammable. In this century there have been two major lootings of the palace: first by the Japanese forces, and second by the Kuomintang, who on the eve of the Communist takeover in 1949 removed thousands of crates of relics to Taiwan, where they are now on display in Taipei's National Palace Museum (worth seeing). Perhaps this was just as well, since the Cultural Revolution turned much of China's precious artwork into confetti. The gaps have been filled by bringing treasures, old and newly manufactured, from other parts of China.

The palace is so large (720,000 sq metres, 800 buildings, 9000 rooms) that a permanent restoration squad moves around repainting and repairing. It's estimated to take about 10 years to do a full renovation, by which time the beginning is due for repairs again. The complex was opened to the public in 1949.

Layout

The palace was built on a monumental scale, one that should not be taken lightly. Whatever you do, try not to miss the delightful courtyards, pavilions (and mini-museums within them) on each side of the main complex. Allow yourself a full day for exploration, or perhaps several separate trips if you're an enthusiast. The information given here can only be a skeleton guide; if you want more detail then tag along with a tour group for explanations of individual artefacts.

There are plenty of western tour groups around – the Forbidden City has 10,000 visitors a day. Tour buses drop their groups off at Tiananmen and pick them up again at the north gate; you can also enter the palace from the east or west gates. Even if you had a separate guidebook on the Forbidden City, it would be rather time-consuming to match up and identify every individual object and building, and a spoken guide has more immediacy. On the north-south axis of the Forbidden City, from Tiananmen at the south to Shenwumen at the north, lie the palace's ceremonial buildings.

Restored in the 17th century, **Meridian Gate** *(wŭmén)* is a massive portal designed exclusively for the emperor. Lesser mortals would use lesser gates – the military used the west gate, civilians the east. The emperor also reviewed his armies from here,

紫禁城

Forbidden City 紫禁城

1 Divine Military Genius Gate
神武门
2 Imperial Peace Hall
钦安殿
3 Thousand Autumns Pavilion
千秋亭
4 Arts & Crafts Exhibit
明清工艺美术馆
5 Imperial Garden
御花园
6 Western Palaces
宫廷史迹陈列
7 Eternal Spring Palace
长春宫
8 Earthly Tranquillity Palace
坤宁宫
9 Ceramics Exhibition
陶瓷馆
10 Hall of Union
交泰殿
11 Jewellery Exhibition
珍馆
12 Character Cultivation Hall
养性殿
13 Imperial Supremacy Hall (Painting Exhibit)
绘画馆
14 Bronzes Exhibition
青铜器馆
15 Palace of Heavenly Purity
乾清宫
16 Mental Cultivation Hall
养心殿
17 Heavenly Purity Gate
乾清门
18 Nine Dragon Screen
九龙壁
19 Hall of Preserving Harmony
保和殿
20 Hall of Middle Harmony
中和殿
21 Hall of Supreme Harmony
太和殿
22 Supreme Harmony Gate
太和门
23 Meridian Gate
午门
24 Beijing Music Hall
北京音乐厅
25 Tiananmen Gate
天安门

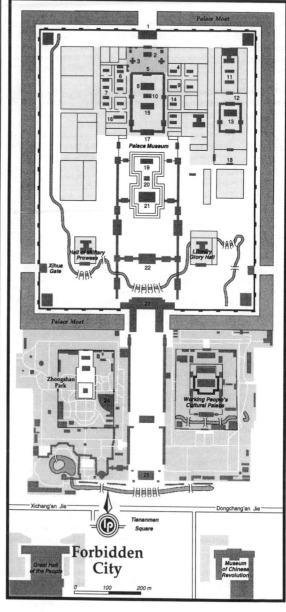

passed judgement on prisoners, announced the new year calendar and surveyed the flogging of troublesome ministers.

Across Golden Stream, which is shaped to resemble a Tartar bow and is spanned by five marble bridges, is **Supreme Harmony Gate** *(tàihémén)*. It overlooks a massive courtyard that could hold an imperial audience of up to 100,000.

Raised on a marble terrace with balustrades are the **Three Great Halls**, the heart of the Forbidden City. The **Hall of Supreme Harmony** *(tàihédiàn)* is the most important and largest structure in the Forbidden City. Built in the 15th century and restored in the 17th century, it was used for ceremonial occasions such as the emperor's birthday, the nomination of military leaders and coronations. Flanking the entrance to the hall are bronze incense burners. The large bronze turtle in the front is a symbol of longevity and stability – it has a removable lid and on special occasions incense was lit inside so that smoke billowed from the mouth.

To the west side of the terrace is a small pavilion with a bronze grain-measure and to the east is a sundial; both are symbolic of imperial justice. On the corners of the roof, as with some other buildings in the city, you'll see a mounted figure with his retreat cut off by mythical and real animals, a story that relates to a cruel tyrant hanged from one such eave.

Inside the hall is a richly decorated Dragon Throne where the emperor would preside over trembling officials. The entire court had to touch the floor nine times with their foreheads (this was the custom known as kowtowing). Thrown in thick veils of incense and the battering of gongs, and it would be enough to make anyone dizzy. At the back of the throne is a carved Xumishan, the Buddhist paradise, signifying the throne's supremacy.

Behind Taihedian is the smaller **Hall of Middle Harmony** *(zhōnghédiàn)* which was used as a transit lounge for the emperor. Here he would make last-minute preparations, rehearse speeches and receive close ministers. On display are two Qing Dynasty sedan chairs, the emperors' mode of transport around the Forbidden City. The last of the Qing emperors, Puyi, used a bicycle and altered the palace grounds to make it easier to get around.

The third hall is the **Hall of Preserving Harmony** *(bǎohédiàn)* used for banquets and imperial examinations. It now houses archaeological finds. The Baohedian has no support pillars, and behind it is a 250-tonne marble block carved with dragons and clouds which was moved into Beijing on an ice path. The outer housing surrounding the Three Great Halls was used for storing gold, silks, carpets and other treasures. The configuration of the Three Great Halls is echoed by the next group of buildings, smaller in scale but more important in terms of power, which traditionally lies at the back door, or in this case, the back gate.

The first structure is the **Palace of Heavenly Purity** *(qiánqīng gōng)*, a residence of Ming and early Qing emperors, and later an audience hall for receiving foreign envoys and high officials.

Immediately behind it is the **Hall of Union**, which contains a clepsydra – a water clock with five bronze vessels and a calibrated scale. Water clocks date back several thousand years; this one

紫
禁
城

was made in 1745. There's also a mechanical clock on display, built in 1797, and a collection of imperial jade seals.

At the northern end of the Forbidden City is the **Imperial Garden**, a large classical garden of fine landscaping with rockeries and pavilions. This is a good place to take a breather, with snack bars, toilets and souvenir shops. Two more gates lead out through the large **Divine Military Genius Gate** *(shénwǔmén)*.

The western and eastern sides of the Forbidden City are the palatial former living quarters, once containing libraries, temples, theatres, gardens and even the tennis court of the last emperor. These buildings now function as museums requiring extra admission fees, but the foreigners' all-inclusive ticket covers them. Opening hours are irregular and no photos are allowed without prior permission. Special exhibits sometimes appear in the palace museum halls, so check the *China Daily* newspaper for details of events coming up.

Zhongshan Park *(zhōngshān gōngyuán)*, otherwise known as Sun Yatsen Park, is in the south-west of the Forbidden City and was laid out at around the same time as the palace. Here you'll find the Altar of Land and Grain, which is divided into five distinct sections, each filled with earth of a different colour (red, green, black, yellow and white) to symbolise all the earth belonging to the emperor. You can also rent boats here for about Y1 and have a paddle around the moat.

The **Working People's Cultural Palace** *(láodòng rénmín wénhuà gōng)*, in the south-east sector of the Forbidden City, is a park with halls dating from 1462 which were used as ancestral temples under the Ming and Qing; they come complete with marble balustrades, terraces and detailed gargoyles. The park is now used for movies, temporary exhibits, cultural performances and the odd mass wedding.

ZHONGNANHAI
(zhōngnánhǎi)

Just west of the Forbidden City is China's 'new Forbidden City', Zhongnanhai. Although closed off to tourists, you can gawk all you want at the entrance. The name means 'central and south seas', after the two large lakes in the compound. The southern entrance is reached via Xinhuamen (Gate of New China) which you'll see on Chang'an Jie; it's guarded by two PLA soldiers stationed beneath the red and gold flag. The gate, built in 1758, was known as the Tower of the Treasured Moon when it was constructed.

The compound was built between the 10th and 13th centuries as a sort of playground for the emperors. Although expanded during Ming times, most of the present buildings making up the complex date from the Qing Dynasty. Empress Dowager Cixi once lived here; after the failure of the 1898 reform movement she imprisoned Emperor Guangxu in the Hall of Impregnating Vitality where, ironically, he died. Yuan Shikai used Zhongnanhai for ceremonies during his brief presidency of the Chinese Republic, after the overthrow of the imperial government. Since the founding of the People's Republic, top Communist Party officials have made Zhongnanhai home.

颐
和
园

SUMMER PALACE
(yíhéyuán)

One of Beijing's most visited sights, the Summer Palace is an immense park containing some newish Qing architecture. The site had long been a royal garden and was considerably enlarged and embellished by Emperor Qianlong in the 18th century. He deepened and expanded Kunming Lake with the help of 100,000 labourers, and reputedly surveyed imperial navy drills from a hilltop perch.

Anglo-French troops badly damaged the buildings during the Second Opium War (1860). Empress Dowager Cixi began rebuilding in 1888 using money that was supposedly reserved for the construction of a modern navy – but she did restore a marble boat that sits immobile at the edge of the lake.

In 1900 foreign troops, apparently a little annoyed by the Boxer Rebellion, had another go at turning the Summer Palace into a towering inferno. Although seriously charred around the edges by the soldiers' efforts, the palace was more or less still recognisable. Restorations took place a few years later and a major renovation occurred after 1949, by which time the long-suffering building had once more fallen into disrepair.

The original palace was used as a summer residence, as its name implies. The residents of the Forbidden City packed up and decamped here for their holidays, so the emphasis was on cool

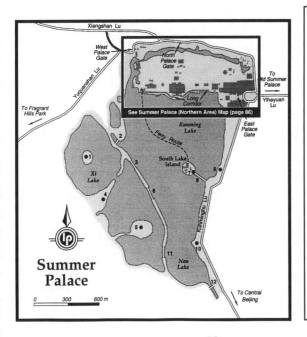

Summer Palace
颐和园

1 Site of the Zhijing Pavilion
   治镜阁址
2 Jade Belt Bridge
   玉带桥
3 Mirror Bridge
   镜桥
4 Changguan Hall
   畅观堂
5 Zaojian Hall
   藻鉴堂
6 Chain Bridge
   练桥
7 Knowing in the Spring Pavilion
   知春亭
8 17-Arch Bridge
   十七孔桥
9 Bronze Ox
   铜牛
10 Phoenix Mound
   凤凰墩
11 Willow Bridge
   柳桥
12 Xiuyi Bridge
   绣漪桥

See Summer Palace (Northern Area) Map (page 86)

颐和园

Summer Palace (Northern Area)
颐和园

1 Boathouse
  船坞
2 Rowing Boat Dock
  划船码头
3 Marble Boat
  清晏船
4 Ferry Dock
  码头
5 Tingliguan
  Restaurant
  听鹂馆
6 Long Corridor
  长廊
7 Cloud Dispelling Hall
  排云殿
8 Buddhist Virtue
  Temple
  佛愀
9 Precious Clouds
  Pavilion
  排云殿
10 Wisdom Sea Temple
  智慧海
11 Buddhist Tenants
  Hall
  香崇宗印之阁
12 Renshou Hall
  仁寿殿
13 Jingfu Pavilion
  景福楼
14 Yishou Hall
  益寿堂
15 Tiaoyuan House
  眺远斋
16 Harmonious Interest
  Garden
  谐趣园
17 Theatre Stage
  戏楼
18 Hall of Benevolence
  & Longevity
  仁寿殿
19 Rowing Boat Dock
  划船码头
20 Wenchang Pavilion
  文昌殿

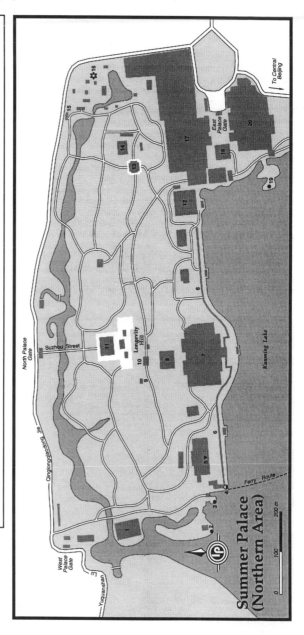

Summer Palace (Northern Area)

features – water, gardens, hills. It was divided into four sections: court reception, residences, temples and strolling areas.

Three-quarters of the park is occupied by Kunming Lake, and most items of architectural interest are to be found towards the east or north gates. The main building is the **Hall of Benevolence & Longevity**, just off the lake towards the east gate. It houses a hardwood throne and has a courtyard featuring bronze animals. It was here that the emperor-in-residence handled state affairs and received envoys.

Along the north shore of the lake is the **Long Corridor** *(cháng láng)*, over 700m long, which is decorated with mythical scenes. If the paint looks new it's because many pictures were white-washed during the Cultural Revolution.

On artificial Longevity Hill *(wànshòushān)* are a number of temples. The **Precious Clouds Pavilion** on the western slopes is one of the few structures to escape destruction by the Anglo-French forces. It contains some elaborate bronzes. At the top of the hill sits the **Buddhist Temple of the Sea of Wisdom**, made of glazed tiles; good views of the lake can be had from this spot.

On public display in a garage on the palace grounds is the first car ever imported to China, a Mercedes-Benz.

Other sights are largely associated with Empress Cixi, like the place where she celebrated her birthdays, and exhibitions of her furniture and memorabilia.

The Tingliguan (Listening to the Orioles) Restaurant serves imperial banquet food – fish from Kunming Lake, velvet chicken and dumplings – on regal tableware lookalikes. With a fantastic alfresco location and exorbitant prices to match, the restaurant is housed in a former imperial theatre; and nowadays there are souvenir shops attached.

Another noteworthy feature is the **17-arch bridge** spanning 150m to South Lake Island; on the mainland side is a beautiful bronze ox. Also note the Jade Belt Bridge on the mid-west side of the lake; and the Harmonious Interest Garden at the north-east end which is a copy of a garden in Wuxi.

You can get around the lake by rowing boat, or on a pair of ice skates in winter. As with the Forbidden City moat, it used to be a common practice to cut slabs of ice from the lake in winter and store them for summer use.

The park is about 12km north-west of the centre of Beijing. The easiest way to get there is to take the subway to Xizhimen (close to the zoo), then a minibus or bus No 375. Bus No 332 from the zoo is slower but will get you there eventually. There are lots of minibuses returning to the city centre from the Summer Palace, but get the price and destination settled before departure. You can also get there by bicycle; it takes about 1½ to two hours from the city centre. Rather than taking the main roads, it's far more pleasant to bike along the road following the Beijing-Miyun Diversion Canal.

Foreigners are charged a fairly outrageous Y45 for admission, which does *not* get you into everything – there are some additional fees to be faced inside. Admission for locals is Y20 – and foreigners need to be Beijing residents (with the appropriate ID)

圆
明
园

to get this price. Opening times are 9 am to 4 pm. By the way, try to avoid visiting this place on a weekend, or the only things you'll see will be camera flashes, cotton candy and a sea of 'I Love Beijing' T-shirts.

OLD SUMMER PALACE
(yuánmíngyuán)
The original Summer Palace was laid out in the 12th century. But it wasn't until the reign of Emperor Qianlong (reigned 1736–1795) that the palace's set of interlocking gardens really came into their own. Qianlong set a team of Jesuit architects to work to come up with several European-style palaces for the gardens, while also overseeing the construction of elaborate fountains and baroque statuary.

During the Second Opium War (1860), British and French soldiers pillaged and torched the imperial family's summer holiday house and sent the booty back to their respective homelands. Since the pavilions and temples were made of wood they too were lost in the fires, but a marble facade, some broken columns and traces of the fountains still stick out of the rice paddies. The effect, while a little melancholy, is charming, and many people enjoy this sedate setting more than the touristy Summer Palace.

The ruins have long been a favourite picnic spot for foreign residents and Chinese twosomes seeking a bit of privacy. More recently, the government has decided to slowly restore the gardens, moats and buildings. It's uncertain yet just how far the restoration will go. Will it be allowed to remain as ruins or will it become another Chinese tourist circus like the Great Wall? At present, it's a very worthwhile place to visit, so make the most of it while you still can.

Right: The doomed Hall of Audience in the grounds of the Old Summer Palace. The hall was destroyed by British and French troops in 1860.

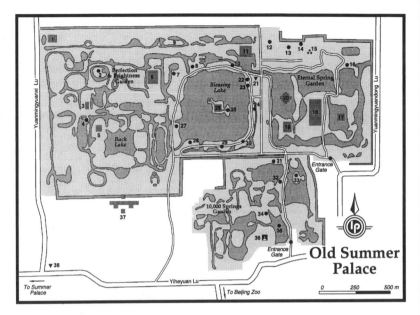

圆明园

Old Summer Palace
圆明园

1 Purple Blue Lodge
紫碧山房
2 Library Pavilion
文源阁
3 Wuling Spring Beauty
武陵春色
4 Universal Peace
万方安和
5 Apricot Blossoms in Spring Lodge
杏花春馆
6 Guards' Citadel
舍卫城
7 Open World to the Public
觳然大公
8 Autumn Moon Over the Calm Lake
平湖秋月
9 Far North Mountain Village
北远山村
10 Collecting Mysteries Tower
藏密楼
11 Square Pots Wonderland
方壶胜境
12 10,000 Flowers Maze
万花阵

13 Oceanic Banquet Hall
海宴堂
14 Exhibition Hall
展览馆
15 Great Fountain Ruins (European Gardens)
西洋楼
16 Lion's Forest
狮子林
17 Exquisite Jade Hall
玉玲珑馆
18 Containing Scriptures Hall
含经堂
19 Everlasting Thoughts Studio
思永斋
20 Open Sea Hill
海岳开襟
21 Fuhai Restaurant
福海酒家
22 Rowboat Dock
船台
23 Clear Reflection of the Void
涵虚朗鉴
24 Grace & Beauty Lodge
接秀山房
25 Blessing Sea Fairy Hill Hall
瀛海仙山亭

26 Jade Terraces on Penglai Isles
蓬岛瑶台
27 Body Bathed in Virtue
澡身浴德
28 Lakes & Hills View
湖山在望
29 Broad Nutrient Palace
广育宫
30 New Fairyland
别有洞天
31 Pine Moon Pavilion
松月亭
32 Contain Autumn Hall
涵秋馆
33 Phoenix & Unicorn Isles
凤麟洲
34 Boat Dock
船台
35 Enjoying Jasper Pavilion
槛碧亭
36 Awareness Temple
正觉寺
37 Great Palace Entrance Gate
大宫门
38 Xiyuan Restaurant
西苑饭店

圓
明
園

The site is enormous – 2.5km from east to west – and divided into three separate compounds. The western section of the Old Summer Palace grounds is the main area, known as the **Perfection & Brightness Garden** *(yuánmíngyuán)*. The southern compound is the **10,000 Springs Garden** *(wànchūnyuán)*. The eastern section is the **Eternal Spring Garden** *(chángchūnyuán)*. It's in the eastern section that you'll find the European Garden with its **Great Fountain Ruins**, considered to be the best preserved relic in the palace and featured prominently in the tourist brochures. In this area is also the fully restored **10,000 Flowers Maze**.

Minibuses connect the new Summer Palace with the old one for about Y5, but a taxi on the same route only costs about Y10. Bus No 375 from Xizhimen subway station (on the circle line) will get you there. Admission is Y5 and opening times are 9 am to 4 pm.

There are some pleasant trips around the area by public transport. Take bus No 332 from the zoo to the Old Summer Palace and the Summer Palace; change to bus No 333 for the Fragrant Hills; then take bus No 360 back to the zoo.

Another round-trip route is to take the subway to Pingguoyuan (the last stop in the west) and then bus No 318 to the Fragrant Hills; change to No 333 for the Summer Palace, and then bus No 332 for the zoo.

PRINCE GONG'S PALACE
(gōng wáng fǔ)
Prince Gong was the son of a Qing emperor and the father of Puyi, the last of China's emperors. As palaces go, Gong's is a small one. But what it lacks in interior space, it more than makes up for in its awe-inspiring grounds. One of the largest private residential compounds remaining in Beijing, the layout includes nine courtyards and numerous elaborate gardens, all hemmed in by imposing walls.

Right: The ornate surrounds of Beijing's palaces and official residences were often as impressive as the buildings themselves.

圆
明
园

Gong, But Not Forgotten

As well as being the last emperor's father, Prince Gong earned an unflattering footnote in history as a failed negotiator with the bellicose British. The issue was a matter of who might live in Beijing's splendid courtyard houses – with the forced signing of the infamous Tianjin Treaty (1858), China was expected to permit foreign ambassadors to reside in the capital.

Most clauses of the treaty – tolerance of Christian missionaries, more 'open' trade and the continued sale of opium (illegal in China) – could be conceded. But while the British were no longer to be referred to as *yi* (barbarians), allowing them to live in the Son of Heaven's city was too much to ask.

Unimpressed, British troops pushed the issue by force, attacking seaside forts east of Beijing. When this didn't work, the British sent negotiators to the capital, some of whom were promptly arrested and executed. By now the situation was critical; the emperor (who had fled to Manchuria) sent his brother Prince Gong to negotiate, but the Prince's efforts were doomed. The British were led by the son of the same Lord Elgin who had removed the Parthenon's famous statuary ('Elgin's marbles') to England 'for safekeeping'. After allowing British and French troops to pillage what they could, the younger Elgin ordered the Summer Palace burned.

This act was distressing enough to the Qing, but it might have been worse: the Forbidden City was only spared because its destruction would have brought down the entire dynasty, and the British considered this a little bad for business. Prince Gong immediately agreed to all the Tianjin Treaty's terms, and further pledged a large payment of silver plus part of Kowloon to British Hong Kong. In exchange, the British agreed to protect their new gains by supporting the Qing against the dangerous Taiping rebellion.

Russ Kerr

The compound is reputed to have been the inspiration for the mansion in the classic work of vernacular literature, *The Dream of the Red Chamber* (translated into English as *The Story of the Stone* by David Hawkes), by 'China's Tolstoy', Cao Xueqin.

 ← READ THIS

To find the palace, you have to get off the main roads and search in the small alleys running around the Shisha Hai Lakes. It's more or less at the centre of the arc created by the lakes running from north to south (Map 5). Admission costs Y5.

continued from page 76

Mei Lanfang Former Residence (Map 5)
(méi lánfāng gùjū)

Beijing opera was popularised in the west by the actor Mei Lanfang (1894-1961) who played *dàn* or female roles, and is said to have influenced Charlie Chaplin. Mei Lanfang's former residence at 9 Huguosi Lu, Xicheng District, has been preserved as a museum. It's closed during winter and also every Monday. Admission costs Y5.

Guo Moruo Former Residence (Map 5)
(guō mòruò gùjū)

Born Guo Kaizhen (1892–1978), Guo Moruo was one of Communist China's most politically correct writers. He was from a wealthy landlord family and received an elite education in Japan. But in spite of his ruling-class roots, he founded the Marxist-inspired Creation Society in 1921. In the same year, a collection of Guo Moruo's poetry, *The Goddesses (nǚshén)*, was partially translated into English. In 1927 he wrote an article criticising Chiang Kaishek, and was thus forced to flee to Japan in 1928. With the outbreak of the Sino-Japanese War, he returned to China and wrote anti-Japanese tracts. When the Communists came to power in 1949, Guo was made director of the Chinese Academy of Sciences. In 1951 he was awarded the Stalin Peace Prize (an oxymoron if ever there was one). He was given several other high-level posts during his twilight years. Unlike many other writers, he survived the Cultural Revolution with barely a scratch.

Guo lived in a garden-like compound in Beijing. His house has been preserved along with many of his books and manuscripts. You'll find it at 18 Qianhai Xijie in the Xicheng District. The house is open from 9 am to 4 pm, but is closed during the winter months and closed on Monday during the other seasons.

Mao Dun Former Residence (Map 6)
(máo dùn gùjū)

Mao Dun (1896–1981) was the pen name of Shen Yanbing. He was born into an elite family in Zhejiang Province but was educated in Beijing. In 1916 he worked in Shanghai as a translator for the Commercial Press (a major state-run publishing operation which is still in business today – check out their store in Hong Kong, which is a brilliant source of books about China). In 1920 he help found the Literary Study Society (the earliest literary society of the New Literature Movement). The society advocated literary realism. Mao Dun joined the League of Left Wing Writers in 1930 and became active in Communist worker activities in Shanghai. He became solidly entrenched in the bureaucracy after the Communists came to power. He laid low during the Cultural Revolution, but briefly returned to writing in the 1970s.

The Mao Dun Former Residence is only open to the public on Tuesday, Thursday and Saturday from 9.30 am to 4.30 pm. Admission costs Y1.

Lao She Former Residence (Map 11)
(lǎo shè gùjū)

A novelist of the early 20th century, Lao She (1899–1966) was the pen name of Shu Sheyu. He's most famous for *The Rickshaw Boy*, also known as *Camel Xiangzi*, a social critique of the living conditions of Beijing rickshaw drivers. Lao She's other works include *Cat City* and the play *Teahouse*.

For his efforts, he was severely persecuted during the Cultural Revolution and died from wounds inflicted by Red Guards.

Lao She lived for 16 years in an undistinguished house with courtyard at 19 Fengfu Hutong, Dengshi Xikou. There really isn't all that much to see here.

TEMPLES
Lama Temple (Map 6)
(yōnghégōng)

This is the most colourful temple in Beijing, with its beautifully landscaped gardens, stunning frescoes and tapestries, and incredible carpentry.

The Lama Temple was once modified to become the official residence of Count Yin Zhen. Nothing unusual in that, perhaps, but in 1723 he was promoted to emperor, and moved to the Forbidden City. His name was changed to Yong Zheng, and his former residence became Yonghe Palace. The green tiles were changed to yellow, the imperial colour, and – as was the custom – the place could not be used except as a temple. In 1744 it was converted into a lamasery, and became a residence for large numbers of monks from Mongolia and Tibet.

In 1792 the Emperor Qianlong, having quelled an uprising in Tibet, instituted a new administrative system involving two gold vases. One was kept at the Jokhang Temple in Lhasa, where it was intended to be used for determining the reincarnation of the Dalai Lama (under the supervision of the Minister for Tibetan Affairs). The other was kept at the Lama Temple for the lottery for the Mongolian Grand Living Buddha. The Lama Temple thus assumed a new importance in ethnic minority control.

The lamasery has three richly-worked archways and five main halls strung in a line down the middle, each taller than the preceding one. Styles are mixed – Mongolian, Tibetan and Han – with courtyard enclosures and galleries.

The first hall, **Lokapala**, houses a statue of the Maitreya (future) Buddha, flanked by celestial guardians. The statue facing the back door is Weituo, the guardian of Buddhism, made of white sandalwood. Beyond, in the courtyard, is a pond with a bronze mandala depicting Xumishan, the Buddhist paradise.

The second hall, **Yonghedian**, has three figures of Buddha – past, present and future.

The third hall, **Yongyoudian**, has statues of the Buddha of Longevity and the Buddha of Medicine (to the left). The courtyard beyond the hall features galleries with some nandikesvaras, or joyful Buddhas, tangled up in multi-armed close encounters. These are coyly draped lest you be corrupted by the sight, and are to be found in other esoteric locations.

The **Hall of the Wheel of Law**, further north, contains a large bronze statue of Tsong Khapa (1357–1419), founder of the Gelukpa or Yellow Hat sect, and frescoes depicting his life. This Tibetan-style building is used for study and prayer.

The last hall, **Wanfu Pavilion**, has an 18m-high statue of the Maitreya Buddha in his Tibetan form, sculpted from a single piece of sandalwood and clothed in yellow satin. The smoke curling up from the yak-butter lamps transports you momentarily to Tibet, which is where the log for this statue came from.

In 1949 the Lama Temple was declared protected as a major historical relic. Miraculously it survived the Cultural Revolution without scars. In 1979 large amounts of money were spent on repairs and it was restocked with several dozen novices from Inner Mongolia, a token move on the part of the government to back up its claim that the Lama Temple is a 'symbol of religious freedom, national unity and stability in China'. The novices study Tibetan language and the secret practices of the Gelukpa (Yellow Hat) sect.

The temple is active again, though some question whether or not the monks in tennis shoes are really monks or PSB. Prayers take place early in the morning, not for public viewing, but if you inquire discreetly of the head lama you might be allowed to return the following morning. No photography is permitted inside the temple buildings, but the postcard industry thrives.

The temple is open daily, except Monday, from 9 am to 4 pm. Get there by subway to the Yonghegong station or else the double-decker bus No 2. Entry costs Y30; the audio tour is Y20 plus a refundable Y50 deposit.

Confucius Temple & Imperial College (Map 6)

(kǒng miào, guózijiān)

Just down the hutong opposite the gates of the Lama Temple is the former Confucius Temple and the Imperial College. The Confucius Temple is the largest in the land after the one at Qufu. The temple was re-opened in 1981 after some mysterious use as an official residence. It's now a museum, in sharp contrast to the Lama Temple.

The steles in the temple courtyard record

the names of those successful in the civil service examinations (possibly the world's first) of the imperial court. To see his name engraved here was the ambition of every scholar, but it wasn't made easy. Candidates were locked in cubicles (about 8000 of them) measuring roughly 1.5m square for a period of three days. Many died or went insane during their incarceration. Imagine that.

The Imperial College was the place where the emperor expounded the Confucian classics to an audience of thousands of kneeling students and professors; this was an annual rite. Built by the grandson of Kublai Khan in 1306, the former college was the only institution of its kind in China. It's now the Capital Library. In the 'collection' are the stone tablets commissioned by Emperor Qianlong. These are engraved with 13 Confucian classics – 800,000 characters (12 years' work for the scholar who did it). There is an ancient 'Scholar-Tree' in the courtyard.

The easiest way to get there is by subway to the Yonghegong subway station.

Great Bell Temple (Map 10)
(dàzhōng sì)
The biggest bell in China, this one at the Great Bell Temple weighs a hefty 46½ tonnes and is 6.75m tall. The bell is inscribed with Buddhist sutras, a total of over 227,000 Chinese characters.

The bell was cast during the reign of Ming Emperor Yong Le in 1406 and the tower was built in 1733. Getting the bell from the foundry to the temple proved problematic, since back in those days it wasn't possible to contract the job out to a Hong Kong company. A shallow canal had to be built which froze over in winter, and the bell was moved across the ice by sled.

Within the grounds of the monastery at this site are several buildings besides the one housing the bell itself. They include the Guanyin Hall, Sutra-keeping Tower, Main Buddha Hall and Four Devas Hall. This monastery is one of the most popular in Beijing and was reopened in 1980.

The Great Bell Temple is almost 2km east of the Friendship Hotel on Beisanhuan Xilu.

White Dagoba Temple (Map 5)
(báitǎ sì)
The White Dagoba Temple can be spotted from the top of Jingshan, and is similar (and close) to the one in Beihai Park. It was used as a factory during the Cultural Revolution but reopened after restoration in 1980. The dagoba dates back to Kublai Khan's days though the halls date only from the Qing Dynasty. It lies off Fuchengmennei Dajie.

Wuta Temple (Map 10)
(wǔtǎ sì)
The Indian-style Wuta Temple has five pagodas and was first constructed in 1473 from a model presented to the imperial court. The temple has been renovated and sits in a small park filled with stone turtles and inscribed stone steles. For this reason, it's also known as the **Carved Stone Museum** *(shíkē bówùguǎn)*. The temple is a delightful place, though it's no longer an active place of worship. The compound currently houses the China Life Sciences Research Institute and the Qigong Club.

The temple is easily found by crossing the canal bridge directly opposite the rear exit of the Beijing Zoo.

Guangji Temple (Map 5)
(guǎngjì sì)
The Guangji (Universal Rescue) Temple is on the north-west side of Xisi intersection, and east of the White Dagoba Temple. It's the headquarters of the Chinese Buddhist Association.

Fayuan Temple (Map 8)
(fǎyuán sì)
In a lane just east of the Niujie Mosque (see the next section) is the Fayuan (Source of Law) Temple. The temple was originally constructed in the 7th century and is still going strong. It's now the China Buddhism College and is open to visitors.

White Cloud Temple (Map 8)
(báiyúnguān)
The White Cloud Temple is in a district directly south of Yanjing Hotel and west of

the moat. Once the Taoist centre of North China and the site of temple fairs, inside you'll find several courtyards containing a pool, bridge, several halls of worship and Taoist motifs. Walk south on Baiyun Lu and cross the moat; continue south along Baiyun Lu, turn into a curving street on the left and follow it for 250m to the temple entrance. Admission costs Y10.

Zhihua Temple (Map 7)
(zhìhuà sì)
Notable for its deep blue tiling, this is a pretty example of Ming architecture (dating from 1443) but there's nothing else of note. If you strain over a bus map looking north of Beijing railway station, you will find a hutong called Lumicang which runs east off Chaoyangmen Nanxiaojie (about 1.5km north of the station). The temple is at the east end of Lumicang. The coffered ceiling of the third hall of the Growth of Intellect Temple is not at the east end of Lumicang – it's in the USA. Lumicang Hutong had rice granaries in the Qing Dynasty but these days it's mostly got traffic.

MOSQUES & CATHEDRALS
Dongsi Mosque (Map 11)
(dōngsì qīngzhēn sì)
The Dongsi Mosque is one of two functioning mosques in Beijing, the other being Niujie Mosque. Dongsi is at 13 Dongsi Nan Dajie, just south of the intersection with Chaoyangmennei Dajie.

Niujie Mosque (Map 8)
(niújiē lǐbài sì)
Beijing is estimated to have some 180,000 ethnic-Chinese Muslims (now officially labelled the 'Hui' minority). There are some 40 mosques in town, the largest of which is the Niujie Mosque. It's in the south-west of Beijing, south of Guang'anmennei Dajie (Beijing's largest Hui neighbourhood).

Bare legs are a no-no inside the compound, but if you show up in shorts or a miniskirt you can borrow a pair of trousers. Although anyone can go into the compound, only Muslims are permitted to enter the main hall of worship.

Near the mosque is Niu Jie (Ox St), an area with a feel all its own and worth a look.

South Cathedral (Map 8)
(nántáng)
This is the main functioning cathedral of Beijing – the others are in a comparatively sorry state. The South Cathedral (also known as St Mary's Church) is built on the site of Matteo Ricci's house – first built in 1703 and destroyed three times since then.

The cathedral is on Qianmen Dajie at the Xuanwumen intersection (north-east side) above the subway station.

Mass is held daily in Latin and Chinese beginning at 6.30 am. English mass is on Sunday at 10 am.

North Cathedral (Map 5)
(beitáng)
Also called the Cathedral of Our Saviour. It was built in 1887 but was badly damaged during the Cultural Revolution then converted into a factory warehouse. It was reopened at the end of 1985 when restoration work was completed. The cathedral is at Xishiku in the Xicheng District.

PARKS
In imperial days the parks were laid out at the compass points: to the west of the Forbidden City lies Yuetan Park; to the north lies Ditan Park; to the south lies Taoranting Park and to the east is Ritan Park. To the southeast of the Forbidden City is the showpiece, Tiantan Park.

All of these parks were venues for ritual sacrifices offered by the emperors. Not much remains of the shaman structures, bar those of the Temple of Heaven in Tiantan Park, but if you arrive early in the morning you can witness taiji, fencing exercises, or perhaps opera-singers and musicians practising. It's well worth experiencing the very different rhythms of the city at this time.

Temporary exhibitions take place in the parks, including horticultural and cultural ones, and there is even the odd bit of open-air theatre as well as some worthy eating establishments. If you take up residence in Beijing, the parks become very important for preserving sanity. They are open late too, typically until 8 pm.

Tiantan Park (Tiantan Park Map & Map 9)
(tiāntán gōngyuán)

The perfection of Ming architecture, Tiantan (Temple of Heaven) has come to symbolise Beijing. Its lines appear on countless pieces of tourist literature and its name serves as a brand name for a wide range of products from tiger balm to plumbing fixtures. In the 1970s the complex got a face-lift and was freshly painted after pigment research. It is set in a 267-hectare park, with four gates at the compass points, and bounded by walls to the north and east. It originally functioned as a vast stage for solemn rites performed by the Son of Heaven who came here to pray for good harvests, seek divine clearance and atone for the sins of the people.

With this complicated mix in mind, the unique architectural features will delight numerologists, necromancers and the superstitious – not to mention acoustic engineers and carpenters. Shape, colour and sound take on symbolic significance. The temples, seen from above, are round, and the bases are square, deriving from the ancient Chinese belief that heaven is round and the earth is square. Thus the north end of the park is semicircular and the south end is square (the Temple of Earth, also called Ditan, is on the northern compass point and the Temple of Heaven on the southern compass point).

Tiantan was considered sacred ground and it was here that the emperor performed the major ceremonial rites of the year. Just before the winter solstice, the emperor and his enormous entourage passed down Qianmen Dajie to the Imperial Vault of Heaven in total silence. Commoners were not permitted to view the ceremony and remained cloistered indoors. The procession included elephant chariots, horse chariots and long lines of lancers, nobles, officials and musicians, dressed in their finest, flags fluttering. The next day the emperor waited

in a yellow silk tent at the south gate while officials moved the sacred tablets to the Round Altar, where the prayers and sacrificial rituals took place. The least hitch in any part of the proceedings was regarded as an ill omen, and it was thought that the nation's future was thus decided. This was the most important ceremony although other excursions to the Temple of Earth took place.

Tiantan, it should not be forgotten, is still an important meeting place. Get there at 6.30 am (before the ticket booth opens) to see *t'ai chi*, dancing to western music and some other games people play. This is how Beijing awakens. It becomes just another Chinese park by 9 am.

If you get a Chinese-priced ticket for Tiantan Park (Y0.50), you must pay an extra Y5 to see the Hall of Prayer for Good Harvests. If you buy the overpriced tourist ticket (Y30), admission to everything is included. The park is open from 6 am to 8 pm.

Round Altar The 5m-high Round Altar was constructed in 1530 and rebuilt in 1740. It is composed of white marble arrayed in three tiers, and its geometry revolves around the imperial number nine. Odd numbers were considered heavenly, and nine is the largest single-digit odd number. The top tier, thought to symbolise heaven, has nine rings of stones, each ring composed of multiples of nine stones, so that the ninth ring has 81 stones. The middle tier – earth – has the 10th to 18th rings. The bottom tier – man – has the 19th to 27th rings, ending with a total of 243 stones in the largest ring, or 27 times nine. The number of stairs and balustrades are also multiples of nine. If you stand in the centre of the upper terrace and say something, the sound waves are bounced off the marble balustrades, making your voice appear louder (nine times?).

Echo Wall Just north of the altar, surrounding the Imperial Vault of Heaven, is the Echo Wall, 65m in diameter. This enables a whisper to travel clearly from one end to

Top Left: A monk in prayer at the Lama Temple, one of Beijing's rare Buddhist sanctuaries.
Top Right: The Great Bell Temple definitely has a ring to it, housing a Ming bell weighing
47 tonnes.
Bottom: Entrance to the Hall of Prayer for Good Harvests, Tiantan Park's crowning glory.

GLENN BEANLAND

Tiantan Park's glorious Hall of Prayer for Good Harvests, where Ming and Qing emperors saw out the winter solstice each year, praying and performing rituals to encourage bumper crops and full tummies. A bad harvest meant the emperor had lost touch with heaven, and in turn, with his subjects.

your friend's ear at the other – that is, if there's not a tour group in the middle.

In the courtyard are the Triple-Sounds Stones. If you stand on the first one and clap or shout, the sound is echoed once, on the second stone twice, and on the third, three times. Should it return four times you will almost certainly not find a taxi during rush hour that day, or any other day that is a multiple of three.

Imperial Vault of Heaven This octagonal vault was built at the same time as the Round Altar, and is structured along the lines of the older Hall of Prayer for Good Harvests, though it is smaller. It used to contain tablets of the emperor's ancestors, which were used in the winter solstice ceremony.

Proceeding up from the Imperial Vault is a walkway: to the left is a molehill composed of excess dirt dumped from digging air-raid shelters and to the right is a rash of souvenir shops.

Hall of Prayer for Good Harvests The grand-daddy of the whole complex is the Hall of Prayer for Good Harvests, which is a magnificent piece mounted on a three-tiered

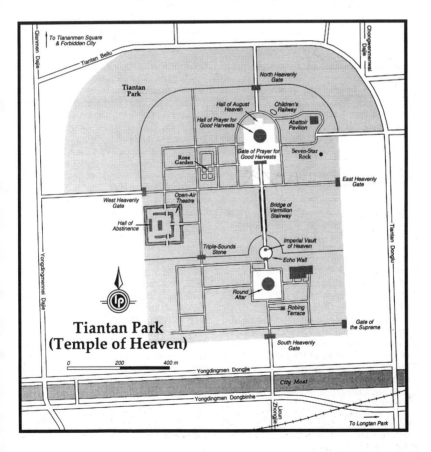

Tiantan Park (Temple of Heaven)

marble terrace. Built in 1420, it was burnt to cinders in 1889 and heads rolled in apportioning blame. The cause seems to have been lightning. A faithful reproduction based on Ming architectural methods was erected the following year, using Oregon fir for the support pillars.

The four central pillars symbolise the seasons, the 12 in the next ring denote the months of the year, and the 12 outer ones represent the day, broken into 12 'watches'. Embedded in the ceiling is a carved dragon, a symbol of royalty. The patterning, carving and gilt decoration of this ceiling and its swirl of colour is a dizzy sight, enough to carry you into the Seventh Heaven.

In fact it looks peculiarly modern, like a graphic from a sci-fi movie of a UFO about to blast into space. All this is made more amazing by the fact that the wooden pillars ingeniously support the ceiling without nails or cement – for a building 38m high and 30m in diameter, that's an accomplishment not matched until Lego was invented. Capping the structure is a deep blue umbrella of tiles with a golden knob and two complementary eaves.

Jingshan Park (Map 11)
(jīngshān gōngyuán)
North of the Forbidden City is Jingshan Park, which contains an artificial mound made of earth excavated to create the palace moat. The mound is known as Jingshan (Prospect Hill), but was formerly called Meishan (Coal Hill). It was the highest point in Beijing during the Ming Dynasty, but it's fair to say the city has grown a bit since then and numerous higher hills have now been incorporated into the megalopolis.

If you clamber to the top pavilions of this regal pleasure garden, you get a magnificent panorama of the capital and a great overview of the russet roofing of the Forbidden City. On the east side of the park is a locust tree (not the original) where the last of the Mings, Emperor Chongzhen, hanged himself (after slaying his family) rather than see the palace razed by the Manchus. The hill supposedly protects the palace from the evil spirits – or

dust storms – from the north, but which didn't quite work for Chongzhen.

Entrance to Jingshan Park is a modest Y0.50, or you can pay over 30 times as much for a souvenir 'tourist passport ticket'; the latter is optional.

Beihai Park (Beihai Park Map & Map 5)
(běihǎi gōngyuán)
Just north-west of the Forbidden City, Beihai Park is the former playground of the emperors. It's also said to have been the private domain of the great dragon-lady/witch Jiang Qing, widow of Mao who, until her death in May 1991, was serving a life sentence as No 1 member of the Gang of Four. Half of the park is a lake. The island in the lower middle is composed of the heaped earth dug to create the lake – some attribute this to the handiwork of Kublai Khan.

The site is associated with the Great Khan's palace, the navel of Beijing before the creation of the Forbidden City. All that remains of the Khan's court is a large jar made of green jade, in the Round City near the south entrance. A present given in 1265, and said to have contained the Khan's wine, it was later discovered in the hands of Taoist priests who used it to store pickles. In the Light Receiving Hall, the main structure nearby, is a 1.5m-high white jade Buddha inlaid with jewels, a gift from Myanmar (Burma) to Empress Dowager Cixi.

From the 12th century on, Beihai Park was landscaped with artificial hills, pavilions, halls, temples and covered walkways. In the present era the structures have been massively restored and Beihai Park is now one of the best examples of a classical garden found in China. Dominating Jade Islet on the lake, the **White Dagoba** is a 36m-high pop-art 'peppermint bottle' originally dating from 1651. It was put up for a visit by the Dalai Lama and was rebuilt in 1741. It's believed that Lamaist scriptures, robes and other sacred objects are encased in this brick-and-stone landmark.

On the north-east shore of the islet is the handsome double-tiered **Painted Gallery**, with unusual architecture for a walkway.

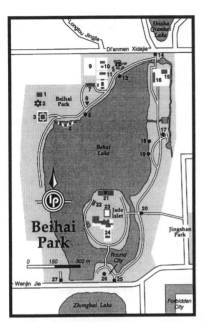

Near the boat-dock is the Fangshan Restaurant, dishing up recipes favoured by Empress Cixi. She liked 120-course dinners with about 30 kinds of desserts. The restaurant is expensive and high class, and reservations are necessary (but check out the decor!). Off to one side, however, is a snack bar that dispenses royal pastries much more cheaply.

The big attraction on the north side of the park is the **Nine Dragon Screen**, 5m high and 27m long, made of coloured glazed tiles. The screen was to scare off evil spirits; it stands at the entrance to a temple which has disappeared. To the south-west of the boat-dock on this side is the Five Dragon Pavilion dating from 1651, where the emperors liked to fish, camp and sing songs around the campfire (a forerunner of karaoke).

Over on the east side of the park are the **Gardens Within Gardens**. These waterside pavilions, winding corridors and rockeries were summer haunts of the imperial family, notably Emperor Qianlong and Empress

Cixi. They date back some 200 years, with structures like the Painted Boat Studio and the Studio of Mental Calmness. Until 1980 the villas were used as government offices.

Beihai Park is a relaxing place to stroll around, grab a snack, sip a beer, rent a rowing boat (Y10, with a Y100 deposit) or, as the Chinese do, cuddle on a bench in the evening. It's crowded at weekends. Swimming in the lake is not permitted, but in winter there's skating. This is nothing new in China – ice skating apparently goes back to the 18th century when Emperor Qianlong reviewed the imperial skating parties here.

Fragrant Hills Park (Fragrant Hills Park Map & Map 3)

(xiāngshān gōngyuán)
Within striking distance of the Summer Palace and often combined with it on a tour are the Fragrant Hills. The hills were formerly a resort for Communist Party brass, but now that most of the leadership is elderly

they prefer to stay in the Zhongnanhai Compound (wheelchairs are hard to manoeuvre in those hills).

You can scramble up the slopes to the top of Incense Burner Peak, or take the crowded chairlift. From the peak you can enjoy an all-embracing view of the countryside. The chairlift is a good way to get up the mountain, and from the summit you can hike further into the Western Hills and leave the crowds behind. Beijingers love to flock here in the autumn when the maple leaves carpet the hillsides in hues of red.

The Fragrant Hills area was razed by foreign troops in 1860 and 1900 but a few bits of original architecture still poke out. A glazed tile pagoda and the renovated **Temple of Brilliance** *(zhāo miào)* – a mock Tibetan temple built in 1780 – are both in the same area. The surrounding heavily wooded park was a hunting ground for the emperors, and once contained a multitude of pavilions and shrines, many of which are being restored.

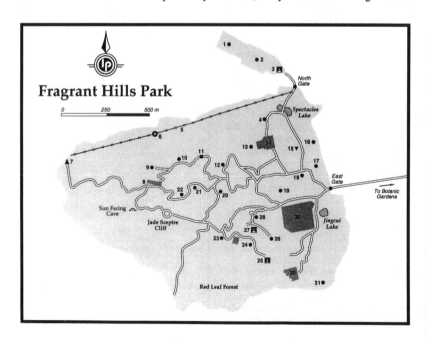

It's a favourite strolling spot for Beijingers and destined to become another Chinese Disneyland – the chair lift and souvenir shops are signs of horrors to come. It's possible to stay the night here at the four-star *Fragrant Hills Hotel (xiāngshān fàndiàn)*, Xiangshan Gongyuan Nei, Haidian District, 100093. Standard twins cost Y580 (☎ 6259-1166; fax 6259-1762).

Within walking distance of the north gate of Fragrant Hills Park is the **Azure Clouds Temple** *(bìyún sì)*, whose landmark is the Diamond Throne Pagoda. Of Indian design, it consists of a platform with a central pagoda and stupas. Built in 1366, and expanded in the 18th century with the addition of the Hall of Arhats, it holds 500 statues of Buddha's disciples. Dr Sun Yatsen's coffin was placed here in 1925 before being moved to Nanjing. The memorial hall still has a picture display of Sun's revolutionary activities.

There are a couple of ways of getting to the Fragrant Hills by public transport: bus No 333 from the Summer Palace, bus No 360 from the zoo, and bus No 318 from Pingguoyuan (the westernmost stop on the East-West Line).

Ditan Park (Map 6)
(dìtán gōngyuán)
Although 'ditan' sounds just like the Chinese word for carpet, in this case it means Temple of Earth. Ditan Park was built around 1530 as a place for the emperors to sacrifice lesser beings to keep on good terms with the Earth God. The park experienced many years of neglect, but reopened in 1984 as a sort of activity centre for the elderly. The park is just north of the magnificent Lama Temple.

Ritan Park (Maps 7 & 9)
(rìtán gōngyuán)
Ritan means Temple of the Sun; it's one of Beijing's older parks and was built in 1530. Ritan Park was built as an altar for ritual sacrifice to the Sun God. Practically in the middle of Jianguomenwai embassy-land, it's a big hit with the diplomats corps, their families and other notables who like to rub elbows with important foreigners. Admission is just Y1.

The Ritan Restaurant is in the park and serves *jiaozi* in an older-style pavilion – this place is very popular with westerners for drinks and snacks.

Fragrant Hills Park
香山公园

1　Diamond Throne Pagoda
　　金刚宝座塔
2　Sun Yatsen Memorial Hall
　　孙中山纪念堂
3　Azure Clouds Temple
　　碧云寺
4　Unbosoming Chamber
　　见心斋
5　Chair Lift
　　游览索道
6　Middle Station
　　中站
7　Incense Burner Peak
　　香炉峰
8　Platform
　　平台
9　Stele of Western Hills
　　Shimmering in Snow
　　西山晴雪

10　Tiered Cloud Villa
　　梯云山馆
11　Fourth Jade Flower Villa
　　玉花四院
12　Hibiscus Hall
　　芙蓉馆
13　Glazed Tile Pagoda
　　琉璃塔
14　Temple of Brilliance
　　昭庙
15　Pine Forest Restaurant
　　松林餐厅
16　Xiangshan Villa
　　香山别墅
17　Administrative Office
　　管理处
18　Peak Viewing Pavilion
　　望峰亭
19　Scattered Clouds Pavilion
　　多云亭
20　Jade Flower Villa
　　玉花山庄

21　Varied Scenery Pavilion
　　多景亭
22　Moonlight Villa
　　栖月山庄
23　Jade Fragrance Hall
　　玉香馆
24　White Pine Pavilion
　　白松亭
25　Xiangshan Temple Site
　　香山寺遗址
26　Halfway Pavilion
　　半山亭
27　Red Glow Temple
　　洪光寺
28　Eighteen Turns
　　十八盘
29　Fragrant Hills Hotel
　　香山宾馆
30　Twin Lakes Villa
　　双清别墅
31　See Clouds Rise
　　看云起

Yuetan Park (Map 5)
(yuètán gōngyuán)

Yuetan Park is another of Beijing's sacrificial parks, where the emperors reduced the surplus population to appease the Moon God. A small park west of the centre, this one's name means 'Temple of the Moon'.

Taoranting Park (Map 8)
(táoràntíng gōngyuán)

Taoranting (Happy Pavilion) Park is in the southern part of Beijing. The park dates back to at least the Qing Dynasty (which kicked off in 1644), when it gained fame chiefly because it was one of the very few leafy city areas accessible to the masses (most of the others were the private playgrounds of the emperors). While it's one of the less inspiring parks in Beijing, it does have a good public swimming pool complete with water slides.

Beijing Botanic Gardens (Beijing Botanic Gardens Map & Map 3)
(běijīng zhíwù yuán)

About halfway between the Fragrant Hills and the Summer Palace are the Beijing Botanic Gardens. While not spectacular, the gardens are a botanist's delight and certainly a pleasant place for a stroll. Most of the time the gardens are uncrowded.

At the north end of the gardens is the **Sleeping Buddha Temple** *(wòfósì)*. This huge reclining Buddha is 5.2m long and cast in copper. Its weight is unknown but could be up to 50 tonnes. The history books place it in the year 1331 but it's more likely to be a copy in the style of that period. Pilgrims used to make offerings of shoes to the barefoot statue. During the Cultural Revolution the Buddhas in one of the halls were replaced by a Mao statue (since removed).

On the east side of the gardens is the **Cao Xueqin Memorial** *(cáo xu'qín jìniànguǎn)*, the former residence of Cao Xueqin (1715–1763). Cao is credited with authoring the classic *The Dream of Red Mansions*, a sort of overly complex Romeo and Juliet saga set in the early Qing period. The official address of the memorial is 39 Zhengbaiqi.

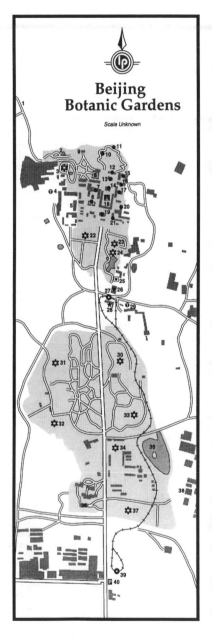

Beijing
Botanic Gardens

Scale Unknown

Beijing Botanic Gardens
北京植物园

1 Cherry Valley
樱桃沟
2 Longjiao Temple Scenic Area
隆教寺景区
3 Assemble Beauty Garden
集秀园
4 Public Toilet
厕所
5 Honey Production Research Institute
农科院养蜂研究所
6 Water Spring Compound
水泉院
7 Xing Palace Compound
行宫院
8 Square River
方河
9 Dragon King Hall
龙王堂
10 Guanyin Pavilion
观音阁
11 Longevity Mountain Pavilion
寿山亭
12 Buddhist Scriptures Building
藏经楼
13 Sleeping Buddha Sanctuary
卧佛殿

14 Three Lives Buddhist Sanctuary
三世佛殿
15 Ancestors' Hall Compound
祖堂院
16 Clear Moon Loft
霁月轩
17 Clear Cool Hall
清凉馆
18 Sleeping Buddha Temple
卧佛寺
19 Moon Tooth River
月牙河
20 Great Meditation Hall
大禅堂
21 Study Hall
斋堂
22 Wooden Orchid Garden
木兰园
23 Old Root Flower Plants Garden
宿根花卉园
24 Water-Bred Plants Garden
水生植物园
25 Sun Chuanfang Tomb
孙传芳墓
26 Sleeping Buddha Temple Restaurant
卧佛寺餐厅
27 Mini-Train Railway Station
小火车站
28 Police Station
派出所

29 Public Toilet
厕所
30 Clove Garden
丁香园
31 Peony Garden
牡丹园
32 Seedling Nursery
苗圃
33 Jasper Garden
碧桃园
34 Treepost Flowerpot Scenic Garden
树桩盆景园
35 Clear Lake Scenery
澄湖揽秀
36 Exhibition Hothouse
展览温室
37 Gorgeous Autumn Garden
绚秋园
38 Cao Xueqin Memorial
曹雪芹纪念馆
39 Mini-Train Railway Station & Ticket Office
小火车站、售票处
40 Car Park
停车场

Zizhuyuan Park (Map 10)

(zǐzhúyuàn gōngyuán)

The park's name means Purple Bamboo, a reference to some of what has been planted here. This place doesn't have much history to distinguish it, being mainly former paddy fields, but during the Ming Dynasty there was a Temple of Longevity here. Zizhuyuan Park is pleasant enough and there is a reasonably large lake which is good for ice skating in winter. Zizhuyuan is in a prestigious neighbourhood just west of the zoo.

Longtan Park (Map 9)

(lóngtán gōngyuán)

Longtan (Dragon Pool) Park, just east of the Temple of Heaven, is probably of most inter-est to budget travellers staying at the nearby Longtan Hotel in south-east Beijing; visit the park at dawn to see taiji performances.

The west side of Longtan Park has been converted into the Beijing Amusement Park, a world of balloons, cotton candy and nau-seating rides (don't eat Sichuan food before getting on the 'Spider').

Grand View Garden (Map 8)

(dàguānyuán gōngyuán)

Unlike most of Beijing's parks, which date back to imperial days, this one is new. Construction started in 1984 and was completed four years later. The park was built as a replica of the family gardens described in the classic Chinese novel *The Dream of the Red*

Chamber (also translated as *The Dream of Red Mansions* and *The Story of the Stone*), written by Cao Xueqin in the late 18th century. While the park is not steeped in history, it could be of interest if you've read the novel. Otherwise, just relax and enjoy the birds, trees and colourful pavilions. The Grand View Garden is in the south-west corner of town just inside the Second Ring Road. You can get there on bus No 59 from Qianmen. Admission costs Y10.

Jade Spring Mountain (Map 3)
(yùquán shān)

About 2.5km west of the Summer Palace is Jade Spring Mountain.The spring's name is derived from the simple observation that the water has a jade-like, crystalline appearance. During the Ming and Qing dynasties, water from this spring was sent daily to the Forbidden City to quench the emperor's thirst – it was believed the water had a tonic effect, an essential consideration with so many concubines to satisfy.

In the 1950s villas were built here for China's top five leaders at the time: Mao Zedong, Liu Shaoqi, Zhou Enlai, Zhu De and Ren Bishi. Mao seldom stayed in his villa

because he was said to be unhappy with the size of the swimming pool (it was made small to make drowning impossible).

It wasn't until the 1990s that this hallowed area was opened to the public as a park. The area is now dressed up with all the usual temples, pagodas and pavilions. At the base of the mountain is the Garden of Light & Tranquility.

OTHER SIGHTS
Ancient Observatory (Map 9)
(gǔguān xiàngtái)

One interesting perspective on Beijing is the Ancient Observatory mounted on the battlements of a watchtower, once part of the city walls. Dwarfed by embassy housing blocks, it's surrounded by traffic loops and highways just west of the Friendship Store, on the south-west corner of Jianguomennei Dajie and the Second Ring Road. The views themselves are worth the visit. There are some English explanations. The observatory dates back to Kublai Khan's days, when it was north of the present site. Khan – as well as later Ming and Qing emperors – relied heavily on the predictions of astrologers to plan his military moves.

Going Underground

In the late 1960s, with the threat of a Soviet invasion hanging over them, the Chinese built huge civil defence systems, especially in northern China. This hobby started before 1949, when the PLA used tunnels to surprise the enemy. For evacuating China's political leaders, a special underground highway was built connecting the Zhongnanhai compound to the Fragrant Hills. For the masses, the East-West subway line was built. Civil defence officials proudly proclaimed that 10,000 shoppers in the Dazhalan area could seek shelter in five minutes (what about the other 70,000?) in the event of an attack.

Pressed for space, and trying to maximise the peacetime possibilities of the air-raid shelters (aside from the fact that the shelters are useless in the event of nuclear attack), Beijing has put them to use as warehouses, factories, shops, restaurants, hotels, roller-skating rinks, theatres and clinics.

The underground city (*dìxià chéng*) was constructed by volunteers and shop assistants living in the Qianmen area – about 2000 people and 10 years of spare-time work with simple tools. The people reap a few benefits now, such as use of warehouse space, and preferential treatment for relatives and friends who can stay in a 100-bed hotel – the views aren't great, but at least they can escape the traffic noise.

It's not one of the most inspiring sights in Beijing, but an estimated 600 people per day pay to catch a glimpse of the 32km underground system. There are roughly 90 entrances to this particular complex and entrances are hidden in shops. One such shop happy to welcome tourists is at 62 Xidamochang Jie, a narrow hutong. To find it, start from the Qianmen subway station and walk east along this hutong for 15 minutes. Admission for foreigners costs Y10. A fluorescent wall map reveals the routing of the entire tunnel system. ■

The present Beijing Observatory was built between 1437 and 1446, not only to facilitate astrological predictions but to aid seafaring navigators. Downstairs are displays of navigational equipment used by Chinese ships. On the 1st floor are replicas of five 5000-year-old pottery jars, unearthed from Henan Province in 1972 and showing painted patterns of the sun. There are also four replicas of Han Dynasty eave tiles representing east, west, north and south. There is a map drawn on a wooden octagonal board with 1420 stars marked in gold foil or powder; it's a reproduction of the original, which is said to be Ming Dynasty but is based on an older Tang map. Busts of six prominent astronomers are also displayed.

On the roof is a variety of astronomical instruments designed by the Jesuits. The Jesuits, scholars as well as proselytisers, found their way into the capital in 1601 when Matteo Ricci and company were permitted to work with Chinese scientists. The emperor was keen to find out about European firearms and cannons from them.

The Jesuits outdid the resident Muslim calendar-setters and were given control of the observatory, becoming the Chinese court's official advisors.

Of the eight bronze instruments on display (including an equatorial armilla, celestial globe and altazimuth), six were designed and constructed under the supervision of the Belgian priest Ferdinand Verbiest, who came to China in 1659 as a special employee of the Qing court.

The instruments were built between 1669 and 1673, and are embellished with sculptured bronze dragons and other Chinese craftwork – a unique mix of east and west. The azimuth theodolite was supervised by Kilian Stumpf, also a missionary. The eighth instrument, the new armilla, was completed in 1744 by Ignaz Kögler. It's not clear which instruments on display are the originals.

During the Boxer Rebellion, the instruments disappeared into the hands of the French and Germans. Some were returned in 1902 and others came back under the provisions of the Treaty of Versailles (1919).

More recently, government officials were caught off guard when local and foreign rock bands got together and staged a dance party in the ancient tower. The observatory is open Wednesday through Sunday from 9 to 11 am and 1 to 4 pm.

Central TV Tower (Map 10)
(zhōngyāng diànshìtái)

Though westerners tend to be less than thrilled by TV towers, these appear to be a major drawcard for Chinese tourists. At 238m, Beijing's Central TV Tower is the tallest structure in the city. For a steep Y50, you can be whisked to the top for a meal at a pricey restaurant with a bird's-eye view. Unfortunately, even the birds look depressed by Beijing's smoggy skyline. With this in mind, the trip is more rewarding at night.

The Central TV Tower is on the western side of Yuyuantan Park. Bus Nos 323 and 374 stop there.

Drum Tower (Map 6)
(gǔlóu)

The tower is an impressive structure with a solid brick base. It was built in 1420 and has several drums which were beaten to mark the hours of the day, in effect the Big Ben of Beijing. Time was kept with a water clock. Most cities in ancient China had similar drum towers, and not too surprisingly they were either torn down or allowed to decay once clocks and watches came into fashion.

During the Cultural Revolution, drum towers were scornfully regarded as yet another reminder of the feudal past – now they are treasured as ancient artefacts and are being restored. Local artisans are particularly keen on Beijing's Drum Tower and exhibitions are occasionally held here. In the interest of raking in some cash, there are plans to add a video game arcade.

Bell Tower (Map 6)
(zhōng lóu)

Don't confuse this structure with the Great Bell Temple in north-west Beijing. The Bell Tower sits just behind the Drum Tower (down an alley directly north). It was originally built at the same time as the Drum Tower but burnt down. The present structure is 18th century. The gigantic bell was moved to the Drum Tower for a while but has now been returned to its original location. Legend has it that the bellmaker's daughter plunged into the molten iron before the bell was cast. Her father only managed to grab her shoe as she did so, and the bell's soft sound resembled that of the Chinese for 'shoe' *(xié)*. The same story is told about a couple of other bells in China – seems like committing suicide in molten iron was a serious social problem. The tower is open daily from 8.30 am to 5 pm.

WALKING TOURS
Walking tours are close to impossible in sprawling Beijing. You can walk a bit in certain neighbourhoods like Wangfujing, Dazhalan and Jianguomenwai, but the city is so spread out that the obvious way to go is by bicycle.

BLOCKBUSTER BICYCLE TOUR
Tiantan Park (west side) – Natural History Museum – Dazhalan – Qianmen – Tiananmen Square – Chinese Revolution History Museum – Great Hall of the People – Mao's Mausoleum – Tiananmen Gate – Forbidden City – Zhongnanhai – Beihai Park – Jingshan Park – Prince Gong's Palace – Song Qingling Museum – Drum Tower – Bell Tower – Confucius Temple – Lama Temple – China Art Gallery – Kentucky Fried Chicken or McDonald's – Wangfujing – Tiantan Park (east side) – Home?

Obviously this tour only gives you a cursory glance at Beijing's many fine sights; indeed, you could spend a full day in the Forbidden City alone. But if you start out early (such as at dawn) you can see a good chunk of town and take in some of Beijing's many moods, and you can always continue the tour the next day if your schedule permits.

For the following tour, cycling time is about two hours – Chinese bike, western legs, average pace. The starting point is the west side of Tiantan Park. The finishing point is the east side of the same park.

The southern end of Qianmen Dajie is called Yongdingmen Dajie; it's here that

you'll find the west entrance of **Tiantan Park**. The park is certainly worth exploring, but you can do that on the way back. Right now, our goal is just a little to the north, the **Natural History Museum** on the east side of Yongdingmen Dajie.

After you've had your dose of natural history, continue north to where Yongdingmen Dajie becomes Qianmen Dajie. Coming up on your left is **Dazhalan**, one of Beijing's most intriguing hutongs. Bikes cannot be ridden into this particular hutong, though you can explore most others on two wheels.

Slightly more than a stone's throw to the north is **Qianmen**, the front gate to the vast expanse of **Tiananmen Square**. Traffic is one way for north-south avenues on either side of the square. If you want to go to Tiananmen, dismount after the archway and wheel the bike to the parking areas along the sidewalk. Bicycles cannot be ridden across Tiananmen Square (apparently tanks are OK), but you can walk the bike. Nearby are the **Chinese Revolution History Museum, Great Hall of the People, Mao's Mausoleum, Tiananmen Gate** and the **Forbidden City** itself.

Over to the west side of the Forbidden City you're heading into the most sensitive part of the capital, the **Zhongnanhai** compound. On the right, going up Beichang Jie, you pass some older housing that lines the moat. On the left is a high wall which shields from view the area where top Party members live and work (it was decided not to rip down this section of the old walls). In 1973, when the new wing of the Beijing Hotel shot up, the police realised that guests with binoculars could observe activity in Zhongnanhai, so a fake building was erected along the western wall of the Forbidden City to block the hotel guests' line of sight. Mysterious buildings abound in this locale – as do rumours of a network of clandestine tunnels connecting such buildings.

Then it's **Beihai Park**, which by this time of day should be bustling with activity. You can exercise your arms as well as your legs by hiring a rowing boat. There's a cafe near the south gate overlooking Beihai Lake, where you can refresh yourself with beer, coffee, tea or cold drinks.

Back on the bike and you'll soon bump into **Jingshan Park**. There's bicycle parking by the entrance. Jingshan Park is a splendid place to survey the smog of Beijing, get your bearings with 360° views and enjoy a good overview of the russet roofing of the Forbidden City opposite.

North of Jingshan Park it gets a bit tricky. You want to get off the main road into the small alleys running around the Shisha Hai Lakes. In this area, and worth checking out for a taste of literary history, is **Prince Gong's Palace**, thought to be the house which Cao Xueqin used as a model in his classic *The Dream of the Red Chamber*.

The lake district is steeped in history; if you consult a Beijing map you will see that the set of lakes connects from north to south. In the Yuan Dynasty, barges sailed through various canals to the top lake *(jīshuǐtán)*, a sort of harbour for Beijing. Later the lakes were used for pleasure-boating, and were bordered by the homes of high officials.

The larger lake to the north-west is the Shisha Houhai (Lake of the Ten Back Monasteries). Below that is the Shisha Qianhai (Lake of the Ten Front Monasteries).

Also around the lakes you'll find the **Song Qingling Museum**, the retirement residence of Sun Yatsen's respected wife.

Make a small detour here. If you go northeast through the hutongs you will arrive at the **Bamboo Garden Hotel**, which is a wonderful example of the surprises that hutongs hold. This place was originally the personal garden of Sheng Xuanhuai, an important Qing official. There are exquisite landscaped gardens and courtyards, renovated compound architecture and a fancy restaurant with an English menu (alfresco in summer). It's a quiet place to sip a drink.

Another small detour brings you to the Kaorouji Restaurant – not necessarily the cheapest place to get your roast chicken, but the balcony dining in summer is pleasant enough.

Back on the main drag you come to the **Drum Tower**, which originally held 24 drums. Only one remains. Directly to the north down an alley is the **Bell Tower** – the bell no longer tolls but it's still impressive.

Back on the road you'll reach the former **Confucius Temple** and Imperial College, now a museum and library complex. Unless you can read stele-calligraphy, you probably won't want to spend much time here. A stele standing in the hutong ordered officials to dismount at this point but you can ignore this unless of course you happen to be travelling on horseback.

By contrast, just down the road is the **Lama Temple**, one of Beijing's finest. Along the way to the Lama Temple you might pass through several decorated lintels; these graceful archways *(páilóu)*, which commemorate mandarin officials or chaste widows, were ripped out of the thoroughfares of Beijing in the 1950s. The reason given was the facilitation of traffic movement. Some have been relocated in parks. The ones you see in this hutong are rarities.

This is the northernmost point of today's journey (you're still with us, aren't you?). Head south, and if you're ready for yet another museum there's the **China Art Gallery**, a slight detour to the west at the northern end of Wangfujing. Unfortunately, Wangfujing itself is closed to cyclists, so head back to the east on Dongsi Xi Dajie and you'll find Kentucky Fried Chicken. If the Colonel's fried chicken delights aren't what you had in mind, you could try McDonald's, at the southern end of Wangfujing. No matter what you think of the food, these restaurants are at least as popular as the Forbidden City – and just remember that none of China's emperors ever had the chance to clog their royal arteries with a big mac, cheeseburger or chicken nuggets.

Launch yourself into the sea of cyclists, throw your legs into cruising speed and cycle the length of Dongdan south to the east entrance of **Tiantan Park**. If this is still day one of your bike tour, you're probably too exhausted to walk inside to see the Temple of Heaven – well, there's always tomorrow. From this point, you're well positioned to head back to where you started from.

ACTIVITIES
Health Clubs

Sporting, recreational and club facilities are to be found in tourist hotels, and the Asian Games Village (National Olympic Sports Centre) on Beisihuan Zhonglu (north-central section of the Fourth Ring Road). The International Club on Jianguomenwai – a place with signs telling you what not to do – can be dull during the daytime but livens up in the evening. You might also want to try the Beijing International Health Land (☎ 6466-1302) at 11 Xinyuan Xijie.

Guests at major hotels can generally use all facilities for free, while non-guests must pay additional requisite fees. These fees can be high if calculated by the hour, but many hotels offer substantial discounts if you pay on a monthly basis (Y500 and up), quarterly or annually. Hotels offering this service include the Jinglun, China World, Capital, Great Wall Sheraton, Holiday Inn Lido, Landmark Towers, Kunlun and Shangri-la. If you don't mind commuting out to the airport, the Mövenpick Hotel has an excellent health club (The Splash) but you are obliged to become a member.

Badminton

(yǔmáo qiú)

The handiest badminton courts are at the Chaoyang Gym *(cháoyáng tǐyù guǎn)* just to the north-east of Tuanjiehu Park. There are also courts at the Asian Games Village.

Basketball

(lánqiú)

This sport hasn't exactly captured the hearts and minds of Beijingers. It's mostly expat Americans who play this, and for this reason the only regular games are played at the US embassy every Sunday at 2 pm. There is now an attempt to get a basketball league started – ask at the US embassy for details.

Bowling

(gǔnmùqiú)

Hotels with bowling alleys include the Capital, China World, Grand View Garden, International, Holiday Inn Lido and Scitech.

You can also find a bowling alley at the Beijing Recreation Centre, north of the Asian Games Village.

Golf

(gāoěrfū qiú)

The art of poking a white ball around a lawn enjoys high prestige in face-conscious China. Check out the Beijing International Golf Club (☎ 6974-6388) *(běijīng guójì gāoěrfū qiú jùlèbù)*. This Sino-Japanese joint venture is considered the best course in Beijing. The 18-hole course is 35km north of Beijing, close to the Ming Tombs. Pushing that little ball around is not cheap, but the course is in top condition and the scenery is spectacular. Green fees are Y1200 on weekdays and Y1400 on weekends and public holidays. You can rent a set of golf clubs and spiked golf shoes for an additional fee. The course is open from 8 am to 5 pm, March through November.

There is a 36-hole golf course which goes by a variety of names. Officially named the Beijing Golf Club (☎ 6944-1005) *(běijīng gāoěrfūqiú jùlèbù)*, it's at Shunyi, north-east of the capital airport. Green fees and equipment rentals will set you back Y750. Open 8 am to 5 pm.

Just next to the preceding is the Beijing Rural Golf Club (☎ 6940-2020) *(běijīng xiāngcūn gāoěrfū qiú jùlèbù)*. This 36-hole course has green fees running from Y400 to Y1000. It's open from 8 am to 4 pm.

Closest to the city centre is the 9-hole Chaoyang Golf Club (☎ 6491-0385) *(cháoyáng gāoěrfūqiú chǎng)*. It includes a driving range, but the course leaves much to be desired. Green fees are Y230 on weekdays and Y340 on weekends.

Miniature Golf Mark Twain used to say that golf was a good walk ruined. If you agree, you might find miniature golf more suitable.

Beijing's first outdoor miniature golf course is in Ditan Park. Playing one 18-hole round costs Y25. The Jinglun Hotel also has a miniature golf course in the basement, but the fee is a perverse Y300 per hour.

continued on page 113

A Stroll Down Memory Lane

Off the wide avenues with their high-rises, fast-food outlets and relentless traffic, an increasingly rare Beijing phenomenon lingers on. Known as *hutongs*, these narrow side lanes which form the skeleton of old Beijing are being bulldozed in the name of progress.

胡
同

Hutong History

The story of Beijing's hutongs is almost as fascinating as a visit to the lanes themselves. The word 'hutong' derives from Mongolian, at the time when the Khan's horsemen camped in the new capital of the Yuan Dynasty, though its original meaning is uncertain. It may have referred to a passageway between *gers* (or 'yurts', the Russian term). Or it may come from *hottog*, meaning a water well – in the dry plain around Beijing, where there was water, there were inhabitants. Either way, the word's been applied to the passageways between Beijing's courtyard houses.

This being China, lots of commerce takes place on hutongs (allowing private enterprise has helped). In a city with abundant labour that lives and works together, specialisation is the rule – lanes dedicated to cotton jacket padding or taxi sign repair thrive just out of sight of state department stores.

Many hutongs were named after the markets (fish, rice, sheep) or trades (hats, bowstrings, trousers) once conducted along them. Others took their names from the seats of government offices or specialised suppliers to the palace (granaries, red lacquer, armour). Yet others were named after dukes now entombed in history books.

Around the Forbidden City there were some rather unusual industries. Wet-Nurse Lane was full of young mothers who breast-fed the imperial offspring. They were selected from around China on scouting trips four times a year. Clothes-Washing Lane was where the women who did the imperial laundry lived. The maids, grown old in the service of the court, were packed off to faraway places until their intimate knowledge of royal undergarments was out of date.

Wind-Water Lanes

Following feng shui and the precepts of the classic *Zhou Li* text, hutongs ideally run east-west, since compound entrances should face south. This maximises sunny southern *yang* (left side; heavenly forces) vibes while minimising northern *yin* (right side; earth forces) ones. These 'regular' hutongs intersect with broader north-south streets and avenues to form a grid, in accord with the symbolism of the earth as a square ('all within the four seas').

Strict rules for the width of lanes, streets and avenues were relaxed over the centuries, and hutongs ranging from the claustrophobic (50cm wide) to the relatively capacious (10m) emerged. Hutong directions vary as well: some are slanted to the south-east, others run north-south for convenient passage between houses. Entering some neighbourhoods is like stepping into a maze.

胡
同

Courtyard Houses

Behind the walls which define the orderly chaos of hutongs lie Beijing's courtyard houses (*siheyuan*), where roughly a quarter of the city's population still lives. Until 'modernisation' got going in a big way and skyscrapers started turning a long-time horizontal city into a vertical eyesore, these one-storey structures formed a dignified, slate-grey backdrop to the auspicious vermilion and yellow imperial palaces.

Make sure you see life on either side of the solid courtyard gates while you still can – the siheyuan are fast disappearing. These houses are where countless generations of Beijing families both rich and poor have lived and died. Only a hard-hearted real estate developer would deny that something more than just traditional architecture is disappearing along with the siheyuan.

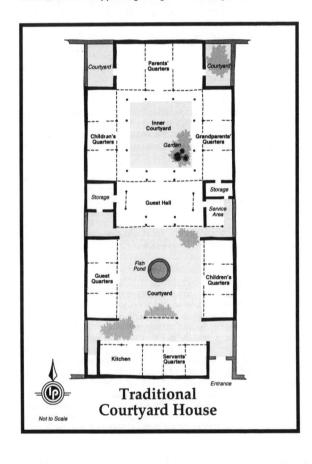

Traditional Courtyard House

Not to Scale

胡
同

Like hutongs, courtyard houses were built according to plan, hardly changed since the Han Dynasty (206 BC–220 AD). Order and harmony are key values – a siheyuan's four-walled enclosure (as opposed to the three-walled sanheyuan found in some parts of China) is a model of symmetry. Like Beijing itself, courtyard houses are oriented to a north-south axis.

Confucian ideals of joining heaven and earth through *jen* ('human-heartedness') and proper filial relations can be seen in the way the siheyuan is laid out. Courtyard arrangements can form heavenly characters on the ground, like the sun (the outer rooms and central guest hall in the floor plan illustration form the 'sun' character).

In a common, one-courtyard house (shaped like the character *kou*, symbolising 'right speech'), ancestral tablets and the family shrine are carefully placed to receive first morning light through the south-east entrance. Ancestor tablets aren't decorations: the most honoured people in the house (eg the grandparents) sleep closest to them. And mirrors aren't just for vanity: they're used to ward off demonic houseguests and help direct a healthy flow of *qi* through the house. Ideal arrangements of rooms and courtyards also depend on the yin and yang balance of elements in the compound.

Courtyards have some less esoteric aspects too: they provide ventilation and light and, if there's a small courtyard off one of the main halls (as in the upper left corner of the illustration), even a little privacy.

Unlike western urban experience, non-modern China didn't see a clear boundary between city and countryside. Courtyards weren't designed to replicate nature in an urban setting. Instead, trees, stones, plants and ponds were treated more like idealised extensions of natural elements.

The size and number of courtyards in a siheyuan originally depended on the owner's status (so a 'seeing clearly' layout, with its three main courtyards, was more prestigious than a 'sun' plan). Nonetheless, aside from the structure's scale, even a humble siheyuan (which had a fence and low gate rather than high walls) shared the same layout as the Son of Heaven's living quarters in the Forbidden City.

The inner and outer aspects of the Forbidden City were repeated in the surrounding siheyuan. The courtyard nearest the entrance was open to just about anyone, while only some were invited into the far courtyard (the guest hall in the floor plan illustration marks the transition area between the two).

From the Ming Dynasty onwards, four main siheyuan pockets were distinguished around the Forbidden City: to the east mainly lived the aristocracy, to the west were officials, while the north and south was largely occupied by labourers, traders and those eking out a marginal living in the capital, often with squalid housing to match.

Beijing's often violent, earthquake-prone history means that most of the courtyard houses you'll see date from the 19th century. The 1976 earthquake destroyed some of these; bureaucrats are taking care of what's left.

胡
同

The Housing Freeze

Though they're damn cold in winter (coal braziers and/or space heaters make life bearable, and Chinese babies aren't wrapped like arctic mummies just for style), given the choice between a high-rise block and a traditional compound, most residents of Beijing would probably opt for the latter. The compounds have a lot more character – and provide space to grow vegetables. On the other hand, with running water, heating, electricity and toilets (all or most of which siheyuan lack), life in new high-rise flats may look tempting to some. Many young Beijingers are also willing to sacrifice a lot of traditional living for a little bit of modern privacy.

Originally, housing one more-or-less extended family (with servants when possible), these days a siheyuan can be pretty cramped. Home to several smaller families, some compounds now hold 30 people. Halls have been divided into smaller rooms and add-ons built to satisfy the allocation of housing space; rental subsidy policies and connections (as well as some free-booting capitalism) dictate who can afford the luxury of having a courtyard house to themselves. Desirable courtyard houses are now astronomically expensive (up to US$3000 per month).

The Fate of Hutongs

The motto of Beijing's developers might be 'Planning grows out of the blade of a bulldozer'. How best to preserve the old city while developing modern infrastructure has been debated for years. Meanwhile, the practice has been to preserve a few worthy siheyuan (which may then be walled in by new high-rises), recreate 'old Beijing' on some gentrified lanes (eg Liulichang), and plough through as many others as possible for new streets and housing.

Exploring Hutongs

Beijing's remaining traditional lanes have become a tourist attraction, but happily, tour buses (thus far) don't fit in them. Hutongs are best explored by bicycle (see On Your Bike, page 71, and the Blockbuster Bicycle Tour, page 106), either self-powered or pedalled for you. Pedicabs (an odd concept in nominally socialist China) ply some of the more memorable lanes along a three hour route which includes the Drum Tower and a stop at Prince Gong's Palace, a fine example of an aristocrat's siheyuan.

Pedicab tours start near the north gate of Beihai Park at least twice daily, and cost about Y200 per person. You can just appear at the gate, but be warned that the tours are very popular. Tours can be arranged at the travel desk (call or drop in) at most large hotels, or ring the Beijing Hutong Tourist Agency (☎ 6615-9097). Be on time, as pedicabs wait for no one.

Beware also of fake hutong tours – the real ones have informative English-speaking guides in uniforms that match their fancy pedicabs; the hustlers don't.

Russ Kerr & Robert Storey

accept foreign students and tuition fees vary considerably.

If you work in the day and want to study part time, the Bridge School (☎ 6494-0243) *(qiáo yǔyán xuéyuàn)*, 12 Yabao Lu, Jianguomenwai, offers Chinese classes three nights a week.

Traditional Medicine

Aside from learning the language, one other subject that continues to draw large numbers of foreign students is the study of traditional Chinese herbal medicine and acupuncture. The best place to go is the University of Chinese Medicine (☎ 6421-3458) *(zhōngyī xuéyuàn)*, 11 Beisanhuan Donglu, Chaoyang District. Prices are reasonable, ranging from about Y1 to Y10 for most prescriptions.

Music

There aren't many places in the west where you can learn to play traditional Chinese musical instruments such as the two-stringed fiddle or three-stringed lute. In Beijing there are two schools offering such courses. One school is the Central Music Conservatory (☎ 6605-3531 ext 228) *(zhōngyāng yīnyuè xuéyuàn)*, 43 Baojia Jie, Xuanwu District; and the other is the China Music Conservatory (☎ 6202-5511 ext 277) *(zhōngguó yīnyuè xuéyuàn)*, at Deshengmenwai Dajie, Weizikeng, Chaoyang District.

Places to Stay

In China, you can't simply stay in any hotel which has a vacancy – the hotel must be designated a 'tourist hotel'. There's not much use trying to charm your way into a Chinese-only hotel; even if the staff would love you to stay they dare not break the rules, which are enforced by the PSB.

During the summer peak season, hotels (especially the cheaper ones) tend to fill up quickly and you may have to scramble to find something affordable. It's advisable to ring ahead before embarking on a long taxi journey in search of that elusive vacant room, although many hotel phone operators cannot speak English. When the operator answers, ask to be put through to the reception desk (*zǒng fúwù tái*).

For more information on the taxes and discounts applicable to hotels in Beijing, see under Costs in the Facts for the Visitor chapter.

The following hotel lists are arranged according to the maps in this book and the standard of the particular hotels.

PLACES TO STAY – BUDGET

Beijing offers little in the way of cheap accommodation, but there are a few budget places – mostly in the outlying areas of town. In China's pricey capital city, any hotel charging under Y500 in the high season would have to be considered 'bottom end'.

At the present time, the two favourite bottom-end haunts for backpackers are the Jinghua Hotel and Lihua Hotel, about the only two places in town with dormitories. Other hotels which get good reviews include the Far East, Longtan, Lüsongyuan and Fangyuan.

The following list of hotels with rooms priced below Y500 is in alphabetical order. Make allowances for the fact that future renovations (and greed) may suddenly drive prices to even more astronomical levels.

Beijing (Map 3)

Desheng Hotel (déshèng fàndiàn), 4 Beisanhuan Zhong Lu, Haidian District. All rooms cost Y372. (☎ 6202-4477; fax 6201-4363)

Huiqiao Hotel (huìqiáo fàndiàn), 19 Huixindong Jie, Chaoyang District, 100101 (near the Sino-Japanese Friendship Hospital). Twins cost Y440. (☎ 6421-4061; fax 6421-8319)

Jiali Hotel (jiālì fàndiàn), 21B Jiuxianqiao Lu, Chaoyang District, 100016. Standard twins cost Y388. (☎ 6436-3399; fax 6436-3366)

Jingfeng Hotel (jīngfēng bīnguǎn), 71 Fengtai Lu, Fengtai District, 100071. Twins cost Y408. (☎ 6381-2233; fax 6381-3307)

Jinghua Hotel (jīnghuá fàndiàn), Xiluoyuan Nanli, Yongdingmenwai, 100077 (southern part of the Third Ring Road). This is the perennial favourite with backpackers. Dorm beds cost Y35 in a four-bed room, or Y26 in a 30-bed room. Twins are Y180. Bus Nos 2 and 17 from Qianmen drop you off nearby. (☎ 6722-2211)

Jingtai Hotel (jīngtài bīnguǎn), 65 Yongwai Jingtaixi (a small alley running off Anlelin Lu). Twins cost Y180. (☎ 6722-4675)

Lihua Hotel (lìhuá fàndiàn), 71 Yangqiao, Yongdingmenwai. A well-established backpackers' hotel; dorms cost Y35 and twins are Y182. Bus No 343 is the easiest way to get there, but bus No 14 will also do. (☎ 6721-1144)

Sea Star Hotel (hǎixīng dà jiǔdiàn), 166 Haihutun, Yongwai (Muxu Yuan). Dorm beds are Y35, twins cost Y180. This is a very popular place with backpackers. (☎ 6721-8855; fax 6722-7915)

Wanshou Hotel (wànshòu bīnguǎn), 12A Wanshou Lu, 100036. Twins cost Y180 to Y360. (☎ 6821-4433; fax 6821-6290)

Yinghua Hotel (yīnghuā bīnguǎn), 17 Huixin Dongjie, Hepingli, Chaoyang District, 100029. Twins cost Y328. (☎ 6493-4455; 6491-8628)

North-West Beijing (Map 5)

Beihai Hotel (běihǎi bīnguǎn), 141 Di'anmenxi Dajie, Xicheng District, 100009. Standard twins cost Y230. (☎ 6616-2229; fax 6616-0905)

Huguosi Hotel (hùguósì bīnguǎn), 125 Huguosi Dajie, Xicheng District, 100035. Twins cost Y218 and Y278. (☎ 6618-1113; fax 6618-0142)

Zhumulangma Hotel (zhūmùlǎngmǎ bīnguǎn), also known as *Qomolangma Hotel*, 149 Gulou Xi Dajie, 100009. Standard twins are Y392. (☎ 6401-8822; fax 6401-1330)

North Beijing (Map 6)

Hebei Hotel (héběi fàndiàn), 11A Cheniandian Hutong, Andingmennei, 100009. Standard twins are Y412. (☎ 6401-5522; fax 6401-5886)

Hualun Hotel (huálún fàndiàn), 291 Andingmennei Dajie, 100009. Standard twins cost about Y250. (☎ 6403-3337; fax 6401-5747)

Lüsongyuan Hotel (lǚsōngyuán bīnguǎn), 22 Banchang Hutong, Dongcheng District, 100007. Twins cost Y298 to Y358, dorm beds are Y60. The dormitory here is currently the only one in China officially recognised by the International Youth Hostel Federation. It can be difficult to find this place – when you approach the one-way hutong from either end, it doesn't seem that there could be a building of such high standard halfway down. The hotel is directly north of the China Art Gallery, second hutong north of Di'anmen, turn left – bus No 104 from Beijing railway station comes close. (☎ 6401-1116, 6403-0416)

Overseas Chinese Hotel (huáqiáo fàndiàn), 5 Beixinqiao Santiao, Dongcheng District, 100007. Standard twins cost Y474. (☎ 6401-6688; fax 6401-2386)

Youhao Guesthouse (yǒuhǎo bīnguǎn), 7 Houyuan Ensi Hutong, Jiaodaokou, 100009. Twins cost Y362. (☎ 6403-3114; 6401-4603)

East Beijing (Map 7)

Guoan Hotel (guóān bīnguǎn), Guandongdianbei Jie, Dongdaqiao, Chaoyang District, 100020. Standard twins are Y350. (☎ 6500-7700; fax 6500-4568)

Huaxia Hotel (huáshà bīnguǎn), Chunxiu Lu, Gongren Tiyuchangbei Lu, Chaoyang District, 100027 (near Workers Stadium). Twins cost Y198. (☎ 6415-5231; fax 6416-5519)

Huayuan Hotel (huáyuán fàndiàn), 28 Beixiaoyun Lu, Dongsanhuan, 100027. Standard twins are Y362. (☎ 6467-8661; fax 6467-8509)

South-West Beijing (Map 8)

Far East Hotel (yuǎndōng fàndiàn), 90 Tieshuxie Jie, Qianmenwai, Xuanwu District, actually on the west end of Dazhalan, 100050. Twins cost Y310 to Y410. (☎ 6301-8811; fax 6301-8233)

Feixia Hotel (fēixiá fàndiàn), Building 5, Xibianmen Xili, Xuanwu District, 100053. Rooms cost Y192. (☎ 6301-2228; fax 6302-1764)

Fenglong Youth Hostel (fēnglòng qīngnián lǚshè), 35 Taiping Jie (just north of Second Ring Road). Beijing's newest backpacker hub. Twin rooms are Y180, four-bed dorms with attached bath Y40 per person. Less classy dorms in the basement have beds for Y25. Any bus going to nearby Beijing South railway station (Yongdingmen) will get you there. From Beijing station, this would include bus Nos 20 and 54. (☎ 6354-5836)

Hualong Hotel (huálóng fàndiàn), 30 Dongdan Bei Dajie, Dongcheng District, 100005 (near Beijing West railway station). Twins cost around Y410. (☎ 6612-3203; fax 6513-8659)

Qiaoyuan Hotel (qiáoyuán fàndiàn), Dongbinhe Lu, Youanmenwai (Second Ring Road). Twins in the old grotty wing cost Y280, but it's Y420 in the new wing. (☎ 6303-8861, 6301-2244)

South-East Beijing (Map 9)

Beiwei Hotel (běiwěi fàndiàn), 13 Xijing Lu, Xuanwu District (western side of Tiantan Park). Standard twins are Y460, superior Y680 and suites Y800. (☎ 6301-2266; fax 6301-1366)

Dabei Hotel (dàběi bīnguǎn), 1A Nan Langjiayuan, Jianguomenwai, 100022 (close to China World Trade Centre). Twins cost Y244. (☎ 6506-5511; fax 6500-5258)

Haoyuan Hotel (hàoyuán bīnguǎn), A9 Tiantandong Lu, Chongwen District (east side of Tiantan Park). Twins cost Y349. (☎ 6701-4499)

Leyou Hotel (lèyóu fàndiàn), 13 Dongsanhuannan Lu (Third Ring Road), 100021, is east of Longtan Park. Twins go for Y288. Take bus No 28 or 52 to the terminus. (☎ 6771-2266; fax 6771-1636)

Longtan Hotel (lóngtán fàndiàn), 15 Panjiayuan Nanli (Second Ring Road), Chaoyang District, 100021. Twins are Y298, Y366, Y508 and Y760. The hotel is opposite Longtan Park. (☎ 6771-2244; fax 6771-4028)

Tiantan Sports Hotel (tiāntán tǐyù bīnguǎn), 10 Tiyutuan Lu, Chongwen District, 100061. Standard twins cost Y272 but the rooms are badly in need of renovation. (☎ 6701-3388; fax 6701-5388)

Traffic Hotel (jiāotōng fàndiàn), 35 Dongsi Kuaiyunan Jie. The 82 comfortable rooms are priced from Y238 to Y268. The hotel is in a narrow alley running south from Tiyuguan Lu – signs in English point the way. Bus No 41 runs on Tiyuguan Lu and drops you off at the alley's entrance. (☎ 6711-2288)

Haidian District (Map 10)

Beilin Hotel (běilín bīnguǎn), Zhongguancun Lu, Xiaozhuang, 100083. Twins are Y280. (☎ 6205-4411; fax 6254-5024)

Big Bell Hotel (dàzhōngsì fàndiàn), 18 Beisanhuanxi Lu, 100086. Standard twins are Y292. (☎ 6225-3388; fax 6225-2605)

Changchunyuan Hotel (chàngchūnyuán fàndiàn), 5 Xiyuan Caochang, (close to Beijing University). Twins cost Y258. (☎ 6256-1177)

Evergreen Hotel (wànniánqīng bīnguǎn), 25 Xisanhuanbei Lu, 100081. Standard twins cost Y282. (☎ 6842-1144)

Hainan Hotel (hǎinán fàndiàn), Zhongguancun. Twins cost Y280. (☎ 6256-5550; fax 6256-8395)

Jimen Hotel (jìmén fàndiàn), Huangtingzi, Xueyuan Lu, 100088. Twins begin at Y232. (☎ 6201-2211; fax 6201-5355)

Lingnan Hotel (lǐngnán fàndiàn), 34 Beiwacun Lu. Twins begin at Y318. (☎ 6841-2288; fax 6841-4392)

Qinghuayuan Hotel (qīnghuáyuán bīnguǎn), 45 Chengfu Lu, 100083. Twins cost Y250. (☎ 6257-3355; fax 6256-2421)

Shangyuan Hotel (shàngyuán fàndiàn), Xie Jie, Xizhemenwai, 100044. The hotel is near Xizhimen (North) Railway Station. Twins are Y298. (☎ 6225-1166; fax 6225-5643)

Shengtang Hotel (shèngtáng fàndiàn), 2 Wanggongfen, Wangquanzhuang, 100080. Twins cost around Y352. (☎ 6256-4433; fax 6256-3092)

Xizhimen Hotel (xīzhímén fàndiàn), 172 Xizhimennei Dajie, 100044, near Xizhimen (North) Railway Station. Twins cost Y238. (☎ 6225-7766; fax 6225-5224)

Ziyu Hotel (zǐyù fàndiàn), 55 Zengguan Lu. Twins cost Y398. (☎ 6841-1188)

Wangfujing Area (Map 11)

Fangyuan Hotel (fāngyuán bīnguǎn), 36 DengShikouxi Jie, Dongcheng District, 100006 (near Wangfujing). Twins cost Y158 and Y198. This place gets good reviews from budget travellers. (☎ 6525-6331; fax 6513-8549)

Hademen Hotel (hādémén fàndiàn), 2A Chongwenmenwai Dajie, 100062. Twins are Y380 to Y490. (☎ 6711-2244; fax 6711-6865)

Inner Mongolia Guesthouse (nèi ménggǔ bīnguǎn), 71 Meishuguan Houjie, 100010 (behind China Art Gallery at north end of Wangfujing). Twins cost Y280. (☎ 6576-2933; fax 6576-2488)

Airport

Capital Airport Hotel (shǒudū jīchǎng bīnguǎn), 1km from the airport terminal. Standard twins are Y312. (☎ 6459-4466; fax 6456-4563)

PLACES TO STAY – MIDDLE

Remember that by Beijing's questionably high standards, a hotel where you can get a regular twin room priced from around Y500 to Y1000 is considered 'mid-range'.

The following establishments fall into this category:

Beijing (Map 3)

Beijing Grand Hotel (yuánshān dà jiǔdiàn), 20 Yumin Dongli, Deshengmenwai, Xicheng District, 100029. Standard twins are Y547. (☎ 6201-0033; fax 6202-9893)

Chongqing Hotel (chóngqìng fàndiàn), 15 Guangximen Beili, Chaoyang District, 100028 (west side of Exhibition Centre). Standard twins cost Y480. (☎ 6422-8888; fax 6422-1189)

Guangming Hotel (guāngmíng fàndiàn), Liangmaqiao Lu, Chaoyang District, 100016. Twins cost Y570. (☎ 6467-8822; fax 6467-7682)

Huabei Hotel (huáběi dà jiǔdiàn), Anhuaqiao, 19 Gulouwai Dajie, 100011. Twins go for Y528 to Y638. (☎ 6202-8888; fax 6202-7196)

Park Hotel (bǎilè jiǔdiàn), 36 Puhuangyu Lu, 100078. Twins cost Y580. Officially a three-star place, but it's poorly managed and not worth it. (☎ 6761-2233; fax 6761-1615).

Yanxiang Hotel (yānxiáng fàndiàn), 2A Jiangtai Lu, Dongzhimenwai (along the way to the airport in north-east Beijing). Rates are from Y680 to Y1160. (☎ 6437-6666; fax 6437-6231)

North Beijing (Map 6)

Bamboo Garden Hotel (zhúyuán bīnguǎn), 24 Xiaoshiqiao Hutong, Jiugulou Dajie, 100009. Twins range from Y520 to Y730. (☎ 6403-2229; fax 6401-2633)

East Beijing (Map 7)

Huadu Hotel (huádū fàndiàn), 8 Xinyuannan Lu, Chaoyang District, 100027. Twins cost Y715. (☎ 6500-1166; fax 6500-1615)

Twenty-First Century Hotel (èrshíyī shìjì fàndiàn), 40 Liangmaqiao. Room prices are from Y600 to Y1300. (☎ 6466-3311)

South-West Beijing (Map 8)

Beijing Commercial Business Complex (běijīng shāngwù huìguǎn), Building No 1, Yulin Li, Youanmenwai, 100054. The official rate for twins is Y520, but it seems to be fairly easy to negotiate it down to Y450 or less. (☎ 6329-2244)

Media Centre Hotel (méidìyǎ zhōngxīn), 11B Fuxing Lu. Room rates are from Y650 to Y1300. (☎ 6851-4422; fax 6851-6228)

Minzu Hotel (mínzú fàndiàn), 51 Fuxingmennei Dajie, 100031 (west of CAAC and Xidan). Twins cost from Y704 to Y862, suites are from Y1194 to Y1782. (☎ 6601-4466; fax 6601-4849)

Qianmen Hotel (qiánmén fàndiàn), 175 Yong'an Lu, Xuanwu District, 100050 (south-west of Qianmen). Standard twins cost Y504. (☎ 6301-6688; fax 6301-3883)

Xinxing Hotel (xīnxīng bīnguǎn), 17 Xisanhuanzhong Lu, 100036. Twins cost Y580. (☎ 6816-6688; fax 6851-4669)

Yanjing Hotel (yānjīng fàndiàn), 19 Fuxingmenwai Dajie (west Beijing). Standard/deluxe twins cost Y400/672. (☎ 6853-6688; fax 6852-6200)

Yuexiu Hotel (yuèxiù dà fàndiàn), 24 Dong Dajie, Xuanwumen, 100051. Standard twins are Y480. (☎ 6301-4499; fax 6301-4609)

South-East Beijing (Map 9)

Dongfang Hotel (dōngfāng fàndiàn), 11 Wanming Lu, 100050 (south of Qianmen). Standard twins are Y500, superior rooms cost Y700. (☎ 6301-4466; fax 6304-4801)

Fengzeyuan Hotel (fēngzéyuán fàndiàn), 83 Zhushikouxi Lu (about 1km south of Qianmen). Twins cost Y513. Very good value for a three-star hotel. (☎ 6318-6688)

Guotai Hotel (guótài fàndiàn), 12 Yongan Xili, Jianguomenwai Dajie, 100022. Twins are Y418. (☎ 6501-3366; fax 6501-3926)

Hua Thai Hotel (huátài fàndiàn), Jinsong Dongkou. Twin rooms are Y400. (☎ 6771-6688; fax 6771-5266)

Rainbow Hotel (tiānqiáo bīnguǎn), 11 Xijing Lu (south-west of Qianmen). Twin rooms are priced from Y630 to Y766. (☎ 6301-2266; fax 6301-1366)

Tiantan Hotel (tiāntán fàndiàn), 1 Tiyuguan Lu, Chongwen District (east of Tiantan Park). Twins cost Y832. (☎ 6711-2277; fax 6711-6833)

Haidian District (Map 10)

Exhibition Centre Hotel (zhǎnlǎn guǎn bīnguǎn), 135 Xizhimenwai Dajie, Xicheng District, 100044. Standard twins cost Y800. (☎ 6831-6633; fax 6834-7450)

Holiday Inn Downtown (jīndū jiàrì fàndiàn), 98 Beilishi Lu, Xicheng District, 100037. Standard twins cost about Y750. (☎ 6833-8822; fax 6834-0696)

Olympic Hotel (aòlínpīkè fàndiàn), 52 Baishiqiao Lu, Haidian District, 100081. Twins cost Y590. (☎ 6217-6688; fax 6217-4260)

Yanshan Hotel (yānshān dà jiǔdiàn), 138A Haidian Lu, Haidian District, 100086. Standard/suite rooms are Y912/1300. (☎ 6256-3388; fax 6256-8640)

Yulong Hotel (yùlóng dàjiǔdiàn), 40 Fucheng Lu, Haidian District. Standard twins cost Y530. (☎ 6841-5588; fax 6841-3108)

Wangfujing Area (Map 11)

Chongwenmen Hotel (chóngwénmén fàndiàn), 2 Chongwenmen Xi Dajie, 100062. Standard twins are Y480, suites Y600. (☎ 6512-2211; fax 6512-2122)

Xinqiao Hotel (xīnqiáo fàndiàn), 2 Dong Jiaomin Xiang, Dongcheng District, 100004. Twins range from about Y660 to Y1100. (☎ 6513-3366; fax 6512-5126)

PLACES TO STAY – TOP END

For definition purposes, a hotel should be considered 'top end' if standard twin rooms cost over Y1000. It's worth noting that while many government-run tourist hotels rate themselves as four-star and five-star (with prices to match), service is often not up to international standards. A good example of this is the State-owned Beijing Hotel, which continues to 'win awards'.

A personal favourite of ours is the Holiday Inn Lido. It's only rated four stars, but in many ways comes out ahead of its five-star competitors.

Beijing (Map 3)

Catic Plaza Hotel (kǎidi'kè dàjiǔdiàn), 18 Beichendong Lu, Chaoyang District, 100101. Standard twins cost Y1000. (☎ 6492-1188; fax 6494-1288)

China Resources Hotel (huárùn fàndiàn), 35 Jianguo Lu, Chaoyang District, 100025. Twins are from Y900 to Y1500. (☎ 6501-2233; fax 6501-2311)

Continental Grand Hotel (wǔzhōu dà jiǔdiàn), 8 Beichendong Lu, Beisihuan Lu, Andingmenwai, 100101 (in the Asian Games Village). Standard rooms are Y830, superior Y1660 and suites Y2490. (☎ 6491-5588; fax 6491-0106)

Holiday Inn Lido (lìdū jiàrì fàndiàn), Jichang Lu, Jiangtai Lu, 100037 (on the road to the airport). Standard twins cost from Y1450 to Y1632, superior rooms are Y1824 and suites are priced up to Y7864. (☎ 6437-6688; fax 6437-6237)

Novotel Parkview Hotel (xīn wànshòu bīnguǎn), 8 Jiangtaixi Lu, Chaoyang District, 100016 (also known as the *Grace Hotel*). Twins cost Y1100. (☎ 6436-2288; fax 6436-1818)

East Beijing (Map 7)

Beijing Asia Hotel (běijīng yàzhōu dà jiǔdiàn), 8 Xinzhong Xijie, Gongren Tiyuchangbei Lu, 100027. Standard twins cost Y1030. (☎ 6500-7788; fax 6500-7291)

Chains City Hotel (chéngshì bīnguǎn), 4 Gongren Tiyuchangdong Lu, Chaoyang District, 100027. Twins are from Y900 to Y1020, suites from Y1280 to Y3600. (☎ 6500-7799; fax 6500-7668)

China Travel Service Tower (zhōnglǚ dàshà), 2 Beisanhuandong Lu (Third Ring Road), 100028. Standard twins cost Y1400. (☎ 6462-2288; fax 6461-2502)

China World Hotel (zhōngguó dà fàndiàn), 1 Jianguomenwai Dajie, 100020 (located inside China World Trade Centre). Twins range from Y2070 to Y3600.

Great Wall Sheraton (chángchéng fàndiàn), 10 Dong-sanhuanbei Lu, Chaoyang District, 100026. Standard twins cost Y2320. (☎ 6500-5566; fax 6500-2580)

Hilton Hotel (xīěrdùn fàndiàn), 1 Dongfang Lu, Dongsanhuanbei Lu, 100027. Twins are from Y2072 to Y2986. (☎ 6466-2288; fax 6465-3052)

Jingguang New World Hotel (jīngguǎng xīn shìjiè fàndiàn), Hujialou, Chaoyang District, 100020. Twins begin at Y1660. (☎ 6501-8888; fax 6501-3333)

Kempinski Hotel (kǎibīnsījī fàndiàn), Lufthansa Centre, 50 Liangmaqiao Lu, 100016. Standard twins begin at Y1370. (☎ 6465-3388; fax 6465-3366)

Kunlun Hotel (kūnlún fàndiàn), 2 Xinyuannan Lu, Chaoyang District, 100004. Standard twins cost Y2155. (☎ 6500-3388; fax 6506-8424)

Landmark Hotel (liàngmǎhé dàshà), 8 Dong-sanhuanbei Lu, 100004. Twins are from Y750 to Y1300. (☎ 6501-6688; fax 6501-3513).

Poly Plaza (bǎolì dàshà), 14 Dongzhimen Nan Dajie, Dongcheng District, 100027. Twins cost Y844. (☎ 6500-1188; fax 6501-0277)

Radisson SAS Hotel (huángjiā dà fàndiàn), 6A Beisanhuandong Lu (Third Ring Road), 100028. Standard/suite rooms cost about Y1575/2275. (☎ 6466-3388; fax 6465-3186)

Swissôtel (běijīng gǎng'aò zhōngxīn) – also called the *Hong Kong-Macau Centre* – Dongsi Shitiao Lijiaoqiao, 100027 (at Gongren Tiyuchangbei Lu and Chaoyangmenbei Dajie). Standard twins cost Y2005. (☎ 6501-2288; fax 6501-2501)

Yuyang Hotel (yúyáng fàndiàn), 18 Zhong Jie, Xinyuan Xili, Chaoyang District, 100027. Standard twins cost Y1150. (☎ 6466-9988; fax 6466-6602)

Zhaolong Hotel (zhàolóng bīnguǎn), 2 Gongren Tiyuchangbei Lu, Chaoyang District, 100027 (at the Third Ring Road). Twins cost Y1290. (☎ 6500-2299; fax 6500-3319)

South-West Beijing (Map 8)

Grand View Garden Hotel (dàguān yuán jiǔdiàn), 88 Nancaiyuan Jie, Xuanwu District, 100054 (beside the Grand View Garden Park). Standard twins are Y1350. (☎ 6353-8899; fax 6353-9189)

South-East Beijing (Map 9)

Gloria Plaza Hotel (kǎilái dà jiǔdiàn), 2 Jianguomennan Dajie, 100022. Twins cost from Y1148 to Y1405, suites range from Y1532 to Y2171. (☎ 6515-8855; fax 6515-8533)

Hotel New Otani (chángfù gōng), 26 Jianguomenwai Dajie, 100022. 500 rooms; twins cost from Y1492 to Y1824, suites range from Y2487 to Y5388. (☎ 6512-5555; fax 6512-5346)

International Club Hotel (guójì jùlèbù fàndiàn), 21 Jianguomenwai Dajie, 100020. Standard twins cost from Y1350. (☎ 6460-6688; fax 6460-3299)

International Hotel (guójì fàndiàn), 9 Jianguomennei Dajie, 100005. Singles/twins start at around Y830/Y1200, suites cost from Y2155 to Y9948. (☎ 6512-6688; fax 6512-9972)

Jianguo Hotel (jiànguó fàndiàn), 5 Jianguomenwai Dajie, 100020. Twins cost from Y1600 to Y1760 and suites are from Y1970 to Y2860. (☎ 6500-2233; fax 6500-2871)

Jinglun Hotel (jīnglún fàndiàn), 3 Jianguomenwai Dajie, 100020 (also known as *Beijing-Toronto Hotel*). Twins are from Y1530 to Y1870, suites Y2210 to Y4080. (☎ 6500-2266; fax 6500-2022)

Scitech Hotel (sàitè fàndiàn), 22 Jianguomenwai Dajie (across from Friendship Store), 341 rooms. Twins are Y1120, suites from Y2155 to Y5140. (☎ 6512-3388; fax 6512-3542)

Traders Hotel (guómào fàndiàn), China World Trade Centre, 1 Jianguomenwai Dajie. Twins cost Y1600, but business discounts are negotiable. (☎ 6505-2277; fax 6505-0818)

Haidian District (Map 10)

Central Garden Hotel (zhōngyuàn bīnguǎn), 18 Xie Jie, Gaoliangqiao, Xizhimenwai (north-west of the Xizhimen railway station). Standard twins are Y1050. (☎ 6831-8888; fax 6831-9887)

Debao Hotel (débǎo fàndiàn), Building 22, Debao Xinyuan, Xizhimenwai Dajie, Haidian District, 100044 (east side of the zoo). Standard twins cost Y1080. (☎ 6831-8866; fax 6833-4571)

Diaoyutai State Guesthouse (diàoyútái guó bīnguǎn), Sanlihe Lu, 100830. Most guests are invited by the government and don't have to pay, but others may fork out Y1000 and up for a standard twin. (☎ 6859-1188; fax 6851-3362)

Friendship Hotel (yǒuyí bīnguǎn), 3 Baishiqiao Lu, Haidian District, 100873 (near the Third Ring Road). Standard rooms cost from Y830 to Y1130. (☎ 6849-8880; fax 6849-8866)

Mandarin Hotel (xīndàdū fàndiàn), 21 Chegongzhuang Lu, Xicheng District, 100044 (south of Beijing Zoo). Standard twins cost around Y1200, suites are about Y1500. (☎ 6831-9988; fax 6833-8296)

New Century Hotel (xīn shìjì fàndiàn), 6 Shoudu Tiyuguannan Lu, Haidian District, 100046 (south-west of Beijing Zoo). Twins are from Y1500 to Y2250. (☎ 6849-2001; fax 6849-1107)

Shangri-La Hotel (xiānggé lǐlā fàndiàn), 29 Zhizhuyuan Lu, Haidian District, 100081. Rates are from Y1980 to Y3600. (☎ 6841-2211; fax 6841-8006)

Xiyuan Hotel (xīyuàn fàndiàn), 1 Sanlihe Lu, Haidian District (immediately south of Beijing Zoo). Twins cost Y1466. (☎ 6831-3388; fax 6831-4577)

Wangfujing Area (Map 11)

Beijing Hotel (běijīng fàndiàn), 33 Dongchang'an Jie, 100004. Rooms go for Y1330 to Y2650. Officially five stars but in our opinion more like three stars. (☎ 6513-7766; fax 6513-7307)

Capital Hotel (shǒudū bīnguǎn), 3 Qianmendong Dajie, 100006. Standard twins are Y1600. (☎ 6512-9988; fax 6512-0309)

Grand Hotel Beijing (guìbīnlóu fàndiàn), 35 Dongchang'an Jie, 100006. Standard twins cost Y2280. (☎ 6513-7788; fax 6513-0038)

Guangdong Regency Hotel (huáqiáo dàshà), 2 Wangfujing Dajie, 100006 (also known as the *Prime Hotel*). Standard twins cost Y1825 (☎ 6513-6666; fax 6513-4248)

Holiday Inn Crowne Plaza (guójì yìyuàn huángguān jiàrì fàndiàn), 48 Wangfujing Dajie, Dengshixikou, 100006. Standard twins are from Y1660. (☎ 6513-3388; fax 6513-2513)

Jinlang Hotel (jīnlǎng dà jiǔdiàn), also known as the *Yashi Jinlang Hotel*, 75 Chongwenmennei Dajie, Dongcheng District. Twins cost Y830, suites are Y1500. (☎ 6513-2288; fax 6512-5839)

Novotel Hotel (sōnghè dà jiǔdiàn), 88 Dengshikou Jie, Dongcheng District, 100006 (north part of Wangfujing). Twins are priced from Y995. (☎ 6513-8822; fax 6513-9088)

Palace Hotel (wángfǔ fàndiàn), 8 Jinyu Hutong, Wangfujing Dajie, 100006. Doubles cost Y2321 to Y2652, suites from Y3316 to Y6632. (☎ 6512-8899; fax 6512-9050)

Peace Hotel (hépíng bīnguǎn), 3 Jinyu Hutong, Wangfujing Dajie. Twins are from Y911 to Y1326, suites range from Y1243 to Y12,435. (☎ 6512-8833; fax 6512-6863)

Taiwan Hotel (táiwān fàndiàn), 5 Jinyu Hutong, Wangfujing Dajie. Twins/suites are Y1000/1825. (☎ 6513-6688; fax 6513-6896)

Tianlun Dynasty Hotel (tiānlún wángcháo fàndiàn), 50 Wangfujing Dajie. Standard twins cost Y1380. (☎ 6513-8888; fax 6513-0028)

Wangfujing Grand Hotel (wángfǔjīng dà fàndiàn), 57 Wangfujing Dajie, 100006. Standard twins cost Y1500. (☎ 6522-1188; fax 6522-3816)

Zijin Guesthouse (zǐjìn bīnguǎn), 9 Chongwenmen Xi Dajie, 100005. Twins cost from Y995 to Y1660. (☎ 6513-6655; fax 6524-9215)

Airport

Mövenpick Hotel (guódū dà fàndiàn) at Capital Airport. Twins start at Y1144. (☎ 6456-5588; fax 6456-5678)

LONG TERM

If you're planning to live, work or study in Beijing, the good news is accommodation options are increasing. Years ago, foreigners had little choice but to live in luxury hotels. The bad news is China's housing market is anything but free. Regulations govern where, when and how a foreigner can live.

The two basic rules are thsee: government policy is to make sure Chinese and foreigners are separated, and foreigners must pay the earth for apartments. If you harbour dreams of living with a Chinese family as a paying guest in their dirt-cheap flat, you can stop dreaming, because it's near impossible. The PSB will eventually find out, you'll be kicked out and your host family will face the consequences. Ditto for finding a quaint Chinese farmhouse in the suburbs.

If you're coming to study, your school will probably have some sort of dormitory. If you teach or work for the government, your housing will likely be provided free or at the Chinese price (next to nothing).

Housing costs really begin to escalate when you go to work for a foreign company or embassy, or if you want to set up your own office. In fact, it's not unusual for foreigners to live in their offices because maintaining two addresses is prohibitively expensive. Beijing's apartment buildings are almost entirely government-owned – and there's no point browsing the Chinese newspapers for real estate ads because there aren't any.

Most foreigners are exiled to special high-priced compounds. You will find occasional ads in the *China Daily* or *Business Beijing* for luxury flats and villas. Foreigners' apartments tend to be in big residential and office towers on Jianguomenwai and the Sanlitun area in north-east Beijing – examples would include the Capital Mansion or the China World Trade Centre. Flats rent for about US$70 to US$90 per sq metre, which typically works out to be US$5000 per month for an average-sized apartment. Villas cost about double this rate.

If making Beijing your permanent home, you can buy a flat or villa. Budget flats start at around US$1700 per sq metre, but double this price is not unusual. In theory, buying a flat or villa gains you a permanent residence visa, though given China's ever-changing regulations, don't bet your life on it.

Places to Eat

FOOD

Eating out in Beijing is a true adventure, one that should be seized with both chopsticks. But pay careful attention to opening times, as most restaurant staff insist on taking their *xiuxi* (afternoon nap) between 2 and 5 pm.

The northern capital has always been supplied with an abundance of produce from the rest of China, and this is reflected in the spectrum of restaurants on offer. From quick snacks at a street stall to a 12-course (or larger) imperial banquet, you're not going to be stuck for variety. You could also spend months working through all Beijing's different variants of Chinese regional cooking.

However, prices are escalating rapidly. The days are gone when a budget traveller could afford to visit an up-market restaurant and rub elbows with Beijing's bloated cadres. On the other hand, even up-market hotels often charge very reasonable prices for breakfast and sometimes for lunch too, though dinner can be pricey. There is a surprisingly wide range of restaurants in the major hotels too.

Despite the relatively small variety of produce which can be grown in the north, Beijing has still developed its own distinctive cuisine, centred on the cold northlands of China. Since this is the country's wheat belt, steamed breads, dumplings and noodles figure more prominently than rice. The other local grain, millet, supplies Beijingers with a hearty winter gruel, usually eaten with beef and pickles, and is very filling.

Beef, chicken and of course duck are the most common meats. The Chinese also do interesting things with fungi (more politely called 'truffles') of which there are numerous species with different tastes. There are relatively few local vegetables, cabbages being the main exception. Others are tomatoes, shallots and leeks.

In general, Beijingers like their food relatively bland and less spicy than elsewhere in China. However, you'll find a wide variety of pickled side dishes to go with your noodles.

One of the most common ways of cooking Chinese food is the *bào* ('explode-frying') method. Food is deep fried (with all the usual popping, sizzling, crackling noises, hence the name) in smoking hot peanut oil for about 60 seconds, to seal in the nutrients and flavours.

Representative dishes in a Beijing-style restaurant might include cold spiced pork as an appetiser, then a choice of at least a dozen chicken recipes. Among these, look for the famed beggar's chicken *(qǐgàijī)*, supposedly created by a beggar who pinched the emperor's chicken and had to bury it in the ground to cook it. The dish is wrapped in lotus leaves and baked all day in hot ashes.

The standard Beijing budget fare is the dumpling (or *jiǎozi*), which can be steamed, boiled or fried. They're normally prepared in small bamboo steamers, stacked on top of each other, and sold on street stalls. Buy them by the *jin* – half a jin is plenty for one person. Smaller alternatives are called *bǎozi* and *shǎomai*. The good old spring roll *(chūn juǎn)* is also common and it comes with a variety of fresh fillings.

Baked sweet potatoes are a cheap (about Y3), filling snack sold at street stalls throughout the city during winter. Vendors attach oil drums to their bikes, which have been converted into mobile ovens. Choose a nice soft sweet potato and the vendor will weigh it and tell you how much it costs.

Chinese crepes with egg are another big favourite on the streets of Beijing. The crepes are made with batter made from millet flour. They're then cooked on a round griddle with a spicy sauce poured on top. The whole thing is then wrapped in brown paper. Look for the glass-topped three-wheeled carts, and expect to pay about Y3 for this delicious morsel.

Useful Terms

restaurant
cāntīng
餐厅

I'm vegetarian.
wǒ chī sù.
我吃素

menu
cài dān
菜单

bill (cheque)
mǎi dān/ jiézhàng
买单/结帐

set meal (no menu)
tàocān
套餐

to eat/let's eat
chī fàn
吃饭

chopsticks
kuàizi
筷子

knife
dāozi
刀子

fork
chāzi
叉子

spoon
tiáogēng/ tāngchí
调羹/汤匙

Have you got any ...?
Nǐ yǒu méiyǒu ...?
你有没有 ...?

Please bring me one order of ...
Qǐng nǐ chǎo yīpán ... gěi wǒ.
请你炒一盘 ... 给我.

How much does this dish cost?
Zhèzhǒng cài duōshǎo qián?
这种菜多少钱?

What's the total cost for everything?
Yígòng duōshǎo qián?
一共多少钱?

Do you have any of the dishes on this list?
Càidān lǐmiàn yǒu méiyǒu zhèzhǒng cài?
菜单里面有没有这种菜?

Rice 饭

steamed white rice
mǐfàn
米饭

watery rice porridge
xīfàn
稀饭

rice noodles
mǐfěn
米粉

Bread, Buns & Dumplings 面类

western-style bread
miànbāo
面包

fried roll
yínsī juǎn
银丝巷

steamed bun
mántou
馒头

steamed meat bun
bāozi
包子

fried bread stick
yóutiáo
油条

dumplings
jiǎozi
饺子

prawn cracker
lóngxiā piàn
龙虾片

Vegetable Dishes 菜类

fried rice with vegetables
shūcài chǎofàn
蔬菜炒饭

fried noodles with vegetables
shūcài chǎomiàn
蔬菜炒面

spicy peanuts
wǔxiāng huāshēng mǐ
五香花生米

fried peanuts
yóuzhá huāshēng mǐ
油炸花生米

spiced cold vegetables
liángbàn shíjǐn
凉拌什锦

Chinese salad
jiācháng liángcài
家常凉菜

fried rape in oyster sauce
háoyóu pácài dǎn
蚝油扒菜胆

fried rape with mushrooms
dōnggū pácài dǎn
冬菇扒菜胆

fried bean curd in oyster sauce
háoyóu dòufǔ
蚝油豆腐

spicy hot bean curd
mápó dòufǔ
麻婆豆腐

bean curd casserole
shāguō dòufǔ
沙锅豆腐

bean curd & mushrooms
mógū dòufǔ
蘑菇豆腐

garlic & morning glory
dàsuàn kōngxīn cài
大蒜空心菜

fried garlic
sù chǎo dàsuàn
素炒大蒜

fried eggplant
sùshāo qiézi
素烧茄子

fried beansprouts
sù chǎo dòuyá
素炒豆芽

fried green vegetables
sù chǎo qīngcài
素炒青菜

fried green beans
sù chǎo biǎndòu
素炒扁豆

fried cauliflower & tomato
chǎo fānqié càihuā 炒番茄菜花
broiled mushroom
sù chǎo mógū 素炒蘑菇
black fungus & mushroom
mù'ěr huákǒu mó 木耳滑口蘑
fried white radish patty
luóbo gāo 萝卜糕
assorted hors d'oeuvre
shíjǐn pīnpán 什锦拼盘
assorted vegetarian food
sù shíjǐn 素什锦

Egg Dishes 蛋类
preserved egg
sōnghuā dàn 松花蛋
fried rice with egg
jīdàn chǎofàn 鸡蛋炒饭
fried tomatoes & eggs
xīhóngshì chǎo jīdàn 西红柿炒鸡蛋
egg & flour omelette
jiān bǐng 煎饼

Beef Dishes 牛肉类
fried rice with beef
niúròusī chǎofàn 牛肉丝炒饭
noodles with beef (soupy)
niúròu tāng miàn 牛肉汤面
spiced noodles with beef
niúròu gān miàn 牛肉干面
fried noodles with beef
niúròu chǎomiàn 牛肉炒面
beef with white rice
niúròu fàn 牛肉饭
beef platter
niúròu tiěbǎn 牛肉铁板
beef with oyster sauce
háoyóu niúròu 蚝油牛肉
beef braised in soy sauce
hóngshāo niúròu 红烧牛肉
beef with tomatoes
fānqié niúròu piàn 番茄牛肉片
beef with green peppers
qīngjiāo niúròu piàn 青椒牛肉片
beef curry & rice
gālí niúròu fàn 咖喱牛肉饭
beef curry & noodles
gālí niúròu miàn 咖喱牛肉面

Chicken Dishes 鸡肉类
fried rice with chicken
jīsī chǎofàn 鸡丝炒饭
noodles with chicken (soupy)
jīsī tāng miàn 鸡丝汤面
fried noodles with chicken
jīsī chǎomiàn 鸡丝炒面
chicken leg with white rice
jītuǐ fàn 鸡腿饭
spicy hot chicken & peanuts
gōngbào jīdīng 宫爆鸡丁
fruit kernal with chicken
guǒwèi jīdīng 果味鸡丁
sweet & sour chicken
tángcù jīdīng 糖醋鸡丁
sauteed spicy chicken pieces
làzi jīdīng 辣子鸡丁
sauteed chicken with green peppers
jiàngbào jīdīng 酱爆鸡丁
chicken slices & tomato sauce
fānqié jīdīng 番茄鸡丁
mushrooms & chicken
cǎomó jīdīng 草蘑鸡丁
chicken pieces in oyster sauce
háoyóu jīdīng 蚝油鸡丁
chicken braised in soy sauce
hóngshāo jīkuài 红烧鸡块
sauteed chicken with water chestnuts
nánjiè jīpiàn 南芥鸡片
sliced chicken with crispy rice
jīpiàn guōbā 鸡片锅巴
chicken curry
gālí jīròu 咖喱鸡肉
chicken curry & rice
gālí jīròu fàn 咖喱鸡肉饭
chicken curry & noodles
gālí jīròu miàn 咖喱鸡肉面

Duck Dishes 鸭肉类
Beijing Duck
běijīng kǎoyā 北京烤鸭
duck with white rice
yāròu fàn 鸭肉饭
duck with noodles
yāròu miàn 鸭肉面
duck with fried noodles
yāròu chǎomiàn 鸭肉炒面

Pork Dishes 猪肉类

pork chop with white rice
páigǔ fàn 排骨饭
fried rice with pork
ròusī chǎofàn 肉丝炒饭
fried noodles with pork
ròusī chǎomiàn 肉丝炒面
pork & mustard greens
zhàcài ròusī 榨菜肉丝
noodles, pork & mustard greens
zhàcài ròusī miàn 榨菜肉丝面
pork with crispy rice
ròupiàn guōbā 肉片锅巴
sweet & sour pork fillet
tángcù zhūròu piàn 糖醋猪肉片
sweet & sour pork fillet
tángcù lǐjī 糖醋里脊
pork fillet with white sauce
huáliū lǐjī 滑溜里脊
shredded pork fillet
chǎo lǐjī sī 炒里脊丝
soft pork fillet
ruǎnzhá lǐjī 软炸里脊
spicy hot pork pieces
gōngbào ròudīng 宫爆肉丁
fried black pork pieces
yuánbào lǐjī 芫爆里脊
sauteed diced pork & soy sauce
jiàngbào ròudīng 酱爆肉丁
spicy pork cubelets
làzi ròudīng 辣子肉丁
pork cubelets & cucumber
huángguā ròudīng 黄瓜肉丁
golden pork slices
jīnyín ròusī 金银肉丝
sauteed shredded pork
qīngchǎo ròusī 清炒肉丝
shredded pork & hot sauce
yúxiāng ròusī 鱼香肉丝
shredded pork & green peppers
qīngjiāo ròusī 青椒肉丝
shredded pork & bamboo shoots
dōngsǔn ròusī 冬笋肉丝
shredded pork & green beans
biǎndòu ròusī 扁豆肉丝
pork with oyster sauce
háoyóu ròusī 蚝油肉丝
boiled pork slices
shuǐzhǔ ròupiàn 水煮肉片

pork, eggs & black fungus
mùxū ròu 木须肉
pork & fried onions
yángcōng chǎo ròupiàn 洋葱炒肉片
fried rice (assorted)
shíjǐn chǎofàn 什锦炒饭
fried rice Cantonese style
guǎngzhōu chǎofàn 广州炒饭

Seafood Dishes 海鲜类

fried rice with shrimp
xiārén chǎofàn 虾仁炒饭
fried noodles with shrimp
xiārén chǎomiàn 虾仁炒面
diced shrimp with peanuts
gōngbào xiārén 宫爆虾仁
sauteed shrimp
qīngchǎo xiārén 清炒虾仁
deep-fried shrimp
zhá xiārén 炸虾仁
fried shrimp with mushroom
xiānmó xiārén 鲜蘑虾仁
squid with crispy rice
yóuyú guōbā 鱿鱼锅巴
sweet & sour squid roll
suānlà yóuyú juǎn 酸辣鱿鱼卷
fish braised in soy sauce
hóngshāo yú 红烧鱼
braised sea cucumber
hóngshāo hǎishēn 红烧海参
clams *gé* 蛤
crab *pángxiè* 螃蟹
lobster *lóngxiā* 龙虾

Soup 汤类

three kinds seafood soup
sān xiān tāng 三鲜汤
squid soup
yóuyú tāng 鱿鱼汤
hot & sour soup
suānlà tāng 酸辣汤
tomato & egg soup
xīhóngshì dàn tāng 西红柿蛋汤
corn & egg thick soup
fènghuáng lìmǐ gēng 凤凰粟米羹
egg & vegetable soup
dànhuā tāng 蛋花汤
mushroom & egg soup
mógu dànhuā tāng 蘑菇蛋花汤

fresh fish soup			pangolin	chuānshānjiǎ	穿山甲	
shēng yú tāng	生鱼汤		(armadillo-like mammal)			
vegetable soup			frog	qīngwā	青蛙	
shūcài tāng	蔬菜汤		eel	shàn yú	鳝鱼	
cream of tomato soup			turtle	hǎiguī	海龟	
nǎiyóu fānqié tāng	奶油番茄汤		Mongolian	huǒguō	火锅	
cream of mushroom soup			hotpot			
nǎiyóu xiānmó tāng	奶油鲜蘑汤					

Condiments 香料

garlic	dàsuàn	大蒜
black pepper	hújiāo	胡椒
hot pepper	làjiāo	辣椒
hot sauce	làjiāo jiàng	辣椒酱
ketchup	fānqié jiàng	番茄酱
salt	yán	盐
MSG	wèijīng	味精
soy sauce	jiàng yóu	酱油
vinegar	cù	醋
sesame seed oil	zhīma yóu	芝麻油
butter	huáng yóu	黄油
sugar	táng	糖
jam	guǒ jiàng	果酱
honey	fēngmì	蜂蜜

pickled mustard green soup — zhàcài tāng 榨菜汤
bean curd & vegetable soup — dòufǔ cài tāng 豆腐菜汤
wanton soup — húntùn tāng 馄饨汤
clear soup — qīng tāng 清汤

Miscellanea & Exotica 其它

kebab	ròu chuàn	肉串
goat, mutton	yáng ròu	羊肉
dogmeat	gǒu ròu	狗肉
deermeat (venison)	lùròu	鹿肉
snake	shé ròu	蛇肉
ratmeat	lǎoshǔ ròu	老鼠肉

DRINKS
Non-alcoholic Drinks

Tea is the most common brew in Beijing; it didn't originate in China but in South-East Asia. Indian tea is not generally available in restaurants, but if you need the stuff, large supermarkets stock Lipton and Twinings.

Real coffee addicts not staying at five-star hotels will have to make do with the instant muck available at supermarkets, or make a desperate dash for Johnny's Coffee (Map 3) in north-east Beijing (see under Bars in the Entertainment chapter).

Coca-Cola, introduced into China by US troops in 1927, is now made in Beijing. Fanta and Sprite are widely available, both genuine and copycat versions. Sugary Chinese soft drinks are cheap and sold everywhere – some are so sweet they'll turn your teeth inside out. Jianlibao is a Chinese soft drink made with honey rather than sugar, and is one of the better brands. Lychee-flavoured fizzy drinks get rave reviews from foreigners. Fresh milk is rare but you can buy imported UHT milk from western-style supermarkets.

A surprising treat is fresh sweet yoghurt, available from street stalls and shops everywhere. It's usually sold in what look like small milk bottles and is consumed by drinking with a straw rather than eating with a spoon. This excellent stuff would make a great breakfast if you could find some decent bread to go with it.

Alcoholic Drinks

If tea is the most popular drink in Beijing then beer must be number two. By any standards the top brands are great stuff. The best known is Tsingtao, made with a mineral water which gives it its sparkling quality. It's really a German beer since the town of Qingdao (formerly spelt 'Tsingtao') where it's made was once a German Concession and the Chinese inherited the brewery. Some claim that draft Tsingtao tastes much better than the bottled stuff.

Beijing has several local beers. The best is said to be Yanjing, while another, Beijing Beer, is like coloured water. San Miguel is brewed in Guangzhou and is available from some shops in Beijing. Western imports are sold in the Friendship Store and five-star hotels, at five-star prices.

China has probably cultivated vines and produced wine for over 4000 years, but westerners give them mixed reviews. The word 'wine' gets rather loosely translated; many Chinese 'wines' are in fact spirits. Rice wine – a favourite with Chinese alcoholics because of its low price – is intended mainly for cooking rather than drinking. Lizard wine is produced in the southern province of Guangxi; each bottle contains one dead lizard suspended perpendicularly in the clear liquid. Wine with dead bees or pickled snakes is also desirable for its alleged tonic (or aphrodisiac) properties. In general, the more poisonous the creature, the more potent are the alleged tonic effects.

Maotai (máotái) is a spirit made from sorghum (a type of millet). It's used for toasts at banquets and tastes like rubbing alcohol.

Chinese women don't drink (except beer) in public; women who hit the booze are regarded as prostitutes. However, western women can easily violate this social taboo without unpleasant consequences, since the Chinese expect weirdness from westerners anyway. As a rule Chinese men are not big drinkers, but toasts are obligatory at banquets. If you really can't drink, fill your wine glass with tea and say you have a bad stomach. In spite of all the toasting and beer drinking, public drunkenness is strongly frowned upon.

Imported alcohol – like XO, Johnny Walker, Kahlua, Napoleon Augier Cognac etc – is highly prized by the Chinese for its prestige value rather than exquisite taste. The snob appeal and steep import taxes translates

Drinks

beer		
píjiǔ	啤酒	
whiskey		
wēishìjì jiǔ	威士忌酒	
vodka		
fútèjiā jiǔ	伏特加酒	
fizzy drink		
qìshuǐ	汽水	
Coca-Cola		
kěkǒu kělè	可口可乐	
tea		
chá	茶	
coffee		
kāfēi	咖啡	
coffee creamer		
nǎijīng	奶精	
water		
kāi shuǐ	开水	
mineral water		
kuàng quán shuǐ	矿泉水	
red grape wine		
hóng pútáo jiǔ	红葡萄酒	
white grape wine		
bái pútáo jiǔ	白葡萄酒	
rice wine		
mǐ jiǔ	米酒	
milk		
niúnǎi	牛奶	
soybean milk		
dòujiāng	豆浆	
yoghurt		
suānnǎi	酸奶	
fruit juice		
guǒzhī	果汁	
orange juice		
chéng zhī	橙汁	
coconut juice		
yēzi zhī	椰子汁	
pineapple juice		
bōluó zhī	波萝汁	
mango juice		
mángguǒ zhī	芒果汁	
hot		
rède	热的	
ice cold		
bīngde	冰的	
ice cube		
bīng kuài	冰块	

into absurdly high prices. If you can't live without western spirits, take advantage of your duty-free allowance on arrival.

RESTAURANTS

Although in 1949 Beijing had an incredible 10,000 snack bars and restaurants, by 1976 that number had dwindled to less than 700. Restaurants, a nasty bourgeois concept, were all to have been phased out and replaced with revolutionary dispensaries dishing out rice. The free enterprise reforms of the past two decades have changed all that. An explosion of privately owned eateries has taken place. Gone are the famines and ration cards, and the connections needed to buy a loaf of bread or a bottle of cooking oil. Nobody is pretending they're all five-star restaurants, but the number of places to eat in Beijing must have climbed back up to 10,000 by now.

Northern Chinese

Beijing Duck This is made on the same principle as that other great delicacy, paté de foie gras, namely by force-feeding ducks. By the time they get to your table, the birds have been plucked, blown up like a balloon (to separate the skin from the flesh), basted in honey and vinegar, wind-dried, and grilled. In the restaurants, the duck is served in stages. First comes boneless meat and crispy skin with a side dish of shallots, plum sauce or sweet flour paste, and crepes. This is followed by duck soup made of bones and all the other parts except the quack.

There are plenty of places which specialise in Beijing duck, but you can also order it from almost any major hotel restaurant that does Chinese cuisine.

Otherwise known simply as the 'Old Duck', *Qianmen Quanjude Roast Duck Restaurant* (☎ 6511-2418) *(qiánmén quànjùdé kǎoyādiàn)* is at 32 Qianmen Dajie, on the east side, near the Qianmen subway station (Map 9). As the nickname implies, this is one of the oldest restaurants in the capital, dating back to 1864. However, it has come right up to date with a fast-food section offering duckburgers. Language shouldn't really be a

problem; you just have to negotiate half or whole ducks. But not everyone is satisfied:

We ate in the Qianmen Quanjude Roast Duck Restaurant. We ordered what they call a 'whole duck', advised by the staff. We got a plate full of skin and no meat, and when we asked for meat they told us in a polite way to piss off. No way to escape, we had to pay Y100 for skin and soup that tasted like dishwater.
Marie-Paule Kellner

The *Bianyifang Duck Restaurant* (☎ 6712-5186) *(biànyífǎng kǎoyādiàn)* is another busy place. At 2 Chongwenmenwai Dajie, by the Hademen Hotel (Map 11), it has a cheap section where the locals will show you the correct way to spit on the floor.

Mongolian Hotpot This is so good in Beijing that it's hard to believe it can be so bad in Mongolia. Nothing like a casserole hotpot in the western sense, it was originally prepared in the helmets and shields of Mongol warriors. Using a brass pot with charcoal inside, you get to cook thick strips of mutton and vegetables yourself, fondue fashion, spicing as you like.

Look for the hotpot symbol on food stalls and restaurants in the *hutongs* (side streets).

Nengren Ju (☎ 6601-2560) is appropriately next to Kublai Khan's creation, the White Dagoba Temple (Map 5). There are also lots of hotpot spots on Dazhalan from Qianmen to the Far East Hotel (Maps 8 & 9).

Muslim Barbecue Muslim barbecue is very cheap if you know the right place to look. The right place is the west end of Baiwanzhuangxi Lu, a street in a neighbourhood known as Ganjiakou not far south of the zoo. This is where Beijing's Uighur minority congregates. It's often best to eat with a small group (two to four persons) so you can get several dishes and sample everything. Alternatively, you can just drift from stall to stall sampling as you go. A standard Uighur meal consists of flatbread (náng) consumed with sweet tea (sānpào tái or bābǎo chá), vegetable dishes, noodles (miàn) and kebabs (ròuchuān).

Out in tourist hotel-land, prices for this

type of cuisine are high, but one place you might like to try is *Hongbinlou* (☎ 6603-8460) *(hóngbīnlóu fànzhuāng)* at 82 Xichang'an Jie, just east of Xidan intersection.

The *Kaorouwan Restaurant* (☎ 6601-9042) *(kǎoròuwǎn fànzhuāng)*, at 93 Fuxingmennei Dajie (Map 8), is one of Beijing's best Muslim barbecue houses.

Shandong The food of Shandong Province is similar to Beijing style, but with more focus on vegies and seafood. 'Confucian food' is considered Shandong style, since Confucius was born in Qufu, Shandong Province.

A major player is the *Confucian Heritage Restaurant* (☎ 6303-0689) *(kǒng shàntáng fànzhuāng)* at 3 Liulichangxi Jie (Map 8). It has fairly long operating hours, from 10.30 am to 2 pm and from 5.30 to 11 pm.

Also superb is the *Fengzeyuan Restaurant* (☎ 6318-6688) *(fēngzéyuán fànzhuāng)*, 83 Zhushikou Xilu, Xuanwu District, inside the Fengzeyuan Hotel (Map 9). Open 11 am to 2 pm and 4.30 to 9 pm.

Imperial Imperial food *(gōngtíng cài* or *mǎnhàn dàcān)* is fit for an emperor and it will clean your wallet out very fast. In 1982 a group of Beijing chefs set about reviving the imperial pastry recipes, and even went so far as to find the last emperor's brother to try their products out on.

You'll find this cuisine served up in the *Fangshan Restaurant* (☎ 6401-1879) in Beihai Park – the official address is 1 Wenjin Jie (Map 5). The Summer Palace houses the *Tingliguan Imperial Restaurant* (☎ 6258-1955) (Summer Palace map, page 85). There's also an imperial restaurant at Fragrant Hills Park (Fragrant Hills Park map, page 100).

The *Li Family Restaurant* (☎ 6601-1915) *(lì jiā cài)* is at 11 Yangfang Hutong, off Deshengmenwai Dajie (Map 5) on the scenic south bank of Shisha Houhai Lake. There's a Y200 per head set menu which includes delicious appetisers. Take note: this place is tiny – in summer, reservations are required two weeks in advance!

Cantonese
No self-respecting tourist hotel in Beijing is without a Cantonese restaurant to keep its Hong Kong clientele happy. A staple of this proud southern Chinese tradition is *dim sum*, a banquet served for breakfast and lunch (but never dinner). It consists of all sorts of little delicacies served from pushcarts wheeled around the restaurant. It's justifiably famous and highly addictive stuff.

Cantonese dinners can be somewhat unattractive to western palates. The Cantonese are said to eat anything with four legs but the table – specialities are 1000-year eggs (traditionally made by soaking eggs in horses' urine), shark's fin soup, snake soup and dog stew. Other culinary exotica include anteaters, pangolins (a sort of armadillo), cats, rats, owls, monkeys, turtles and frogs.

For something that's not inside a tourist hotel, you might like to try the *Renren Restaurant* (☎ 6511-2978) *(rénrén dà jiǔlóu)* at 18 Qianmendong Dajie (Map 11).

Windows on the World (☎ 6500-3335) offers reasonably priced dim sum and the western 'executive lunch' is quite a deal at Y40 per person. On Sunday, the restaurant sets up a children's area with toys and videos. This place is on the 28th floor of the CITIC building on Jianguomenwai Dajie (Map 9).

Hong Kong Food City (☎ 6466-8886) *(xiānggǎng měishí chéng)* has a number of branches. The most accessible one for foreigners is just west of the Lufthansa Centre (Map 7). It has long dinner hours – 11.30 am to 2 pm and from 5.30 pm to 3.30 am.

Chaozhou
This is similar to Cantonese food, though the emphasis is less on dim sum and more on seafood. Specialities are abalone, shark's fin soup, roast pig and a snake dish known as 'Dragon's Duel Tiger', which is a combination of wild cat and snake meat.

Zuihong Chaozhou Food City (☎ 6303-6530) *(zuìhóng cháozhōu chéng)*, Building 3, Zhengyang Market, looks like it was lifted lock, stock and lobsters out of Hong Kong. The *Zhongqiao Chaozhou Restaurant* (☎ 6306-6220) *(zhōngqiáo cháozhōu jiǔlóu)* is in the same building. The building itself is a little hard to find, stuck in an alley near Dazhalan (Map 9).

Fairly easy to find is the *Chaofuyuan Restaurant* (☎ 6256-4433) inside the Shengtang Hotel at 2 Wanggongfen, Wangquanzhuang, Haidian District (Map 10).

In the western area of town, try the *Crystal Palace Chaozhou Restaurant* (☎ 6852-2487) *(shuǐjīnggōng cháozhōu jiǔlóu)*, 15A Nanlishi Lu (Map 8). The emphasis here is heavily on seafood.

Hunan

This style of cooking is similar to Sichuan cuisine, but also borrows the Cantonese concept of making anything palatable. If the French can do it with frogs, why not the Chinese with dogs? Anyone for hot dog? Hunan menus typically include onion dog, dog soup (reputed to be an aphrodisiac) and dog stew.

But for those a little sensitive to the culinary culling of canines, perhaps a switch to Hunan-style duck spiced with hot pepper, or some seafood, and several styles of noodles would be better.

The *Shaoshan Mao's Restaurant* (☎ 6421-9340) *(sháoshān máojiā càiguǎn)*, at 4 Hepinglizhong Jie near Ditan Park (Map 6), serves revolutionary cuisine that's actually prepared by the late chairman's townsfolk.

Then there's the rather odd *CPPCC Cultural Restaurant* (☎ 6602-5758) *(zhèngxié wénhuà cāntīng)*, A23 Taipingqiao Dajie (Map 5), which is at least unique for being in the auditorium of the Chinese Communist Party. Also intriguing is the fact that it's open 24 hours.

The gloriously named *Recall One's Past Sufferings and Think About One's Present Happiness Restaurant* (☎ 6617-5752) *(yìkǔsītián dàzáyuàn fànzhuāng)* actually offers 'revolutionary nostalgia cuisine', with a menu divided into 'past suffering' and 'present happiness' (go with the latter unless you're feeling brave ... or masochistic). The restaurant is hidden down a little lane at 17 Picai Hutong, Xicheng District (Map 5).

Sichuan

Sichuan food is China's spiciest cuisine – we're talking chillies that can do damage here. One speciality is smoked duck cooked in peppercorns, marinated in wine for 24 hours soaked in tea leaves and cooked again on a charcoal fire. Also worth a try is the salted shrimp with garlic, dried chilli beef, and eggplant with garlic.

Next to the main building of the Holiday Inn Lido is a charming wooden house where you'll find the *Sichuan Yandianzi Restaurant* (☎ 6437-3561 ext 6028) (Map 3).

Another place with a charming setting is the *Fuhai Restaurant* (☎ 6256-8867) within the grounds of the Old Summer Palace (Old Summer Palace map, page 89), but it has quite short hours (10 am to 3 pm).

Near the south-west gate of Ritan Park is *Yuyuan Restaurant* (☎ 6502-5985) *(yúyuán fànzhuāng)* (Map 9). As a rule, reservations are necessary.

Less charming but still excellent is the *Douhua Restaurant* (☎ 6771-8392) *(dòuhuā fànzhuāng)* (Map 9). The location at Guangqumenwai Majuan is also a little odd.

Right in the heart of the Sanlitun tourist combat zone is the *New Douhua Village Restaurant* (☎ 6462-9097) *(xīn dòuhuā cūn cāntīng)* at 3 Sanlitun Lu (Map 7).

Vegetarian

The brilliant *Gongdelin Vegetarian Restaurant* (☎ 6511-2542) *(gōngdélín sùcàiguǎn)*, at 158 Qianmennan Dajie (Map 9), is probably the best place in the city for herbivores. It serves up wonderful vegetarian cuisine with great names to match. How's about the 'peacock in pride' or 'the fire is singeing the snow-capped mountains'? Open 10.30 am to 8.30 pm.

Buried behind the White Cloud Temple in the Xicheng District is the *Taoist Family Healthfood Restaurant* (☎ 6346-3531 ext 28) *(dàojiā yǎngshēng cāntīng)* (Map 8). Open 11 am to 2 pm, and 4.30 pm to 9 pm.

Just off of Wangfujing is the *Green Angel Vegetarian Restaurant* (☎ 6524-2349) *(lütiānshǐ sùshí guǎn)* at 57 Dengshikou Dajie in the Dongcheng District (Map 11). Open 8 am to midnight.

See also the *Omar Khayyam Restaurant* under Other Asian Cuisine, Indian.

Health Food

The average Chinese notion of 'health food' *(yàoshàn)* differs somewhat from that of the west. While western health food emphasises low fat, high fibre and a lack of chemical additives, the Chinese version puts its main emphasis on the use of traditional ingredients and herbs. Because of the high price and concern about endangered species, you probably won't be served tiger meat or rhino horn in Beijing's health food restaurants. However, you may be treated to exotic items such as ganoderma mushrooms or angelica.

Well worth a try is the *Sichuan Hometown Restaurant* (☎ 6595-7687) *(sìchuān jiāxiāng jiǔjiā)*, a cheap hole-in-the-wall eatery specialising in fiery Chinese health food. Recommendations include the eggplant and the spicy chicken with red peppers. A hot favourite of businesspeople and journalists, it's at Yong'an Xili (a small alley east of the Scitech Hotel near Jianguomenwai) (Map 9).

Inside the Xiyuan Hotel you'll find the *Yangshengzhai Restaurant* (☎ 6831-3388 ext 10213) – the name translates as 'health-preserving food') (Map 10). The Rainbow Hotel chips in with its *Healthfood Restaurant* (☎ 6301-2266) *(shízhēn yuàn)* (Map 9).

Cheap Eats

The hutongs are so packed with cheap eateries it would take a gigantic book to list them all. Areas to explore include the Qianmen region at the south end of Tiananmen Square, and Wangfujing around parks such as Tiantan, Ritan and Beihai.

An extra special mention should go to the *Dong'anmen Night Market* which gets going from around 6 to 9 pm daily. All sorts of exotic snacks are available, including a few roasted and skewered beasties that westerners might ordinarily regard as domestic pets. The market is at the north end of Wangfujing near the Bank of China (Map 11).

Other Asian Cuisine

Let it not be forgotten that Beijing is one of the most cosmopolitan Chinese cities. Foreign embassy staff, business people and tourists have carved quite a culinary niche.

Indian The *Shamiana Indian Restaurant* (☎ 6832-2288 ext 7107) in the Holiday Inn Downtown (Map 10) is where you can get your chapattis and tandoori chicken. The tariff will run upwards of Y100 per person.

The *Omar Khayyam Restaurant* (☎ 6513-9988 ext 20188) can be found in the Asia Pacific Building at 8 Yabao Lu, near Ritan Park (Map 7). Indian bread (naan), fish tikka and the many vegetarian dishes are all good choices here. Expect to pay about Y125 per person.

Indonesian *Rasa Sayang* (☎ 6437-6688 ext 1847) is buried within the cavernous corridors of the Holiday Inn Lido (Map 3).

Japanese Japanese restaurants seem to be expensive no matter where you go in the world. In keeping with this tradition, you'll find Beijing's Japanese restaurants located in up-market hotels. Hotels with stylish Japanese restaurants include: the Hilton Hotel, the Hong Kong-Macau Centre, and the Kunlun Hotel (Map 7); the Media Centre Hotel (Map 8); the Hotel New Otani, the China World Trade Centre & Hotel, and the Rainbow Hotel (Map 9); the New Century Hotel (Map 10); and the Capital Hotel (Map 11).

Korean There are lots of Korean students at the Beijing Language Institute in the Haidian District, and they've staked out an ethnic cuisine enclave in the nearby neighbourhood of Wudaokou (Map 10). You'll find dozens of great Korean restaurants here. Look for the picture of a hotpot (Korean barbecue).

Classier surroundings and higher prices can be found at numerous other Korean restaurants – mostly inside up-market hotels. These options include: *Sorobol* (☎ 6501-6688 ext 5119) inside the Landmark Hotel (Map 7); the *Lido Garden Korean Restaurant* (☎ 6437-1517), Holiday Inn Lido Hotel

(Map 3); *Bobea Won* (☎ 6512-9844), 1st and 3rd floors, International Hotel (Map 9); the *Suraksan* (☎ 6831-9988); *Meigetsukan Restaurant* (☎ 6501-2032) 2nd floor, Jingguang New World Hotel (Map 7); and *The Golden Turtle* (☎ 6515-8855 ext 3255), 2nd floor, Gloria Plaza Hotel (Map 9).

Malaysian Big points here for the *Asian Star Restaurant* (☎ 6591-6716) *(yàzhōu zhīxīng xīnmǎyìn cāntīng)* (Map 7), an excellent combination eatery with a busy and jovial atmosphere. Cuisine on offer includes dishes from Malaysia, Singapore and India – a delight for curry enthusiasts. Dinner comes to about Y125 per head and reservations are recommended on the weekend.

Thai The *Red Basil Restaurant* (☎ 6460-2342), Beisanhuandong Lu in north-east Beijing (Map 7), has the usual fiery hot Thai dishes. A relatively new place, it has high ceilings, beautiful decorations and an atmosphere that is decidedly un-Chinese.

The superb *Borom Piman Thai Restaurant* (☎ 6437-6688 ext 2899) inside the Holiday Inn Lido (Map 3) is worth more than one visit.

The Novotel Hotel (Map 11) chips in with *Sawasdee* (☎ 6513-8822 ext 2430).

Vietnamese The *Saigon Inn* (☎ 6515-8855) is in the Gloria Plaza Hotel (Map 9). *Ma Cherie* (☎ 6500-3388 ext 5247) is in the Kunlun Hotel (Map 7).

Western Fast Food

From the day of its grand opening in 1992, *McDonald's (màidāngláo)* has been all the rage with Beijingers. Indeed, it's one of the city's most prestigious restaurants, the venue for cadre birthday parties and a popular hang-out for the upper crust. Despite this, a Beijing Big Mac, at Y9.50, is one of the world's cheapest burgers.

Beijing's first McDonald's, on Wangfujing, was recently reduced to rubble by the reconstruction hammers, but there are more than 40 new branches to replace it. For backpackers camped out at the Jinghua Hotel (Map 3) in south Beijing, Ronald McDonald

can be visited just half a block west of the hotel. A more up-market branch (but same menu of course) exists next to the Hotel New Otani on Jianguomenwai Dajie (Map 9). Most branches are open from 7 am to 11 pm.

KFC first spread its deep-fried wings here in 1987, when it was still going by the name Kentucky Fried Chicken. The store opposite Mao's Mausoleum (Map 11) was China's first, and for a time it was the largest KFC in the world – you may want to visit for historical reasons. Another KFC has hatched on Chaoyang Lu near Dongdaqiao Lu (Map 11).

Pizza Hut (bìshèngkè) has grabbed a large slice of the fast-food market. Its Beijing branches can be a bit grotty and a bit crowded, but they're relatively cheap and the service is quick. The most conspicuous branch is part of the Friendship Store on Jianguomenwai (Map 9). Another is at 27 Dongzhimenwai Dajie in the Sanlitun area (next to the Australian embassy).

Good ol' *Uncle Sam's Fastfood (shānmǔ shūshū kuàicān)* is on the south side of Jianguomenwai near McDonald's (Map 9). Don't mistake it for the US embassy, which is on the other side of the street.

Subway sandwiches has two branches in Beijing. In the north-east part of town there is one at Liangmaqiao Lu by the Lufthansa Centre (Map 7). The other is in the north-west area by the west gate of North Jiaotong University on Xizhimenwai Dajie (close to the Beijing North railway station) in the Haidian District (Map 10).

Down in the basement of Scitech Plaza on Jianguomenwai (Map 9) is *Lotteria*, a South Korean fast-food chain which all the locals believe is 100% American.

Hotel Food

Most major hotels have a western coffee shop, but few of these are particularly thrilling. There are, however, several western restaurants in five-star hotel-land that have distinguished themselves with the expat community.

Peppino's (☎ 6841-2211 ext 2727) is a trendy Italian restaurant. It's not outrageously expensive considering its location inside the Shangri-la Hotel (Map 10). It's open from 6 to 10.30 pm. Kudos also go to *Pino Pizzeria* in the Kunlun Hotel (Map 7).

The *Brauhaus* (☎ 6505-2266 ext 6565), in the China World Hotel (Map 9), is a great place for Bavarian beer and big servings of German food (meat, meat, and more meat). At about Y200 per person, it's not cheap – but with the huge all-you-can-eat rolls and liverwurst that come with each meal, you won't have to eat for a week after this.

If it's French food you crave, you can satisfy the urge at *La Fleur* (☎ 6505-2266 ext 38) in the China World Hotel (Map 9). Despite the Chinese name, the *Old Peking Grill* in the Grand Hotel Beijing, 35 Dong Chang'an Dajie (Map 11), is a French restaurant. *Maxim's* in the Chongwenmen Hotel, 2 Chongwenmen Xi Dajie (Map 11), is not quite as good as it's Parisian cousin with the same name.

The *Atrium Cafe* in the Gloria Plaza Hotel (Map 9), is a sophisticated all-purpose western restaurant.

Pub Grub

Most westerners hardly eat Chinese food in Beijing at all. Fast-food joints aside, there are many pubs doing fantastic western food. Some open for lunch, but many do dinner only and stay open well past midnight. There is often live music and the clientele leans towards heavy drinking and socialising. For these reasons, it seems more fitting to list these places as 'nightlife' (see the Entertainment chapter).

Miscellaneous

The *Moscow Restaurant* (☎ 6831-6677 ext 4331) *(mòsīkē cāntīng)* is on the west side of the Soviet-designed Beijing Exhibition Centre in the zoo district (Map 10). The vast interior has chandeliers, a high ceiling and fluted columns. You can get a table overlooking the zoo (which has, by the way, no connection with the menu). Unlike Moscow, there are no queues here, but the food is genuinely Russian. It's moderately priced. Open 10.30 am to 2.30 pm and 4.30 to 8 pm.

Self Catering

Bakeries Chinese bread is about as tasty as a dried-out sponge, but a few entrepreneurs have introducedf edible baked goods to the masses. One fine effort in this direction is *Delifrance (dà mòfáng miànbāo diàn)*, which has croissants and baguettes for a fraction of what you'd pay in Paris. This bakery has one branch in front of the Friendship Store (Map 9), and another at the Qianmen Zhengyang Market, south-west of Mao's Mausoleum (Map 11).

In a bid to lift Beijing's baking standards, some of the big hotels have gone as far as to send their kitchen staff off to Europe for a crash course in making German black bread and Danish pastries. It's not surprising then that hotel prices tend to be high for tasty pastries. The delicatessen in the *Holiday Inn Lido* (Map 3) stocks delectable chocolate cakes and sourdough bread, as well as other western foods like mustard, Swiss cheese, salami and pickles.

Supermarkets The quality and range of goods on offer in Beijing's supermarkets has improved enormously in the past few years.

Certainly one of the best-stocked supermarkets is in the basement of *Scitech Plaza*, a department store on the south side of Jianguomenwai (Map 9).

On the eastern fringe of Jianguomenwai is the China World Trade Centre (Map 9) – head for the basement to find a fully fledged *Wellcome* supermarket, imported lock, stock and shopping carts from Hong Kong.

Close to the north-east corner of the Workers Stadium, there's the *Blue Bridge Market (lán qiáo dàshà* (Map 7) – it offers a range of Chinese and imported delicacies.

In the Sanlitun area is the duet *Friendship Supermarket (yǒuyì chāojí shāngchǎng)* and International *(guójì shāngdiàn)* (Map 7). This is Sanlitun's answer to the more famous Friendship Store on Jianguomenwai.

Just north of the Great Wall Sheraton Hotel is the *Lufthansa Centre* (Map 7). Yes, it *is* a German airline office, but it also has a shopping mall with a great supermarket in the basement packed with imported goods.

Entertainment

Back in the days of Mao, 'nightlife' often meant revolutionary operas featuring evil foreign and Kuomintang devils who eventually were defeated by heroic workers and peasants inspired by the 'little red book'. Fortunately, performances have improved considerably. The *China Daily* carries a listing of cultural evenings recommended for foreigners; also worth checking is *Beijing Weekend*, which is published once a week. Offerings include concerts, theatre, ethnic minority dancing and some cinema. You can make reservations by phoning the box office via your hotel, or by picking up tickets at CITS (for a surcharge) – or take a risk and just roll up at the theatre.

FILM

Chinese movies *(diànyǐng)* are out of the boring stage and starting to delve into some more contemporary issues, even verging on Cultural Revolution aftershock in a mild manner (see Film in the Facts About Beijing chapter). There are about 50 cinemas in the capital, but the big problem is that they show mostly Chinese films and these are seldom subtitled. The Chinese government limits imported foreign films to just 10 a year, which rather puts a damper on variety. On the other hand, films made in Hong Kong usually have English subtitles and Mandarin dialogue.

Some embassies have special film showings for foreigners only, but it's certainly hit or miss. If you really want to see foreign films, you may have to content yourself with STAR TV or video tapes.

Sophia's Choice (Map 7; ☎ 6500-4466), Sino-Japanese Youth Exchange Centre, 40 Liangmaqiao Lu, is a little to the east of Lufthansa Centre. This has Chinese films with English subtitles. The place is very popular with expats, but the big problem is that there is only one film showing every two weeks (always on a Friday night). Perhaps in the future the schedule will be increased, so ring up and check.

One cinema that generally shows most of the 10 imported foreign films is the Star Cinema. Premiers of foreign films are shown at many other theatres. The current line-up of cinemas in Beijing includes:

Dahua Cinema (dàhuá diànyǐng yuàn), 82 Dongdan Dajie, Dongcheng District (Map 11; ☎ 6525-5654).
Dizhi Cinema Hall (dìzhì lǐtáng), 30 Yangrou Hutong, Xicheng District (Map 5; ☎ 6617-1598)
Huashi Cinema (huāshì diànyǐng yuàn), 135 Xihuashi Dajie, Chongwen District (☎ 6712-2828)
Kaiming Cinema (kāimíng diànyǐng yuàn), 28 Zhushikouxi Dajie, Xuanwu District (Map 9; ☎ 6303-3350)
Shoudu Cinema (shǒudū diànyǐng yuàn), Xichang'an Jie (Map 8; ☎ 6605-5510)
Star Cinema (míngxīng diànyǐng yuàn), 537 Dongsibei Dajie, Dongcheng District (Map 11; ☎ 6405-8932)
Tuxin Cinema (túxīn diànyǐng yuàn), National Library, 39 Baishiqiao Lu, Haidian District (Map 10; ☎ 6841-5566 ext 5731)
Ziguang Cinema (zǐguāng diànyǐng yuàn), 168 Chaoyangmenwai Dajie, Chaoyang District (Map 7; ☎ 6502-2006)

THEATRE

Entertainment is cheap compared to the West, but prices are rising. Beijing is on the touring circuit for foreign troupes and these are also listed in the *China Daily*. They're somewhat screened for content, but they've been beefing up what's available. When Arthur Miller's *Death of a Salesman* was acted out by Chinese at the Capital Theatre, it was held over for two months by popular demand.

The same theatre staged some avant-garde Chinese theatre. It put on two plays by Gao Xingjian, incorporating theatre of the absurd and traditional Chinese theatrical techniques. One of the plays, *Bus-stop*, is based on eight characters who spend 10 years at a bus stop, only to discover that the service was cancelled long ago. It's either a vicious comment on the Beijing bus service, or a sly reference to Gao's stint in a re-education camp during the Cultural Revolution.

The likeliest venue for Western-style drama is the big *Capital Theatre* (Map 11; ☎ 6524-9847) *(shǒudū jùchǎng)* at 22 Wangfujing Dajie, otherwise known as the Beijing People's Art Theatre *(běijīng rénmín yìshù jùyuàn)*. The other likely spot is the *Central Academy of Drama Experimental Theatre* (☎ 6401-7894) *(zhōngyāng xìjù xuéyuàn shíyàn jùchǎng)*, at 39 Dongmianhua Hutong, Jiaodaokou, Dongcheng District (near the China Music Conservatory; Map 3).

CLASSICAL MUSIC

In the classic concert department they've presented Beethoven's Ninth Symphony played on Chinese palace instruments, such as tuned bells copied from those found in an ancient tomb. Other classical instruments are being revived for dance-drama backings.

If it's Beethoven or Mozart you want to hear, the place to go is the *Beijing Concert Hall* (Map 8; ☎ 6605-7006) *(běijīng yīnyuè tīng)*, at 1 Bei Xinhua Jie, Liubukou, Xichang'an Jie. Go to Hepingmen subway station and walk north; it's just before Xichang'an Jie. To hear (in Chinese) a listing of upcoming events dial ☎ 6204-7755 ext 56789, but only dial the extension number after you hear the beep. If you do this with a fax machine you can get a faxed schedule.

Another option is the *Central Music Conservatory* (Map 3; ☎ 6605-3531) *(zhōngguó yīnyuè xuéyuàn lǐtáng)*, 43 Baojia Jie, Xicheng District. There are also concerts in the lobby of the *Swissôtel*, also known as the *Hong Kong-Macau Centre* (Map 7; ☎ 6501-2288 ext 2213).

JAZZ & ROCK

Real culture shock strikes when East meets West over the music score. China's leadership had a hard time deciding how to react – in the beginning, Western music was vehemently denounced by the government as yet another form of 'spiritual pollution'. China's first concert featuring a foreign rock group

was in April 1985, when the British group *Wham!* was allowed to perform. The audience remained deadpan – music fans who dared to get up and dance in the aisles were hauled off by the PSB. Since then, things have become considerably more liberal and China has produced some notable bands (see Music in the Facts for the Visitor chapter).

Sanwei Bookstore (☎ 6601-3204), 60 Fuxingmennei Dajie (opposite the Minzu Hotel; Map 8) has a trendy bookshop on the ground floor, and on the 2nd floor is a charming Chinese teahouse. Jazz bands play here on Friday evening and classical music plays on Saturday night. Business hours are from 9.30 am until 10.30 pm, but the live music begins at around 8 pm. Cover charge is Y30.

Big rock concerts, when they happen, will be announced well in advance in Beijing's English-language publications which cater to foreigners. Possible venues include the *Workers Stadium* (Map 7; ☎ 6502-4558) *(gōngrén tǐyù guǎn)* in the Chaoyang District and the *Capital Gymnasium* (Map 10; ☎ 6831-3926) *(shǒudū tǐyù guǎn)* on the west side of the Beijing Zoo (Haidian District). Admission fees typically run from Y50 to Y250.

BARS

(jiǔbā)

New bars open and old ones close so rapidly in Beijing that even the city's licensing bureaucracy can barely keep up with the changes. What follows should be thought of as a brief snapshot in time – remember that if you find any great new nightlife spots, we hope you'll write and tell us about them.

Chaoyang District

The Chinese government may be claiming sovereignty, but the Chaoyang District of North-East Beijing appears to have been taken over by expats.

Sanlitun Lu Beijingers refer to Sanlitun Lu as the 'Golden Street', which may have as much to do with the price of real estate as the fact that business is booming here. Sanlitun

Lu must account for about 75% of the expat bar-cafes in town.

Jazz Ya (Map 7; ☎ 6415-1227) is an enormous place, and is one of the busiest expat night spots in Beijing. The official address is 18 Sanlitunbei Lu though it's actually hidden in a small alley just to the east of the main road. Open 10.30 am to 2 am (but only gets busy after 8 pm).

Public Space Bar & Cafe (Map 7; ☎ 6416-0759), 50 Sanlitun Lu, has a festive and pleasing atmosphere. It seems to have inspired its near neighbour, the *Upside Down Cafe* (Map 7; ☎ 6416-4191) at No 54 to adopt a similar motif.

Dai Sy's Pub (Map 7; ☎ 6416-4043) at No 48 is a very popular spot with outdoor tables. It opens early and is a good spot for lunch and dinner.

Bella's Gourmet Restaurant (Map 7; ☎ 6416-8785), 20 Sanlitun Lu, is one of the finest Italian restaurants in town. They do a mean bruschetta and spaghetti Napoli. Open 11 am to 2 pm and 6 to 11 pm.

Annie's Cafe (Map 7; ☎ 6594-2894) is an early opener at the intersection of Gongren Tiyuchangbei Lu and Nan Sanlitun Lu.

My Place Cafe (Map 7; ☎ 6415-3242) is on the east side of Sanlitun Lu and offers an Italian-German menu. Open 11 am to 2 am.

La Terrasse (Map 7; ☎ 6415-5578) is a popular place on the west side of Sanlitun Lu. The food is French, the ambience is Paris roadside cafe. Reservations are usually necessary on the weekend. It's open from 11 am to 11 pm.

The *Redwood Bar* (Map 7; ☎ 6462-9143) is a cosy place around the corner from Sanlitun Lu. It's in the Sanlitun Diplomatic Apartments, across from the Zhaolong Hotel. Jazz bands play here and the hamburgers can match anything in the West. Open 10.30 am to 2 am.

With their emphasis on hot barbecues and cool music, Brazilian establishments have quickly proven themselves to be a hit with Beijing's expats. *Parati Restaurant* (Map 7; ☎ 6595-8039), 120 Nan Sanlitun Lu, has great Brazilian food and an appropriately enthusiastic expat clientele.

Workers Stadium Area On the east side of the Forbidden City, the Workers Stadium is bordered by Gongren Tiyuchang Lu and Gongren Tiyuchangdong Lu, where you will find Chain's City Hotel plus six of Beijing's best pub/cafes.

On the north side of Chain's City Hotel is the *Owl Cafe* (Map 7; ☎ 6509-3833).

The first pub-cafe on the south side of Chain's City Hotel the *Park Bar* (Map 7; ☎ 6507-1331). It's a brand new place and still hasn't established its reputation yet, but it does look promising. At present, it appears to be more pub than cafe.

Next in line is the *Downtown Cafe* (Map 7; ☎ 6507-3407). The decor is more or less British (there's even a dartboard hidden in a corner). The cafe's owner is very friendly, and both food and service are excellent here. Open 11.30 am to 2 am.

Just a hop, skip and a jump to the south is *Frank's Place* (Map 7; ☎ 6507-2617), a beer-garden setting popular with expats. You may have to compete for space at the crowded outdoor tables on summer weekends. Steaks, burgers and big screen TV are major attractions. Open 11.30 am to 2 am.

The next place in this particular line-up is *Berena's Bistro* (Map 7; ☎ 6592-2628), at 6 Gongren Tiyuchangdong Lu. The food is mostly Cantonese, making this one of the few western-style pubs to dish up Cantonese cuisine. The cheap draft beer also helps drawn in the expat crowd. It's open from 11 am to 2 am.

On the opposite (west) side of Gongren Tiyuchangdong Lu is *Carella Cafe* (Map 7; ☎ 6501-6655), also known as the *Car Wash*. After a few too many drinks, inebriated foreigners have been know to run themselves through the car wash whether they have a vehicle or not. And it's perhaps the best spot in Beijing if you want to eat and drink outdoors. The house specialty is barbecued steak. Open 2 pm to midnight, but until 2 am on weekends.

The west side of the Workers Stadium is bordered by Gongren Tiyuchangxi Lu. At No 6 is the *Metro Cafe* (Map 7; ☎ 6552-7828). The place is famous for Italian cuisine. It's open 11.30 am to 2 pm, and from 5.30 pm to midnight. On Friday and Saturday nights business hours are extended until 2 am.

The south side of the Workers' Stadium is bordered by Gongren Tiyuchang Nanlu. This is home to the *Curry Cafe* (Map 7; ☎ 6506-7738) and its not hard to guess what's on the menu. San Miguel beer is offered three for the price of two every Friday.

The north side of the Workers' Stadium is ringed by Gongren Tiyuchangbei Lu. At No 4 is *Shanghai Nights* (Map 7; ☎ 6506-9988 ext 218). This place has free live jazz performances from 9 pm to midnight on Thursday, Friday and Saturday evenings.

Dongdaqiaoxi Jie This narrow lane is to the east of the Workers' Stadium but west of Sanlitun Lu (and runs parallel to it). A lot of pubs have set up shop here in the past few years and it's an extremely popular spot with expats. Most of the cafes here do not open until after 7 pm, and may stay open well past midnight. But darkening the horizon are rumours that the area is scheduled for a major redevelopment project. If this comes to pass, all of the following pubs could disappear literally overnight.

Enter the alley from the north side and walk south. The first place you encounter is the *Minder Cafe* (Map 7; ☎ 6500-6066). This is one of the largest and busiest pub-cafes in Beijing. Steak is the specialty, and there is live music on Thursday, Friday and Saturday evenings. Open 11 am to 2 am.

Nashville (Map 7; ☎ 6502-4201) is a large and busy place specialising in country music. There are live performances every night. Open 11 am to 2 am.

The *Hidden Tree* (Map 7; ☎ 6509-3642) is a chic restaurant-pub with a Greek and Spanish menu. It's one of the liveliest spots on this alley with good rock music. Open 5 pm to 1 am.

Cafe Cafe (Map 7; ☎ 6507-1331 ext 5127), Dongdaqiaoxie Jie, is another beer garden-sort-of-place with good pub grub. It's very popular but the atmosphere is quiet, making it a fine meeting, drinking and socialising spot. Open 11 am to 2 am.

North-East Third Ring Road The northeast section of the third ring road is called Dongsanhuan Beilu, and is a veritable expat playground.

The *Hard Rock Cafe* (Map 7; ☎ 6501-6688 ext 2571) is in the west wing of the Landmark Towers, 8 Dongsanhuan Beilu. Many have said that this place is not up to standard of its Hong Kong sister, but at least the decor is good. Cover charge is Y100 and it's open from 11.30 am to 2 am.

South of the Hilton Hotel is the *Amazon Bar* (Map 7; ☎ 6462-5044). A feature here is the Brazilian barbecue and live jazz at night. Open 11 am to 2 am.

All major hotels have coffee shops, but *Johnny's Coffee* (Map 3; ☎ 6461-0827), Xibahedongli Building 11, is worth a special mention. It's *the* place to get your cappuccino and croissants, and also boasts live jazz music. You'll find it opposite the International Exhibition Centre, and it's open daily from 10 am to 11 pm.

As anyone who has ever run a business knows, the devil is in the details. *Schiller's Bar & Restaurant* (Map 7; ☎ 6461-9276) seems to do it right – the place is notable for its diligent and friendly service. You'll find it on Liangmahenan Lu, across from the Lufthansa Centre. Open 7 am to 1 am.

The *CD Cafe* (Map 7; ☎ 6501-8877 ext 6156) not only has a good CD collection, but also live bands weekend nights. The veranda offers a superb view of bustling Beijing and is a great place to sit and drink when the weather is fine. It's open 11 am to 2 am.

Rick's Cafe (Map 7; ☎ 6502-2331 ext 554), is at 23 Dongsanhuanbei Lu (across from the Jingguang New World Hotel). In summer, you can enjoy Italian food on the open-air patio. Open 11 am to 10.30 pm.

Sprawled across the 1st floor of the huge Lufthansa Centre (Map 7) is the *Paulaner Brauhaus* (☎ 6465-3388 ext 5732), an excellent German pub cum restaurant. This place brews its own genuine German beer! Open 10 am until midnight.

It's easy to confuse the foregoing with the *Hof Brauhaus* (Map 7; ☎ 6591-4598), 15 Dongsanhuan Beilu, 100m south of the

Zhaolong Hotel. The decor and beer are German, but the food is an unusual German-Cantonese mix. Open 10 am until midnight.

Maggie's Bar (Map 7; ☎ 6463-1166 ext 2109), Xinyuan Lu (opposite the Kunlun Hotel) is *the* place to go if you want to stay out all night. Though there are no fixed times, though 6 pm to 5 am is usual.

TGI Friday's (Map 7; ☎ 6595-1380) is at 19 Dongsanhuanbei Lu (Third Ring Road). It could just about be considered a Mexican restaurant given the tortilla chips, quesadillas and fajitas that you'll find on the menu, but the steak and French fries give it an American flavour. Prices tend towards the high side but the food is awesome. Open 11 am until midnight.

The *Atrium Tea Garden* (Map 7; ☎ 6500-5566) at the Great Wall Sheraton Hotel is unusual for having live jazz music every evening from around 6 to 10 pm. Bands also perform during the Sunday luncheon buffet.

Jianguomenwai Jianguomenwai embassy-land is on the north side of Jianguomenwai Dajie, though some of the nightlife action spills out onto the south side of the boulevard. It's here you'll find good restaurants, bars and the worst traffic jams in Beijing.

Mexican Wave (Map 9; ☎ 6506-3961) is on Dongdaqiao Lu near the intersection with Guanghua Lu. This is one of Beijing's oldest and best established expat pub-restaurants. Mexican Wave serves set lunches (western not Mexican food) from noon until 2.30 pm; dinners (Mexican style) are from around 6 pm onwards. Prices here tend towards the upper end. Open 10 am to 2 am.

The *Hawaii Bar* (Map 9; ☎ 6594-0155), 6 Gaunghuaxili, is just around the corner from the famous Mexican Wave. The theme is 'Hawaii' though the brew and food are very cosmopolitan. Open 11 am to 11 pm.

The *Water Hole* (Map 9; ☎ 6507-4761), 3 Guanghuaxili, is also close to Mexican Wave. This place does good beer and burgers to the accompaniment of fine music. Open 10 am to 3 am.

The *Goose & Duck Pub* (Map 7; ☎ 6509-3777), Ritan Donglu, is a few blocks to the

north of Jianguomenwai Dajie. The decor is British but the food is mixed western. There is live music every Friday and Saturday from 9 pm until midnight, though it tends more towards classical – not a place to rage, but certainly very social.

El Gaucho Restaurant (Map 9; ☎ 6502-2198), 12 Jianhua Nanlu, is in an alley on the south side of Jianguomenwai Dajie (south of the Friendship Store). The cuisine is Brazilian. There is a special salad, barbecue and dessert menu for Y88 per person.

The *Phoenix Bar* (Map 9; ☎ 6502-2851), 12 Jianhua Nanlu, is in a lane south of the Friendship Store and next door to El Gaucho Restaurant. This is another place with live rock music on weekends, and the patio is really relaxing. Open 6 pm to 2 am.

Ritan Park (north of the Friendship Store) is the venue of several outstanding pubs. On the south side of the park is Guanghua Lu, where you'll find the all-new *John Bull Pub* (Map 9), which looks like it was cloned out of London. At 1 Guanghua Lu is the *Sunflower Jazz Club* (Map 9; ☎ 6594-0515), which has a beautiful setting in a Chinese-style courtyard and features great live bands (open 11.30 am to 2 am). Just next door is the *Sun Garden Bar* (Map 9; ☎ 6501-8942), also a nice Chinese courtyard with outdoor seating. On the north side of the park at 17 Ritanbei Lu is the *Elephant Bar* (Map 7; ☎ 6502-4013) which features Russian food and is open from 10 am to 2 am.

Ted's Cafe (Map 7; ☎ 6506-0329) at 56 Guangdongnan Jie is one block north of the China World Trade Centre. This smallish bar is open for lunch and dinner, and does some Chinese food specials. An interesting feature is the art exhibition daily between 2 and 6 pm. There is live music (usually blues and jazz) every Friday, Saturday and Sunday night. It's open from 11 am to 2 pm, and 5 pm to 2 am.

Others The over-the-top *San Francisco Brewing Company* (Map 7; ☎ 6500-7788 ext 7156) is west of the Beijing Asia Hotel (near the Second Ring Road). It shows movies on a large video screen every night starting from

7 pm (6 pm on Sunday) during which you can guzzle homemade brew for Y35per half litre. There are hamburgers on tap too. Open from 11 am until nobody is left in the place.

The *Rasput-Inn* (Map 7; ☎ 6507-1331 ext 5050) is at 1 Sanlitun Lu, alongside the Liangma River just south of the towering Capital Mansion. It's a Sino-Russian joint venture, featuring chess matches and satellite TV. Open 11 am to 11 pm.

Opposite the Canadian embassy on Dongzhimenwai at Xindong Lu is *Xanadu Bar & Grill* (Map 7; ☎ 6416-2272). The New Zealand steaks are unsurpassed. Open 11 am to midnight.

Haidian District

Most of Beijing's big universities are in the Haidian District. With lots of young students, the neighbourhood has a colourful collection of low-cost night spots.

NYX Sports Bar (Map 10; ☎ 6262-7260) is just 100m west of the Beijing University south gate. If not hungry, you can hang out and watch sports on the tube while munching on snacks and a drink for Y20. It's open 10.30 am to 2 am.

Kenny Rogers Roasters (Map 10) is a chain operation with rapidly proliferating branches around Beijing. You'll find one at 86 Haidian Lu. The restaurant features American-style barbecue including roast chickens and barbecued ribs, complete with salad, mashed potatoes and dessert. It has more of a fast food restaurant feel than bar atmosphere.

The *Character Bar* (Map 10) is in an alley at the east gate of Beijing University. The place certainly does have character with its rustic wooden decor and wall posters. Open from around 6 pm to 5 am.

Shadow Cafe and *Club X* (Map 10; ☎ 6261-8587), 31 Kexueyuan Nanlu, are two adjacent places which nicely complement one another. This very trendy hangout has live jazz bands performing from around 7 pm onwards. Cover charge is Y20.

Boss American Barbecue (Map 10; ☎ 6255-7825), 22 Haidian Dajie, is true to its name. Aside from the fine barbecued beef

meal, it's a good place to sit with a beer. Open 11 am to 11 pm.

Blue Jays Pub (Map 10), 40 Haidian Caochang, is a huge pub in an old warehouse. The extra space gives enough room to include a dance floor. Open 8 pm to 2 am.

Angel's Bar (Map 10; ☎ 6205-9580), 1 Wudaokou, is in the Korean enclave. The bar has an avant-garde feel and on the weekend there's live music from 8 pm to midnight.

Richmond Brewery (Map 10; ☎ 6253-1040), 29B Haidian Lu, is the largest bar in the Zhongguancun computerland. Open 10 am to 2 am.

Nook Bar (Map 10) is a most unusual place, having been constructed from several derelict buses welded together. Thus it's Chinese moniker, *Gonggong Qiche Jiuba* meaning 'the bus bar'. This pub has is now one of most chic spots in the Haidian area. You'll find it on Zhongguancun Lu, about 100m west of Xueyuan Lu.

Solutions Pub (Map 10) is opposite the west gate of Beijing University.

Wangfujing Area

For something different, take a look at the *Banpo Primitive Hotpot Beer Hut* (Map 11; ☎ 6525-5583), at 26 Wangfujing Dajie. It's designed to look like something out of *The Flintstones*, and you can try some primitive tasty treats like chocolate-covered ants and fried grasshoppers. They do, of course, serve hotpot, and there is plenty of conventional beer on tap. Open 10 am to midnight.

The *Traders' Bar* (Map 9), 28 Dongdanbei Dajie, is one of the largest pubs in town with a full two storeys of tables.

Branch No 2 of the *Richmond Brewery* is at 46 Dongdanbei Dajie. This large place has something of a teahouse-pub motif.

DISCOS
(dísīkě)

Some of Beijing's discos are open daily, but the vast majority are either closed or very quiet except on Friday and Saturday nights, when they rage.

The *Poacher's Inn* (Map 7; ☎ 6595-8357, 6500-8391) deserves top billing. Currently it's only open on Friday and Saturday nights from 9 pm to 4 am. There is live music on Saturday night starting from 9.30 pm. Poacher's is on an island in Tuanjiehu Park, which is on the third ring road in east Beijing (enter from the park's west gate). Admission costs Y50. If you'll be going to Poacher's every weekend, it's worthwhile to become a member, in which case admission costs Y30. Membership costs Y200 for six months, Y300 for one year.

NASA Disco (Map 10; ☎ 6203-2906) advertises 'advanced designed style appealing to radicals'. It can accommodate 1500 dancers, and on weekends they easily get that many. It's opposite the Jimen Hotel at the corner of Xueyuan Lu and Xitucheng Lu, just north of the third ring road.

JJ's Disco (Map 5; ☎ 6618-9305) is an enormous Chinese dance venue at 74 Xinjiekoubei Dajie. Your admission ticket buys you a chance in JJ's lottery – first prize is a bicycle. The cover charge is Y50 but rises to Y80 on Friday and Saturday night. This place is incredibly popular, and gay friendly.

Nightman Disco (Map 7; ☎ 6466-2562) is yet another ultra-hot gay and hetero spot. It's at the corner of Xikanhezhong Jie and Qisheng Nanlu. Admission is Y35 but rises to Y50 on weekends. Foreign students (with ID card) can get it free.

Jackson's (Map 10; ☎ 6201-7285), at 23 Chengfu Lu, Haidian District, is a low-budget disco appealing to students who lack rich parents. This place seems to be most busy on weekdays, which presumably means that the students spend their weekends studying (or partying elsewhere?).

The *Glass House Disco* (☎ 6500-3388 ext 5328) is an up-market disco on the 2nd floor of the towering Kunlun Hotel (Map 7). The glass facade makes it very clear where the name derived from. The cover charge is a cool Y100 on weekends when the place stays open until 3.30 am.

V-One Disco (☎ 6522-3931) is a very slick disco on the 3rd floor of the Wangfujing Grand Hotel (Map 11). Unfortunately, it's priced beyond the budget of most Beijing youth. If you show up before 8 pm it's only Y35, but after that women pay Y100 and men Y120 – on weekends there is an additional Y30 surcharge. Drinks are pretty pricey too.

Freezer Disco (☎ 6437-6688) is inside the plush Holiday Inn Lido (Map 3). It boasts foreign bands every evening, and on weekends stays open until 3.30 am. Lots of good lighting effects – you might need to wear sunglasses.

Talk of the Town (☎ 6505-2266) is something less than that. Basically, it's you're standard five-star hotel disco and the cover charge tends to keep the locals at bay. You'll find it in the China World Hotel (Map 9) at 1 Jianguomenwai.

It's more of the same at *Passion* (Map 7; ☎ 6500-5566 ext 219) in the Great Wall Sheraton Hotel at 10 Dongsanhuanbei Lu (Third Ring Road). Cover is Y100 weekdays and Y120 on weekends.

KARAOKE

(kǎlā OK)

Want to be a singing star? Karaoke bars give you an opportunity to stand in front of the microphone and croak along with a music tape. It's all the rage with Chinese, though to many Westerners it makes as much sense as underwater bungey jumping. As a foreigner, the Chinese audience will probably give you polite applause, though for the sake of international relations you should probably limit yourself to no more than two show-stopping numbers.

There's really no need to list the karaoke venues of Beijing because there are so many around town that you'll have a hard enough time avoiding them. Just remember that some of the karaoke places try to cheat customers in a big way, with outrageous service charges for 'talking to the hostesses'. Some of these hostesses hang around on the street near their place of employment and try to lure unsuspecting males (even domestic tourists) into going inside for 'a few drinks'. The bill for a couple of Cokes could amount to six months in wages for the average Chinese worker.

SONG & DANCE SHOWS
(chànggē/tiàowǔ biǎoyǎn)
These come in different varieties, from Western style to Chinese or occasionally in the style of China's ethnic minorities. They advertise in the *China Daily*, but may be cancelled despite being advertised in the newspapers.

For song & dance, the *Poly International Theatre* (Map 7; ☎ 6500-1188 ext 5682) *(bǎolì dàshà guójì jùyuàn)* in Poly Plaza – a hotel at 14 Dongzhimennan Dajie – is your best bet.

The Twenty-First Century Hotel (Map 7; ☎ 6466-3311 ext 3149) *(èrshíyī shìjì fàndiàn)* houses *Century Theatre (shìjì jùychǎng).*

ACROBATICS
(tèjì biǎoyǎn)
Two thousand years old, and one of the few art forms condoned by Mao, acrobatics is the best deal in town.

The best place to catch an acrobatics performance is probably the *Chaoyang Theatre (cháoyáng jù-chǎng)* (Map 7; ☎ 6507-2421) at 36 Dongsanhuanbei Lu (opposite Jingguang New World Hotel). Shows run from 7.15 to 8.40 pm and cost Y60.

The *Beijing Amusement Park* (Map 9), which is adjacent to Longtan Park and east of Tiantan Park, often has performances.

PUPPET SHOWS
(mù'ǒu biǎoyǎn)
Puppetry is known to have existed in China for more than 2000 years. While not exactly all the rage with the masses, most Chinese enjoy the occasional puppet show on TV.

Seeing a show live is possible, although the dialogue is in Chinese only. The *China Puppet Art Troupe* (☎ 6425-4846) has an auditorium at A1 Anhua Xili. If you can speak Chinese, ring up for information on the latest performances. Shows are between 6.30 and 8.30 pm. Admission costs Y50.

BEIJING OPERA
(jīngjù)
Special performances of Beijing opera are put on for foreigners nightly at 7.30 pm in the Liyuan Theatre *(líyuán jùchǎng)* which is inside the Qianmen Hotel (Map 8; ☎ 6301-6688). Ticket prices are from Y80 to Y180 depending on seat location. A mid-priced ticket buys you a seat at a table where you can enjoy snacks and tea while watching the show. The top-end tickets get you get better snacks and a table with a better location. Performances here last just 1½ hours with sporadic translations flashed on an electronic signboard. You can get dressed up in an opera costume (with full facial makeup) for a photo session.

Another establishment offering Beijing opera for foreigners is the Chang'an Grand Theatre (Map 9; ☎ 6510-1308) *(cháng'ān dà jùchǎng)* at 7 Jianguomennei Dajie (just west of the International Hotel). There is speculation that the Liyuan Theatre will eventually be closed and foreigners will move to this newer theatre. Prices and show times here are identical to what you'll find at the Liyuan.

The *Zhengyici Theatre* (Map 8; ☎ 6318-9454) *(zhèngyǐcí jùchǎng)* is a beautiful old restored theatre. Performances are from 7.30 to 9.15 pm and Y120, or Y230 if you want a complete dinner thrown in. The theatre is at 220 Qianmen Xiheyan Jie, a lane to the south of Qianmen Dajie. Hidden within this building is a wonderful teahouse, in itself worth a visit.

You can also see opera at the *Grand View Garden Theatre* (Map 8; ☎ 6351-9025) *(dàguānyuán jùchǎng).* The Grand View Garden is a park south-west of central Beijing. Performances are nightly from 7.30 to 8.40 pm and cost Y50 to Y80.

The *Lao She Teahouse* (Map 9; ☎ 6303-6830) *(lǎo shè cháguǎn),* 3rd floor, 3 Qianmenxi Dajie, has nightly shows although they're mostly in Chinese. The performances vary from comedy acts to musical routines. Prices depend on the type of show and where you sit – the range is typically from about Y40 to Y130. Show time is usually from 7.30 to 9.30 pm.

Along similar lines is the *Tianqiao Happy Teahouse* (Map 9; ☎ 6304-0617) *(tiānqiáo lè cháguǎn)* at A1 Beiwei Lu, Xuanwu District.

It's open daily except Monday from 7 to 9 pm and has an admission charge of Y180 to Y330. The lower price admission charge gets you snacks while the higher price includes a full-course dinner.

THEME PARKS

If you want to avoid being smothered by cotton candy (fairy floss) and blinded by popping camera flashes, it's important to avoid Beijing's theme parks on weekends

Beijing Opera

It used to be the Marx Brothers, the Gang of Four and the Red Ballet – but it's back to the classics these days. Beijing opera has been revived, and is still regarded as the *crème de la crème* of all the opera styles prevalent in China. Traditionally it's been the opera of the masses. The themes are usually inspired by disasters, natural calamities, intrigues or rebellions. Many have their source in the fairy tales and stock characters and legends of classical literature. Titles like *The Monkey King*, *A Drunken Beauty* and *A Fisherman's Revenge* are typical.

The music, singing and costumes are products of the opera's origins. Formerly, opera was performed mostly on open-air stages in markets, streets, teahouses or temple courtyards. The orchestra had to play loudly and the performers had to develop a piercing style of singing which could be heard over the throng. The costumes are a garish collection of sharply contrasting colours because the stages were originally lit by oil lamps.

The movements and techniques of the dance styles of the Tang Dynasty are similar to those of today's opera. Provincial opera companies were characterised by their dialect and style of singing, but when these companies converged on Beijing they started a style of musical drama called *kunqu*. This developed during the Ming Dynasty, along with a more popular variety of play-acting with pieces based on legends, historical events and popular novels. These styles gradually merged by the late 18th and early 19th centuries into the opera we see today.

The musicians usually sit on the stage in plain clothes and play without written scores. The *erhu* is a two-stringed fiddle which is tuned to a low register, has a soft tone and generally supports the *huqin*, a two-stringed viola tuned to a high register. The *yueqin*, a sort of moon-shaped four-stringed guitar, has a soft tone and is used to support the erhu. Other instruments are the *sheng* (a reed flute) and the *pipa* (lute), as well as drums, bells and cymbals. Last but not least is the *ban*, a time-clapper which virtually directs the band, beats time for the actors and gives them their cues.

There are four types of actors' roles: the *sheng*, *dan*, *jing* and *chou*. The sheng are the leading male actors, and they play scholars, officials, warriors and the like. They are divided into the *laosheng* who wear beards and represent old men, and the *xiaosheng* who represent young men. The *wensheng* are the scholars and the civil servants. The *wusheng* play soldiers and other fighters, and because of this are specially trained in acrobatics.

The dan are the female roles. The *laodan* are the elderly, dignified ladies such as mothers, aunts and widows. The *qingyi* are aristocratic ladies in elegant costumes. The *huadan* are the ladies' maids, usually in brightly coloured costumes. The *daomadan* are the warrior women. The *caidan* are the female comedians. Traditionally, female roles were played by male actors.

The jing are the painted-face roles, and they represent warriors, heroes, statesmen, adventurers and demons. Their counterparts are the *fujing*, ridiculous figures who are anything but heroic.

The chou is basically the clown. The *caidan* is sometimes the female counterpart of this male role.

Apart from the singing and music, the opera also incorporates acrobatics and mime. Few props are used, so each move, gesture or facial expression is symbolic. A whip with silk tassels indicates an actor riding a horse. Lifting a foot means going through a doorway. Language is often archaic Chinese, music is earsplitting (bring some cotton wool), but the costumes and make-up are magnificent. The only action that really catches the western eye is a swift battle sequence – the female warriors involved are trained acrobats who leap, twirl, twist and somersault into attack.

There are numerous other forms of opera. The Cantonese variety is more 'music hall', often with a 'boy meets girl' theme. Gaojia opera is one of the five local opera forms from Fujian province and is also popular in Taiwan, with songs in the Fujian dialect but influenced by the Beijing opera style.

When you get bored after the first hour or so, and are sick of the high-pitched whining, the local audience is with you all the way – spitting, eating apples, breast-feeding an urchin on the balcony, or plugging into a transistor radio (important sports match?). It's a lively prole audience entertainment fit for an emperor. ■

and holidays. On more sedate weekdays, you are far more likely to be able to enjoy what's on offer.

World Park (Map 3)
(shìjiè gōngyuán)

A monument to kitsch, Beijing's World Park has miniaturised reproductions of world-famous architectural wonders. Exhibits include France's Eiffel Tower, the pyramids of Egypt, America's Statue of Liberty and the White House. Since most Chinese are unable to travel abroad, this is as close as they can come to an overseas holiday. Perhaps this explains why the World Park is the largest theme park in China.

The park is south-west of the centre, about 3km due south of Fengtai railway station. If you don't plan to travel by taxi, you'll have to take a bus to Fengtai railway station and a minibus from there to the park. Bus Nos 309 and 406 also get you there.

China Ethnic Minorities Park (Map 3)
(zhōnghuá mínzú yuán)

Far more hallucinogenic than World Park, this is where you get to see China's 55 nationalities in their native habitat. Or rather, to see Han Chinese dressed up in minority costumes. Actually, 56 nationalities are represented if you count the highly dubious 'Gaoshan' nationality which is what China calls Taiwan's nine aboriginal tribes (the Taiwanese aborigines vehemently reject this label of course).

The park is also dressed up with small-scale imitations of famous Chinese scenic spots such as a fake Jiuzhaigou Dragon Waterfall. Ethnic holidays are re-enacted on the appropriate dates – the Water-Splashing Festival of the Dai minority, for example. Perhaps the best thing about the place is the opportunity to sample some ethnic minority speciality foods.

The China Ethnic Minorities Park is to the west of the Asian Games Village. Double decker bus No 2 goes there. The park is open daily from 8 am to 10 pm and admission costs Y60.

Western Han Tombs Museum (Map 3)
(xī hàn mù bówùguǎn)

Just 1km from World Park is the Western Han Tombs Museum. A taxi should cost no more than Y10. There are English-speaking guides here and most travellers find this place more worthwhile than the nearby World Park.

Beijing Amusement Park (Map 9)
(běijīng yóulè yuán)

China's answer to Disneyland, this one is a cut above other Beijing parklands largely because it's a joint-venture with an American company. The rides are in good nick, and the 360-degree rollercoaster is not for coronary patients. Admission is a rather steep Y45, but all rides and shows are included free except for the go-carts and boats. If you're under 140cm, you get in free (we're not making this up). The amusement park is on the west side of Longtan Park in the south-east corner of the city. Bus Nos 60 and 116 from Chongwenmen Dajie will get you there.

Tuanjiehu Park (Map 7)
(tuánjiēhú gōngyuán)

Baywatch in Beijing? Although the city lacks an ocean, it does have a 'wave pool' in Tuanjiehu Park. Sand has been imported to create a real beach scene. Surfing isn't feasible and you won't find dune buggies, but the park has proven popular.

There are a number of kiddy rides of the general amusement park category here, though none is particularly heart-stopping.

Another feature here is Poacher's Inn, Beijing's top-rated rage pub/disco.

The park is in the super-trendy Chaoyang District of north-east Beijing on the third ring road, very close to the Jingguang New World Hotel.

Shijingshan Amusement Park (Map 3)
(shíjǐngshān yóulè yuán)

It's one of Beijing's oldest amusement parks and used to be known for its rusted-out equipment. Fortunately, it's had a recent facelift. There's swimming in summer, and the water slides are the steepest (and thus most exciting) in Beijing. There are also Ferris wheels, roller coasters and other vomit-inducing contraptions.

Shijingshan Amusement Park is in the far west of Beijing on Shijingshan Lu (the western tentacle of Chang'an Dajie). Take the east-west subway line to Bajiaocun station.

Yuyuantan Park (Maps 8 & 10)
(yùyuāntán)

This is Beijing's largest water-theme park, though in truth the waterslides at Shijingshan are more exciting. Most of the water entertainment is on the west side of Yuyuantan (Jade Hole Pool) Park.

The east side of the park is notable for the palatial Diaoyutai State Guesthouse, the stomping ground of visiting diplomats and high-ranking cadres. Tourists wandering around in front of the main gate of the guesthouse will probably be politely told to get lost. Yuyuantan Park is just north of the Military Museum.

ZOO
Beijing Zoo (Map 10)
(běijīng dòngwùyuán)

For humans the zoo may be OK – an enormous park, pleasant lakes, good birds – but after you've been there you'll probably look as pissed-off as the animals. No attempt has been made to re-create their natural environments; they live in tiny cages with little shade or water. The Panda House, right by the gates, has four dirty specimens that would be better off dead, and you'll be happier looking at the stuffed toy pandas on sale in the zoo's souvenir shop. Parents can buy their children miniature plastic rifles with which they can practise shoot the animals. The children also enjoy throwing rocks at the monkeys and jabbing them with sticks. Some of the monkeys fight back by throwing their faeces.

The zoo got its start as a private garden for a Qing Dynasty aristocrat. Credit for creating the zoo goes to Empress Dowager Cixi – she imported 700 animals from Germany for her own amusement. The quality of the zoo hasn't improved much since Cixi's time,

though the number of animals has increased nearly 10-fold, making this the largest zoo in all of China.

Admission is a modest Y10, but there is an extra charge for the Panda House and other surcharges for special exhibits.

Getting to the zoo is easy enough; take the subway to the Xizhimen station. From there, it's a 15-minute walk to the west or a short ride on trolley bus Nos 105, 107 or 111.

Next to the zoo is the **Beijing Planetarium** *(běijīng tiānwén guǎn)* and the bizarre Soviet-style **Beijing Exhibition Hall** (Map 10) *(běijīng zhǎnlǎn guǎn)* which looks like a cross between a missile and a wedding-cake decoration.

SPECTATOR SPORT
(yùndòng huì)

The main place to see national (and rarely international) athletic competitions is the Asian Games Village (Map 3), otherwise known as the National Olympics Sports Centre. Another possibility is the Workers Stadium (Map 7) in the Sanlitun area.

Soccer
(zú qiú)

If there is any spectator sport the Chinese have a true passion for, it's soccer. Games are devoutly covered in the mass media and it's possible to see live matches when the team comes to Beijing. China has dreams of taking the World Cup eventually, and the government has been throwing money into the project by importing players and coaches. The season runs approximately from April through November.

Basketball
(lán qiú)

Although it hasn't quite fired the Chinese imagination in the way that soccer has, basketball does provide the masses with entertainment during the long winter when playing outdoors means risking frostbite. There are now two professional basketball leagues, and players have been recruited from the USA.

DAMIEN SIMONIS

GLENN BEANLAND

GLENN BEANLAND

DIANA MAYFIELD

Beijing has a wide range of culinary adventures for the hungry visitor: an ideal place to try China's unofficial national bird, Beijing duck (middle left), or to hoe into a Mongolian hotpot (bottom left), a northern Chinese speciality. There's also a smorgasbord of goodies available out in the open – either at noodle stalls (top) or in the many neighbourhood markets (right).

Pedal power and people power combine to make the bike Beijing's most popular beast of burden. The city's flat, wide streets are perfect for cycle sightseeing, and trusty steeds can be hired all over town.

Baseball

(bàng qiú)

The government has decided that the nation also needs a 1st class baseball team. To that end, has-been foreign players long forgotten in the West have been recruited to play on the Chinese team. The game is nowhere close to soccer or basketball when it comes to stirring up nationalistic zealotry, but it does provide yet another safe avenue for the masses to vent their frustrations.

Rugby

(gǎnlǎn qiú)

Known to the Chinese as 'olive ball' (because of the shape of the ball), rugby has yet to emerge as a serious sport among the Chinese. One reason perhaps is that it gets confused with American football (which also uses an 'olive ball'). Right now, the capital's sole rugby team is the Beijing Foreign Devils, but the Chinese have shown interest.

Martial Arts

(wǔshù)

Aside from boarding the buses, you can witness live demonstrations of martial arts skills at the Asian Games Village (Map 7). Otherwise, just rent a Hong Kong-made video.

Horse Racing

Gambling is illegal in China, but the government has made an exception for horse racing. The fact that the revenue goes into the government's coffers of course had nothing to do with this decision.

The race track *(pǎo mǎ chǎng)* (Map 2) is about 10km north of the Capital Airport, on the way to Huairou. It's on the east side of the road near the Beijing Golf Course and some new super expensive housing. Race times vary according to the season, so you will have to check with local punters for the current schedule.

It's Just a Game

Dictatorships have long recognised the potential of international sporting events to drum up nationalism and support for the government. China's government only seems to have become aware of this around 1990. Since then, millions of Yuan have been poured into crash programs to outfit China with an Olympic team. When the Eastern Bloc collapsed in 1991, the PRC government brought East Germany's famous (and infamous) Olympic coaches to China. From virtually nowhere, Chinese athletes have sprung onto the world stage and now typically walk away with a sizeable percentage of the medals at all international sporting events. To the Chinese, this is a source of great national pride.

What the Chinese public doesn't get to hear are the accusations about their athletes using steroids. The Chinese government claims their teams use nothing stronger than traditional herbal medicines, but they've been caught with their pants down on several occasions.

However, it takes more than drugs to make a star athlete – training is rigorous. Potential Olympic stars are identified at around age eight to 12, and are then subjected to five or more years of harsh round-the-clock training. Despite the promise of big rewards, the dropout rate is high and sometimes results in embarrassing defections and revelations when the team goes abroad.

China's big dream is to host the Olympic Games, but the dream has been frustrated by protests over China's human rights record. China didn't win any friends in 1993 when the International Olympic Committee rolled into Beijing to check out China's bid for hosting the year 2000 games – locals had their heat and hot water turned off because the government didn't want the committee to see the pollution caused by burning coal. Street urchins were bussed out of town during the three-day visit; workers were stopped and fined for gobbing on the footpaths; streets were cleaned, potholes were patched and squatters' shacks were bulldozed; and most people were prohibited from driving their vehicles so the committee would see no traffic jams. These tactics backfired – the foreign press soon picked up the story about how the visit was being stage-managed and the committee finally chose Sydney, Australia. However, China will no doubt put in a bid for the 2008 games. ■

Shopping

The Chinese produce some interesting items for export – tea, clothing and Silkworm missiles, although the latter are not generally for sale to tourists.

Within China the consumer boom has arrived, though the types of goods on offer are markedly different from what gets exported. A notable difference is that goods produced for the domestic market are often of inferior quality. There is an awful lot of junk on sale, such as zips which break literally the first time you use them, imitation discmans which last a week, electrical appliances which go up in smoke the first time they're plugged in. Keep in mind the Latin expression *caveat emptor* ('let the buyer beware'). Always test zips, examine stitching and, in the case of electrical appliances, plug them in and make sure they won't electrocute you before handing over the cash. Chinese sales clerks expect you to do this; they'll consider you a fool if you don't.

A word about antiques – most are fakes. There is, of course, nothing wrong with buying fakes as long as you're paying the appropriate prices. Remember that you need special certificates to take genuine antiques out of China. For fakes, be sure you have receipts to prove that they are fakes, otherwise the goods may get confiscated.

There are several notable Chinese shopping districts offering abundant goods and low prices: Wangfujing, Qianmen (including Dazhalan Hutong), Xidan, Dongsi and Silver St. More luxurious shopping areas can be found in the embassy areas of Jianguomenwai and Sanlitun. There are also some specialised shopping districts such as Liulichang and Zhongguancun (see further on for details).

Tourist attractions like the Forbidden City and Tiantan, as well as major hotels, have garish souvenir shops stocking arts and crafts. Otherwise, speciality shops are scattered all around the city centre. Stores are generally open from 9 am to 7 pm seven days a week; some are open from 8 am to 8 pm. Bargaining is not a way of life in the government stores, but it certainly is on the free market.

Down jackets are one of the best bargains you can find in Beijing and are essential survival gear if you visit northern China during winter. Good buys are stationery (chops, brushes, inks), prints, handicrafts, clothing and antiques. Small or light items to buy are silk scarves and underwear, T-shirts, embroidered purses, papercuts, wooden and bronze Buddhas, fold-up paper lanterns and kites.

New department stores have been springing up all around the capital. Most are open daily from 9 am to 9 pm.

A description of the shopping districts and bargains to be found follows:

WANGFUJING (Map 11)

This prestigious shopping street is just east of the Beijing Hotel – it's a solid block of stores and a favourite haunt of locals and tourists seeking bargains. For a while it became known as 'McDonald's St' because of the restaurant which once occupied the southern intersection (it was torn down in 1996 to make way for a new commercial project). In pre-1949 days it was known as Morrison St and catered mostly to foreigners. The name Wangfujing derives from a 15th-century well.

At the time of writing, Wangfujing was in the middle of a major three-year renovation. When finished, there will be an 800m-long underground street with three levels. It will be a solid mass of stores, restaurants, pubs and karaoke lounges.

Wangfujing's biggest emporium is the Beijing Department Store *(běijīng bǎihuò dàlóu)*. Of prime interest to foreigners is the Foreign Languages Bookstore *(wàiwén shūdiàn)* at shop No 235. This is not only *the* place in China to buy English-language books, but the music tape section upstairs is pretty impressive as well.

Soon to open is the Xindong'an Shopping Centre, which will be one of the biggest shopping malls in the land.

Wangfujing is a good place to buy film, though the Friendship Store also offers very competitive prices. You can even find slide film here, but check the expiry dates.

DONGSI (Map 11)

The very northern end of Wangfujing is known as Dongsi, and is a thriving commercial district. The centre of action is the Longfu Department Store *(lóngfú shāngyè dàshà)*, built on the site of the old Longfu Temple. Surrounding streets and hutongs are also very busy.

SILVER ST (Map 11)

A few blocks east of the Forbidden City in the Wangfujing area is Dongdanbei Dajie, which is also known as Silver St *(yín jiē)*. This is another area for fashionable clothes and small specialty shops.

XIDAN (Map 8)

Officially known as Xidan Beidajie, this street aspires to be a little Wangfujing. It's certainly a popular place with the locals. As for foreign tourists, the Xidan area (west of the Zhongnanhai compound) is a bit disappointing. There is no shortage of things to buy, but it's mostly of the 'cheap junk that breaks easily' variety. However, it's a good street for budget travellers in search of practical everyday items. The major store is the high-rise Xidan Shopping Centre *(xīdān gòuwù zhōngxīn)* (Map 5).

XICHENG DISTRICT (Map 8)

A couple of very interesting department stores have sprung up to the west of Xidan. About 1km to the west of Xidan by the Fuxingmen subway station is the plush Parkson Department Store *(bǎishèng gòuwù zhōngxīn)*.

If you're looking for Beijing's best, then look no further than the Vantone New World Shopping Centre *(wàntōng xīn shìjiè shāngchǎng)* at 2-8 Fuchengmenwai Dajie. If this American managed shopping mall looks like it was transplanted from Los Angeles, that's because it was. From Friday through Sunday it stays open until 10 pm. Take the circle line subway to Fuchengmen station.

DAZHALAN (Map 9)

If Wangfujing is too organised for you, the place to go and rub shoulders with the proletariat is Dazhalan, a hutong running west from the top end of Qianmen. It's a heady jumble of silk shops, department stores, theatres, herbal medicine, food and clothing specialists and some unusual architecture.

Dazhalan has a definite medieval flavour to it, a hangover from the days when hutongs (laneways) sold specialised products – one would sell lace, another lanterns, another jade. This particular one used to be called 'Silk Street'. The name Dazhalan actually refers to a wicket-gate that was closed at night to keep prowlers out.

In imperial Beijing, shops and theatres were not permitted near the city centre, and the Qianmen-Dazhalan District was outside the gates. Many of the city's oldest shops can be found along or near this crowded hutong.

Just off the beginning of Dazhalan at 3 Liangshidian Jie is Liubiju, a 400-year-old pickle and sauce emporium patronised by discriminating shoppers. Nearby is the Zhimielou Restaurant , which serves imperial snacks. On your right as you go down Dazhalan is a green concave archway with columns at No 5; this is the entrance to Liufuxiang, one of the better-known material and silk stores and a century old.

Another famous shop is the Tongrentang at No 24, selling Chinese herbal medicines. It's been in business since 1669, though it doesn't appear that way from the renovations. It was a royal dispensary in the Qing Dynasty, and creates its pills and potions from secret prescriptions used by royalty. All kinds of weird ingredients – tiger bone, rhino horn, snake wine – will cure you of anything from fright to encephalitis, or so they claim. Traditional doctors are available on the spot for consultation; perhaps ask them about fear of Chinese railway ticket offices (patience pills?).

Dazhalan runs west off Qianmen Dajie (Map 9). At the far end where the hubbub dies down there's a bunch of Chinese hotels. Dazhalan was once the gateway to Beijing's red-light district; folklore has it that the Tongzhi emperor would frequently disguise himself as a peasant, slip out of the Forbidden City at night and patronise the brothels. In 1949, the brothels were shut down and the women packed off to factories.

Qianmen Dajie, and Zhushikouxi Dajie leading off to the west, are interesting places in which to meander. On Qianmen Dajie there are pottery stores at Nos 99 and 149, ethnic-minority musical instruments at Nos 18 and 104, and a nice second-hand shop at No 117. At 190 Qianmen Dajie is the Army Store, just the place to stock up on green PLA overcoats and Snoopy hats.

LIULICHANG (Maps 8 & 9)

Not far to the west of Dazhalan is Liulichang, Beijing's antique street. Although it's been a shopping area for quite some time, only recently has it been dressed up for foreign tourists. The stores here are all designed to look as if they're straight out of an ancient Chinese village, and this makes for good photographs even if you don't want to buy anything.

Nearly all of the shops are State-run and seem to specialise in surly service and ridiculously high prices. Almost everything on sale looks antique, but most are fakes. Overall, you'll probably do better hunting for those olde worlde knick-knacks in Tianjin's antique market, which is particularly impressive on the weekend (see the Excursions chapter).

A few shops here also carve name chops, though again expect to pay 10 times the actual value.

Making a Name for Yourself

The traditional Chinese name chop or seal has been used for thousands of years. It's likely that people began using name chops because Chinese characters are so complex and few people in ancient times were able to read and write. And as a means of positive identification, chops predate ID cards and government computer files by a good millennium.

A chop served both as a unique personal statement and as a valid signature. All official documents in China needed a chop to be valid. Naturally, this made a chop quite valuable, for with another person's chop it was possible to sign contracts and other legal documents in their name.

Today, most Chinese are literate, but the tradition lives on. In fact, without a chop it is difficult or impossible to enter into a legally binding contract in China. A chop is used for bank accounts, entrance to safe-deposit boxes and land sales. Only red ink is used for a name chop.

If you live in China for work or study, you will almost certainly need to have a chop made. If you're staying a short time, a chop makes a great souvenir. A chop can be made quickly, but first you will need to have your name translated into Chinese characters.

There are many different sizes and styles of chops. Inexpensive small chops can be carved from wood or plastic, while expensive ones can be carved from ivory, jade, marble or steel. Most Chinese people have many chops to confuse a possible thief, though they run the risk of confusing themselves as well. One chop might be used for their bank account, another for contracts and another for a safe-deposit box. Obviously, a chop is important and losing one can be a big hassle.

Since the people who carve chops don't check your ID, it might occur to you that obtaining a fake or forged chop would be very easy. Indeed, it is. It's also a very serious crime in China. ■

Above: Chopping and changing. Shown on top is how Mao Zedong made his mark, while the seal below came from the chop of an emperor.

JIANGUOMENWAI (Map 9)

The Friendship Store *(yŏuyí shāngdiàn)*, at 17 Jianguomenwai, is the largest in the land – this place stocks both touristy souvenirs and practical everyday items. Not long ago, the Friendship Store was *the* place to shop in Beijing – so exclusive that only foreigners and cadres were permitted inside. But these days anyone can go in. The touristy junk is upstairs, but the ground floor is where the really useful items are found – tinned and dried foods, tobacco, wines, spirits, coffee, Chinese medicines and film. The book and magazine section is a gold mine for travellers long starved of anything intelligent to read. To the right are a supermarket and deli.

Just down the street from the Friendship Store is the newer Guiyou Department Store *(guìyŏu dàshà)*.

Scitech Plaza *(sàitè gòuwù zhōngxīn)* is a huge department store with an enormous selection – pragmatic shoppers will probably most enjoy the supermarket in the basement. Upstairs is where you'll find the more upscale items: the latest fashion, cosmetics and perfumes. Kitchen wares are in basement No 2. Scitech Plaza is on the south side of Jianguomenwai, opposite the CITIC building.

Landao (Blue Island) Department Store *(lándăo dàshà)*, 8 Chaoyangmenwai Dajie, is a new store to the north of Jianguomenwai. Prices here are relatively low. Just next door is the even newer Kama Department Store *(kămă shāngchăng)*.

The Xiushui Silk Market *(xiùshuĭ dōngjiē)* is on the north side of Jianguomenwai between the Friendship Store and the Jianguo Hotel. Because of the prestigious location amid the luxury hotels, this place is elbow to elbow with foreign tourists at times – go early to avoid crowds and forget it on Sundays. This market is one of the best places to pick up good deals in up-market clothing – everything from silk underwear and negligee to leather money belts. Bargaining is expected here, although it can sometimes be difficult because of all the foreign tourists willing to throw money around like water. Prices are marked, but

nevertheless the real price is sometimes only a quarter of the marked price.

Ritan Park is north of the Friendship Store – on the west side of the park and intersecting with it at a 90° angle is Yabao Lu Clothing Market. This place is enormous – no Beijing department store could hope to match the variety and low prices on offer here. Bargaining is *de rigueur*.

SANLITUN (Map 7)

The Sanlitun embassy compound is in northeast Beijing, close to the Great Wall Sheraton Hotel. Like Jianguomenwai, the stores here are decidedly up-market.

The gigantic Lufthansa Centre *(yānshā shāngchéng)*, also known as the Kempinski Hotel *(kăibīnsījī fàndiàn)*, falls into a category by itself, being Beijing's first flashy multi-storey shopping mall. You can buy everything here from computer floppy disks to bikinis (but who in China wears the latter?). A supermarket is in the basement.

HAIDIAN (Map 10)

The Haidian District is in the north-west part of Beijing, not far from the Summer Palace. The Beijing Language Institute is here, and the on-campus bookshop is a goldmine for students of Chinese.

Buried within the Haidian District is a neighbourhood called Zhongguancun. South of the Old Summer Palace, it's in the vicinity of Zhongguancun (bus stop). This area is Beijing's hi-tech answer to California's Silicon Valley. The big attractions here are the computer shops and some fledgling Internet cafes. If you're ready to put their money where your mouse is, Zhongguancun is Beijing's best venue for finding cheap knock-off PCs. While prices are reasonably low, so is the quality, and it's only recommended you buy a machine in Beijing if you'll be staying a while so that you can take advantage of the one-year warranty. Buy only desktop PCs in Beijing – if you need a portable machine, you'll do better to pick one up in Hong Kong, Taiwan or elsewhere.

Much of the world's Chinese-language software originates in Zhongguancun, and if

Dumb and Dharma

From grandma's mantlepiece at home to Beijing's temples and souvenir shops abroad, little 'Laughing Buddha' statues are China's most familiar religious icon. They're distinctive, cute and interactive (grandma might have told you to rub its ample belly for luck) – but how did a monk who ate nothing but a piece of fruit, a sesame seed and a grain of rice each meal for years get to be so fat and happy? It wasn't the dharma of enlightenment that did it for him (Buddhas elsewhere aren't typically round and jolly). Actually, the Laughing Buddha (*Mi lo fo*) is a case of a folktale meeting philosophy at the crossroads of Buddhist religion in China.

The folk tale concerns a certain 'Hemp Bag monk' who wandered the 10th century countryside around Chekiang. His ability to predict the weather made him popular with peasants, but most intriguing were his foolish Zen-like answers (the Chinese school of Ch'an became Zen in Japan) to questions about the contents and purpose of his bag.

A cult of sorts arose around the monk. Poems attributed to him spoke of his innumerable rebirths and of how 'men of the age' would not recognise him. Portraits drawn of him were said not to fade in the elements (just as the monk was cheerfully unaffected by extreme heat and cold).

The new cult inspired locals to re-examine old images of the Indian Buddha Maitreya (a sect had formed in the area during the 5th and 6th centuries AD in the hope that Maitreya, the 'Future Buddha', would return and restore the dharma to a dark age). When a story about the Hemp Bag monk emerged with details of Maitreya returning as a fool, laughing and rubbing his big belly, the transformation of the obscure monk into the revered Future Buddha, now in Laughing Buddha form, was complete.

Russ Kerr

Chinese computing is something you plan to do then check out the racks of CD ROMs. Pirating software is a big local industry too, but it's kept low-key because of China's international promises (usually broken) to protect intellectual property rights.

Just off Zhongguancun is the low-tech shopping area (for music tapes, clothes, food etc) known as Haidian Tushucheng.

The two big department stores in Haidian are Modern Plaza (*dāngdài shāngchéng*) and the Shuang'an Shopping Centre *shuāng'ān shāngchǎng*). The Modern Plaza is the fancier of the two.

In the northern outlying reaches of the Haidian District is the Price Smart Member Mart (*pǔ'ěr sīmǎtè huìyuán shāngdiàn*). This is Beijing's first experiment with a members-only megastore, and if the idea catches on then you'll probably see more such places. Prices are low and most items are sold in large sizes. You'll find it at 18A Xueqing Lu – Xueqing Lu is the northern extension of Xueyuan Lu.

MISCELLANEOUS

If there's anything you think is impossible to buy in Beijing, check out Watson's (*qū-chénshì*), in the Holiday Inn Lido (Map 3). This place sells every vitamin known to humankind: sunscreen (UV) lotion, beauty creams, balms, tampons and scented toilet paper.

The duty-free shop inside the airport departure hall is no bargain. Like other duty-free shops around the world, there's a heavy emphasis on macadamia nuts, perfume, watches and cameras. You can probably buy this stuff more cheaply at home. There are a still a few locally made commodities of interest such as scroll paintings and pottery, but the airport is hardly the place to get a once-in-a-lifetime deal on these items ... it *is* a handy place to get a plane from though.

If you're looking more to get away from the city and mingle with the masses, you could always try shopping at the Urban-Rural Trade Centre (Map 8) (*chéngxiāng màoyì zhōngxīn*).

Excursions

All the places in this chapter can be visited as day trips from Beijing, although in several cases you might find it worth your while to stay overnight.

TOMBS

Dying is a big deal in China, especially if you're an emperor. Not willing to accept poverty in the next world, the emperors decided they could take it all with them. Around Beijing there are three major tomb sites, and each tomb holds (or held) the body of an emperor, his wives, girlfriends and funerary treasures. At least you have to admit that the royal families went out in style. All the tombs have been plundered at one time or other, but recent efforts at restoration have benefited China's cultural pride, not to mention the tourist industry.

The three tomb sites around Beijing open to tourists are the Ming Tombs, Western Qing Tombs and Eastern Qing Tombs. Of the three, the Ming Tombs are by far the most frequently visited.

Ming Tombs

(shísānlíng)

The travellers' consensus on the Ming Tombs (see Ming Tombs Map & Map 2) is that you'd be better off looking at a bank vault which is, roughly, what the tombs are. However, the scenery along the way is charming.

The 7km road known as the 'spirit way' starts with a triumphal arch then goes through the Great Palace Gate, where officials had to dismount, and passes a giant tortoise (made in 1425) bearing the largest stele in China. This is followed by a guard of 12 sets of stone animals. Every second one is in a reclining position, legend has it, to allow for a 'changing of the guard' at midnight. If your tour bus driver whips past them, insist on stopping to look – they're far more interesting than the tombs. Beyond the

stone animals are 12 stone-faced human statues of generals, ministers and officials, each distinguishable by headgear. The stone figures terminate at the Lingxing Gate.

Unfortunately, the Chinese drivers don't care much about the statues and usually prefer to spend half an hour at the Shisangling (Ming Tombs) Reservoir. The reservoir itself is dead boring, though the history behind it is mildly interesting. It was Mao's brainchild, constructed in 1958 as part of a massive nationwide water conservancy project. The reservoir was constructed entirely by hand using armies of 'volunteers' working around the clock. Mao himself showed up and shovelled dirt for 30 minutes while the event was recorded for the world news media. Even some foreign embassy staff based in Beijing lent a hand while the cameras rolled. It was great demonstration of socialist solidarity, and a precursor to the disastrous 'Great Leap Forward' launched later that year.

Thirteen of the 16 Ming emperors are buried in this 40-sq-km area, hence it's other name: the Thirteen Tombs. Dingling was the first of the tombs to be excavated and opened to the public. Two others, Changling and Zhaoling, are now open to the public.

Dingling, the tomb of Emperor Wan Li (1573–1620), is in fact the second largest tomb. Over six years the emperor used half a million workers and a heap of silver to build his necropolis and then held a wild party inside the completed chambers. It was excavated between 1956 and 1958 and you can now visit the underground passageways and caverns. The underground construction covers 1195 sq metres, is built entirely of stone and is sealed with an unusual lock stone. The tomb yielded 26 lacquered trunks of funerary objects, some of which are displayed on site, while others have been removed to Beijing's museums and replaced with copies.

Wan Li and his royal spouses were buried in double coffins surrounded by chunks of uncut jade. The jade was thought to have the power to preserve the dead (and could have bought millions of bowls of rice for starving peasants), or so the Chinese tour literature relates. Meanwhile experts on cultural relics as well as chefs are studying the ancient cookbooks unearthed from Dingling with a view to serving Wan Li's favourite dishes to visitors, using replicas of imperial banquet tableware.

Another tomb, Changling, was started in 1409 and took 18 years to complete. This is the final resting place of Emperor Yong Le. According to the story, 16 concubines were buried alive with his corpse. This was the second of the Ming Tombs to be excavated and opened to the public. It consists mainly of displays of funerary objects.

Zhaoling is the ninth of the Ming Tombs and was opened to visitors in 1989. This is the tomb of Emperor Longqing, who died in 1572, and three of his wives.

Aware of the fact that many visitors consider the tombs a bit of a wipeout, the Beijing municipal government is busy dressing up the area. New facilities include a golf course, the Nine Dragons Amusement Park, an archery and rifle range, shops, cafes, a 350-room hotel, swimming pool, aquarium, camp site, picnic area, fountain (with a 200m waterjet), fishing pier (on the Ming Tombs Reservoir), helicopter rides, racecourse, cross-country skiing area and Mongolian yurts for use as a summer hotel.

The **Ming Dynasty Waxworks Palace** (*míng huáng làxiàng gōng*) is the notorious wax museum that foreigners are herded through if they book a Ming Tombs tour with a Chinese group. For what it's worth, this is claimed to be the largest wax museum in the world. The wax figures are all well-known Chinese historical personages, and they will 'talk' to you thanks to some cleverly hidden speakers.

Just next door to the above-mentioned Ming Dynasty Waxworks Palace is the Qing dynasty's rejoinder, the **Ancient Beijing Mini-Landscape Park** (*lǎo běijīng wēisuō*

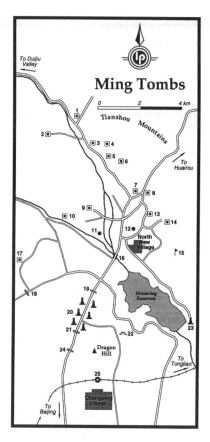

jǐngguǎn). This is another must-see for the Chinese but leaves foreigners yawning. The park contains a full-fledged model of Beijing as it used to be. Conspicuously absent from the model áre the pubs in Sanlitun and the backpacker dormitories.

About 10km east of Changping at Xiaotangshan and also on some of the Great Wall Tour circuits is the **China Aviation Museum** (*zhōngguó hángkōng bówùguǎn*). Chairman Mao's personal shuttle plane is on display here, but most of the aircraft on show were designed for destroying the Motherland's arch enemies.

Ming Tombs 十三陵

1 Tailing Tomb
泰陵
2 Kangling Tomb
康陵
3 Maoling Tomb
茂陵
4 Yuling Tomb
裕陵
5 Qingling Tomb
庆陵
6 Xianling Tomb
献陵
7 Changling Tomb
长陵
8 Jingling Tomb
景陵
9 Dingling Tomb
定陵

10 Zhaoling Tomb
昭陵
11 International Friendship
Forest
国际友谊林
12 Heliport
空中旅游机场
13 Yongling Tomb
永陵
14 Deling Tomb
德陵
15 Beijing International
Golf Club
北京国际高尔夫球具植
16 Seven Arch Bridge
七孔桥
17 Siling Tomb
思陵
18 Small Palace Gate
小宫门

19 Lingxing Gate
棂星门
20 Stone Statues
石像生
21 Great Palace Gate
大宫门
22 Fairy Cave
仙人洞
23 Shisanling Reservoir
Memorial
十三陵水库纪念碑
24 Stone Arch
石牌坊
25 Changping North
Railway Station
昌平北火车站

Getting There & Away The Ming Tombs lie 50km north-west of Beijing and 4km from the small town of Changping. Tour buses make their early-morning departures from Qianmen, the Chongwenmen Hotel area, Landao Shopping Centre (Dongdaqiao) and the Zhanlanguan Lu Tour Bus Station near the Beijing Zoo. The tour will likely include Badaling as well as the wax museum and other peculiar sights. You can also go by local bus. From Deshengmen, take bus Nos 919 or 920 to Changping – you may need a taxi for the last stretch.

Western Qing Tombs
(qīng xīlíng)
The Western Qing Tombs are in Yixian County, 110km south-west of Beijing. If you didn't see enough of Dingling, Yuling, Yongling and Deling at the Ming Tombs, there's always Tailing, Changling, Chongling and Muling at the Western Qing Tombs.

The vast tomb area houses the corpses of the emperors, empresses, princes, princesses and other members and hangers-on of the royal family. The tomb of Emperor Guangxu (reigned 1875 – 1908), called Chongling, has been excavated. Guangxu's was the last of

the imperial tombs, constructed between 1905 and 1915.

Not many tours go to these tombs, so your only hope may be to share a chartered taxi.

Eastern Qing Tombs
(qīng dōng líng)
The Eastern Qing Tombs (see Eastern Qing Tombs Map & Map 2) valley could be called Death Valley, housing as it does five emperors, 14 empresses about 130 imperial consorts. In the surrounding mountains are buried princes, dukes, imperial nurses etc.

The approach to the tomb area is a common 'spirit way', similar to that of the Ming Tombs but with the addition of marble-arch bridges. The materials for the tombs come from all over China, including 20-tonne logs which were pulled over iced roads, and giant stone slabs.

Emperor Qianlong (reigned 1736–1795) started preparations for his inevitable demise when he was only 30, and by the time he was 88 the old boy had managed to use up 90 tonnes of his silver on the affairs of the hereafter. How the emperor's accountant managed to deal with this great tax write-off in the sky is anybody's guess.

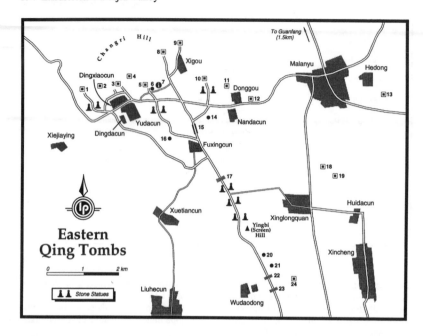

Qianlong's resting place ended up covering about 500 sq metres. Some of the beamless stone chambers of the tomb are decorated with Tibetan and Sanskrit sutras; while the doors bear bas-relief bodhisattvas.

Empress Dowager Cixi also got a head start. Her tomb, Dingdong, was completed some three decades before her death. The phoenix (the symbol of the empress) appears *above* that of the dragon (the symbol of the emperor) in the artwork at the front of the tomb. On other tombs, such symbols appear side by side. Sadly, both tombs were plundered in the 1920s.

In Zunhua County, about 125km east of Beijing, the Eastern Qing Tombs offer a lot more to see than the Ming Tombs, although you may be a little jaded after the Forbidden City.

Getting There & Away It's a rather long haul by public bus to the Eastern Qing Tombs. Tour buses are considerably more comfort-able than the local rattletraps and take three or four hours to get there; you have about three hours on site. Some people actually prefer to go from Tianjin.

DUIJIU VALLEY
(duìjiù yù)

After you've dried out from the trip to the Ming Tombs, you might want to explore a scenic hiking area which is just 10km to the north. Duijiu (Pestle & Mortar) Valley (Map 2) is notable for its small river, waterfalls and pools set out among the boulders. Although the area is well-known to the Chinese and the car park area is crowded, rather few visitors venture very far up the gorge because the journey has to be made on foot. The upper end of the gorge becomes quite steep, but should be well within the capabilities of the average traveller.

To reach the entrance, you should take a taxi from the Ming Tombs. Once there, it's a Y10 admission fee to get in.

Eastern Qing Tombs 清东陵	8 Xiaoling Tomb 孝陵 9 Xiaodong Tomb 孝东陵	17 Longfeng (Dragon- Phoenix) Gate 龙凤门 18 Huifei Tomb
1 Dingling Tomb 定陵 2 Dingfei Tomb 定妃陵 3 Dingdong (Empress Cixi) Tomb 定东陵 4 Yufei Tomb 裕妃陵 5 Yuling (Emperor Qianlong) Tomb 乾隆裕陵 6 Foreign Guest Reception Centre 外宾招待中心 7 Tourist Office 旅游 事处	10 Jingling Tomb 景陵 11 Jingfei Tomb 景妃陵 12 Taifei (Two Concubines of Emperor Kangxi) Tombs 太妃陵 13 Princess Tomb 公主陵 14 Stele Tower 石碑楼 15 Seven-Arch Bridge 七孔桥 16 Stele Tower 石碑楼	惠妃陵 19 Huiling Tomb 惠陵 20 Stele Tower 石碑楼 21 Robing Hall 理服廊 22 Great Palace Gate 大宫门 23 Stone Archway 石孔门 24 Zhaoxi Tomb 昭西陵

TANZHE TEMPLE
(tánzhè sì)

About 45km directly west of Beijing is Tanzhe Temple (Map 2), the largest of all the Beijing temples, occupying an area 260m by 160m. The Buddhist complex has a long history dating as far back as the 3rd century (Jin Dynasty). Structural modifications date from the Tang, Liao, Ming and Qing dynasties. It therefore has a number of features such as dragon decorations, mythical animal sculptures and grimacing gods – all of which are no longer found in most temples in the capital.

Translated literally, Tanzhe means Pool Cudrania. The temple takes its name from its proximity to the Dragon Pool *(lóng tán)* and some rare Cudrania *(zhè)* trees. Locals come to the Dragon Pool to pray for rain during droughts. The Cudrania trees nourish silkworms and provide a striking yellow dye, and the bark of the tree is believed to cure women of sterility, which may explain why there are so few of these trees left at the temple entrance.

The Tanzhe Temple complex is open to the public daily from 8.30 am until 6 pm. To get there, to take bus No 336 from Zhanlanguan Lu, which runs off Fuchengmenwai Dajie

(north-west of Yuetan Park), to the terminal at Mentougou and then hitch or take a taxi.

A more direct route to the temple is available by taking bus No 307 from Qianmen to the Hetan terminal and then a numberless bus to the temple. Alternatively, you can take the subway to Pingguoyuan, then bus No 336 to Hetan and then the aforementioned numberless bus to the temple.

JIETAI TEMPLE
(jiètái sì)

About 10km south-east of the Tanzhe Temple is a compound similar to Tanzhe, only smaller. The name Jietai Temple (Map 2) roughly translates as the Temple of Ordination Terrace. The temple was built around 622 AD, during the Tang Dynasty, with major improvements made by later tenants during the Ming Dynasty. The main complex is dotted with ancient pine trees, all of which have been given quaint names. One of these, Nine Dragon Pine, is claimed to be over 1300 years old.

It is approximately 35km from Jietai Temple to Beijing, and the journey out here is usually combined with a visit to Tanzhe Temple.

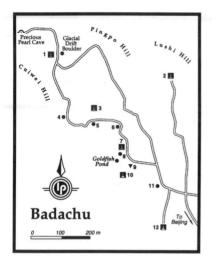

Badachu

0   100   200 m

BADACHU

(bādàchù)

Badachu (see Badachu Map & Map 2) is also known as Eight Great Temples *(bādà sì)* or Eight Great Sights. It has eight monasteries or temples scattered in wooded valleys. The Second Site has the Buddha's Tooth Relic Pagoda, built to house the sacred fang and accidentally discovered when the Allied army demolished the place in 1900.

The mountain has numerous apricot trees, which makes for some cheerful and sweet-smelling scenery around April when the trees briefly bloom.

Since 1994, the ancient culture has been dressed up with an unusual amusement park adventure – a terrifying roller-toboggan course. A chairlift will carry you up the hill to the top of the roller-toboggan course. The rollerway has a length of 1700m and it can send you hurtling downwards at speeds of up to 80 km/h.

Admission to Badachu costs around Y5. The easiest way to reach it is by taking the east-west subway to Pingguoyuan and catching a taxi (for Y10) from there. You can also take bus No 347, which runs from Badachu to Beijing Zoo.

FAHAI TEMPLE

(fǎhǎi sì)

A little further to the west of Badachu is the Fahai Temple (Map 2). Set among the fir trees on Maanshan (Saddle Hill), the temple is notable for its enormous altar (10m by 10m with a height of 3.3m).

To get there, take the East-West subway line to the Pingguoyuan subway. Then it's either bus No 311 (exit at the Moshikou stop) or take a taxi. The temple is open daily from 9 am to 5 pm. Admission is Y10.

STONE FLOWER CAVE

(shí huā dòng)

By following the same highway westwards that takes you to Jietai Temple you'll reach Stone Flower Cave (Map 2). This is considered the most scenic set of caves in the Beijing area – so of course it's lit with coloured lights and has souvenir stands outside.

The cave is 55km south-west of central Beijing. From the Tianqiao Bus Station take bus No 917 to Fangshan and from there get a tour bus or taxi. Admission to the caves is Y64 for foreigners.

MARCO POLO BRIDGE

(lúgōuqiáo)

Publicised by the great traveller himself, the Marco Polo Bridge (Map 3) is made of grey marble, is 260m long and has over 250 marble balustrades supporting 485 carved stone lions. First built in 1192, the original arches were washed away in the 17th century. The bridge is a composite of different eras and was widened in 1969. It spans the Yongding River near the little town of Wanping.

About than 200 years before CITS started shoving travelles in this direction, the Qing Dynasty overlord, Emperor Qianlong, was doing his bit to promote the bridge. In 1751 he put his calligraphy to use and wrote some poetic tracts about Beijing's scenic wonders. His *Morning Moon Over Lugou Bridge* is now engraved into stone tablets and placed on steles next to the bridge. On the opposite bank is a monument to Qianlong's inspection of the Yongding River.

Despite the publicity campaign by Marco and Qianlong, the bridge wouldn't rate more than a footnote in Chinese history were it not for the famed 'Marco Polo Bridge Incident' which ignited a full-scale war with Japan.

On the night of 7 July 1937, Japanese troops illegally occupied a railway junction outside Wanping, which prompted Japanese and Chinese soldiers to start shooting at each other, and that gave Japan enough of an excuse to attack and occupy Beijing (then Peking). The Chinese were more than a little displeased by this turn of events, especially since Japan had already occupied Manchuria and Taiwan. The day of the Marco Polo Bridge Incident is considered by China watchers to be the day the Chinese became part of WWII.

A relatively recent addition to this ancient site is the Memorial Hall of the War of Resistance Against Japan, built in 1987. Besides Qianlong's Morning Moon stele, there is also a stele commemorating his inspection of the Yongding River. Also on the site is the Wanping Castle, the Daiwang Temple and a tourist hotel.

You can get to the bridge by taking bus No 339 from Lianhuachi Bus Station. Another option is bus No 917 which can be picked up at Tianqiao bus station (west of Tiantan Park) and goes straight to the bridge. By bicycle it's about a 16km trip one way.

PEKING MAN SITE

(zhōukǒudiàn)

The old stamping ground of those primeval Chinese, the Peking men (and women, of course), Zhoukoudian Village is approximately 50km south-west of Beijing at the town of Fangshan (see Peking Man Site Map & Map 2).

There's an 'Apeman Cave' on a hillside here above the village, along with several lesser caves and a number of archaeological dig sites. There is also a fossil exhibition hall, although you'd have to be a bit of a fossil yourself to hang around here for more than 15 minutes.

Skullduggery

There is an interesting story behind the skull of the Peking Man. Early this century, villagers around Zhoukoudian found fossils in a local quarry and took them to the local medicine shop for sale as 'dragon bones'. This news got back to Beijing and archaeologists – foreign and Chinese – poured in for a dig.

Many years later, a molar was extracted from the earth, and the hunt for a skull was on. They finally found it in the late afternoon of December 1929, *Sinanthropus pekinensis* – a complete skull cap. The cap was believed to be over half a million years old – if so, then it rates as one of the missing links in the evolutionary chain.

Unfortunately, research on the skull was never carried out. When the Japanese invaded in 1937 the skull cap was packed away with other dig results and the whole lot swiftly vanished. The Chinese accused the Americans, the Americans accused the Japanese and the mystery remains. Other fragments surfaced from the site after 1949, but no comparable treasure was found. ∎

Peking Man Site

0   100   200 m

Peking Man Site 周口店猿人遗址

1 No 2 Dig Site
  第二地点
2 Peking Man Exhibition Hall
  北京猿人展览馆
3 Hostel
  招待所
4 Foreigners' Reception Room
  外宾接待室
5 Car Park
  停车场
6 Front Gate
  大门
7 Pigeon Hall Cave
  鸽子堂洞
8 Apeman Cave
  猿人洞
9 Upper Cave
  山顶洞
10 No 15 Dig Site
  第十五地点
11 No 4 Dig Site
  第四地点
12 No 12 Dig Site
  第十二地点
13 No 3 Dig Site
  第三地点
14 Zhoukoudian Railway Station
  周口店火车站

There are three distinct sections to the Peking Man exhibition hall: one dealing with pre-human history, one introducing the life and times of Peking Man, and the last dealing with recent anthropological research. There are ceramic models, stone implements and the skeletons of several prehistoric creatures. The exhibition hall is open daily from 9 am to 4 pm.

To get there, you could get a suburban train from Beijing south railway station (also known as Yondingmen) and get off at Zhoukoudian. Alternatively, bus No 917 from Tianqiao bus station (on the west side of Tiantan Park) goes to Fangshan, from where you can take a bus or taxi to the site.

Another possibility is bus No 309 from Changchun Jie (the south-west corner of the Second Ring Road); or bus No 339 from Lianhuachi bus station. If combined with a trip to Tanzhe Temple and the Marco Polo Bridge, approaching the site by taxi is certainly not unreasonable considering the time you'll save.

There is also a guesthouse on the site where archaeological groupies can spend the night with Peking Man ... well, in a manner of speaking.

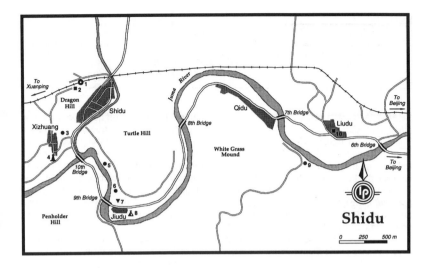

Shidu 十渡

PLACES TO STAY
2 Longshan Hotel
    龙山饭店
8 Campground
    帐篷村
10 Liudu Hotel
    六渡旅馆

OTHER
1 Shidu Railway Station
    十渡火车站
3 Dragon Mountain Buddhist
    Character
    龙山佛字
4 Anti-Japanese War
    Memorial
    平西抗日烈士纪念馆

5 Rowboat Rentals &
    Swimming Area
    划船场
6 Viewing Buddhas Pavilion
    望佛亭
7 Xiaoyao Restaurant
    逍遥餐厅
9 Wangyu Pavilion
    望浴亭

SHIDU
(shídù)
This is Beijing's answer to Guilin. The pinnacle-shaped rock formations, small rivers and general beauty of the place make it a favourite spot with expatriate students, diplomats and business people.

Situated 110km south-west of central Beijing, Shidu (see Shidu Map & Map 2) means Ten Ferries or Ten Crossings. Before the new road and bridges were built, it was necessary to cross the Juma River 10 times while travelling along the gorge between Zhangfang and Shidu village.

The gorge can be visited as a day trip, but it's really worth spending one night. The

Longshan Hotel (lóngshān fàndiàn), opposite the Shidu railway station, is the main accommodation. Down near Jiudu (Ninth Ferry) there is a camp site, conveniently located on a flood-plain.

To get to Shidu, take bus No 917 from Beijing's Tianqiao bus station (west side of Tiantan Park). Get off the bus in Fangshan and then get another minibus or taxi.

Getting to Shidu is fastest by train, but there are only two departures daily. Trains leave from the Beijing South railway station (probably the only chance you'll have to use this station). If you take the morning train, the trip can be done in one day. See the following train schedule for more details.

Beijing – Shidu Train Schedule				
No	From	To	Depart	Arrive
795	Beijing South Railway Station	Shidu	6.38 am	9.03 am
897	Beijing South Railway Station	Shidu	5.40 pm	8.10 pm
796	Shidu	Beijing South Railway Station	7.42 pm	10.02 pm
898	Shidu	Beijing South Railway Station	9.07 am	11.28 am

SHANGFANG MOUNTAINS

(shāngfāng shān)

The scenic Shangfang Mountains (Map 2) are approximately 70km south-west of central Beijing. It's not far north of the highway between the Peking Man Site and Shidu.

A major attraction is the Yunshui Caves *(yúnshuǐ dòng)*. Don't expect to be the first human to explore these depths because you'll find coloured lights, souvenir shops and snack bars. About 1km to the east of the cave entrance is the Doulü Temple, a large monastery complex in the foothills.

The best way to reach the mountains is to take a train from the Beijing South Station and get off at Gushankou.

YUNJU TEMPLE

(yúnjū sì)

The Chinese have a long history of establishing Buddhist shrines in caves, although the really legendary shrines (Datong, Luoyang, Dunhuang etc) are far from Beijing.

Just south of the Shangfang Mountains are some limestone hills riddled with small cave temples, some of which date back to the Sui Dynasty (589–618 AD). The best-known cave temple in the area is the Yunju (Cave Dwelling) Temple (Map 2). China's State-controlled Buddhist association declared in 1987 that a box found in the temple contained two bone fragments that belonged to none other than Siddhartha Gautama (563–483 BC) himself, the founder of Buddhism. Of course, lacking a DNA analysis of the Great Siddhartha, it would be rather difficult to prove or disprove this claim. Although the two pieces of Siddhartha are in fact hardly bigger than a grain of sand, the 'discovery' has greatly changed the temple's fortunes.

Money has poured into the temple's coffers from various overseas Buddhist asso-

ciations. This has set off quite a construction boom. In 1990 a new structure was erected to house more than 77,000 engraved wooden blocks containing the Chinese *tripitaka* (Buddhist scriptures). These tripitaka did not originate in Yunju Temple, but have been shipped in from other collections throughout China, such as the one at Beijing University. Only eight sets of tripitaka are known to exist in China.

To get there, at Tianqiao bus station (west side of Tiantan Park) in Beijing take bus No 917 to Fangshan. In Fangshan change to a tourist bus. Admission is Y20.

KANGXI GRASSLANDS

(kǎngxī cǎoyuán)

The grasslands (Map 2) are actually in a beautiful hilly region 80km north-west of the city. This is considered the best place in Beijing municipality for horse riding. It is also possible to spend the night here in a Mongolian yurt, but rug up and be prepared for surprisingly chilly nights – even in the summer.

Unfortunately, the area is being dressed up for tourism and is rapidly developing a carnival atmosphere. There is already the gaudy City of the Three Kingdoms, as well as the Folklore Holiday Village, camel rides and a roller skating rink.

To get there, take a train from the Beijing North railway station to Kangzhuang.

LONGQING GORGE

(lóngqìngxiá)

About 90km north-west of Beijing is Longqing Gorge (see Longqing Gorge Map & Map 2), a canyon in Yanqing County. The gorge was probably more scenic before the dam and reservoir flooded the area. Rowing and hiking are the big attractions in summer.

From mid-December to the end of January this is the site of Beijing's deservedly famous Ice Lantern Festival (*bīngdōng jié*). The 'lanterns' are enormous ice carvings into which coloured electric lights are inserted. The effect (at least during the night) is quite stunning. Children (yes, including adult children) are welcome to amuse themselves to their chilled bottoms' content on the ice slide.

The ride from Beijing takes two hours one way. There are currently three hotels in Longqing Gorge and plenty more are on the drawing board.

HONGLUO TEMPLE
(*hóngluó sì*)

About 65km north-east of central Beijing near Huairou is Hongluo (Red Conch Shell) Temple (Map 2). The name derives from a legend that two conch shells started emitting a red light here one evening.

The temple was built sometime during the Tang Dynasty (618–907 AD) and it has since been rebuilt, renovated and renamed several times.

Hongluo Temple is large as far as such temples go, with several courtyards, halls and the quaint Conch Shell Pagoda. It was

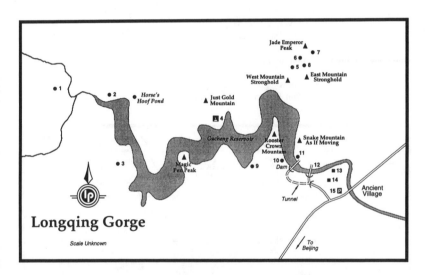

Longqing Gorge

Longqing Gorge 龙庆峡	3 18 Plates 十八盘	9 General Crag 将军岩
PLACES TO STAY	4 Just Gold Temple Site 金刚寺遗址	10 Stone Bear Jumping Cliff 石燕眺崖
13 Yudu Hotel 玉都山庄宾馆	5 Devil Tree 魔人树	11 Rowboat Dock 划船码头
14 Longqing Gorge Hotel 龙庆峡宾馆	6 Fairy Chessman 仙人棋	12 Bow-Shaped Bridge 弓形桥
OTHER	7 Sky King Rock 天王石	15 Car Park 停车场
1 Dianjiang Platform 点将台	8 Magic Fairy Hall 神仙院	
2 Make Money Stove 造钱炉		

an important Buddhist pilgrimage site, even drawing the Tang, Ming and Qing emperors.

Adjacent to the temple is (get ready for this) the Sino-Interest Mars Sports Centre (☎ 6491-2233 ext 316) where weekenders go to play paintball (*pītèbó*).

To get there, take a bus from Dongzhimen bus station in north-east Beijing to Huairou, then change to a bus or taxi to Hongluo Temple. A visit to the temple can also be included on an excursion to the Great Wall at Mutianyu.

MIYUN RESERVOIR
(mìyún shuǐkù)

Some 90km north-east of Beijing is Miyun Reservoir (see Miyun Reservoir Map & Map 2), the city's water supply and largest lake in Beijing municipality. Since this is drinking water, swimming is prohibited, but the lake is impressive for its scenery.

Chinese entrepreneurs know a good thing when they see it, and Miyun Reservoir has

Miyun Reservoir 密云水库

1 Fengjiayu
  冯家峪
2 Banchengzi
  半诚子
3 Bulaotun
  不老屯
4 Taishitun
  太师屯
5 Yunhu Holiday Resort
  云湖渡假村
6 In Front of the Dam Park
  坝前公园
7 Xiwengzhuang
  溪翁庄
8 Miyun International
  Amusement Park
  密云国际游乐场
9 Miyun Railway Station
  密云火车站
10 Mujiayu
  穆家峪
11 Dachengzi
  大城子

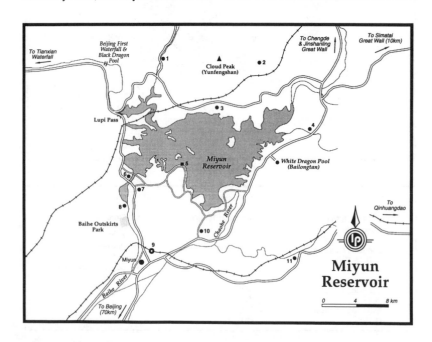

acquired a number of commercial recreation sites. Most important is the **Miyun International Amusement Park** *(mìyún guójì yóulè chǎng)*, not on the lake itself but 20km to the south-west, about 7km outside Miyun town. Facilities include a merry-go-round, monorail, car race track, and souvenir shops – just about everything you could possibly want in life.

If the carnival atmosphere gets to be too much, there are less touristy scenic sites around the reservoir. On the east side of the lake is **White Dragon Pool** *(bái lóng tán)*. While also being developed for tourism, it retains much of its former charm. During the Qing Dynasty, emperors on their way to Chengde would drop in for a visit, so the area is dotted with temples and pavilions which recently have been renovated.

Believe it or not, right in front of the dam is the **In Front of the Dam Park** *(bàqián gōngyuán)*, though this is mainly just a place for Chinese tourists to get their pictures taken. On the shores of the reservoir itself is the *Yunhu Holiday Resort* (☎ 6994-4587; fax 6994-4190) *(yúnhú dùjiàcūn)* where you can stay for Y380.

North-west of Miyun Reservoir are the less visited scenic spots. These sights include **Black Dragon Pool** *(hēi lóng tán)*, **Beijing First Waterfall** *(jīngdū dìyī pùbù)*, **Tianxian Waterfall** *(tiānxiān pùbù)*; due north is **Cloud Peak** *(yúnfēng shān)*.

Trains running to Chengde stop at Miyun. Buses to Miyun depart from the Dongzhimen Bus Station.

YANQI LAKE
(yànqi hú)

A small reservoir near Huairou (60km north-east of central Beijing), Yanqi Lake (Map 2) is perhaps Beijing municipality's best venue for water sports. Apart from swimming, paddleboating and waterskiing, you can also go parasailing (towed by a speedboat while dangling from a parachute).

The main place to stay is the *Yanming Hotel* (☎ 6966-1124) *(yànmíng lóu)*, where standard twins are Y300. There is also a campground here.

Take a bus from Dongzhimen bus station to Huairou, then change to a bus or taxi to Yanqi Lake. The bus stop at Yanqi Lake is in front of the Yanming Hotel, and from there you can catch buses or taxis to Hongluo Temple and the Great Wall at Mutianyu.

HAIZI RESERVOIR
(hǎizi shuǐkù)

At the far eastern end of Beijing municipality is Haizi Reservoir (Map 2), an artificial creation that is being promoted for tourism. The park around the lake is called Jinhai (Golden Sea) Lake Park *(jīnhǎi hú gōnguán)*. The reservoir is distinguished by the fact that it was the site of the aquatic sports (waterskiing etc) during the 1990 Asian Games.

Because of the games (which were poorly attended), the area has decent recreation facilities, though it's hard to say if everything will be kept in good nick or be allowed to become dilapidated. At the present time, modern amenities include the *Jinhai Hotel* *(jīnhǎi bīnguǎn)* and the *Jinhai Restaurant* *(jīnhǎi cāntīng)*. There is a pier *(yóuchuán mǎtóu)* where you can sometimes catch a cruise across the lake to the aquatic sports area *(shuǐshàng yùndòng chǎng)*. The shore of the reservoir is dotted with some recently-built pavilions to remind you that this is indeed China.

Buses going to the lake depart from Dongzhimen bus station.

TIANJIN
(tiānjīn)

The fourth largest city in China, Tianjin (see Tianjin Map, Tianjin Central Map & Map 1) is a major port about 2½ hours by bus to the south-east of Beijing. For centuries, it has served as Beijing's outlet to the sea and has often been referred to as 'the Shanghai of the north'.

For the sea-dog western nations of the 19th century, Tianjin was a trading bottleneck too good to be passed up. British gunboats persuaded the Chinese to sign the Treaty of Tianjin (1858) which opened the port up to foreign trade. The Brits were soon joined by the French, Japanese, Germans,

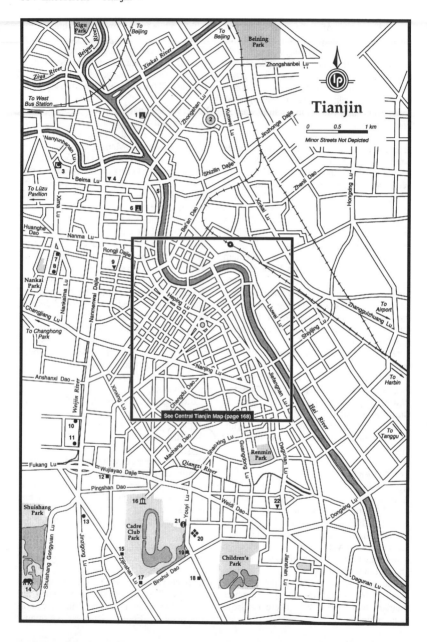

Tianjin 天津	9 Food Street 食品街	10 Tianjin University 天津大学
PLACES TO STAY	22 18th Street Dough-Twists Shop 桂发祥麻花店	11 Nankai University 南开大学
7 Cairnhill Hotel 金禧大酒店		13 TV Tower 电视塔
12 Caesar's Palace Hotel 凯撒皇宫大酒店	**OTHER**	14 Zoo 动物园
15 Sheraton Hotel 喜来登大酒店	1 Dabeiyuan Monastery 大悲院	16 Natural History Museum 自然博物馆
17 Dickson Hotel 带城酒店	2 Zhongshan Park 中山公园	20 Friendship Store 友谊商店
18 Geneva Hotel 津利华大酒店	3 Grand Mosque 清真寺	21 CITS 中国国际旅行社
19 Crystal Palace Hotel 水晶宫饭店	5 Ancient Culture Street 古文化街	
	6 Confucius Temple 文庙	
PLACES TO EAT	8 Zhou Enlai Memorial Hall 周恩来纪念馆	
4 Eardrum Fried Spongecake Shop 耳朵眼炸糕店		

Austro-Hungarians, Italians and Belgians. Since 1949 Tianjin has been a focus for major industrialisation. But despite new high-rises, factories and a busy container port, much of Tianjin's old European architecture has been left intact – the city still has a good deal of charm and a very different flavour than Beijing.

For business people, the big event of the year is the Tianjin Export Commodities Fair held every March. It's for invited guests only – to get an invite, contact CITS or CTS well in advance.

Information

The Tianjin Tourism Bureau (☎ 2835-4860; fax 2835-2324) is at 18 Youyi Lu (almost opposite the Friendship Store). Just next door at 22 Youyi Lu is CITS (☎ 2835-8499; fax 2835-2619), just opposite the Friendship Store.

Antique Market
(gǔwán shìcháng)
The sheer size and variety of the Antique Market makes it fascinating to stroll through. Among the many items on sale include stamps, silver coins, silverware, porcelain, clocks, photos of Mao, Cultural Revolution exotica and old books.

The antique market runs seven days a week, but on weekdays it occupies only a section of Shenyang Dao in the centre of town. On weekends it expands enormously and spills out into side streets in every direction. Operating hours are from 7.30 am until around 3 pm – it's best to arrive around 8 am to get the widest selection. Sunday morning is best.

Ancient Culture Street
(gǔ wénhuà jiē)
The Ancient Culture Street is a fair attempt to recreate the appearance of a long-gone Chinese city. Besides the traditional buildings, the street is lined with vendors plugging every imaginable type of cultural memento from Chinese scrolls, paintings and name chops to the latest heavy metal sounds on CD. During public holidays street operas are often staged here as well.

Within the confines of the recreated street is the small Tianhou Temple *(tiānhòu gōng)*. Tianhou (Heaven Queen) is the goddess of the sea, and is known by various names (such as Matsu in Taiwan and Tin Hau in Hong Kong). It is claimed that Tianjin's Tianhou

Temple was built in 1326, but it has seen a bit of renovation work since then.

The Ancient Culture Street is a major drawcard for tourists, both foreigners and Chinese. The street is in the north-west part of town.

Confucius Temple
(wén miào)
On the north side of Dongmennei Dajie, one block west of the Ancient Culture Street, is Tianjin's Confucius Temple. It was originally built in 1463 during the Ming Dynasty. The temple, and Confucianists in general, took quite a beating during the Cultural Revolution. By 1993 however, the buildings had been restored and opened to the public.

Grand Mosque
(qīngzhēn sì)
Although it has a distinctly Chinese look, the Grand Mosque is an active place of worship for Tianjin's Muslims. The mosque is on Dafeng Lu, not far south of the west railway station.

Dabeiyuan Monastery
(dàbēiyuàn)
This is one of the largest and best-preserved monasteries in the city. Dabeiyuan was built between 1611 and 1644, was expanded in 1940, battered during the Cultural Revolution and finally restored in 1980. The temple is on Tianwei Lu in the northern part of the city.

Catholic Church
(xīkāi jiāotáng)
This is one of the most bizarre looking churches you'll ever see. Situated on the southern end of Binjiang Dao, the twin onion domes of the cathedral, also known as the Xikai Church, form a dramatic backdrop to the 'Coca-Cola Bridge' (a pedestrian overpass crossing Nanjing Lu). It's definitely worth a look. Church services are again being permitted on Sunday, which is about the only time you'll have a chance to view the inside.

Earthquake Memorial
(kàngzhèn jìniànbēi)
Just opposite the Friendship Hotel on Nanjing Lu there is a curious pyramid-shaped memorial. Although there's not much to see here, this Earthquake Memorial is a pointed reminder of the horrific events of 28 July 1976, when an earthquake registering eight on the Richter scale struck north-east China.

It was the greatest natural disaster of the decade. Tianjin was severely affected and the city was closed to tourists for two years. The epicentre was at nearby Tangshan – that city basically disappeared in a few minutes.

Hai River Park
(hǎihé gōngyuán)
Stroll along the banks of the Hai River (a popular pastime with the locals) and see photo booths, fishing, early-morning *taiji*, opera-singing practice and old men toting bird cages. The esplanades of the Hai River Park have a peculiarly Parisian feel, in part because some of the railing and bridge work is French.

Tianjin's sewage has to go somewhere and the river water isn't so pure that you'd want to drink it. It's not Venice, but there are tourist boat cruises on the Hai River which start not far from the Astor Hotel.

TV Tower
(diànshì tái)
In an attempt to whip the masses into patriotic fervour and prove that Tianjin is a modern metropolis, the TV Tower has been declared the great wonder of the city. Indeed, it's proven to be a major drawcard for domestic tourists. You can visit the summit for a whopping Y100 fee and enjoy the warm feeling you get being atop the pride and joy of Tianjin. Views from the top aren't spectacular in the daytime, but things get better at night. The tower is also topped by a revolving restaurant.

You won't have any trouble locating the TV Tower – it dominates the skyline on the south side of town.

Shuishang Park
(shuǐshàng gōngyuán)

The large Shuishang Park is in the southwest corner of town, not far from the TV Tower. The name in Chinese means Water Park and over half the surface area is a lake. The major activity here is renting rowboats and pedal boats.

It's one of the more relaxed places in busy Tianjin, except on weekends when the locals descend on the place like cadres at a banquet. The park features a Japanese-style floating garden and a decent zoo.

Getting to the park from the railway station requires two buses. Take bus No 8 to the terminus and from there hop onto bus No 54, also to the terminus which is just outside the park entrance.

Art Museum
(yìshù bówùguǎn)

The Art Museum is easy to get to and pleasant to stroll around. Housed in an imposing rococo mansion, it has a small but choice collection of paintings and calligraphy on the ground floor and Tianjin folk art including kites, clay figurines and posters on the second floor. The top floor features special displays.

It's at 77 Jiefangbei Lu, one stop from the main railway station.

Zhou Enlai Memorial Hall
(zhōu ēnlái jìniàn guǎn)

Zhou Enlai is perhaps China's most respected revolutionary, in part because he tried to keep Mao's chaotic Cultural Revolution in check. Zhou grew up in Shaoxing in Zhejiang Province, but he attended school in Tianjin, so his classroom is enshrined and there are photos and other memorabilia from his time there (1913–1917). His memorial hall is on the western side of the city in the Nankai District, and occupies the eastern building of Nankai School.

Places to Stay

Tianjin has an adequate supply of up-market accommodation. Where the crunch comes is on the bottom end – the city is devoid of dormitories and even the 'budget hotels' require a pretty big budget. If money is a major consideration, it's probably better to stay in Beijing and do Tianjin as a day trip.

The cheapest place that accepts foreigners is the *Guomin Hotel* (☎ 2711-3353) *(guómín fàndiàn)*. It's on the corner of Heping Lu and Chifeng Dao. Budget doubles with broken plumbing range from Y164 to Y172. More cushy rooms are Y348 to Y480.

The second cheapest place to stay is the nearby *Bohai Hotel* (☎ 2712-3391) *(bóhǎi fàndiàn)* at 277 Heping Lu. Single rooms are Y258, twins cost Y240 to Y328 while suites are Y408 to Y508.

The *Huizhong Hotel* (☎ 2711-0086) *(huìzhōng fàndián)* is at 2 Huazhong Lu. Except for the central location, it hardly seems worth the Y403 tariff.

From here on it gets pricey. The *Cairnhill Hotel* (☎ 2735-3143; fax 2735-4784; 423 rooms) *(jǐnxī dà jiǔdiàn)*, 2 San Malu, is a new luxury-looking high-rise where twins are Y746.

Caesar's Palace Hotel (☎ 2231-1717; fax 2337-4922), 4 Qixiangtainan Lu, Hexi District, is no relation to the same-named Las Vegas pleasure palace. Standard twins cost Y720.

The *Tianjin First Hotel* (☎ 2330-9988; fax 2312-3000) *(tiānjīn dìyī fàndiàn)* is at 158 Jiefangbei Lu opposite the Hyatt. The place boasts a bit of old world charm, which perhaps will make you feel better about having to fork out Y664 for a standard room. Suites cost Y747 to Y1245.

The *Imperial Palace Hotel* (☎ 2230-0888; fax 2230-0222) *(tiānjīn huánggōng fàndiàn)*, 177 Jiefangbei Lu, is an old building that's been beautifully renovated. This Singapore joint venture has standard twins for Y523, plus cushier rooms from Y647 to Y1000.

The newish *Dickson Hotel* (☎ 2836-4888; fax 2836-5018) *(dàichéng jiǔdiàn)* is at 18 Binshui Dao, Hexi District. Standard twins are Y700.

The *Friendship Hotel* (☎ 2331-0372) *(yǒuyí bīnguǎn)* charges rather unfriendly prices. Doubles are Y700. The hotel is at 94 Nanjing

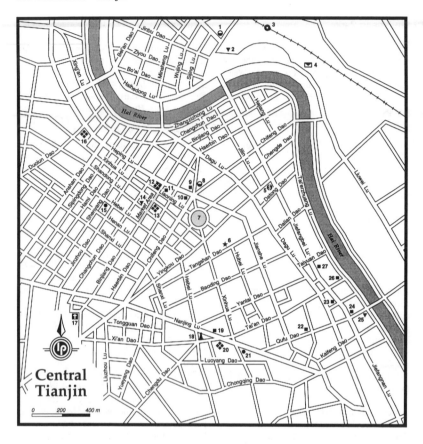

Central Tianjin

0   200   400 m

Lu. The well hidden *Geneva Hotel* (☎ 2835-2222; fax 2835-9855) *(jīnlìhuá dàjiǔdiàn)*, 32 Youyi Lu, is tucked in behind the World Economy & Trade Exhibition Centre (one of the most perverse architectural nightmares in China). However, the hotel is fine, and twins cost Y760 to Y1514.

You can bask in luxury at the *Hyatt Hotel* (☎ 2331-8888; fax 2331-1234) *(kǎiyuè fàndiàn)*, 219 Jiefangbei Lu. Economy rooms are a mere Y1450 while otherwise it's Y1823 to Y9948.

The *New World Astor Hotel* (☎ 2331-1112; fax 2331-6282) *(lìshùndé fàndiàn)* at 33 Tai'erzhuang Lu dates from early this century but has been completely refurbished. There are 222 rooms; twins cost from Y1077 to Y1243, suites are Y1823 to Y7295.

Tianjin's top glamour spot is the 346-room *Crystal Palace Hotel* (☎ 2835-6888; fax 2835-8886) *(shuǐjīnggōng fàndiàn)* at 28 Youyi Lu. Facilities include a swimming pool, tennis court, health club and French restaurant. A standard room is Y1062 and suites are Y1892 to Y5544.

The *Sheraton Hotel* (☎ 2334-3388; fax 2335-8740) *(xǐláidēng dàjiǔdiàn)* is on Zijinshan Lu in the south of Tianjin. The

Central Tianjin
天津市中心

PLACES TO STAY

9 Bohai Hotel
渤海饭店
10 Guomin Hotel
国民大酒店
11 Huizhong Hotel
惠中饭店
19 Friendship Hotel
友谊宾馆
22 Qishilin Hotel;
Kiessling's Bakery
天津起士林酒店
23 Tianjin First Hotel
天津第一饭店
24 Hyatt Hotel
凯悦饭店
26 New World Astor Hotel
利顺德大饭店
27 Imperial Palace Hotel
天津皇宫饭店

PLACES TO EAT

2 McDonald's; Wing On
Department Store
麦当劳、永安百货
14 Goubuli Restaurant
狗不理总店
25 Cosy Cafe & Bar
客思特西餐酒吧

OTHER

1 Buses to Beijing
往北京汽车站
3 Main Railway Station
天津火车站
4 Dongzhan Post
Office
东站邮局
5 Bank of China
中国银行
6 PSB
公安局外事科
7 Zhongxin Park
中心公园

8 Bus Station No 1
(To Tanggu)
一路汽车站（往塘沽）
12 Quanyechang Department
Store
劝业场
13 Binjiang Shangsha
Department Store
滨江商厦
15 Antique Market
古玩市场
16 Tianjin Department Store
百货大楼
17 Catholic Church
西开教堂
18 Earthquake Memorial
抗震纪念碑
20 Isetan Department Store
伊势丹百货
21 International Building;
Korean Air
国际大厦
大韩航空售票处

hotel dishes up 281 rooms priced between Y1500 and Y1750, plus 49 suites ranging from Y3125 to Y6250.

Places to Eat

The *Cosy Cafe & Bar* (☎ 2312-7870) *(kèsītè xīcān jiǔbā)* is one of those somewhat up-market expat havens that will make you forget you're in China. The atmosphere is very western, the menu is in English, there is MTV and popcorn served at the beginning of every meal. The cafe has an unusual location hidden underneath the Daguangming Bridge by the Hyatt Hotel.

You'll be confronted by a *McDonald's* right outside the main railway station next to Wing On Department Store.

The place to go for Chinese food is *Food Street (shípǐn jiē)*, a covered alley with two levels of restaurants. Old places close and new ones open all the time here, but there are approximately 40 to 50 restaurants on each level. You need to check prices – some of the food stalls are dirt cheap but a few up-market restaurants are almost absurdly expensive. You can find some real exotica here, like

snake (expensive), dog meat (cheap) and eels (mid-range). Food Street is a couple of blocks south of Nanma Lu, about 1km west of the centre.

King of the dumpling shops is *Goubuli* (☎ 2730-0810) *(gǒubùlǐ)* at 77 Shandong Lu, between Changchun Dao and Binjiang Dao. The shop has a century-old history. The staple of the *maison* is a dough bun, filled with high-grade pork, spices and gravy. Watch for the *bāozi* (steamed buns) with the red dot since this indicates a special filling like chicken or shrimp. Goubuli has the alarming literal translation of 'dogs won't touch them' or 'dog doesn't care'. The most satisfying explanation of this seems to be that Goubuli was the nickname of the shop's founder, an unfortunate man with an outrageously ugly face – so ugly even dogs were said to be scared of him.

The *Eardrum Fried Spongecake Shop (ěrduǒyǎn zhàgāo diàn)* takes its extraordinary name from its proximity to Eardrum Lane. This shop specialises in cakes made from rice powder, sugar and bean paste, all fried in sesame oil. These special cakes have been named (you guessed it) 'eardrum fried spongecake'. You can in fact find these cakes sold at various venues all around Tianjin, even at the railway station.

Another Tianjin food speciality that takes its name from its location is the *18th Street Dough-Twists (máhuā)*. The dough-twists in question (made from sugar, sesame seeds, nuts and vanilla) aren't exclusive to this shop though – they can be bought all over town.

Kiessling's Bakery (qǐshìlín cāntīng), built by the Austrians back in foreign concession days (1911), is a Tianjin institution. It's at 33 Zhejiang Lu, in the same building as the Qishilin Hotel. Again, you needn't go to the shop as the cakes are distributed all around the city at various shops and restaurants.

Getting There & Away

Air If you like, you can even make your exit from China at Tianjin. Korean Air flies Tianjin-Seoul. Dragonair and CAAC both offer daily direct flights between Hong Kong and Tianjin. CAAC of course connects Tianjin with just about everywhere in China.

CAAC (☎ 2490-2950) is at 242 Heping Lu. Dragonair (☎ 2330-1234) has a booking office in the Hyatt Hotel. Korean Air (☎ 2319-0088 ext 2800) has a booking office in room 2415 of the International Building *(guójì dàshà)* at 75 Nanjing Lu. CITS can book tickets on most airlines.

Bus The opening of the Beijing-Tianjin Expressway has greatly reduced travel time between the two cities – the journey takes about 2½ hours. Buses to Beijing depart from in front of Tianjin's main railway station and cost Y30. In Beijing, catch the bus to Tianjin from the Zhaogongkou bus station on the south side of town, but be careful you get a bus to Tianjin railway station *(tiānjīn huǒchē zhàn)* and not to the outlying districts of Kaifa or Tanggu (unless you want to go to Tanggu). Buses run about once very 15 minutes throughout the day.

There is a direct bus linking Beijing's Capital Airport with Tianjin. It costs Y70.

There are four long-distance bus stations,

with buses running to places that the average foreign visitor may have little interest in. Bus station No 1 *(yīlù qìchē zhàn)*, which is opposite the *Bohai Hotel*, has buses to Tanggu which is Tianjin's port. Tanggu is the place to go if you want to catch a boat to South Korea or Japan.

Train For Beijing trains you'll want the main station in Tianjin. Some trains stop at both main and west, and some go only through the west station (particularly those originating in Beijing and heading south). Through trains to north-east China often stop at the north station.

Foreigners can avoid the horrible queues by purchasing tickets at the soft-seat ticket office which is on the 2nd floor of the departure hall in the railway station.

Express trains take just under two hours for the trip between Tianjin and Beijing. Local trains take about 2½ hours.

Boat Tianjin's harbour is Tanggu, 50km (30 minutes by train) from Tianjin proper. This is one of China's major ports, offering a number of possibilities for arriving and departing by boat. International passenger ferries ply the route between Tianjin and Inch'ŏn (South Korea), while another runs to Kobe, Japan. Tickets and schedules for these boats are available in Tianjin from CITS and other travel agencies (see the Getting There & Away chapter for more details).

THE GREAT WALL
(chángchéng)

Perhaps the most famous of all Beijing's nearby sights are the choice chunks of Great Wall that pass within about 100km of the capital and make for great day trips, or more intensive expeditions. It's no accident that some of the greatest wall restoration jobs have been carried out within spitting distance of Beijing, and the best of these are: Badaling, Mutianyu, Simatai and (the more remote) Haunghua. See the following Great Wall section for all the details.

The Great Wall

Also known as the '10,000 Li Wall', the Great Wall stretches from Shanhaiguan Pass on the east coast to Jiayuguan Pass in the Gobi Desert.

Standard histories emphasise the unity of the wall. The 'original' wall was begun 2000 years ago during the Qin Dynasty (221–207 BC), when China was unified under Emperor Qin Shihuang. Separate walls, constructed by independent kingdoms to keep out marauding nomads, were linked up. The effort required hundreds of thousands of workers, many of them political prisoners, and 10 years of hard labour under General Meng Tian. An estimated 180 million cubic metres of rammed earth was used to form the core of the original wall, and legend has it that one of the other building materials used was decidedly human – the bodies of deceased workers.

The wall never really did perform its function as a defence line to keep invaders out. As Genghis Khan supposedly observed, 'The strength of a wall depends on the courage of those who defend it'. There was always the chance that sentries could be bribed. However, the wall did work well as a kind of elevated highway, transporting people and equipment across mountainous terrain. Its beacon tower system, using smoke signals generated by burning wolves' dung, transmitted news of enemy movements quickly back to the capital. To the west was Jiayuguan Pass, an important link on the Silk Road, where there was a customs post of sorts and where unwanted Chinese were ejected through the gates to face the terrifying wild west.

During the Ming Dynasty a determined effort was made to rehash the whole project, this time facing it with bricks and stone slabs – some 60 million cubic metres of them. This Ming project took over 100 years, and the costs in human effort and resources were phenomenal.

The wall was largely forgotten after that. Lengthy sections of it have returned to dust. The wall might have disappeared totally had it not been rescued by the tourist industry. Several important sections (which just happen to be within a comfortable tour bus jaunt from Beijing) have recently been rebuilt, dressed up with souvenir shops, restaurants and amusement park rides. Oddly, the depiction of the wall as an object of great beauty is a bizarre one. It's often been a symbol of tyranny, as the Berlin Wall once was.

BADALING GREAT WALL (Badaling Great Wall Map page 174)
(bādálǐng chángchéng)

Title Page: With a past as long and twisted as its famous serpentine contours, the Great Wall has been a friend, foe and folktale to travellers for more than 2000 years. This view was recorded by Thomas Allom in the early 1800s.

The majority of visitors see the Great Wall at Badaling, 70km north-west of Beijing at an elevation of 1000m. This section of the wall was restored in 1957, with the addition of guard rails. Since the 1980s, Badaling has become exceedingly crowded so a cable car was added to enhance the flow of tourist traffic.

The Great Wall Circle Vision Theatre was opened in 1990 – a 360-degree amphitheatre showing 15-minute films about the Great Wall. The latest innovation at Badaling is the millennium clock in the KFC fast-food restaurant.

There is an admission fee of Y25, which also gets you into the

The Only Man-Made Myth You Can See from the Moon

The Great Wall is surely China's most famous feature, the 'symbol of the Chinese nation' to many Chinese and foreigners alike – but is it actually what it seems? A visit to one of the world's great sights is well worth the effort; but far from providing evidence of a single people whose conception of the world is expressed through their most monumental achievement, the reality of the Great Wall appears inseparable from the ideas (and myths) about it.

Reputable guidebooks, newspapers and history books confidently quote the wall's length (anywhere from 2500km to 6000km). But since China's walls and earthen ramparts have never been adequately surveyed (satellite surveying spotted a few forgotten walls in late 1997), and even assuming the existence of a single 'wall', these numbers are fanciful. The same sources often note that 'the wall is the only man-made structure visible from space'. Ironically, this claim originated in the West early this century (ie long before *Sputnik*); and it gained currency in a marvellous 'Ripley's Believe It Or Not' column in 1932.

Factoids aside, are we looking at one wall built for a single purpose? Visitors might imagine that the familiar crenellated Ming wall near Beijing flows on over the rest of China's old northern frontier. In fact it doesn't – the wall is no more continuous in space than it is over time. Frontier walls were built long before the Qin Dynasty, but more interesting than who built walls is who did not (such as the Tang and the Sung). In contrast to the idea of a continuous 'Chinese' approach to borders, wall building was only one of several security options available to succeeding dynasties (trade and diplomacy were others).

The discontinuous array of (ineffective) fortifications occasionally and controversially deployed as a political option has only recently become 'Great'. Eighteenth century European enthusiasm for China's 'great work', which dwarfed the Egyptian pyramids in 'utility and immensity' (Voltaire), was not matched in China until the modernising Republicanism of Sun Yatsen. Until then, when conceived at all, the wall was a handy backdrop for recycled tales (such as the legend of the virtuous widow whose tears originally toppled a city wall, not a 'Great' one), or served as a metaphor for tyranny and despotism.

Allusions to Qin Shihuang and his 'despotic' wall were available to cautious critics of Mao's Cultural Revolution (which explains Qin's rehabilitation in the 1970s, especially after his terracotta army was unearthed near X'ian). Meanwhile, peasants carted off chunks of the real thing to build houses. In recent years some sections of the wall have been restored for tourism while others have been dynamited to make room for cement factories, roads and railway lines.

As the major symbol of China, 'the Great Wall' is probably better known to foreigners than it is to the people it is supposed to symbolise. Patriotic campaigners for wall renovation projects have been chagrined to learn that many people in remote regions know the wall only as 'old frontier', using the word (*bian*) employed by the Ming. As some critical historians suggest, these 'ignorant' peasants may be the only ones who've got the story right.

Russ Kerr

China Great Wall museum. You can spend plenty more for a tacky 'I Climbed the Great Wall' T-shirt, a talking panda doll, a cuckoo clock that plays *The East Is Red* or a plastic reclining buddha statue with a lightbulb in its mouth. And if it tickles your fancy, you can pay an additional fee to have your snapshot taken aboard a camel and pretend to be Marco Polo.

长
城

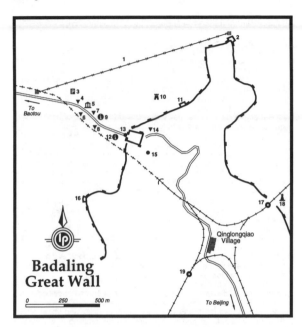

Badaling Great Wall
八达岭长城

PLACES TO EAT
4 Yanshan
  Restaurant
  燕山餐厅
6 Reclining Dragon
  Restaurant
  卧龙餐厅
7 KFC
  肯德基家乡鸡
8 Restaurant
  餐厅
14 Foreigners'
  Restaurant
  外宾餐厅

OTHER
1 Cable Car
  缆车
2 North No 8 Tower
  北八楼
3 Car Park
  停车场

5 Great Wall Museum;
  Circle Vision Theatre
  长城博物馆
  长城全周影院
9 Tourist Shop
  商店
10 Fort
  炮台
11 North No 4 Tower
  北四楼
12 Tourist Shop
  商店
13 North Gate Lock & Key
  北门锁钥
15 Former Outpost of
  Juyong Pass
  居庸外镇
16 South No 4 Tower
  南四楼
17 Qinglongqiao Station
  青龙桥站
18 Zhan Tianyou Statue
  詹天佑像
19 Qinglongqiao New Station
  青龙桥新站

长
城

shop some day. But at least for the moment, Simatai is still an enjoyable outing, and if you want to do the wall in Beijing, then this is the best spot.

The Simatai section of the wall dates all the way back to the Ming Dynasty and has some unusual features like 'obstacle-walls', which are walls-within-walls originally used for defending against enemies who managed to clamber over the Great Wall itself. There are 135 watchtowers at Simatai, the highest being Wangjinglou. Small cannons have been discovered in this area, as well as evidence of nasty rocket-type weapons involving flying knives and flying swords.

Simatai is not for the faint-hearted – this section of the wall is very steep. A few slopes have a 70-degree incline and you need both hands free, so bring a day-pack to hold your camera and other essentials. One narrow section of footpath has a 500m drop – it's no place for acrophobics. However, the steepness and sheer dropoffs help keep out the riffraff (well, at least the riffraff who suffer from vertigo).

In the early 1970s a nearby PLA unit destroyed about 3km of the wall to build barracks, setting an example for the locals who used stones from the wall to build houses. In 1979 the same unit was ordered to rebuild the section they tore down.

The wall at Simatai is being renovated, but most of it still remains in its pristine crumbling condition. Seeing the wall *au naturel* is a sharp contrast to Badaling and Mutianyu, which are so well restored that you may get the impression the wall was built just yesterday to serve CITS tour groups. Perhaps it was.

Admission to the site at Simatai costs Y15.

Getting There & Away

Simatai is 110km north-east of Beijing, and due to the distance and lack of tourist facilities there is little public transport. Buses to Simatai cost Y22 for the round-trip and depart just once daily from the Dongzhimen bus station at 6.10 am. The journey takes from two to three hours, and the bus departs Simatai at 3 pm (but ask to be sure).

For budget travellers, the best deal around is offered through the Jinghua Hotel – Y80 for the return journey by minibus. Ring up their booking office (☎ 6761-2582 after 4 pm) for more details.

If you don't do a tour through the Jinghua Hotel, you can hire a microbus taxi for the day for about Y400. Tour operators also gather at Qianmen and ask ridiculous prices for foreigners.

JINSHANLING GREAT WALL
(jīnshānlǐng cháng chéng)
Though not as steep (and therefore not as impressive) as Simatai, the Great Wall at Jinshanling is considerably less developed than any of the previously mentioned wall sites.

This section of the wall has been renovated and souvenir vendors have moved in, but so far there is no cable car and visitors are relatively few. Many of the tourists stopping here are on an excursion between Beijing and Chengde in Hebei Province, with Jinshanling thrown in as a brief stopoff.

长
城

Perhaps the most interesting thing about Jinshanling is that it's the starting-off point for a hike to Simatai. You can of course do the walk in the opposite direction, though getting a ride back to Beijing from Simatai is much easier than from Jinshanling. Getting a ride should be no problem as long as you have made arrangements with your driver to pick you up (and didn't pay him in advance). The distance between Jinshanling and Simatai is only about 10km, but it takes nearly four hours because the trail is quite steep and stony.

Admission to the Great Wall at Jinshanling is Y40.

Getting There & Away
Unfortunately, there is no public transport from the Jinshanling area, so unless you have a horse or two saddled up, access is only by chartered car, taxi or tour bus.

Walking the Wild Wall

A safe distance from the heavily touristed areas of the Great Wall, long sections of wall stride across the region's lofty mountain ranges (see Huanghua Great Wall Walking Routes map, page 179). This wild-wall territory is remote, lonely, unspoilt, overgrown and crumbling. There are no tickets, no tour guides, no signposts, no hassles from trinket-sellers, no coach parks and no garbage to spoil the fantastic view. It's here that travellers can set out along narrow footpaths winding uphill from tiny villages in Beijing's backwoods and discover what may well turn out to be their ultimate Chinese experience.

For a hike that's both easy to access and close to Beijing, the Huanghua (*huánghuā cháng chéng*, or 'Yellow Flower Fortress') section is just ideal. The wall at Huanghua clings to a high hillside adjacent to a reservoir. Around 60km north of Beijing, Huanghua is a classic and well-preserved example of Ming defence with high and wide ramparts, intact parapets and sturdy beacon towers.

It is said that one Lord Cai was responsible for building this section, and he was meticulous about its quality. Each *cun* or inch of the wall reputedly represented a whole day's work for one labourer. When the Ministry of War heard that his lordship's efforts had been so extravagant, he was beheaded and his family lost their privileges and fell into disgrace. Many years later (and far too late for the Cai family), a general judged Lord Cai's wall to be one of the best sections of the Great Wall and the official was consequently posthumously rehabilitated.

WEST TO ZHUANGDAOKOU (4km; 3 hours return)
The obvious place to start this walk is at the point where the wall meets the road. However, the wall is in quite a poor state here, and it's easier to walk about 100m to the south.

After passing a small, deep quarry and old toilet, you'll see a well-trodden path leaving the roadside and heading up along a creek. This path keeps to the left-hand side of the creek and is

长
城

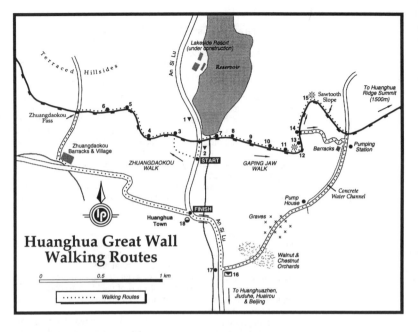

Huanghua Great Wall Walking Routes

Huanghua Great Wall Walking Routes	9 Third Tower
	10 Perfectly Preserved Tower
1 Restaurant	11 Battle Platform
2 Shuang Long Zhu Jin Jia Restaurant	12 Panorama Point
3 Second Watchtower	13 Ming-Renovated Tower
4 Derelict Tower	14 Tablet Tower
5 Stone Ceiling Tower	15 Panorama Point
6 Three-eyed Tower	16 Post Office
7 First Tower	17 61km Milestone Marker of An Si Lu
8 Second Tower	18 Buses to Huairou

clear and easy to follow. After about 300m the creek starts to veer towards the wall, and fades out among the terraces, but by this point your first target is in sight.

Second Watchtower
To get to this tower (the first, lower tower is derelict) make your way to an arched entrance just past the tower itself. As you pass

长
城

through the archway, straight ahead is an engraved tablet embedded in the wall. It details construction of a length of wall in the 7th year of the Wanli period (1579) by a group of commanders and their workforce. The name of the stonemason who carved the tablet, Wu Zongye, is in the bottom left-hand corner.

The tower itself has three windows along both its northern and southern faces. Locals describe towers by referring to the number of openings along one face, referring to them as holes (keng) or eyes (yan). So this tower is a three-hole or three-eyed tower, san keng lou or san yan lou. It once had a wooden roof which supported a second-storey structure, but these days its central area is open to the sky. You can see holes in the course of brick (about half a metre above the archway apexes) where roof/floor beams were originally positioned.

Leaving the tower, make your way west along the ramparts towards a derelict tower. From this high point, you get panoramic views of the area.

Derelict Tower

Looking east, the Huanghua reservoir is in full view. Beyond the reservoir, four towers dot the wall on its lower slopes, while a roofless battle platform can be seen near the summit. The wall then turns north and plunges out of sight. It reappears with a side view of the inverted, U-shaped stretch of wall known evocatively as the Gaping Jaw. Further on, the wall can be seen snaking up the Huanghua ridge.

Looking north, a few seemingly free-standing watchtowers can be seen in the vicinity of the towering Fenghuangtuo Mountain (1530m). The watchtowers are connected by walls, but they are quite small and of inferior quality.

Looking south, you can see the town of Huanghua and the wide river valley leading towards Huanghuazhen. The view starkly illustrates the strategic importance of the pass between the mountains at this point.

From the corner tower the wall swings north, running level through conifer woods before turning west again and dropping to a three-eyed tower, notable for its stone ceiling.

Stone Ceiling Tower

Large slabs of igneous rock have been incorporated into the ceiling of this tower. Normally, rock was used only in foundations, with bricks employed throughout the upper levels. Given that the slabs are almost 1m long and about 40cm wide, it's difficult to explain their use; the effort required to hoist such heavy slabs into position would have been considerable.

Leave the tower through the western door and follow the wall as it plummets through a thick conifer plantation. The parapets around here are in pretty poor condition and the wall's pavement is overgrown and, in some places, totally derelict.

After 200m and another three-eyed tower, the ramparts cross a small valley where a pass, or gate, in the wall once existed. In compensation for the condition of the ramparts here, the gate is in excellent condition.

长
城

Zhuangdaokou Pass

This pass, a passageway through the wall, is about 2.5m wide and is in the form of a brick archway founded on large igneous blocks. It is most striking for its engraved tablets which are different on either side of the archway. On a tablet on the southern side there are the three large characters – *zhuang*, *dao* and *kou* from right to left. There's also a number of smaller characters recording the name of the official who put the tablet in place, Liu Xun, and the date, in the fifth year of the Wanli reign (1577). Farmers continue to use this gate to reach terraced hillsides beyond the wall to tend their fruit trees or coppice conifers for firewood.

The tablet on the northern face, also dated 1577, bears three large characters which read from right to left *zhen lu guan*, or Suppress Captives Pass.

Zhuangdaokou was originally fortified in 1404 during the early

Left: One of three passes constructed north of Beijing during the late 15th century, Zhuangdaokou Pass was designed to stop Mongols on horseback from invading.

years of the Ming Dynasty. It was one of three passes (along with Juyongguan at Badaling and Gubeikou in the north-east) deemed to be critical in keeping out large Mongol armies who tended to attack on horseback, and preventing them from reaching the capital unencumbered. Between these passes, where sturdy walls and towers were constructed, there were only lines of watchtowers and beacon towers. It was left up to later dynasties to connect them with walls.

Zhuangdaokou Pass to Zhuangdaokou Village
From the archway turn south and follow the path downhill. It is about 500m to the village of Zhuangdaokou, a marvellous little settlement half nestled within the walls of an ancient army barracks. The path is as ancient as the pass itself, linking the barracks with the wall.

As you enter the village, the barracks is the large walled structure on the left; it's possible to climb its wall at the near corner. The barracks average seven courses of stone blocks in height, and the blocks are of the same provenance and shape as those used as foundations for the wall. About half the foundation of the structure remains; it now encloses some farmhouses.

From the top of its walls you can see carved granite water spouts protruding from inside. All other structures, and half the walls, have been removed – probably during the Cultural Revolution.

Village to Bus Stop or Restaurant
Follow your nose down through the narrow alleyways (note the Cultural Revolution slogans in yellow and the faded images of Mao Zedong's trademark noggin on the crumbling plaster walls) to the southern edge of the village. From there, turn left at the bank of the stream and follow the main road for about 1km to a T-junction. Regular buses for Huairou and Changping head off from here.

If you want to return to the starting point, or if you need to refuel at the Shuang Long Zhu Jiu Jia Restaurant (the name translates literally as 'Pair of Dragons Playing with a Pearl Alcohol House'), turn right (north) at the T-junction.

EAST TO GAPING JAW (4km; 4 hours)
From the restaurant walk north for 50m and cross the top of the dam holding back Huanghua Reservoir (see Huanghua Great Wall Walking Routes map, page 179). The dam occupies the site of the main Huanghua Gate – only the foundations of this once-glorious structure remain. From the far end of the dam, climb up the footpath on the northern side and enter the first tower through one of its north-facing windows.

It is a short but steep climb to the second tower. Here parapets have fallen down, plunderers have removed the bricks, and they have also taken away bricks which once topped the stone block foundations of the rampart. The wall drops in height at this point before climbing to the third tower. This is of a conventional shape – being more of a quadrangle than a rectangle – and is offset well to the north.

长
城

Perfectly Preserved Tower

A gradual 200m climb takes you to the fourth tower. It is quite standard in shape, and is in exceptionally good condition. The ramparts before and beyond the tower are also in excellent condition (with parapets still standing and brick-work intact) as are its upper story battlements and loopholes.

The tower is a three-eyed structure with its central area open to the sky. On the floor of the tower is an engraving dating from the Longqing period (1567–1572). At the time of writing, a wooden ladder in the tower gave access to the tower's top storey. Just outside the eastern door of the tower there's a flight of steps cut down into the ramparts and leading to a perfectly preserved granite archway. On the wall facing the archway is a gap which once housed a tablet.

Battle Platform

Exiting the tower, the ramparts climb to a short steep section featuring small observation platforms in front of a large battle platform. This is like a roofless watchtower, asymmetrically offset to the north for observation and enfilading (flanking) fire. Within its parapets are two rows of loopholes, each topped with bricks of different designs. The platform, close to the summit, commands a strategic position for cannon fire to the valley below.

From the battle platform, the wall reaches the summit and then turns north to a tower which provides a fine place for views of the entire area.

Panorama Point

Looking north, you can see the distinctive shape of the section of the wall called Gaping Jaw. Looking east, the wall streaks up the Huanghua ridge towards the summit (from the south, the ridge profile looks like a camel's back and is called 'the camel's back which breaks the wind'). Heading north, the ramparts lead to a well-preserved four-eyed tower.

Ming Renovated Tower

In good light, the colour of the top half-dozen courses of bricks – especially on the southern face of the tower – appears to differ from the rest. Inside, some parts of the brickwork seems to have been repaired with mortar of a different colour. These features suggest that the top of the tower was rebuilt and other parts inside were repaired. The reason why these efforts were made is open to debate. It seems unlikely that the tower, which is in such a dominant, high position, could have been attacked and damaged. It is more likely that the tower dates from the early Ming Dynasty and was repaired in the later Ming period, or that it was damaged by an earthquake and repaired.

Tablet Tower

About 100m downhill is another fine four-eyed tower. Just before the tower there are steps down from the wall leading through an archway off the wall and down the gully.

长
城

The second chamber on the right (south) houses an engraved tablet from the third year of the Longqing period (1570). It is etched with 206 characters and edged with a simple vine design.

You now have two options. The shorter route is to leave by the southern door, exit the wall via the steps and archway, and head down the gully path to the valley floor. This is route is easy and reaches the valley near a small water pumping station.

If you feel like a longer and tougher walk, leave the tower by the north door and walk around the Gaping Jaw and its steep cousin to the east – Sawtooth Slope. This option will appeal to those who enjoy a scramble because the Sawtooth Slope (named for its zigzag profile) is an extremely steep and slippery descent. It is possible to continue east along Huanghua ridge, but beware: it's a tough hike and you'll encounter some very steep and very challenging terrain.

Barracks
Both routes end up at the pumping station. From there you can wander about 50m south-west to reach an old army barracks. The structure's south-facing wall has an intact archway, and all four of its perimeter walls are standing.

These barracks are thought to have housed about 200 men who were stationed to keep an eye on this section of the wall, taking advantage of a sheltered position and a reliable water source.

Right: Almost perfectly intact, the tablet tower is home to a distinctive 16th-century engraved tablet.

长
城

To the Main Road

To return to the main road, walk south on the stony track which swings gradually to the west, crossing a concrete-channelled waterway after about 600m. There is a small pump house nearby on the right, and a fork off and up a bank to the right (west). Avoid this and keep on the main track, passing conical grave mounds on either side of the track and walking through walnut and chestnut orchards.

You'll know you're nearing your target when the track starts to swing right, eventually reaching the road alongside a post office and beside the 61km milestone marker of An Si Lu (as the main road is known). Head north to the bridge for transport to Huairou and Changping.

PLACES TO STAY & EAT

A resort by the reservoir was being built at the time of writing, but building had been underway for more than a year without much sign of completion. Check it out when you get up there.

If you want to spend a night on the wall, it's possible to sleep in the watchtowers. It's unlikely that the PSB would bother you there, but we couldn't predict their reaction if they did find you there.

As the zhaodaisuo in Huanghuazhen doesn't accept foreigners, the nearest accommodation is in Changping or Huairou, but you'll struggle to find anything under Y100 and it's a long way away.

The Shuang Long Zhu Jiu Jia restaurant, just to the south of the wall, is run by a local family and serves a wide variety of cheap dishes. There's another restaurant north of the wall on the left-hand side of the road. It serves up a similar sort of fare. Otherwise, there's a string of restaurants well worth investigating on An Si Lu in Huanghuazhen.

GETTING THERE & AWAY
Bus & Minibus

There is no direct bus available to Huanghua town, but there are two indirect routes which work well enough.

The first option is to take a public bus or minibus to Huairou from the Dongzhimen long-distance bus station near the subway station of the same name. Bus No 916 leaves every 15 minutes from 5:30 am to 6:30 pm (Y4) and takes just over an hour to get to Huairou. Minibuses *(xiao gong gong qi che)* adopt the same number (916) and run the same route for Y5, although they are a little quicker. Alight in Huairou and change to a minibus for Sihai, which passes through Huanghua. The whole journey takes a little over an hour and costs Y6.

The second option takes you via Changping. Hop on to minibus No 345 at Deshengmen intersection, just east of Jishuitan subway station. The ride to Changping will cost you Y8 and can take anything up to an hour.

In Changping, change buses for Huanghua on the same street at which you pull up. (Don't take the 345 scheduled large-bus service, which is non-express with more than 20 stops.)

The route from Changping to Huanghua passes through the

长
城

valley of the auspicious Ming tombs. It takes more than one hour and costs Y7.

Cycling

It is feasible and straightforward to cycle to Huanghua. Bicycles can be hired from many of Beijing's hotels or from opposite the Friendship Store. Only ride if you are in reasonable shape for the 62km distance, which includes a mountain pass. Cycling time is four to seven hours depending on your fitness, the weather, frequency of stops and bike problems. The roads are excellent, and there are many places where punctures, rattles and squeaks can be repaired.

William Lindesay

William Lindesay has walked the length of the wall, from Jiayuguan to Shanhaiguan. This piece is based on his second book about the wall, Hiking on History – Exploring Beijing's Great Wall on Foot, *due for publication in late 1998. The illustrations in this section are based on sketches by John Macdonald.*

Glossary

bei – north
Beiping – literally 'Northern Peace', the official name of the capital from 1368 to 1403 before changing to Beijing ('Northern Capital')

CAAC – China Aviation Administration of China, which controls most of China's domestic and foreign airlines
catty – Chinese unit of weight, one catty *(jīn)* equals 0.6kg (1.32lbs)
CITS – China International Travel Service
Concessions – small foreign colonies in all but name, commonly found in big eastern cities like Shanghai and Tianjin; all Concessions were abolished when the Communists came to power in 1949
CTS – China Travel Service
Cultural Revolution – a mass movement started by Mao Zedong which lasted from 1966 to 1970, causing enormous chaos and perhaps a million deaths
CYTS – China Youth Travel Service

dadao (or dao) – boulevard
Dadu – the 'Great Capital', Beijing's ancient name during the Mongol period, or Yuan Dynasty (1215–1368)
dajie – avenue
dong – east

fengshui – an ancient form of divination based on geographical features

gongfu – a form of Chinese martial arts, usually called *kung fu* in the West; see also *t'ai chi*

hutong – a narrow backstreet or alleyway

jie – the most common word for street

Kuomintang – the Nationalist Party which controlled mainland China from 1911 to 1949, and still controls Taiwan

laobaixing – common people, the masses
little red book – the name commonly used in the West for the *Quotations of Chairman Mao Zedong*, the book universally read and studied in China before and during the Cultural Revolution
lu – road

Manchus – a non-Chinese ethnic group from Manchuria (present-day north-east China) which took over China and established the Qing Dynasty (1644–1911)
men – gate

nan – south

Overseas Chinese – Chinese people who have left China permanently to settle overseas

Peking – the spelling of 'Beijing' before the Communists adopted the Pinyin romanisation system in 1958
ping – Chinese unit of area, one ping equals 1.82 sq metres (5.97 sq feet)
Pinyin – the phonetic romanisation system adopted by the Communist Party in 1958
PLA – People's Liberation Army
PRC – People's Republic of China – China's official name
PSB – Public Security Bureau, the police
putonghua – the standard form of the Chinese language used since the beginning of this century, based on the dialect of Beijing

qigong – a variation of *gongfu*, claimed to be capable of causing miracle cures

Red Guards – fanatical devotees of Mao Zedong during the Cultural Revolution
RMB – Renminbi (or 'people's money'), China's currency
ROC – Republic of China, the nation's name from 1911 to 1949; the Kuomintang in Taiwan still uses this title

Siheyuan – traditional Chinese courtyard house

tael – Chinese unit of weight, one tael *(liǎng)* equals 37.5g (1.32oz) and there are 16 taels to the *catty*

t'ai chi – slow-motion shadow boxing, a form of exercise; commonly shortened to *taiji* (called *t'ai chi* in the West)

tripitaka – Buddhist scriptures

xi – west

Yanjing – the 'Capital of Yan', Beijing's name during the Liao Dynasty (907–1125 AD)

Yuan – the main unit of Chinese currency

Index

Maps

Text

LONELY PLANET PHRASEBOOKS

Nepali phrasebook

Ethiopian Amharic phrasebook

Latin American Spanish phrasebook

Ukrainian phrasebook

Greek phrasebook

Vietnamese phrasebook

Building bridges,
Breaking barriers,
Beyond babble-on

Listen for the gems

Speak your own words

Ask your own questions

Master of your own image

- handy pocket-sized books
- easy to understand Pronunciation chapter
- clear and comprehensive Grammar chapter
- romanisation alongside script to allow ease of pronunciation
- script throughout so users can point to phrases
- extensive vocabulary sections, words and phrases for every situation
- full of cultural information and tips for the traveller

'...vital for a real DIY spirit and attitude in language learning' – Backpacker

'the phrasebooks have good cultural backgrounders and offer solid advice for challenging situations in remote locations' – San Francisco Examiner

'...they are unbeatable for their coverage of the world's more obscure languages' – The Geographical Magazine

---

Arabic (Egyptian)
Arabic (Moroccan)
Australia
  Australian English, Aboriginal and Torres Strait languages
Baltic States
  Estonian, Latvian, Lithuanian
Bengali
Brazilian
Burmese
Cantonese
Central Asia
Central Europe
  Czech, French, German, Hungarian, Italian and Slovak
Eastern Europe
  Bulgarian, Czech, Hungarian, Polish, Romanian and Slovak
Ethiopian (Amharic)
Fijian
French
German
Greek

Hindi/Urdu
Indonesian
Italian
Japanese
Korean
Lao
Latin American Spanish
Malay
Mandarin
Mediterranean Europe
  Albanian, Croatian, Greek, Italian, Macedonian, Maltese, Serbian and Slovene
Mongolian
Nepali
Papua New Guinea
Pilipino (Tagalog)
Quechua
Russian
Scandinavian Europe
  Danish, Finnish, Icelandic, Norwegian and Swedish

South-East Asia
  Burmese, Indonesian, Khmer, Lao, Malay, Tagalog (Pilipino), Thai and Vietnamese
Spanish (Castilian)
  Basque, Catalan and Galician
Sri Lanka
Swahili
Thai
Thai Hill Tribes
Tibetan
Turkish
Ukrainian
USA
  US English, Vernacular, Native American languages and Hawaiian
Vietnamese
Western Europe
  Basque, Catalan, Dutch, French, German, Irish, Italian, Portuguese, Scottish Gaelic, Spanish (Castilian) and Welsh

---

LONELY PLANET JOURNEYS

JOURNEYS is a unique collection of travel writing – published by the company that understands travel better than anyone else. It is a series for anyone who has ever experienced – or dreamed of – the magical moment when they encountered a strange culture or saw a place for the first time. They are tales to read while you're planning a trip, while you're on the road or while you're in an armchair, in front of a fire.

JOURNEYS books catch the spirit of a place, illuminate a culture, recount a crazy adventure, or introduce a fascinating way of life. They always entertain, and always enrich the experience of travel.

'Idiosyncratic, entertainingly diverse and unexpected . . . from an international writership'
– The Australian

'Books which offer a closer look at the people and culture of a destination, and enrich travel experiences'
– American Bookseller

LOST JAPAN
Alex Kerr

Originally written in Japanese, this passionate, vividly personal book draws on the author's experiences in Japan over thirty years. Alex Kerr takes us on a backstage tour, as he explores the ritualised world of Kabuki, retraces his initiation into Tokyo's boardrooms during the heady Bubble Years, tells how he stumbled on a hidden valley that became his home . . . and exposes the environmental and cultural destruction that is the other face of contemporary Japan.

Alex Kerr is an American who lives in Japan. He majored in Japanese studies at Yale, collects Japanese art and has founded his own art-dealing business. Simultaneously 'a foreigner' and 'an insider', Alex Kerr brings a unique perspective to writing about contemporary Japan.

Winner of Japan's 1994 Shincho Gakugei Literature Prize.

'This deeply personal witness to Japan's wilful loss of its traditional culture is at the same time an immensely valuable evaluation of just what that culture was' **– Donald Ritchie, Japan Times**

'Brilliantly combines essays and autobiography, chronicling Kerr's love affair with Japan' **– The Times**

LONELY PLANET TRAVEL ATLASES

Lonely Planet has long been famous for the number and quality of its guidebook maps. Now we've gone one step further and produced a handy companion series: Lonely Planet travel atlases – maps of a country produced in book form.

Unlike other maps, which look good but lead travellers astray, our travel atlases have been researched on the road by Lonely Planet's experienced team of writers. All details are carefully checked to ensure the atlas corresponds with the equivalent Lonely Planet guidebook.

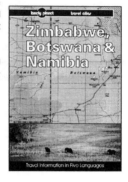

The handy atlas format means no holes, wrinkles, torn sections or constant folding and unfolding. These atlases can survive long periods on the road, unlike cumbersome fold-out maps. The comprehensive index ensures easy reference.

- full-colour throughout
- maps researched and checked by Lonely Planet authors
- place names correspond with Lonely Planet guidebooks
  – no confusing spelling differences
- legend and travelling information in English, French, German, Japanese and Spanish
- size: 230 x 160 mm

Available now:
Chile & Easter Island • Egypt • India & Bangladesh • Israel & the Palestinian Territories •Jordan, Syria & Lebanon • Kenya • Laos • Portugal • South Africa, Lesotho & Swaziland • Thailand • Turkey • Vietnam • Zimbabwe, Botswana & Namibia

---

LONELY PLANET TV SERIES & VIDEOS

Lonely Planet travel guides have been brought to life on television screens around the world. Like our guides, the programmes are based on the joy of independent travel, and look honestly at some of the most exciting, picturesque and frustrating places in the world. Each show is presented by one of three travellers from Australia, England or the USA and combines an innovative mixture of video, Super-8 film, atmospheric soundscapes and original music.

Videos of each episode – containing additional footage not shown on television – are available from good book and video shops, but the availability of individual videos varies with regional screening schedules.

Video destinations include: Alaska • American Rockies • Australia – The South-East • Baja California & the Copper Canyon • Brazil • Central Asia • Chile & Easter Island • Corsica, Sicily & Sardinia – The Mediterranean Islands • East Africa (Tanzania & Zanzibar) • Ecuador & the Galapagos Islands • Greenland & Iceland • Indonesia • Israel & the Sinai Desert • Jamaica • Japan • La Ruta Maya • Morocco • New York • North India • Pacific Islands (Fiji, Solomon Islands & Vanuatu) • South India • South West China • Turkey • Vietnam • West Africa • Zimbabwe, Botswana & Namibia

The Lonely Planet TV series is produced by:
Pilot Productions
The Old Studio
18 Middle Row
London W10 5AT UK

For video availability and ordering information contact your nearest Lonely Planet office.

Music from the TV series is available on CD & cassette.

PLANET TALK

Lonely Planet's FREE quarterly newsletter

We love hearing from you and think you'd like to hear from us.

When...is the right time to see reindeer in Finland?
Where...can you hear the best palm-wine music in Ghana?
How...do you get from Asunción to Areguá by steam train?
What...is the best way to see India?

For the answer to these and many other questions read PLANET TALK.

Every issue is packed with up-to-date travel news and advice including:

* a letter from Lonely Planet co-founders Tony and Maureen Wheeler
* go behind the scenes on the road with a Lonely Planet author
* feature article on an important and topical travel issue
* a selection of recent letters from travellers
* details on forthcoming Lonely Planet promotions
* complete list of Lonely Planet products

To join our mailing list contact any Lonely Planet office.

Also available: Lonely Planet T-shirts. 100% heavyweight cotton.

LONELY PLANET ONLINE

Get the latest travel information before you leave or while you're on the road

Whether you've just begun planning your next trip, or you're chasing down
specific info on currency regulations or visa requirements, check out Lonely
Planet Online for up-to-the minute travel information.

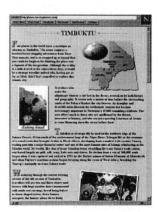

As well as travel profiles of your favourite destinations (including maps and
photos), you'll find current reports from our researchers and other travellers,
updates on health and visas, travel advisories, and discussion of the
ecological and political issues you need to be aware of as you travel.

There's also an online travellers' forum where you can share your experience
of life on the road, meet travel companions and ask other travellers for their
recommendations and advice. We also have plenty of links to other online
sites useful to independent travellers.

And of course we have a complete and up-to-date list of all Lonely Planet
travel products including guides, phrasebooks, atlases, Journeys and videos
and a simple online ordering facility if you can't find the book you want
elsewhere.

www.lonelyplanet.com
or
AOL keyword: lp

LONELY PLANET PRODUCTS

Lonely Planet is known worldwide for publishing practical, reliable and no-nonsense travel information in our guides and on our web site. The Lonely Planet list covers just about every accessible part of the world. Currently there are nine series: *travel guides, shoestring guides, walking guides, city guides, phrasebooks, audio packs, travel atlases, Journeys – a unique collection of travel writing and Pisces Books - diving and snorkeling guides.*

EUROPE

Amsterdam • Andalucia • Austria • Baltic States phrasebook • Berlin • Britain • Canary Islands• Central Europe on a shoestring • Central Europe phrasebook • Czech & Slovak Republics • Denmark • Dublin • Eastern Europe on a shoestring • Eastern Europe phrasebook • Estonia, Latvia & Lithuania • Finland • France • French phrasebook • Germany • German phrasebook • Greece • Greek phrasebook • Hungary • Iceland, Greenland & the Faroe Islands • Ireland • Italian phrasebook • Italy • Lisbon • London • Mediterranean Europe on a shoestring • Mediterranean Europe phrasebook • Paris • Poland • Portugal • Portugal travel atlas • Prague • Romania & Moldova • Russia, Ukraine & Belarus • Russian phrasebook • Scandinavian & Baltic Europe on a shoestring • Scandinavian Europe phrasebook • Slovenia • Spain • Spanish phrasebook • St Petersburg • Switzerland •Trekking in Spain • Ukrainian phrasebook • Vienna • Walking in Britain • Walking in Italy • Walking in Switzerland • Western Europe on a shoestring • Western Europe phrasebook

Travel Literature: The Olive Grove: Travels in Greece

NORTH AMERICA

Alaska • Backpacking in Alaska • Baja California • California & Nevada • Canada • Chicago • Deep South• Florida • Hawaii • Honolulu • Los Angeles • Mexico • Mexico City • Miami • New England • New Orleans • New York City • New York, New Jersey & Pennsylvania • Pacific Northwest USA • Rocky Mountain States • San Francisco • Seattle • Southwest USA • USA phrasebook • Washington, DC & the Capital Region

Travel Literature: Drive thru America

CENTRAL AMERICA & THE CARIBBEAN

• Bahamas and Turks & Caicos • Bermuda • Central America on a shoestring • Costa Rica • Cuba • Eastern Caribbean • Guatemala, Belize & Yucatán: La Ruta Maya • Jamaica

Travel Literature Green Dreams: Travels in Central America

SOUTH AMERICA

Argentina, Uruguay & Paraguay • Bolivia • Brazil • Brazilian phrasebook • Buenos Aires • Chile & Easter Island • Chile & Easter Island travel atlas • Colombia Ecuador & the Galápagos Islands • Latin American Spanish phrasebook • Peru • Quechua phrasebook • Rio de Janeiro • South America on a shoestring • Trekking in the Patagonian Andes • Venezuela

Travel Literature: Full Circle: A South American Journey

ISLANDS OF THE INDIAN OCEAN

Madagascar & Comoros • Maldives • Mauritius, Réunion & Seychelles

AFRICA

Africa - the South • Africa on a shoestring • Arabic (Moroccan) phrasebook • Cairo • Cape Town • Central Africa • East Africa • Egypt • Egypt travel atlas• Ethiopian (Amharic) phrasebook • The Gambia & Senegal • Kenya • Kenya travel atlas • Malawi, Mozambique & Zambia • Morocco • North Africa • South Africa, Lesotho & Swaziland • South Africa, Lesotho & Swaziland travel atlas • Swahili phrasebook • Tunisia • Trekking in East Africa • West Africa • Zimbabwe, Botswana & Namibia • Zimbabwe, Botswana & Namibia travel atlas

Travel Literature: Mali Blues • The Rainbird: A Central African Journey • Songs to an African Sunset: A Zimbabwean Story

MAIL ORDER

Lonely Planet products are distributed worldwide. They are also available by mail order from Lonely Planet, so if you have difficulty finding a title please write to us. North American and South American residents should write to 150 Linden St, Oakland CA 94607, USA; European and African residents should write to 10a Spring Place, London NW5 3BH; and residents of other countries to PO Box 617, Hawthorn, Victoria 3122, Australia.

NORTH-EAST ASIA

Beijing • Cantonese phrasebook • China • Hong Kong • Hong Kong, Macau & Guangzhou • Japan • Japanese phrasebook • Japanese audio pack • Korea • Korean phrasebook • Kyoto • Mandarin phrasebook • Mongolia • Mongolian phrasebook • North-East Asia on a shoestring • Seoul • Taiwan • Tibet • Tibet phrasebook • Tokyo
Travel Literature: Lost Japan

MIDDLE EAST & CENTRAL ASIA

Arab Gulf States • Arabic (Egyptian) phrasebook • Central Asia • Central Asia phrasebook • Iran • Israel & the Palestinian Territories • Israel & the Palestinian Territories travel atlas • Istanbul • Jerusalem • Jordan & Syria • Jordan, Syria & Lebanon travel atlas • Lebanon • Middle East • Turkey • Turkish phrasebook • Turkey travel atlas • Yemen

Travel Literature: The Gates of Damascus • Kingdom of the Film Stars: Journey into Jordan

ALSO AVAILABLE:

Brief Encounters • Travel with Children • Traveller's Tales• Not the Only Planet

INDIAN SUBCONTINENT

Bangladesh • Bengali phrasebook • Bhutan • Delhi • Goa • Hindi/Urdu phrasebook • India • India & Bangladesh travel atlas • Indian Himalaya • Karakoram Highway • Nepal • Nepali phrasebook • Pakistan • Rajasthan • South India • Sri Lanka • Sri Lanka phrasebook • Trekking in the Indian Himalaya • Trekking in the Karakoram & Hindukush • Trekking in the Nepal Himalaya
Travel Literature: In Rajasthan • Shopping for Buddhas

SOUTH-EAST ASIA

Bali & Lombok • Bangkok • Burmese phrasebook • Cambodia • Ho Chi Minh City • Indonesia • Indonesian phrasebook • Indonesian audio pack • Indonesia's Eastern Islands • Jakarta • Java • Laos • Lao phrasebook • Laos travel atlas • Malay phrasebook • Malaysia, Singapore & Brunei • Myanmar (Burma) • Philippines • Pilipino phrasebook • Singapore • South-East Asia on a shoestring • South-East Asia phrasebook • South-West China • Thailand • Thailand's Islands & Beaches • Thailand travel atlas • Thai phrasebook • Thai audio pack • Thai Hill Tribes phrasebook • Vietnam • Vietnamese phrasebook • Vietnam travel atlas

AUSTRALIA & THE PACIFIC

Australia • Australian phrasebook • Bushwalking in Australia • Bushwalking in Papua New Guinea • Fiji • Fijian phrasebook • Islands of Australia's Great Barrier Reef • Melbourne • Micronesia • New Caledonia • New South Wales • New Zealand • Northern Territory • Outback Australia • Papua New Guinea • Papua New Guinea phrasebook • Queensland • Rarotonga & the Cook Islands • Samoa • Solomon Islands • South Australia • Sydney • Tahiti & French Polynesia • Tasmania • Tonga • Tramping in New Zealand • Vanuatu • Victoria • Western Australia
Travel Literature: Islands in the Clouds • Sean & David's Long Drive

ANTARCTICA

Antarctica

THE LONELY PLANET STORY

Lonely Planet published its first book in 1973 in response to the numerous 'How did you do it?' questions Maureen and Tony Wheeler were asked after driving, busing, hitching, sailing and railing their way from England to Australia.

Written at a kitchen table and hand collated, trimmed and stapled, *Across Asia on the Cheap* became an instant local bestseller, inspiring thoughts of another book.

Eighteen months in South-East Asia resulted in their second guide, *South-East Asia on a shoestring*, which they put together in a backstreet Chinese hotel in Singapore in 1975. The 'yellow bible', as it quickly became known to backpackers around the world, soon became *the* guide to the region. It has sold well over half a million copies and is now in its 9th edition, still retaining its familiar yellow cover.

Today there are over 350 titles, including travel guides, walking guides, language kits & phrasebooks, travel atlases and travel literature. The company is the largest independent travel publisher in the world. Although Lonely Planet initially specialised in guides to Asia, today there are few corners of the globe that have not been covered.

The emphasis continues to be on travel for independent travellers. Tony and Maureen still travel for several months of each year and play an active part in the writing, updating and quality control of Lonely Planet's guides.

They have been joined by over 80 authors and 200 staff at our offices in Melbourne (Australia), Oakland (USA), London (UK) and Paris (France). Travellers themselves also make a valuable contribution to the guides through the feedback we receive in thousands of letters each year and on our web site.

The people at Lonely Planet strongly believe that travellers can make a positive contribution to the countries they visit, both through their appreciation of the countries' culture, wildlife and natural features, and through the money they spend. In addition, the company makes a direct contribution to the countries and regions it covers. Since 1986 a percentage of the income from each book has been donated to ventures such as famine relief in Africa; aid projects in India; agricultural projects in Central America; Greenpeace's efforts to halt French nuclear testing in the Pacific; and Amnesty International.

'I hope we send people out with the right attitude about travel. You realise when you travel that there are so many different perspectives about the world, so we hope these books will make people more interested in what they see. Guidebooks can't really guide people. All you can do is point them in the right direction.'

– Tony Wheeler

LONELY PLANET PUBLICATIONS

Australia
PO Box 617, Hawthorn 3122, Victoria
tel: (03) 9819 1877 fax: (03) 9819 6459
e-mail: talk2us@lonelyplanet.com.au

USA
150 Linden St
Oakland, CA 94607
tel: (510) 893 8555 TOLL FREE: 800 275-8555
fax: (510) 893 8572
e-mail: info@lonelyplanet.com

UK
10a Spring Place,
London NW5 3BH
tel: (0171) 428 4800 fax: (0171) 428 4828
e-mail: go@lonelyplanet.co.uk

France:
1 rue du Dahomey, 75011 Paris
tel: 01 55 25 33 00 fax: 01 55 25 33 01
e-mail: bip@lonelyplanet.fr

World Wide Web: http://www.lonelyplanet.com
or *AOL* keyword: lp

Beijing Map List

GLENN BEANLAND

GLENN BEANLAND

DIANA MAYFIELD

Rugged and generally unspoilt, this mountainous Great Wall region is an easy drive north of Beijing.

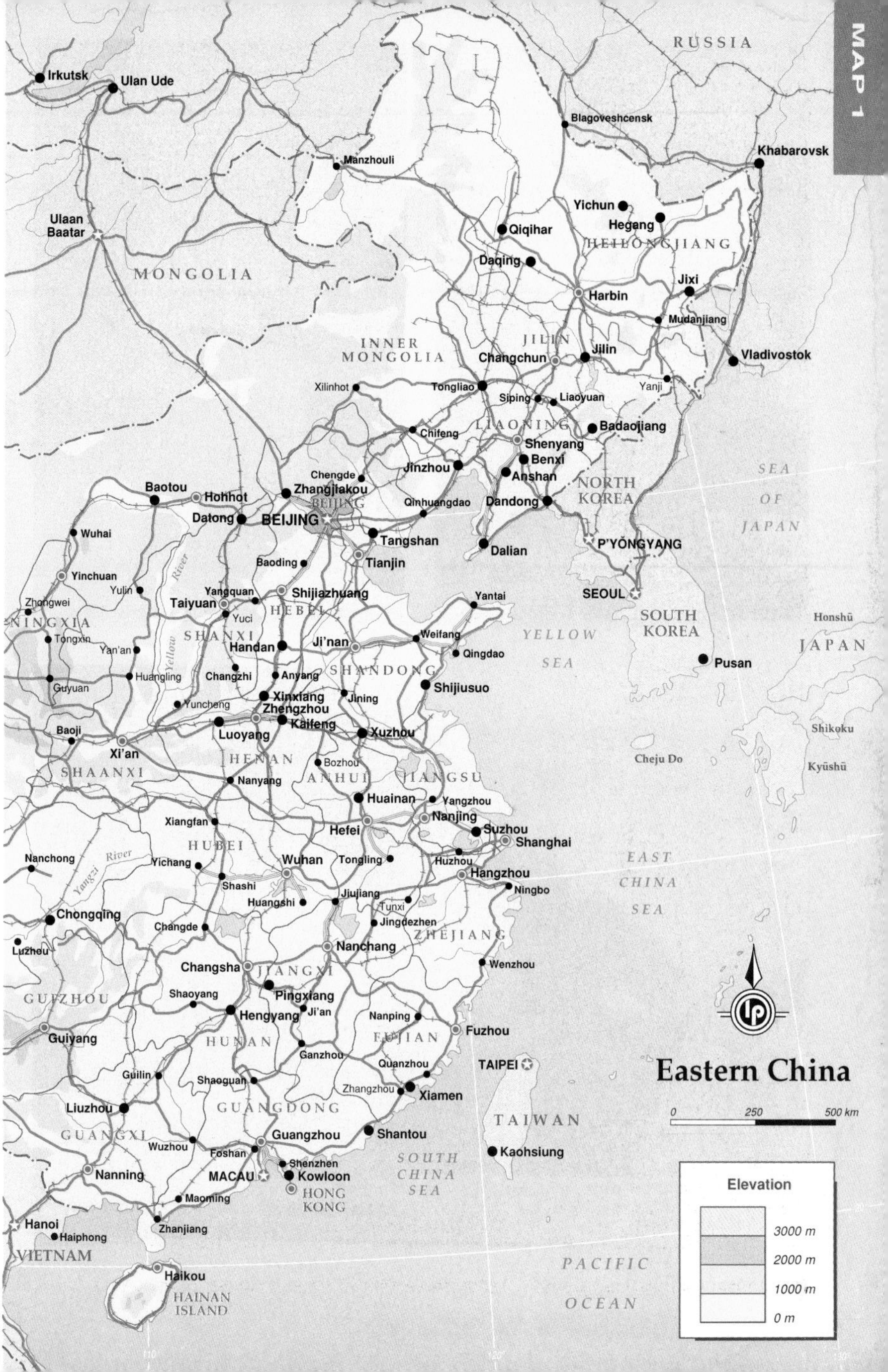

MAP 1

Eastern China

RUSSIA

Irkutsk
Ulan Ude
Manzhouli
Blagoveshcensk
Khabarovsk
Ulaan Baatar
MONGOLIA
Yichun
Hegeng
Qiqihar
HEILONGJIANG
Daqing
Jixi
Harbin
Mudanjiang
JILIN
Xilinhot
Changchun
Jilin
Vladivostok
INNER MONGOLIA
Tongliao
Siping
Liaoyuan
Yanji
Chifeng
LIAONING
Badaojiang
Baotou
Hohhot
Chengde
Shenyang
SEA
Zhangjiakou
Jinzhou
Benxi
NORTH
OF
Datong
BEIJING
Qinhuangdao
Anshan
KOREA
JAPAN
Wuhai
Tangshan
Dandong
Yinchuan
Baoding
Tianjin
Dalian
P'YŎNGYANG
Zhongwei
Yulin
Yangquan
Shijiazhuang
SEOUL
NINGXIA
Tongxin
Yan'an
Taiyuan
Yuci
HEBEI
Yantai
SOUTH
Honshū
Guyuan
SHANXI
Ji'nan
Weifang
YELLOW
KOREA
JAPAN
Huangling
Handan
Anyang
SHANDONG
Qingdao
SEA
Pusan
Baoji
Changzhi
Jining
Shijiusuo
Xi'an
Yuncheng
Xinxiang
Shikoku
SHAANXI
Luoyang
Zhengzhou
Kaifeng
Xuzhou
Kyūshū
HENAN
Bozhou
Cheju Do
Nanyang
ANHUI
JIANGSU
Xiangfan
Huainan
Yangzhou
Nanchong
Hefei
Nanjing
Suzhou
HUBEI
Yichang
Wuhan
Tongling
Huzhou
Shanghai
Shashi
Jiujiang
Hangzhou
EAST
Chongqing
Huangshi
Tunxi
Ningbo
CHINA
Luzhou
Changde
Jingdezhen
ZHEJIANG
SEA
GUIZHOU
Nanchang
Changsha
JIANGXI
Wenzhou
Shaoyang
Pingxiang
Ji'an
Guiyang
Hengyang
HUNAN
Nanping
Guilin
Ganzhou
FUJIAN
Fuzhou
Shaoguan
Quanzhou
TAIPEI
Liuzhou
Zhangzhou
Xiamen
GUANGDONG
TAIWAN
GUANGXI
Guangzhou
Shantou
Nanning
Wuzhou
Foshan
Shenzhen
Kaohsiung
Maoming
MACAU
Kowloon
SOUTH
Zhanjiang
HONG KONG
CHINA
SEA
Hanoi
Haiphong
VIETNAM
Haikou
PACIFIC
HAINAN ISLAND
OCEAN

0   250   500 km

Elevation

3000 m
2000 m
1000 m
0 m

About 50km north-west of Beijing, the Ming Tombs has 36 stone sentries to keep an eye on the tourists.

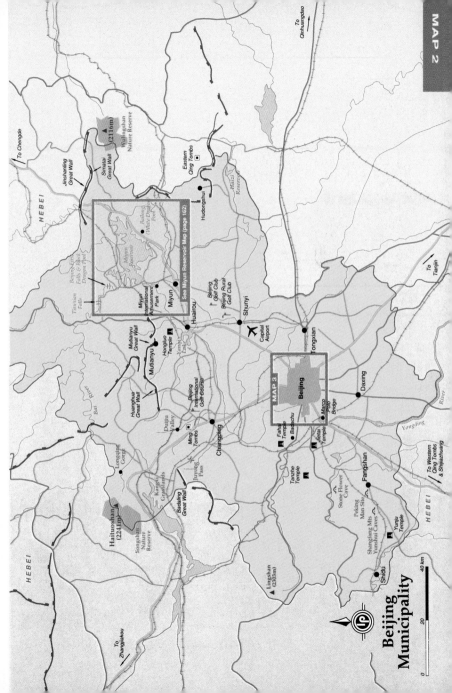

MAP 3

See Fragrant Hills Park Map (page 100)

See Summer Palace Map (page 85)

MAP 10

See Old Summer Palace Map (page 89)

Yiheyuan Lu

2

3

4

Kunming Lake

5

Wanquanhe Lu

1

HAIDIAN DISTRICT

MAP 4

Zizhuyuan Park

Beijing Zoo

Xisanhuanbei Lu

SHIJINGSHAN DISTRICT

Fourth Ring Road

Yuyuantan Park

47

52

46

45

M

48

M

Shijingshan Lu

49

M

50

M

51

Fuxing Lu

53

M

M

M

M

M

To Guchenglu & Pingguoyuan Subway Stations

Wuluan Lu

Wukesong Lu

44

Lianhuachi Park

FENGTAI DISTRICT

Beijing—Shijiazhuang Expressway

Guang'an Lu

Third Ring Road

41

42

43

40

To Shijiazhuang

39

Fourth Ring Road

Beijing

MAP 3 Beijing

PLACES TO STAY

6 Desheng Hotel
德胜饭店
7 Huabei Hotel
华北大酒店
8 Beijing Grand Hotel
圆山大酒店
14 Catic Plaza Hotel
凯迪克大酒店
15 Continental Grand Hotel
五洲大酒店
16 Yinghua Hotel
樱花宾馆
17 Huiqiao Hotel
惠桥饭店
19 Chongqing Hotel
重庆饭店
21 Novotel Parkview Hotel
新万寿饭店
22 Holiday Inn Lido; Watson's
丽都假日饭店、
屈臣氏
23 Yanxiang Hotel
燕翔饭店
24 Jiali Hotel
佳丽饭店
26 Guangming Hotel
光明饭店
30 China Resources Hotel
华润饭店
31 Park Hotel
百乐酒店
33 Jingtai Hotel
景泰宾馆
35 Sea Star Hotel
海兴大酒店
36 Jinghua Hotel
京华饭店
37 Lihua Hotel
丽华饭店
41 Jingfeng Hotel
京丰宾馆
51 Shousong Hotel
寿松饭店
52 Wanshou Hotel
万寿宾馆

OTHER

1 Fragrant Hills Park
香山公园
2 Xiangshan Botanic Gardens
香山植物园
3 Jade Spring Mountain
玉泉山
4 Summer Palace
颐和园
5 Old Summer Palace
圆明园遗址
9 Beijiao (Deshengmen) Long-Distance Bus Station
北郊长途汽车站
10 China Conservatory of Music
中国音乐学院
11 China Ethnic Minorities Park
中华民族园
12 Asian Games Village
亚运村
13 Beijing International Convention Centre
国际会议中心
18 Sino-Japanese Friendship Hospital
中日友好医院
20 Johnny's Coffee
真的咖啡
25 Sino-Japanese Youth Exchange Centre
中日青年交流中心
27 Chaoyang Park
朝阳公园
28 Chaoyang Gymnasium
朝阳体育馆
29 New Subway Station (unnamed)
地铁站
32 Zhaogongkou Bus Station (Buses to Tianjin)
赵公口汽车站
34 Haihutun Long-Distance Bus Station
海户屯公共汽车站
38 Wanfangting Park
万芳亭公园
39 World Park
世界公园
40 Fengtai Railway Station
丰台站
42 Anti-Japanese War Memorial
抗日战争纪念馆
43 Marco Polo Bridge
卢沟桥
44 South-West Suburban Greenhouse
西南郊苗圃
45 Bajiaocun Subway Station
八角村地铁站
46 Shijingshan Amusement Park
石景山游乐场
47 Motorcycle Training Ground
摩托车训练场
48 Babaoshan Subway Station
八宝山地铁站
49 Yuquanlu Subway Station
玉泉路地铁站
50 Wukesong Subway Station
五棵松地铁站
53 Wanshoulu Subway Station
万寿路地铁站

DAMIEN SIMONIS

Detail of the façade on the Hall of Sea of Wisdom, Summer Palace

Kunming Lake, which dominates the Summer Palace grounds, is an icy playground during winter.

MAP 4

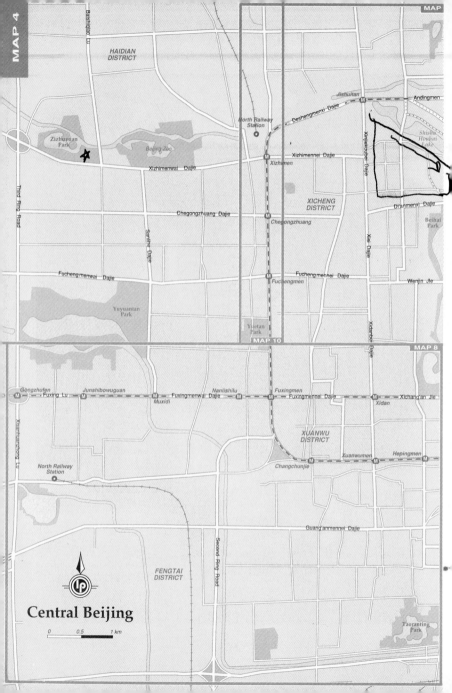

HAIDIAN
DISTRICT

Baishiqiao Lu

North Railway
Station

Jishuitan M

Andingmen

Deshengmenxi Dajie

Shisha
Houhai
Lake

Zizhuyuan
Park

Beijing Zoo

Xizhimennei Dajie

Xinjiekoubei Dajie

Xizhimenwai Dajie

Xizhimen

XICHENG
DISTRICT

Di'anmenxi Dajie

Beihai
Park

Third Ring Road

Chegongzhuang Dajie

Chegongzhuang M

Xisi Dajie

Sanlihe Dajie

Fuchengmenwai Dajie

Fuchengmennei Dajie

Wenjin Jie

Fuchengmen M

Yuyuantan
Park

Yuetan
Park

Xidanbei Dajie

MAP 10

MAP 8

Gongzhufen M

Fuxing Lu

Junshibowuguan M

Nanlishilu

Fuxingmen

M

Xichang'an Jie

Muxidi M

Fuxingmenwai Dajie

M

Fuxingmennei Dajie

M

Xidan

Xisanhuanzhong Lu

North Railway
Station

XUANWU
DISTRICT

Xuanwumen M

Hepingmen M

Changchunjie M

Guang'anmennei Dajie

Second Ring Road

FENGTAI
DISTRICT

Taoranting
Park

Central Beijing

0   0.5   1 km

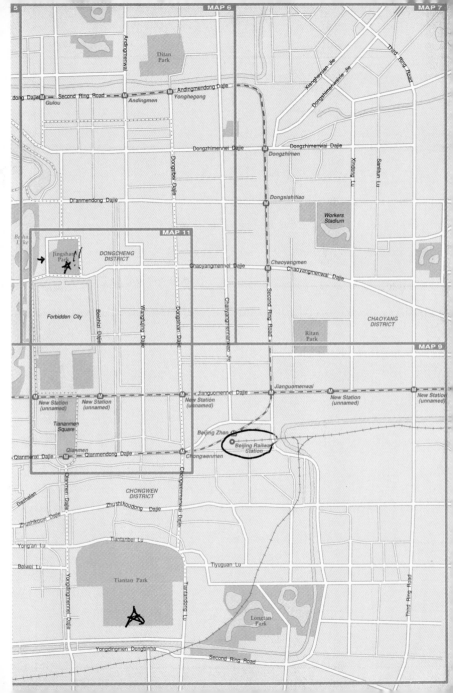

MAP 5

North-West Beijing

0   250   500 m

MAP 5

Xueyuannan Lu

1 ●

2

Second Ring Road

5 ●

🏛 6

Deshengmenwai Dajie

Deshengmenxi Dajie

North Railway Station

3 🏛 ▼ 4

Xinjiekoubei Dajie

▼ 7

Shisha Houhai Lake

Xizhimenwai Dajie

Xizhimennei Dajie

MAP 10

XICHENG DISTRICT

● 8

MAP 6

12 ▼

11 ■

● 9

■ 10

Di'anmenxi Dajie

Chegongzhuang Dajie

Beihai Park

Xisi Dajie

Beihai Lake

ℹ 13

Fuchengmenwai Dajie

Fuchengmennei Dajie

🏛 15   🏛 14

Wenjin Jie

● 16

Second Ring Road

Xidanbei Dajie

Yuetan Park

Zhongnanhai Lake

MAP 8

✤ 17

DIANA MAYFIELD

The jewel of Beihai Park, the 27m-long Nine Dragon Screen, was built in 1756.

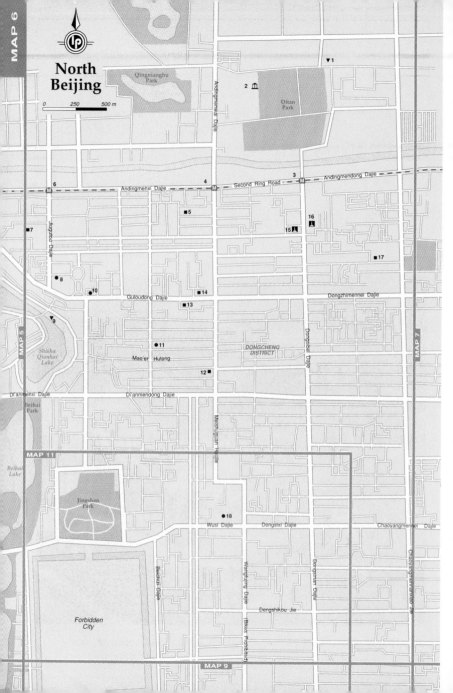

MAP 6

North Beijing

0   250   500 m

Qingnianghu Park

Ditan Park

▼1

2 🏛

Andingmenwai Dajie

Andingmenxi Dajie   4   Second Ring Road   3   Andingmendong Dajie

6

■5

■7   Jinguru Dajie

16
🏯
15 ▲   ■17

● 8

■14

■10   Guloudong Dajie

Dongzhimennei Dajie

■13

▼9

Shisha Qianhai Lake

Dongsidi Dajie

● 11

DONGCHENG DISTRICT

Mao'er Hutong

12■

MAP 5

Di'anmenxi Dajie   Di'anmendong Dajie

Beihai Park

MAP 7

MAP 11

Beihai Lake

Meishuguan Houjie

Jingshan Park

● 18

Wusi Dajie   Dongsixi Dajie   Chaoyangmennei Dajie

Beiheyan Dajie

Wangfujing Dajie (Bikes Prohibited)

Dongsinan Dajie

Chaoyangmennanxiao Jie

Forbidden City

Dengshikou Jie

MAP 9

GLENN BEANLAND

Roar energy: the Lama Temple is a heady mix of Han, Manchu, Mongol and Tibetan architecture.

MAP 7

East Beijing

MAP 6

0   250   500 m

To Airport

Third Ring Road

Airport Expressway

To Sino-Japanese
Youth Exchange
Centre

Dongzhimenwaiwie Jie

Xinyuan Jie

Dongsan huanbei Lu

Liangmaqiao Lu

Liangma River

Xiangheyuan Jie

Liangmahe Nanlu

SANLITUN
EMBASSY
AREA

Dongzhimennei Dajie   22   Dongzhimenwai Dajie

Xindong Lu

Sanlitun Lu

Gongren Tiyuchang Lu

Gongren Tiyuchangbeng Lu

Workers'
Stadium

Yaojiayuan Lu

Second Ring Road

75
74   72 71
73

69

67
68

78

51
Tuanjiehu
Park

Third Ring Road

Chaoyangmennei Dajie   76

Chaoyangmenwai Dajie

77

79

80

81
82

Chaoyang Dajie

Dongsanhuanbei Lu

Tangguomeidei Dajie

90 89
91   Ritan Beilu

94

92
93   Yabao Lu

Ritan
Park

87   86
88   85

JIANGUOMENWAI
EMBASSY AREA

84

MAP 9

MAP 7 East Beijing

PLACES TO STAY

3 Radisson SAS Hotel;
Nightman Disco
皇家大饭店、
菜特曼迪斯可广场
5 China Travel Service
Tower
中旅大厦
6 Huayuan Hotel
华园饭店
8 Hilton Hotel
希尔顿饭店
11 21st Century Hotel
二十一世纪饭店
12 Lufthansa Centre;
Kempinski Hotel
燕沙商城、
凯宾斯基饭店
13 Kunlun Hotel
昆仑饭店
16 Huadu Hotel
华都饭店
19 Yuyang Hotel
渔阳饭店
33 Landmark Towers & Hotel
亮马河大厦
35 Great Wall Sheraton
长城饭店
55 Zhaolong Hotel
兆龙饭店
62 Chains City Hotel;
Owl Cafe
城市宾馆、敦煌西餐
70 Huaxia Hotel
华厦宾馆
72 Beijing Asia Hotel
北京亚洲大酒店
73 Poly Plaza
保利大厦
74 Hong Kong-Macau Centre;
Swissôtel
北京港澳中心、
瑞士酒店
80 Guoan Hotel
国安宾馆
82 Jingguang New World
Hotel
京广新世界饭店
91 Ritan Hotel
日坛宾馆

PLACES TO EAT

2 Exhibition Centre
Restaurant
展览中心餐厅
7 Red Basil Thai Restaurant
红罗勒泰国餐厅
10 Schiller's Bar & Restaurant
西乐酒吧

13 Ma Cherie (Kunlun Hotel)
昆仑饭店
15 Hong Kong Food City
香港美食城
17 Rasput-Inn
拉斯布丁
18 Duoweizhai Restaurant
多味斋餐厅
23 Pizza Hut
必胜客
24 Xanadu Bar & Grill
上都酒吧
42 My Place Cafe
我的地方咖啡
43 La Terasse
拉德莱斯
44 Bella's Gourmet
Restaurant
蓓拉餐厅
46 New Douhua Village
Restaurant
新豆花村餐厅
47 Public Space; Upside
Down Cafe
公共场所、颠倒咖啡
49 CD Cafe
CD咖啡
52 Asian Star Restaurant
亚洲之星新马印餐厅
54 Hof Brauhaus
德国酒吧
56 Shanghai Nights
夜上海
57 Parati Restaurant
葩拉逊餐厅
58 Nashville; Hidden Tree
乡谣俱乐部、
隐蔽的树
59 Annie's Cafe
阿密咖啡
60 Minder Cafe
明大西餐厅
63 Downtown Café; Park Bar
城市咖啡、公园酒吧
64 Frank's Place
万龙酒吧
65 Cafe Cafe
咖啡咖啡
66 Berena's Bistro
柏瑞娜酒家
67 Carella Cafe (Car Wash)
洗车酒吧
68 Metro Cafe
意大利咖啡店
78 Curry Cafe
咖喱咖啡
83 Rick's Cafe
瑞克士咖啡
84 Ted's Cafe
铁芝咖啡

93 Omar Khayyam
Restaurant
味美佳餐厅

ENTERTAINMENT

9 Amazon Bar
亚马逊
14 Maggie's Bar
麦姬酒吧
34 Hard Rock Cafe
硬石餐厅
45 Jazz Ya; Dai Sy's Pub
李波餐厅、
戴普小屋
48 Redwood Bar
红杉吧
53 TGI Friday's
星期五餐厅
71 San Francisco Brewing
Company
旧金山啤酒屋
77 Ziguang Cinema
紫光电影院
81 Chaoyang Theatre
朝阳剧场
87 Goose & Duck Pub
鹅和鸭酒吧
89 Elephant Bar
大象酒吧

EMBASSIES

21 Russian
俄罗斯大使馆
28 Australia
澳大利亚大使馆
29 Malaysia
马来西亚大使馆
30 Cambodia
柬埔寨大使馆
31 Germany
德国大使馆
32 Singapore
新加坡大使馆
37 France
法国大使馆
38 Laos
老挝大使馆
39 Canada
加拿大大使馆
40 UNICEF
联合国儿童基金会
41 Netherlands
荷兰大使馆
85 UK
英国大使馆
86 New Zealand
新西兰大使馆
88 India
印度大使馆

GLENN BEANLAND

DAMIEN SIMONIS

PATRICK HORTON

Top: Lizard tonic, a reputed cure for premature ejaculation, is as easy to come by as a bottle of beer.
Bottom: A pair of working-glass heroes take a break.

The view from the former regal pleasure gardens of Jingshan Park, just north of the Forbidden City.

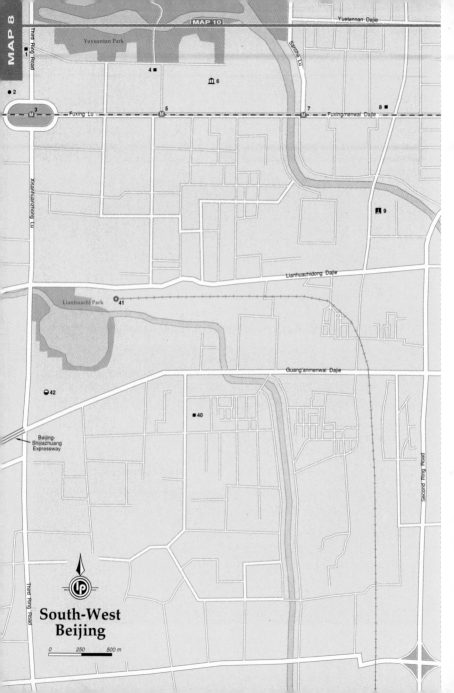

MAP 8

Yuetennan Dajie

MAP 10

Yuyuantan Park

Third Ring Road

■ 1

● 2

4 ■

🏛 6

M 3   Fuxing Lu   5   7   Fuxingmenwai Dajie   8 ■

M   M

Xisanhuanzhong Lu

🎌 9

Lianhuachidong Dajie

Lianhuachi Park ○ 41

● 42

Guang'anmenwai Dajie

■ 40

Beijing-
Shijiazhuang
Expressway

Second Ring Road

Third Ring Road

LP

South-West
Beijing

0   250   500 m

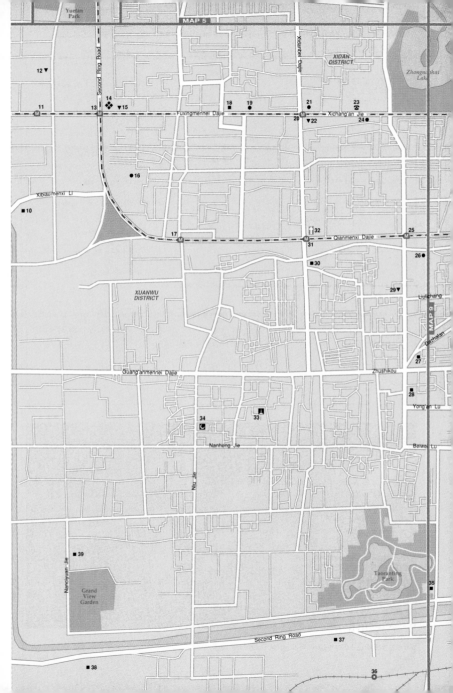

MAP 5

Yuetan Park

Second Ring Road

Xidanbei Dajie

XIDAN DISTRICT

Zhongnanhai Lake

12 ▼

14 ◆◆◆
▼15

18 ■   19 ●

21 ●

23 ☎

11 Ⓜ   13 ■   Ⓜ   Fuxingmennei Dajie   Xichang'an Jie

20 ●
▼22   24 ●

16 ●

Xibiaomenxi Li

■ 10

17 Ⓜ   ╏ 32   Qianmenxi Dajie   Ⓜ 25

31

■ 30   26 ●

XUANWU DISTRICT

29 ▼

Liulichang

MAP 9

Dazhalan

Guang'anmennei Dajie   Zhushikou

27

■ 28   Yong'an Lu

34 ☾   🏯 33

Nanheng Jie   Beiwei Lu

Niu Jie

■ 39

Nanchizi Jie

Grand View Garden

Taoranting Park

■ 35

Second Ring Road   ■ 37

■ 38   36 ◎

MAP 8 South-West Beijing

PLACES TO STAY
1 Xinxing Hotel
新兴宾馆
4 Media Centre Hotel
梅地亚中心
8 Yanjing Hotel
燕京饭店
10 Feixia Hotel
飞霞饭店
18 Minzu Hotel
民族饭店
27 Far East Hotel
远东饭店
28 Qianmen Hotel
前门饭店
30 Yuexiu Hotel
越秀大饭店
35 Fenglong Youth Hostel
凤龙青年旅社
37 Qiaoyuan Hotel
侨园饭店
38 Beijing Commercial
Business Complex
北京商务会馆
39 Grand View Garden Hotel
大观园酒店
40 Hualong Hotel
华隆饭店

PLACES TO EAT
12 Crystal Palace Chaozhou
Restaurant
水晶宫潮州海鲜酒楼
15 Kaorouwan Restaurant
烤肉宛饭庄

22 Hongbinlou Restaurant
鸿宾楼
29 Confucian Heritage
Restaurant
孔膳堂饭庄

OTHER
2 Urban-Rural Trade Centre
城乡贸易中心
3 Gongzhufen Subway
Station
公主坟地铁站
5 Junshibowuguan Subway
Station
军事博物馆地铁站
6 Military Museum
军事博物馆
7 Muxidi Subway Station
木樨地地铁站
9 White Cloud Temple;
Taoist Family Health Food
白云观;
道家养生餐厅
11 Nanlishilu Subway Station
南礼士路地铁站
13 Fuxingmen Subway
Station
复兴门地铁站
14 Parkson Department
Store
百盛购物中心
16 Central Music
Conservatory
中央音乐学院
17 Changchunjie Subway
Station
长春街地铁站

19 Nationalities Cultural
Palace
民族文化宫
20 Xidan Subway Station
西单地铁站
21 Aviation Building (CAAC &
Airport Bus)
民航营业大厦
23 Telegraph Service Centre
电报局
24 Shoudu Cinema
首都电影院
25 Hepingmen Subway
Station
和平门地铁站
26 Zhengyici Theatre
正乙祠剧场
31 Xuanwumen Subway
Station
宣武门地铁站
32 South Cathedral
南堂
33 Fayuan Temple
法源寺
34 Niujie Mosque
牛街礼拜寺
36 Beijing South Railway
Station (Yongdingmen)
北京南站、
永定门火车站
41 Beijing West Railway
Station
西火车站
42 Lianhuachi Bus Station
莲花池长途汽车站

DAMIEN SIMONIS

Bicycle parking lot outside Hepingmen subway station

Bike on down and buy a few calligraphy scrolls in Liulichang, Beijing's street of antiques.

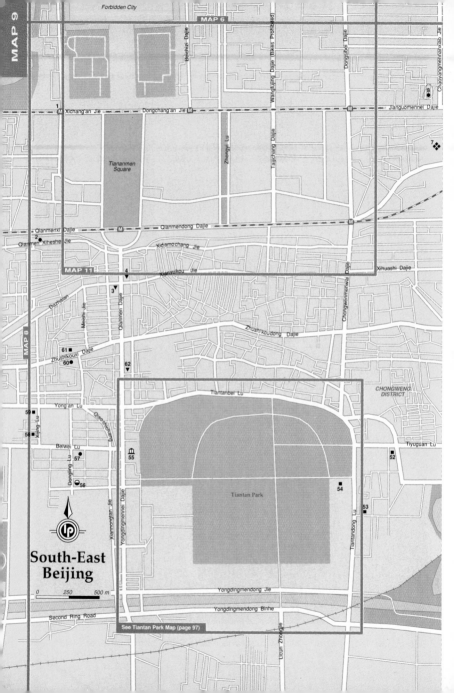

MAP 9 South-East Beijing

PLACES TO STAY
9 International Hotel
国际饭店
11 Gloria Plaza Hotel
凯莱大酒店
12 Scitech Hotel
赛特饭店
14 Hotel New Otani
长富宫饭店
17 International Club Hotel
国际俱乐部饭店
30 Guotai Hotel
国泰饭店
41 Jianguo Hotel
建国饭店
42 Jinglun Hotel
京伦饭店
44 China World Trade Centre
& Hotel
国际贸易中心
46 Dabei Hotel
大北宾馆
49 Leyou Hotel;
Hua Thai Hotel
乐游饭店、
华泰饭店
50 Longtan Hotel
龙潭饭店
51 Tiantan Hotel
天坛饭店
52 Tiantan Sports Hotel
天坛体育宾馆
53 Traffic Hotel
交通饭店
54 Haoyuan Hotel
昊园宾馆
58 Rainbow Hotel;
Beiwei Hotel
天桥宾馆、
北纬饭店
59 Dongfang Hotel
东方饭店
61 Fengzeyuan Hotel
丰泽园饭店

PLACES TO EAT
3 Dazhalan Entrance;
Liubiju Pickle Shop
大栅栏、六必居
4 Qianmen Quanjude Roast
Duck Restaurant
前门全聚德烤鸭店
13 Uncle Sam's Fastfood;
McDonald's
山姆叔叔快餐店、
麦当劳
21 Yuyuan Restaurant
渝园饭庄
24 Windows on the World
(CITIC Building)
国际大厦
28 El Gaucho Restaurant
艾高袤餐厅
29 Sichuan Hometown
Restaurant
拇   蚁缇萍
37 Mexican Wave
墨西哥波涛
47 Douhua Restaurant
豆花饭庄
58 Healthfood Restaurant
(Rainbow Hotel)
天桥宾馆、北纬饭店
62 Gongdelin Vegetarian
Restaurant
功德林素菜馆

EMBASSIES
19 Philippines
菲律宾大使馆
20 Thailand
泰国大使馆
33 Mongolia
蒙古大使馆
34 Vietnam
越南大使馆
35 USA
美国大使馆
36 USA
美国大使馆

OTHER
1 New Subway Station
(unnamed)
地铁站
2 Lao She Teahouse
老舍茶馆
5 Beijing Railway Station
北京火车站
6 Beijingzhan Subway
Station
北京站地铁站
7 Beijing Ceroil Plaza
北京中粮广场
8 Chang'an Grand Theatre
长安大剧场
10 Ancient Observatory
古观象台
15 CITS
中国国际旅行社
(旅游大厦)
16 Jianguomen Subway
Station
建国门地铁站
18 International Post Office
国际邮店局
22 Sunflower Jazz Club;
Sun Garden Bar
向日葵爵士俱乐部、
花园酒吧
23 John Bull Pub
地道的英式酒吧
24 CITIC Building
国际大厦
25 Friendship Store;
Pizza Hut
友谊商店
必胜客
26 Scitech Plaza
赛特购物中心
27 Phoenix Bar
风凰酒吧
31 New Subway Station
(unnamed)
地铁站
32 Xiushui Silk Market
秀水东街
38 Hawaii Bar
夏威夷酒吧
39 Water Hole
水洞酒吧
40 Guiyou Shopping Centre
贵友商场
43 Traders' Hotel
国贸饭店
45 New Subway Station
(unnamed)
地铁站
48 Majuan Long-Distance
Bus Station
马圈(马甸)长途汽车
55 Natural History Museum
自然博物馆
56 Tianqiao Bus Station
天桥长途汽车站
57 Tianqiao Happy Teahouse
天桥剧场
60 Kaiming Cinema
开明电影院

Everyone from twilight kite-flyers (top) to smiling soldiers flock to the famous, or infamous, expanse of Tiananmen Square.

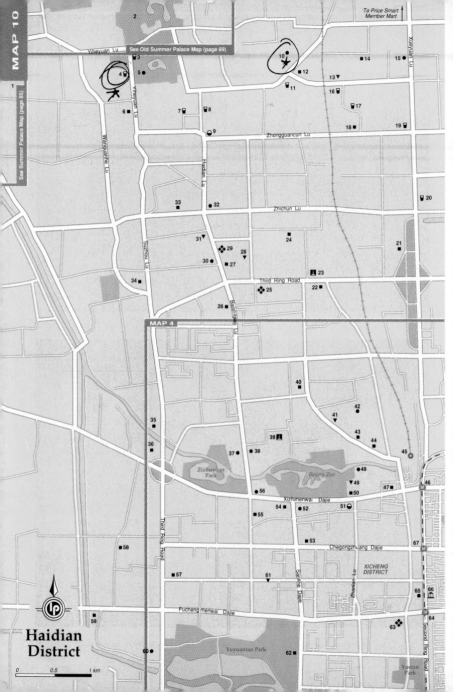

MAP 10 Haidian District
海淀区

PLACES TO STAY
6 Changchunyuan Hotel
畅春园饭店
12 Qinghuayuan Hotel
清华园宾馆
14 Xijiao Hotel
西郊宾馆
18 Beilin Hotel
北林饭店
21 Jimen Hotel
蓟门饭店
22 Big Bell Hotel
大钟寺饭店
24 Cuigong Hotel
翠宫饭店
26 Friendship Hotel
友谊宾馆
27 Yanshan Hotel
燕山大酒店
33 Hainan Hotel
海南饭店
34 Shengtang Hotel
盛唐饭店
35 Evergreen Hotel
万年青宾馆
36 Shangri-La Hotel
香格里拉饭店
38 Olympic Hotel
奥林匹克饭店
40 Central Garden Hotel
中苑宾馆
43 Shangyuan Hotel
上园饭店
44 Xizhimen Hotel
西直门饭店
47 Debao Hotel
德宝饭店
50 Exhibition Centre Hotel
北京展览饭店
53 Mandarin Hotel
新大都饭店
54 Xiyuan Hotel
西苑饭店
55 New Century Hotel
新世纪饭店
57 Ziyu Hotel
紫玉饭店
58 Lingnan Hotel
领南饭店
59 Yulong Hotel
裕龙大酒店

62 Diaoyutai State Guesthouse
钓鱼台国宾馆
65 Holiday Inn Downtown
金都假日饭店

PLACES TO EAT
13 Wudaokou Korean Restaurants
五道口
31 Boss American Barbecue
老板美国烤肉
34 Chaofuyuan Restaurant (Shengtang Hotel)
盛唐饭店
41 Subway Sandwiches
潜水艇三明治餐厅
49 Moscow Restaurant
54 Yangshengzhai Reataurant (Xiyuan Hotel)
西苑饭店
61 Muslim Restaurants
百万庄西路
(回民餐馆)
65 Shamiana Indian Restaurant (Holiday Inn Downtown)
金都假日饭店

OTHER
1 Summer Palace
颐和园
2 Old Summer Palace
圆明园
3 NYX Sports Bar
尼古斯西餐厅
4 Solutions Pub
5 Beijing University
北京大学
7 Character Bar
8 Richmond Brewery
猪奇门
9 Zhongguancun (Bus Stop)
中关村
10 Qinghua University
清华大学
11 Blue Jays Pub
15 Beijing Language Institute
北京语言学院
16 Jackson's Disco
17 Angel's Bar
天使吧
19 Nook Bar
公共汽车酒吧

20 NASA Disco
NASA迪斯可
23 Great Bell Temple
大钟寺
25 Shuang'an Shopping Centre
双安商场
28 Club X; Shadow Cafe
X俱乐部;
阴影咖啡
29 Modern Plaza
当代商城
30 People's University
人民大学
32 Kenny Roger's Roasters
海淀路86号
37 Beijing National Library; Tuxin Cinema
北京图书馆
39 Wuta Temple
五塔寺
42 North Jiaotong University
北方交通大学
45 Xizhimen (North) Railway Station
西直门火车站
46 Xizhimen Subway Station
西直门地铁站
48 Beijing Exhibition Centre
北京展览中心
51 Zhanlanguan Lu Tour Bus Station
展览馆路旅游车售票
52 Planetarium
北京天文馆
56 Sparkice Internet Café; Capital Gymnasium
赛华网络咖啡室、首都体育馆
60 Central TV Tower
中央电视塔
63 Vantone New World Shopping Centre
万通新世界商场
64 Fuchengmen Subway Station
阜城门地铁站
66 Lu Xun Museum
鲁迅博物馆
67 Chegongzhuang Subway Station
车公庄地铁站

MAP 11

Jingshan
Park

Jingshan Qianjie

Wusi Dajie

Qianliang Hutong

1 ■

2 ✿

3 ●

🏛 7

6 ■

Dongsixi Dajie

4 ▼

DONGSI
DISTRICT

5 🄯

Dongsinan Dajie

See Forbidden City Map (page 82)

Beichizi Dajie

Qihelou Jie

Donghuangchenggennan Jie

Baihayan Dajie

8 ■

9 ●

10 ☕

11 ●

Dengshikouxi Jie

13 ■

14 ▼

16 ■

Dengshikou Jie

15 ■   17 ■

Wangfujing Dajie

Dengdanbei Dajie

Forbidden
City

12 ✦

Donghuamen Dajie

23 ■

22 ✦

Dong'anmen Dajie

20 ■   19 ■

Jinyu Hutong

21 ✿

18 ■

MAP 9

24 ●

MAP 6

Nanchizi Dajie

Chenguang Jie

Nanheyan Dajie

25 ✿

(Bikes Prohibited)

26 ✦

27 ●

Silver Street

Zhongshan
Park

Working People's
Cultural Palace

🏛 30

29 ■

28 ■

Xichang'an Jie

Dongchang'an Jie

Ⓜ

Ⓜ

Chongwenmennei Dajie

32

🏛 33

🏛 34

Tianjcheng Dajie

Wangfujing Area

0   250   500 m

Zhengyi Lu

Tiananmen
Square

35

🏛 45

48 ■

36

47 ■

50 ■

37 ☕

Qianmenxi Dajie

44 ■   46 ■

Qianmendong Dajie

49 ■

39 ▼   ☕ 40

42 ▼

43 ●

51 ▼

38 ▼

41 ●

MAP 11 Wangfujing Area
王府井地区

PLACES TO STAY
1 Inner Mongolia
 Guesthouse
 内蒙古宾馆
6 Guangdong Regency
 Hotel
 华侨大厦
8 Wangfujing Grand Hotel
 王府井大饭店
13 Fangyuan Hotel
 芳园宾馆
15 Tianlun Dynasty Hotel
 天伦王朝饭店
16 Holiday Inn Crowne Plaza
 国际艺苑皇冠
 假日饭店
17 Novotel Hotel
 松鹤大酒店
18 Palace Hotel
 王府饭店
19 Peace Hotel
 和平宾馆
20 Taiwan Hotel
 台湾饭店
28 Beijing Hotel
 北京饭店
29 Grand Hotel Beijing
 北京贵宾楼饭店
44 Capital Hotel
 首都宾馆
46 Zijin Guesthouse
 紫金宾馆
47 Xinqiao Hotel
 新桥饭店
48 Jinlang Hotel
 金朗大酒店
49 Hademen Hotel
 哈德门饭店
50 Chongwenmen Hotel
 崇文饭店

PLACES TO EAT
4 KFC
 肯德基家乡鸡
14 Green Angel Vegetarian
 Restaurant
 绿天使素食馆
23 Dong'anmen Night Market
 东安门夜市
38 Zhengyang Market;
 Chaozhou Restaurants
 正阳市场
39 McDonald's; Vie de
 France; KFC
 麦当劳；大磨坊面包
 肯德基家乡鸡
42 Renren Restaurant
 人人大酒楼
51 Bianyifang Restaurant
 便宜坊烤鸭店

OTHER
2 Longfu Department Store
 隆福商业大厦
3 Star Cinema
 明星电影院
5 Dongsi Mosque
 东四清真寺
7 China Art Gallery
 中国美术馆
9 Capital Theatre
 首都剧场
10 Banpo Primitive Beer Hut
 半坡啤酒屋
11 Lao She Former
 Residence
 老舍故居
12 PSB (Visa Extensions)
 公安局外事科
21 Xindong'an Shopping
 Centre
 新东安 谐
22 Bank of China
 中国银行

24 Foreign Languages
 Bookstore
 外文书店
25 Beijing Department
 Store
 北京百货大楼
26 Beijing Union Hospital
 协和医院
27 Dahua Cinema
 大华电影院
30 Imperial Archives
 Museum
 皇史城
31 Tiananmen Gate
 天安门
32 Great Hall of the
 People
 人民大会堂
33 Monument to the
 People's Heroes
 人民英雄纪念碑
34 Chinese Revolution
 History Museum
 中国革命历史博物馆
35 Mao Zedong
 Mausoleum
 毛主席纪念堂
36 Qianmen - Main Gate
 正阳门
37 Qianmen Tour
 Bus Station
 前门、旅游车发车站
40 Qianmen Tour
 Bus Station
 前门、旅游车发车站
41 Qianmen - Arrow Tower
 箭楼
43 Entrance to Underground
 City
 地下城门口
 （西打磨厂街62号）
45 CYTS
 中国青年旅行社

GLENN BEANLAND

A detail of the Monument to the People's Heroes in Tiananmen Square. The monument's foundation stone was put in place by Mao Zedong himself in 1949.

Map Legend

BOUNDARIES

.... International Boundary
.... Provincial Boundary

ROUTES

A25 .... Freeway, with Route Number
.... Major Road
.... Minor Road
.... Minor Road - Unsealed
.... City Road
.... City Street
.... City Lane
.... Train Route, with Station
.... Metro Route, with Station
.... Cable Car or Chairlift
.... Ferry Route
.... Walking Track
.... Walking/Bicycle Tour

AREA FEATURES

.... Building
.... Cemetery
.... Non-Christian Cemetery
.... Hotel
.... Market
.... Park
.... Pedestrian Mall
.... Urban Area

HYDROGRAPHIC FEATURES

.... Canal
.... Coastline
.... Creek, River
.... Intermittent Lake
.... Lake
.... Rapids, Waterfalls
.... Salt Lake

SYMBOLS

CAPITAL ...... National Capital
CAPITAL ..... Provincial Capital
CITY .... City
Town .... Town
Village .... Village

■ .... Place to Stay

▼ .... Place to Eat

▮ .... Pub or Bar

✈ .... Airport
.... Ancient Wall
Θ .... Bank
.... Cathedral, Church
⌒ .... Cave
... Cliff or Escarpment
⚲ .... Embassy
Ä .... Fort
✿ .... Gardens
↑ .... Golf Course
⊕ .... Hospital
※ .... Lookout
⚐ .... Monument
◖ .... Mosque
▲ .... Mountain/Hill

血 .... Museum
Ⓟ .... Parking
)(......... Pass/Tunnel
▮ .... Petrol Station
★ .... Police Station
✉ .... Post Office
∴ .... Ruins
❖ ..... Shopping Centre
○ .... Spring
☎ .... Telephone
▥ .... Temple
▣ .... Tomb
❶ ... Tourist Information
◒ .... Transport
🐘 .... Zoo

Note: not all symbols displayed above appear in this book